THE OCHBERG ORPHANS
AND THE HORRORS FROM WHENCE THEY CAME

THE RESCUE IN 1921 OF 177 JEWISH ORPHANS BY ISAAC OCHBERG,
THE REPRESENTATIVE OF THE SOUTH AFRICAN JEWISH COMMUNITY,
FROM THE HORRORS OF THE 'PALE OF SETTLEMENT'

Volume Two

The Ochberg Orphans were placed in the care of
The South African Jewish Orphanage (now Arcadia Jewish Children's Home) and
The Cape Jewish Orphanage (now Oranjia Jewish Child and Youth Centre)
The full proceeds from the sale of these books, as with my other compilations,
go to Arcadia and Oranjia which still care for children
in Johannesburg and Cape Town and need our support.

Book compiled by
David Solly Sandler

National Library of Australia Cataloguing-in-Publication entry

Title: The Ochberg orphans and the horrors from whence they came.
Volume two / compiled by David Solly Sandler.

ISBN: 9780994619235 (paperback)

Subjects:
　　Ochberg, Isaac.
　　Ochberg Orphans.
　　Arcadia (The South African Jewish Orphanage, Johannesburg)
　　Oranjia (The Cape Jewish Orphanage, Cape Town)
　　Pale of settlement--History.
　　Isaac Ochberg Heritage Committee.
　　Orphanages--South Africa--History.

Other Creators/Contributors:
　　Sandler, David Solly, 1952- compiler

Cover designed by Sarah Natasha Myra Sandler

Every effort has been made to incorporate correct information, dates, statistics and photos. The publisher regrets any errors and omissions, and invites readers to contribute their up-to-date or additional relevant information to

David Solly Sander, E-mail: <sedsand@iinet.net.au>

All rights reserved. No part of this publication may be reproduced, stored in a retrieval system or transmitted in any form or by any means, electronic, mechanical, photocopying, recording or otherwise, without the prior written permission of the copyright holder.

Copyright © David Solly Sandler 2017

ISBN 978-0-9946192-3-5

*Isaac Ochberg was born in Uman, Russia on 31 May 1879
and died on the Pretoria Castle on 11 December 1937.
He was buried in Cape Town on 13 December 1937.*

*"He never refused to support a worthy cause; on the contrary, his creed was that since he had been
enabled to achieve success in his own enterprises, he had a moral duty to help those less fortunate."*

THE OCHBERG ORPHANS - VOLUME TWO
FOREWORD

This volume two is a sequel to **The Ochberg Orphans and the horrors from whence they came,** published in April 2011, and includes not only additional histories of Ochberg Orphans (initially known as Ukrainian War and Pogrom Orphans) that have come to light since 2011 but also the many events and celebrations that have taken place over the past six years to remember Isaac Ochberg and the good work done by the Isaac Ochberg Heritage Committee in Israel that was established mainly through the efforts of Bennie Penzik, the son of two Ochberg Orphans.

This volume commences with an introduction to the Ochberg Orphans by the late Sir Martin Gilbert. It is followed by details of the horrors that faced the Jews in *The Pale of Settlement* in the 1920s and the help given to them by the Jewish communities around the world

The next section of the book is devoted to the three Pinsker Orphanages that are very much part of the Ochberg Orphan story as 44 children were selected from these orphanages to go to South Africa. They were accompanied by Alter Bobrow who had helped establish these orphanages together with his comrades and their story is included in this volume.

We also include **The Work of the Pinsker Orphan Relief Fund of London** by John Cooper, whose grandfather was on the committee of the fund. The fund brought out 19 Pinsker Orphans in 1924 and 34 in 1926 for adoption in London.

The book includes histories of Ochberg Orphans newly uncovered and those that were previously published in **More Arc Memories** in 2008 and for completeness a limited amount of material from the first volume.

We now fast forward to the twenty-first century and reveal the events, ceremonies, books and the documentary, to honour Isaac Ochberg since his death in 1937. The main event, no doubt, was the two day ceremony held in Israel in July 2011 culminating in the Dedication of Memorial Site at Ramat Menashe to Isaac Ochberg and the Orphans he saved.

We end off by detailing the good work done by The Isaac Ochberg Heritage Committee and an addendum.

As with the original volume this edition has three aims:
- To record the forgotten history, the horrors suffered by Jews in the 'Pale of Settlement' from 1914 to 1922 and the help given to them by their brethren, the Jewish Communities worldwide.
- To provide a legacy for the descendants of each of the Ochberg Orphans; a book which presents the history of the original Ochberg Orphans and preserves the life stories of their descendants.
- To raise funds for Arcadia and Oranjia, the two Jewish Orphanages in South Africa, in whose care the Ochberg Orphans were placed. Both of these institutions still exist today and continue to take care of Jewish children in need. All the proceeds from the sale of this book, as with my previous compilations, will be donated to them.

I feel honoured to be the compiler of this volume and the catalyst for its creation. I regard these volumes of life stories collected, as the property of the Jewish Community.

A special thank you goes to Bennie Penzik and Lionel Slier, both descendants of Ochberg Orphans, who always encouraged, helped and contributed towards the creation of this volume. I also thank all the many people who have helped me collect the life stories, and those who have opened their hearts and shared their, or their parents' stories. I dedicate the book to the Ochberg Orphans and Arcadians who have passed away and to the generosity of the South African Jewish community which has always taken care of its own. In these difficult times in South Africa, I appeal to all ex South Africans to support their needy community left behind.

I end with the blessing that Doctor Lichtigfeld (Arcadia's Superintendent from 1952-1971) often bestowed on the congregation at Arcadia.

May the Lord bless you and keep you and make his face shine on you and give you peace and happiness and may there be peace in Israel soon.

Shalom

David Solly Sandler

The Ochberg Orphans – Volume Two

Acknowledgements and Thanks

This book belongs to the Jewish Community and has been a grand collaboration with many people and organisations helping to shape it and nurture it along.

Our first and greatest thanks go to all the Ochberg Orphans and their descendants, who entrusted me with their memories, especially those who bravely opened up and shared their more sensitive and private stories.

Much thanks go to Bennie Penzik, son of two Ochberg Orphans, who like a benevolent older brother was always there to help and guide me. He contributed and shared many articles. Likewise Lionel Slier, the son of an Ochberg Orphan, contributed many articles and was a friend who encouraged and supported my endeavours.

Much thanks are due to Veronica Belling (Jewish Studies Library UCT) for her invaluable and professional help. Not only did she send us archival information of the Cape Jewish Orphanage but also the book is peppered with her translations of letters and documents from Yiddish to English.

Thanks are due to Solly Kaplinski, Misha Mitsel and Lisa Margolin of the American Jewish Joint Distribution Committee for taking the time and trouble to help with information for the book.

I must thank my daughter Sarah, who helped design the cover and a very great thanks must go to Antoinette Weber, my partner of the past nine years, who gave very generously of her time and assisted with the typing and proofreading. I have once again tried to copy the very high standard of formatting she set in the first volume. Thanks also go to Danielle Durbach who helped with the proofreading.

Thanks must again go to two very close Arc 'brothers', David Kotzen and Dr Solly Farber who passed away in July 2002 a day apart. They both inspired and encouraged and helped me and set me on the path to compiling the volumes on Arcadia, the first volume of The Ochberg Orphans and now this second volume. I sometimes feel that it is not by chance that I share with them my names David and Solly. I hope that David and Solly, as well as Doc and Ma and all Old Arcs who have 'bunked over the hill' enjoy the book from above.

Also a very big thank you goes to all those that helped sell and store the books that I have compiled on South African Jewry: Bennie Penzik in Israel; Denise Sheer and Monty Koppel in London; Sharmaine Palmer in the USA and in South Africa: Jules Gordon in Johannesburg and Colin Rosenkowitz in Cape Town. Lastly I thank Barry Berelowitz who generously helped in sponsoring the printing and distribution of the first volume of The Ochberg Orphans.

As mentioned in the foreword one of the aims of the books I have compiled on South African Jewry is to raise funds for Arcadia and Oranjia, the two Jewish Orphanages in South Africa, in whose care the Ochberg Orphans were placed. Both of these institutions still exist today and continue to take care of Jewish children in need. All the proceeds from the sale of this book, as with my previous compilations, will be donated to them.

My compilations on South African Jewry (see details at the back of this book) are on sale all around the world and I encourage you all to promote the books with friends and to give them away as gifts. You can pay for them locally and have them delivered to friends overseas. So far we have raised over R1,300,000 for Arcadia, R60,000 for Oranjia and over $1,000 for the JDC from online sales. Please help us to reach our next milestone to raise R2,000,000 for Arcadia.

I plan next PG to publish in English The Keidan Yizkor Book. This was originally published in 1977 in Hebrew by the US, Israeli and South African Keidan Associations. This book has been translated partly with the help of Bella Golubchik and with the joint effort of Aryeh Shcherbakov of the Israel Keidan Society, Andrew Cassel from the US and I and PG it will be in print shortly. I also plan PG to re-publish with all the Yiddish articles translated into English Krakenowo the story of a world that has passed. This booklet on Krakenowo, a shtetle in Lithuania, was compiled by the Krakenowo Sick Benefit and Benevolent Society in 1961. Over many years I have also gathered my family history and PG My Inheritance may well be another book.

Please contact me if you need help publishing or reprinting a book on South African Jewry.

Best wishes and good health to you all and may there soon be peace in Israel.

David Solly Sandler sedsand@iinet.net.au

THE OCHBERG ORPHANS - VOLUME TWO

TABLE OF CONTENTS

Chapter		Page
	Foreword	iv
	Acknowledgements and thanks	v
	Section 1	
	Introducing the Ochberg Orphans	**1**
1	Introducing the Ochberg Orphans	2
2	Group Passport Photos and Names	5
3	The *Edinburgh Castle* Passenger List	14
4	Remembering the Orphans left behind	21
	Section 2	
	The Horrors in the 'Pale of Settlement' and the help given by Jewish Communities around the world	**23**
5	The Horrors faced by the Jews in the 'Pale of Settlement'	24
6	Jewish Life in Poland	36
7	Starvation in the Ukraine	39
8	The Help Given by the JDC (The American Jewish Joint Distribution Committee)	42
9	The Rescue of Ukrainian Orphans by the Canadian Jewish Community in 1921	50
10	The Help of the South African Jewish Community	59
11	The Cape Jewish Orphanage – 1920 Bulletin	62
12	The Ochberg Orphans	68
13	Isaac Ochberg (1878-1937)	71
14	The Bequests of Isaac Ochberg	73
	Section 3	
	The Pinsker Orphans	**77**
15	The Forty Four Ochberg Orphans selected from the Three Pinsk Orphanages	78
16	Alter Bobrow and the Pinsk Orphans	91
17	The Three Pinsk Orphanages	98
18	Remembering the Pinsker Orphans Left	102
	Section 4	
	The Pinsker Orphan Relief Fund of London	**109**
19	The Jewish Orphanages in Pinsk	110
20	The Pinsker Orphans Relief fund of London	114
21	More about the Pinsker Orphan Relief Fund	120
22	About the Children	124
23	Group Photos	130

Chapter			Page
	Section 5		
	Life stories of the Ochberg Orphans		**137**
	The children placed in the care of Oranjia		**138**
24	Naomi (Stein) Miller (Nachama Lerman)	1917-1970	139
25	Hymie Rosier (Chaim Razu)	1913	140
26	Malka Schapira (Molly Cohen)	1913-2013	143
27	Szlema (Solomon) Shtern later called Solly Chideckel	1912-1942	146
28	Feyga Shtrasner later called Fanny Goldberg	1915-1974	148
29	Yakov Yagalkovsky	1909-1956	152
	The children placed in the care of Arcadia		**154**
30	**Group Photos of the Arcadia Children**		154
31	Sarah (Altuska) Slier	1910-2001	157
32	Leah (Altuska) Rosenblatt	1912-1993	161
33	Sarah, Eva and Harry Gayer	1909 onwards	167
34	Harry Lidven (Herschel Lidvenitsky)	1908-1957	171
35	Rosa Lila later called Rosa Braude	1912-1956	174
36	Beila Nemet later called Judith Smith	1915-2012	175
37	David Penzik and Clara Gabbe	1907 onwards	176
38	Minnie Davidow (Mina Penzik)	1905-1956	179
39	Helen Green (Meyerovitz) (Chaia Penzik)	1916-1990	181
40	Judith, Natie and Phyllis Ratzer	1908 onwards	183
41	Chaim and Abram Reichman		188
42	Rubin Reisender		198
43	Gdalia Rosenblit (later called Gerald Nadelman)	1913-1956	199
44	Szamay Rosenblatt later called Sam Rosen	1912-1957	202
45	Harry Roth (Herman Roht)	1910-1952	205
46	Letters and photos to the Steiner Brothers		207
47	Samuel and Cecele (Olga) Zolkow		210
48	General Observations		211
	Section 6		
	Remembering Isaac Ochberg and the Ochberg Orphans		**213**
49	Honouring and Remembering Isaac Ochberg		215
50	Books and Documentary		216
51	The Work Leading up to the Creation of the Isaac Ochberg Memorial site		220
52	The Dedication Ceremony of the Ochberg Memorial Site - Israel 19th and 20th July 2011		222
53	Day One - Kibbutz Dalia - 19th July 2011		225
54	Day Two - Kibbutz Gal-Ed - 20th July 2011		237
55	Day Two - The Dedication Ceremony of the Ochberg Memorial Site at Ramat Menashe - 20th July 2011		246
56	The Unveiling of A Plaque in Honour of Isaac Ochberg at 'Villa Arcadia' 1st November 2011		258
57	Isaac Ochberg Exhibition in Brest Belarus		262
58	Gala Dinner Held in Edmonton Canada		270
59	75th Yahrzeit of Isaac Ochberg		273
60	A Communal Kaddish for Isaac Ochberg		277

Chapter		Page
	Section 7	
	The Work of the Ochberg Heritage Committee	**281**
61	Righting a Wrong	282
62	If only Isaac could see it all	285
63	WIZO South Africa visits the Ochberg Memorial	287
64	Ochberg Memorial Committee Newsletters	288
65	Spreading the Legacy of Isaac Ochberg	296
66	The Isaac Ochberg Heritage Committee News	297
67	Forgotten Man Remembered	300
	Section 8	
	Addendum	**303**
68	**Plaques on the Wall of Names**	304
69	**Index of the Ochberg Orphans**	318
	Reviews of books and documentaries on Isaac Ochberg and the Ochberg Orphans	**321**
70	*The Man from Africa* - the documentary	321
71	*The Ochberg Orphans and the horrors from whence they came* reviewed by Lionel Slier.	324
72	*This Was a Man* - the life story of Isaac Ochberg	326
73	*The Night of the Burning*	327
74	*My Dear Children - The Untold Story of the Pogroms*	328
	Charities supported with the sale of books	
75	The children were placed in the care of The South African (Arcadia) and The Cape Jewish Orphanages (Oranjia)	330
76	Proceeds on sale of books go to Arcadia, Oranjia and the JDC	334
77	Oranjia Jewish Child and Youth Centre	335
78	The New Arcadia - opened 15th March 2017	337
79	The Johannesburg Chevrah Kadisha	339
	David Solly Sandler and his Compilations	
80	Books on South African Jewry	342
81	Art Books	351
82	About David Solly Sandler, the compiler of the book	353

SECTION 1

INTRODUCING THE OCHBERG ORPHANS

This section starts with an article by the late Sir
Martin Gilbert introducing the Ochberg Orphans.
His article was based primarily on the
first volume of The Ochberg Orphans.

It is followed by Group Passport photos of the children
and the Passenger List of the *Edinburgh Castle* that
brought the children to Cape Town in September 1921

We also remember the children left behind

Chapter 1 – INTRODUCING THE OCHBERG ORPHANS

THE OCHBERG ORPHANS
Written by Sir Martin Gilbert

That part of Eastern Europe lying east of the Polish city of Warsaw, saw great upheavals in the Twentieth Century. These upheavals reached a harsh climax during the First World War (1914-1918), during the Russian civil war that followed the Bolshevik revolution of 1917, and during the pogroms, epidemics, and hunger of 1919 and 1920.

During 1919, as the region's competing ideological and national claims became more and more violent, the troops of the anti-Bolshevik Russian leader General Denikin murdered tens of thousands of Jews throughout southern Russia, in what is now Ukraine. In late 1919 and early 1920, during Simon Petlyura's rule over the briefly independent Ukraine as many as 60,000 Jews were murdered in pogroms. Several thousand Jews were killed between June and October 1920 in the Belorussian region of Russia by the troops of Stanislaw Bulak-Balachowicz, a Belorussian nationalist who in November 1920 became President of the short-lived Belarussian Provisional Government.

In August 1920, Bolshevik Russian forces, hoping to bring Communist revolution to Germany, advanced as far west as the outskirts of Warsaw. They were then driven back by Polish forces to beyond Kiev. On 18 March 1921, the Treaty of Riga established the eastern border of the newly created Republic of Poland, bringing under Polish rule all the areas – including the Polish provinces of Polesia and Volhynia – in which Isaac Ochberg sought out orphans four months later.

Armies marched back and forth in the struggle of ideologies and nationalities. The ravages of hunger and disease, and the savage of the marauding armies, created as many as 150,000 Jewish orphans. The ability of the local Jewish communities to cope with such numbers and such distress was severely limited: their own resources were minimal. Hunger stalked the region. From a sample of just over half of the parents of Ochberg's orphans, some sixty percent had died of hunger and disease; some fifteen percent had been murdered in the pogroms.

Isaac Ochberg was born in the Russian city of Uman (now in Ukraine) in 1878. At the age of sixteen he followed his father to South Africa, and was apprenticed to a watchmaker. He returned to Uman when he was

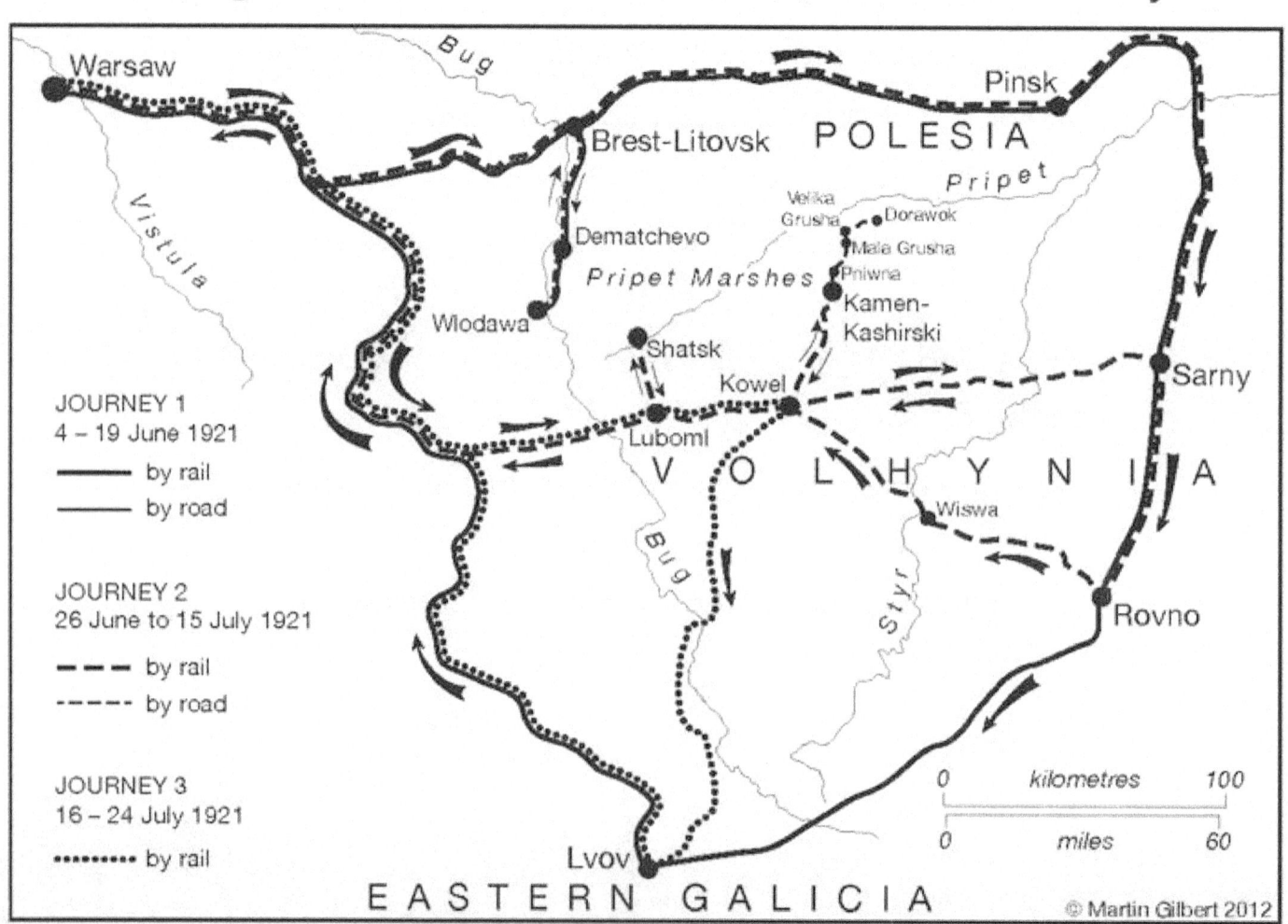

twenty-one, having learned that his mother, who still lived there, had been taken ill. Returning to South Africa in 1900, he became successful in several aspects of business, including property, agriculture and scrap metal. By the time news of the terrible persecutions and poverty in the eastern regions of newly independent Poland reached South Africa, Ochberg was President of the Cape Jewish Orphanage in Cape Town. Learning of the desperate plight of orphans east of Warsaw, he determined to find a way to bring some of them to South Africa.

South African Jews had been active in seeking to help the Jewish communities ravaged by war. As early as December 1914 the Cape Relief Fund for Jewish War and Pogrom Victims had been established in Cape Town. On 18 March 1921, the same day that the Treaty of Riga confirmed Polish rule over the regions to which Ochberg planned to travel, he left Cape Town by sea to London. He had already helped raise the funds needed to bring up to 200 Jewish orphans to South Africa. He reached London on 4 April, and began discussion with the Federation of Ukrainian Jews in London, to provide accommodation for the orphans whom he would bring back with him from Poland.

On 18 May 1921, Ochberg left London for Paris, where on the following day he met Dr Bogen, the Paris head of the American Jewish Joint Distribution Committee ('The Joint'). Dr Bogen promised Ochberg to help him 'in every way' in his 'undertaking' (as Ochberg called it) in 'selecting and transporting a number of Jewish Pogrom orphans from Eastern Europe to South Africa'. From Paris, Ochberg went by train to Warsaw, the capital of the new Polish Republic. In June and July, after spending a week in Warsaw preparing for the reception of the orphans in Warsaw, he made three journeys eastward, returning to Warsaw for a few days at a time with the orphans he had chosen for the journey to South Africa. (I have mapped these journeys on the map that goes with this article..) (See prior page)

Ochberg could only bring back with him to Warsaw those who were well enough to travel. Many of the orphans he saw on his three journeys from Warsaw were too sick to be able to make the onward journey. Typhus was taking a daily toll.

Each of the 181 Jewish orphans whom Ochberg brought from Warsaw to South Africa had a heart-rending story to tell. Typically, the Ochberg mission's notes on eleven-year-old Abi Ellstein, from Pinsk, record: 'Father killed by the Denikins in 1919. The mother died of hunger in 1920 after living in very difficult circumstances.'

In the town of Kamien Koszyrski, in the devastated region in which Ochberg travelled collecting orphans, more than a hundred Jews had been killed in a pogrom a year earlier. One of his orphans, Bracha Gisis, later recalled the fate of the son of Shimon the builder: 'They shot Shimon's son in the back and he fell forward on his face liked a felled tree in the forest.... My father and Shimon dragged the dead body into the house and laid it together with the other dead. 'Later, on entering a barn next to her house, she saw her own father 'hanging there on a length of wire, snorting his last breaths'.

Thanks to the pioneering research of David Solly Sandler, the documentation (such as that above) of the orphans' stories is voluminous and revealing, often painfully so.

Among the Ochberg orphans was eight-year-old Molly Schapira, from Sarny, one of whose earliest memories was of seeing her parents bodies 'in a room full of people crying, sobbing'. They had died from typhus, as had her two sisters. The mission's notes for one twelve-year-old boy from Lvov describe how 'both parents were killed by Petlyurists ... and a Petlyurist chopped off his left hand. The child suffered greatly and was left alone. 'Typical of the orphans' stories was that of Saul Zvengel, from Wlodawa, aged eight. His notes read: 'The father was killed by the Balachowicz. The mother died of typhoid. The child left with no relatives to look after him.' Or the five Pinsky orphans, aged between twelve and five, from Pinsk: 'Father died of hunger and the struggle to survive. The mother ... contracted syphilis after being raped.... The children had nowhere to go.'

Ochberg's mission was a ray of hope. A Jewish woman in the Pinsk district was looking after three orphans, aged 10, 8 and 6, after their widowed father's death. She wrote to the 'African Mission' in Warsaw, Ochberg's headquarters: 'I intend to better their well-being. I freely give them up.'

Half a century later, Ochberg's daughter Bertha I Epstein wrote: 'Most of the children were in shocking state. They were starving, clad in rags and verminous. Many of them were ... in a state of shock from seeing their parents murdered before their eyes or having to watch their mothers and sisters being raped.'

In the orphanages that Ochberg visited, the orphans were surviving mostly on food provided by the Joint. In Pinsk, Ochberg found thirty-eight-year-old Alexander Obrov (Alter Bobrow), a former Analytical Chemist in a sugar factory who in 1916 had helped set up three orphanages in Pinsk, and who offered to help choose those who could go to South Africa, and to accompany them there. In fact, the Pinsk Orphanage Committee would not allow the children to leave unless Obrov went with them. During the journey, Obrov was given the care of sixty orphans.

The children gathered in Warsaw, some arriving destitute, in slow, dirty local trains. The *Cape Jewish Chronicle* later reported them 'clutching a precious doll or a dog-eared photograph'. In Warsaw, they received condensed milk, cocoa and clothes that had arrived for them from South Africa. The Polish authorities helpfully provided collective passports, each one for between twenty and thirty children on each passport, with a single group photograph pasted in it, instead of individual photographs and passports. (See example on next page)

Thirty-seven of the children, having lived in fear for so long, decided at the last moment not to continue on the

Group Passport Four

journey, and ran away. Two were taken ill just before leaving Warsaw. Their names were crossed out on the collective passport photograph lists before the other orphans left Poland. Ochberg appointed several older orphans, whose age made them ineligible for the journey to South Africa, as nurses and tutors, so that they could travel with the others.

On 1 August 1921, Ochberg left Warsaw with his orphans by train to Danzig. The train stopped at many stations on the way. At each station the Jews of that town met them with food and flowers. The children got down from the train, and, with Obrov playing his mandolin, sang and danced on the platform with the local Jews.

From Danzig, the orphans sailed on a small, slow British cargo ship, the *Baltara*, to London. Molly Schapira from Sarny later recalled: 'We stopped in England. I didn't know it was England.' Also stopping briefly in England at this time were several hundred Jewish orphans from Ukraine brought out by the Canadian Jewish Congress, who were taken by ship to Canada.

British newspapers reported on the arrival of the Ochberg orphans on 24 August 1921. Ochberg told the reporters who gathered to watch his orphans come ashore: 'They are all victims of some pogrom or disturbance and when I found them they were roaming about the towns or in the forests, filthy, worse than naked, and starving. In most of the places there was no food, and disease was rampant....' Ochberg added that the Dominion Government in South Africa had given him 'every assistance possible, especially in the way of withdrawing the restrictions against the immigration of orphan children.'

In London for eight days, the orphans slept at the Atlantic Passengers' Hostels for immigrants in transit. During the day, members of the Federation of Ukrainian Jews in London – encouraged by the Federation's Chairman, Dr D Jochelman – gave them hospitality. From London, Ochberg and his orphans went by train from Waterloo Station to Southampton. The *Daily Mail* had a photograph of them at the train window just as it was about to leave, with the headline 'Off to South Africa.'

On 2 September 1921, Ochberg and his orphans sailed from Southampton on the Union Castle liner *Edinburgh Castle* to Cape Town. By then, writes Ochberg's daughter, the children were calling him 'Daddy Ochberg' and during the voyage 'clustered around him like the proverbial lost sheep'. The Union Castle line allowed the orphans greatly reduced fares, and provided them with kosher food. After seventeen days at sea, the *Edinburgh Castle* reached Cape Town. A new life, and a renewal of hope, had begun.

Chapter 2 – GROUP PASSPORT PHOTOS AND NAMES

The following passport photos and names accompanying the photos were kindly provided by the Jewish Museum in Cape Town and Lauren Snitcher.

I understand that the lists of names below accompanying the photos are generally in no particular order in relation to the passport photo and that the number after the name is the age of the child and this was not always accurate. These ages were sometimes less than the ages found on other documents.

Lastly children who are crossed out on the photo for various reasons did not finally come out to South Africa.

GROUP PASSPORT ONE

LIST OF NAMES ACCOMPANYING GROUP PASSPORT ONE

GROUP PASSPORT TWO

LIST OF NAMES ACCOMPANYING GROUP PASSPORT TWO

GROUP PASSPORT THREE

LIST OF NAMES ACCOMPANYING GROUP PASSPORT THREE

GROUP PASSPORT FOUR

LIST OF NAMES ACCOMPANYING GROUP PASSPORT FOUR

GROUP PASSPORT FIVE

LIST OF NAMES ACCOMPANYING GROUP PASSPORT FIVE

GROUP PASSPORT SIX

LIST OF NAMES ACCOMPANYING GROUP PASSPORT SIX

OPIS OSOBY — SIGNALEMENT

DZIECI — ENFANTS

1 Gajer Chane 6 l.
2 [illegible] 5
3 Pinsec Feiga 3
4 Mennes [illegible] 4
5 [illegible] 2
6 Borowitz Chane 12
7 Kolodun Jente 4
8 Faifer Blume 8
9 Rondas Symcha 9
10 Rasur Jente 8
11 Rasur Itzak 5
12 Feldman Mendel 6.
13 [illegible] Mirrea 6 l.
14 [illegible] [illegible] 8.

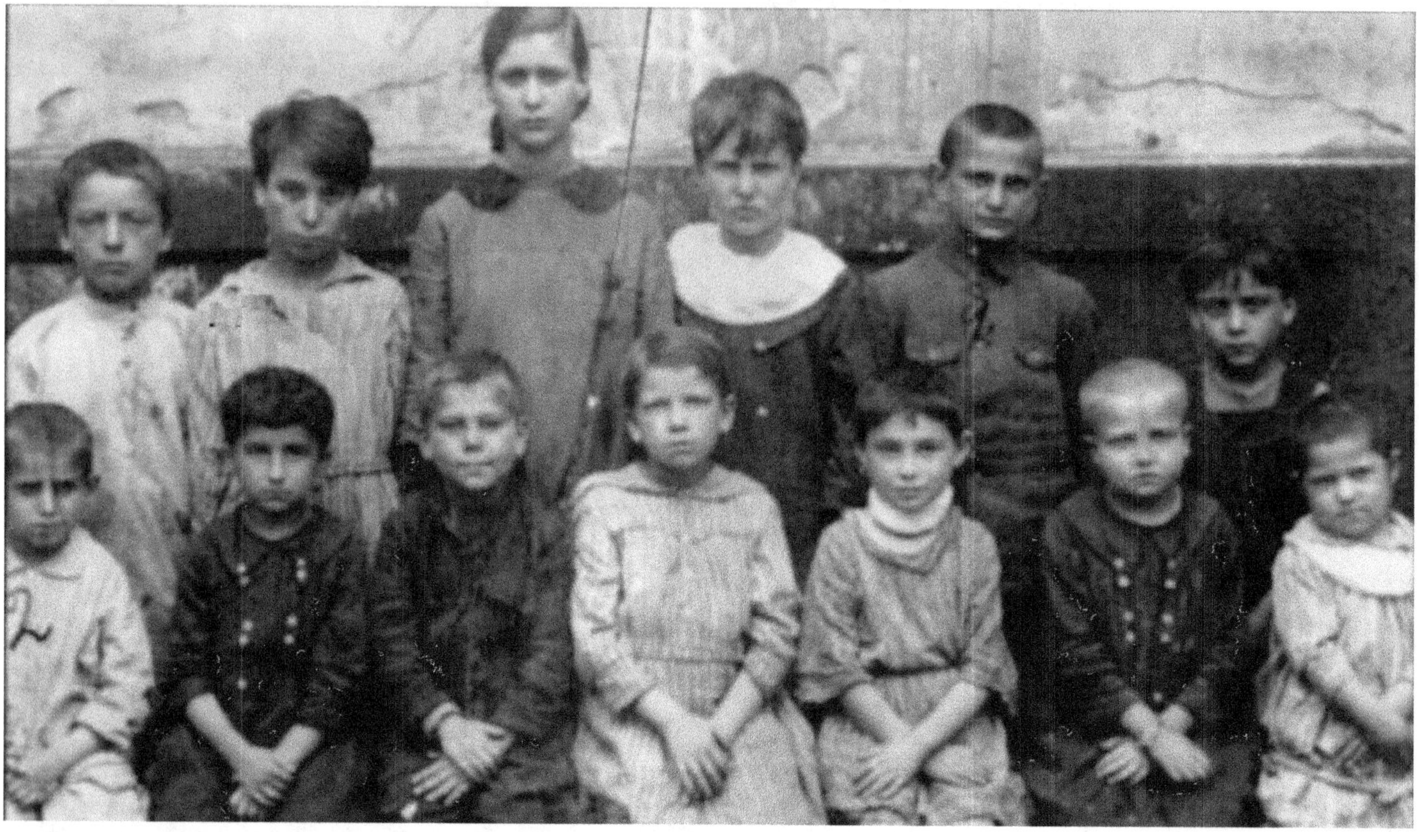

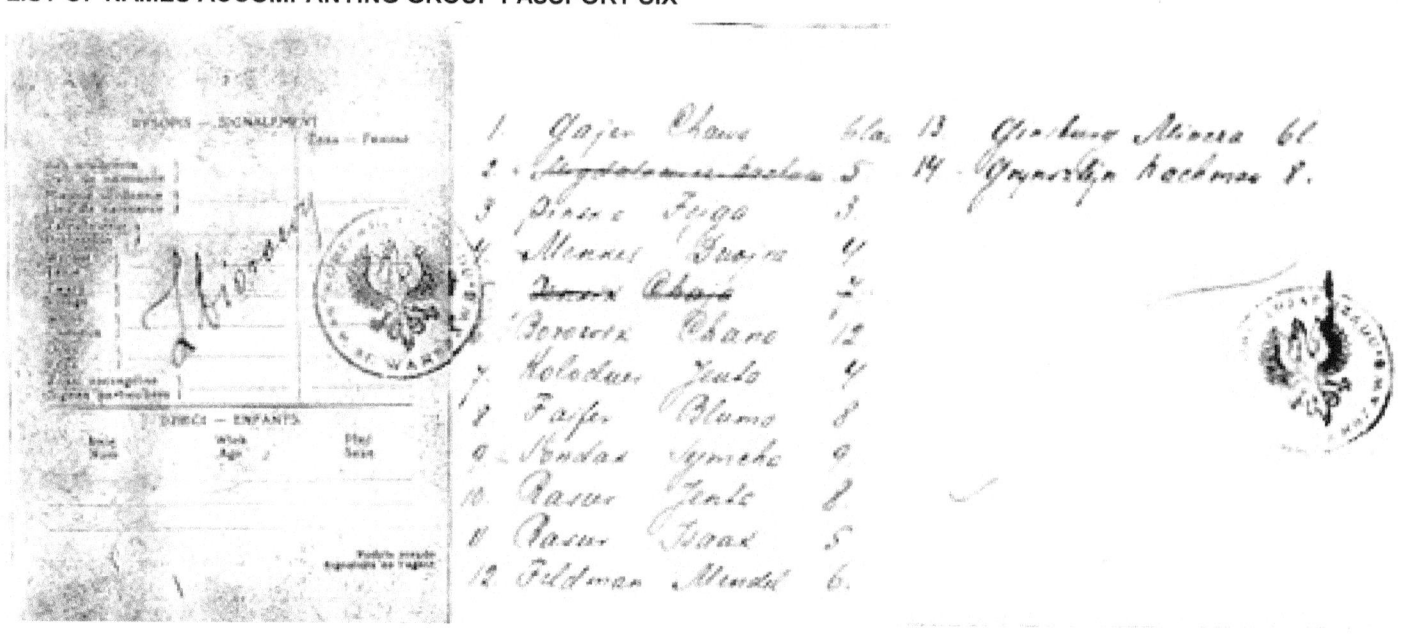

GROUP PASSPORT SEVEN

LIST OF NAMES ACCOMPANYING GROUP PASSPORT SEVEN

#	Name		#	Name		#	Name	
1	Elman Bluma	3	13	Lerman Dwojra	6	25	Joffe Frejdl	9
2	Lerman Nechama	3	14	Hefl Rasia	7	26	Genefas Gitl	12
3	Jaka Pesa	4	15	Mauschblait pesa	8	27	Zaika Mania	8
4	Perevies Regina	4	16	Haus Roza	7	28	Zaika Sisl	5
5	Perler Leja	9	17	Haus Nesia	8	29	Dragif Chasia	7
6	Elman Fejga	5	18	Goldman Tryfra	10	30	Dragif Dwojra	5
7	Margolin Sara	7	19	Majrejer Frances	8			
8	Gunderman Jocha	5	20	Blind Salna	8			
9	Genefas Malka	7	21	Majsenman Rosa	8			
10	Gabaj Gitla	6	22	Derlowez Chana	8			
11	Nejsztejn Sala	5	23	Gesunherman Srjno Rook	10			
12	Massman Reizel	4	24	Sarmurna Ztula	9			

GROUP PASSPORT EIGHT

LIST OF NAMES ACCOMPANYING GROUP PASSPORT EIGHT

GROUP PASSPORT NINE

LIST OF NAMES ACCOMPANYING GROUP PASSPORT NINE

Chapter 3 – EDINBURGH CASTLE PASSENGER LIST – 2 SEPTEMBER 1921

On this passenger list are the names of all the children, nurses and attendants that accompanied Isaac Ochberg to South Africa in September 1921. The Edinburgh Castle left Southhampton on 2 September 1921 and arrived in Cape Town on 21 September 1921.

Names of Passengers		Last Address in the United Kingdom	Port at which Passengers have contracted to land	Profession, Occupation or Calling	Age	Country of Citizen or Subject	Country of Last Permanent Residence	Country of Intended Future Permanent Residence
Alyfrom	Miss Frida	193 Bow Road, London E.	Capetown	Attendant	22 F	Poland	1	S Africa
Kagan	Miss Golda			Nurse	17 F		1	
Altiotka	Jasha			Saitoress	21 F		1	
Morduchowitz	Rosa			Nurse	19 F		1	
Faran-Glasman	Rachel			—	21 F		1	
Morduchowitz	Chanda			Saitoress	16 F		1	
—	Liza			Nurse	16 F		1	
Laika	Liza			—	19 F		1	
Alysfrom	Malka			Attendant	26 F		1	
Wilchuk	Feyga			Nil	4		1	
Lewin	Picha				4		1	
Leisenterman	Brayndel				9		1	
Samurina	Sima				4		1	
Gornstein	Channa				6		1	
Pinska	Slaia				5		1	
Kaufman	Cypora				5		1	
Joffe	Shiwa				6		1	
Scholin	Fauba				4		1	
Kreindel	Pepel				4		1	
Miler	Brayndel				4		1	
Jayfer	Liba				9		1	
Penoyk	Chana				8		1	
Birnfield	Chaya				10		1	
Borowik	Rochela				9		1	
Lenebaum	Sara				10		1	
Helman	Chasia				8		1	
Geeber	Chaya				8		1	
Lipshyts	Kerel				11		1	
Shapiro	Malka				6		1	
Elman	Bluma				3		1	
Lerman	Nechma				3		1	
Bekler	Leya				4		1	
Elman	Feyga				5		1	
Ganefro	Malka				4		1	
Gabay	Gitel				6		1	
Nischolin	Sala				5		1	
Nusoman	Reisel				4		1	
Lerman	Dwoyna				6		1	
Heft	Rosia				4		1	
Mandelblat	Peas				8		1	
Hans	Rosa				4		1	
—	Nechm				8		1	

P.M. 25.

Name of Ship "Edinburgh Castle" Date of Departure 2nd September 1921

Steamship Line Union Castle Mail Steamship Company Ltd Where Bound South Africa

NAMES AND DESCRIPTIONS OF ALIEN PASSENGERS EMBARKED AT THE PORT OF Southampton

B.—NON-TRANSMIGRANTS, that is Alien Passengers other than those included under A.

(1) Contract Ticket Number	(2) Names of Passengers	(3) Last Address in the United Kingdom	(4) Class	(5) Port at which Passengers have contracted to land	(6) Profession, Occupation, or Calling	(7) Ages – Adult Males	Adult Females	Children M	Children F	Infants	(8) Country of which Citizen or Subject	(9) Country of Last Permanent Residence	(10) Country of Intended Future Permanent Residence
			Third Class Continued										
				Forward	42	—	—	9	53	—		42	42
	Meikefer Miss	Franzichka	93 Bow Road London	Capetown	Nil				8		Poland	1	S. Africa
	Blind	Salka							8			1	
	Deklovich	Chana							8			1	
	Youngman	Seria Rachel							10			1	
	Joffe	Freida							4			1	
	Yanfas	Gitel					12						1	
	Jarka	Maria							8			1	
	—	Sysel							3			1	
	Walchuk	Toybe							8			1	
	Gabay	Chaja					12						1	
	Kimbowetz	Itzia							11			1	
	Yabay	Pesia							9			1	
	Altinsky	Soya							6			1	
	Yanipas	Leifa							5			1	
	Pinska	Freyga							6			1	
	Garper	Chawa							4			1	
	Wankes	Delara							12				1	
	Borowich	Chana							4			1	
	Kolodner	Jenia							8			1	
	Fayver	Bluma							8			1	
	Basur	Jenta							6			1	
	Ginsburg	Myncha							9			1	
	Altuska	Sara							6			1	
	Shrayer	Feyga							8			1	
	Pimka	Chawa							7			1	
	Birkowich	Chawa							3			1	
	Gilernter	Lehwa							8			1	
	Barnath	Sara										7	
	Berchman	Jenta							5			1	
	—	Shindal							8			1	
	Broder	Sara										1	
		Bina							7			1	
	Lille	Rosa							5			1	
	Nomet	Beyla							5			1	
	Rasmer	Ides							4			1	
	—	Fira							4			1	
	Weidman	Shindal							4			1	
	Kubin	Chana							4			1	
	Shraver	Feyga										1	
	Rachel	Sora										1	
				Forward				12	70				42	

C. No. 440 C.

Name of Ship "Edinburgh Castle" **Date of Departure** 2nd September 1921
Steamship Line Union Castle Mail S.S. Coy Ltd. **Where Bound** South Africa

NAMES AND DESCRIPTIONS OF ALIEN PASSENGERS EMBARKED AT THE PORT OF Southampton
B.—NON-TRANSMIGRANTS, that is Alien Passengers other than those included under A.

(1) Contract Ticket Number	(2) Names of Passengers		(3) Last Address in the United Kingdom	(4) Class	(5) Port at which Passengers have contracted to land	(6) Profession, Occupation, or Calling of Passengers	(7) Ages of Passengers — Adults Male Acc	Adults Female Acc	Adults Male Not Acc	Adults Female Not Acc	Children 1–12 M	Children 1–12 F	Infants	(8) Country of which Citizen or Subject	(9) England	Wales	Scotland	Ireland	British Poss.	Foreign	(10) Country of Intended Future Permanent Residence
				Third Class	Continued	Forward			12	70										82	82
	Steinger	Miss Pepy	93 Bow Rd London		Capetown	Nil				9				Poland						1	S. Africa
	Mordochowitz	Rivka								8										1	
	—	Etel		6						6										1	
	Gurwitz	Rosa								8										1	
	Szames	Riesel								8										1	
	Wainer	Maril Riva						21												1	
	Lewin	Sara								5										1	
	Huber	Scharna								4										1	
	Korber	Rywke								8										1	
	Kolodner	Liba								4										1	
	Tsunterman	Joche								5										1	
	Sannvine	Slata								9										1	
	Margolin	Sara								7										1	
	Penayk	Chaye								7										1	
	Teier	Sara								9										1	
	Belman	Chane								10										1	
	Karant	Mrs Issak				Doctor	28													1	
	Tkasnov	Auron				Typist	23													1	
	Bobrow	Godtie Sender				Teacher	28													1	
	Neichelyan	Master Solomon				Nil					5									1	
	Stillerman	Hursh									10									1	
	Reht	Herman									8									1	
	Freppel	Jacob									5									1	
	Frema	Max									9									1	
	Rusender	Rubin									4									1	
	Megdalowitch	Simon									6									1	
	Ruchocky	Aron									4									1	
	Litwinicky	Hersch									10									1	
	Ushlein	Schlama									8									1	
	Kahan	Mordock									10									1	
	—	Chahne									7									1	
	Pinsky	Fajwal									6									1	
	Pierchodinsky	Iser									10									1	
	—	Shepsel									4									1	
	Meiner	Gaskel									5									1	
	Reichman	Abraham									9									1	
	Ruchocky	Fajwel									6									1	
	Elman	Benjamin									6									1	
	Megdalowich	Chanon									4									1	
	Steiner	Isac									6									1	
	Gorenshtein	Abram									10									1	

C. No. 440 C.

Name of Ship "Edinburgh Castle"
Steamship Line Union-Castle Mail S.S. Co. Ltd.
Date of Departure 2nd September 192[?]
Where Bound South Africa

NAMES AND DESCRIPTIONS OF ALIEN PASSENGERS EMBARKED AT THE PORT OF Southampton
B.—NON-TRANSMIGRANTS, that is Alien Passengers other than those included under A.

(1) Contract Ticket Number	(2) Names of Passengers	(3) Last Address in the United Kingdom	(4) Class	(5) Port at which Passengers have contracted to land	(6) Profession, Occupation, or Calling	(7) Ages — Adult M	Adult F	Child M (1-12)	Child F	Inf M	Inf F	(8) Country of which Citizen or Subject	(9) Country of Last Permanent Residence — Foreign Countries	(10) Country of Intended Future Permanent Residence
			Third Class Continued											
					Forward	23	—	—	16	28	—	—		123	123
	Elman Master	Jontel	193 Bow Rd London	Capetown	Nil			7				Poland	1	S. Africa
	Altiocha	Chaim						8					1	
	Brengel	Saul						4					1	
	Bouriick	Chaya						9					1	
	Dchtein	Sylema						7					1	
	Echstein	Josef						6					1	
	Pinoyk	David						10					1	
	Haverberg	Mayer						10					1	
	Hanifao	Becadel						8					1	
	Welchuk	Chaim						8					1	
	Bernfeld	Hirsh						4					1	
	Welchuk	Leyba						6					1	
	Rosenblit	Ydalia						4					1	
	Musaman	Isaak						6					1	
	Echstein	Leibel						6					1	
	Elstein	Libel						5					1	
	Baow	Isaac						5					1	
	Sondak	Symcha						9					1	
	Feldman	Mendel						6					1	
	Grinshlein	Nachman						8					1	
	Shleiner	Yoshi						8					1	
	Serchenabel	Moishe						8					1	
	Sagolkowisky	Jacob						8					1	
	Berenshtein	Isaac						8					1	
	Orbansky	Abram						8					1	
	Pinsky	Moisha						8					1	
	Feinshmidt	Seydel						9					1	
	Bechman	Solomon						7					1	
	Druling	Juda						8					1	
	Raomer	Natali						5					1	
	Rosenbaum	Leon						7					1	
	Ringler	Chaskel						8					1	
	Rubin	David						7					1	
	Lwign	Gryash						4					1	
	—	Berner						6					1	
	Sjames	Manno						9					1	
	Wainer	Israel Mote					14							1	
	Dorfman	Moses					14							1	
	Schwarz	Josef						9					1	
	Farbus	Shmel						9					1	
	Olshtein	Abe						8					1	

P.M. 25

Name of Ship: Edinburgh Castle
Date of Departure: 2nd Sept 192[ ]
Steamship Line: Union-Castle Mail S.S. Co. Ltd.
Where Bound: South Africa

NAMES AND DESCRIPTIONS OF ALIEN PASSENGERS EMBARKED AT THE PORT OF Southampton
B.—NON-TRANSMIGRANTS, that is Alien Passengers other than those included under A.

(1) Contract Ticket Number	(2) Names of Passengers	(3) Last Address in the United Kingdom	(4) Class	(5) Port at which Passengers have contracted to land	(6) Profession, Occupation, or Calling of Passengers	(7) Ages — M Adult	F Adult	M 1-12	F 1-12	M Inf	F Inf	(8) Country of Citizen	(9) Eng	Wal	Scot	Ire	Brit Dom	Foreign	(10) Future Residence
					Forward		21	4	15									Nil	S. Africa
	Lewin Mad[ ]	Chaim	193 Bow Rd London E	Capetown	Nil			4				Poland						1	
	Nuchasky	Studin						4										1	
	Shraw	Arieh						4										1	
	Raychman	Chaim						4										1	
	Kaufman	Shlene						5										1	
	Yaier	Moishe						4										1	
	Harman	Benjamin						5										1	
	Rosenblat	Dzaney						6										1	
	~~Cujelin~~																		
	Migdalowich	Nachman							5									1	
	Raser	Chaim							4									1	
	Ylobanov	Isaac							3									1	
	Shraw	Jakob							4									1	
	Golarich	Miss Rebecca				Typist	26											1	
	Gartner	Perla				Attendant		28										1	
	—	Hinda						28										1	
	Lochow	Cecile						24										1	
	Tennenbaum	Chaia						15										1	
	Zebenhole	Ruchla						14										1	
	Rosenberg	Leah						19										1	
	Midman	Mrs Florence Pricilla						32				France	1						
	—	Mr Halil					32						1						
	—	Miss Rita				Nil					1			1					
	Morduchowitz	Mr Shimon				Attendant	27					Poland						1	
	Kowal	Mojzesz					26											1	
	Glasman	Jewla						26										1	
	Benytik	Miss Mindla				Nil		13										1	
	Kolsow	Mr Samuel				Photographer	33											1	
	Weinstein	Mr Moses				Teacher	21					Poland						1	
						192	1 1 7 21 73 86 — —						3 — — — 189					192	

SUMMARY OF BRITISH AND ALIEN PASSENGERS.

NATIONALITIES	NUMBER OF PERSONS							
	Adults of 12 years of age and upwards				Children between 1 and 12 years		Infants	
	Accompanied by husband or wife		Not accompanied by husband or wife					
	Males	Females	Males	Females	Males	Females	Males	Females
British Subjects	108	108	118	146	45	60	1	1
Aliens — Transmigrants								
Aliens — Non-transmigrants	2	2	31	40	74	86		
TOTAL	110	110	149	186	119	146	1	1

	Souls	Equal to Statute Adults
Total Number of Adults	555	555
Total Number of Children between 1 and 12 years	265	132½
Total Number of Infants	2	—
GRAND TOTAL	822	687½

We hereby Certify that the above is a correct List of the Names and Descriptions of all the Passengers who embarked at the Port of Southampton

Countersigned _J M Bale_ Emigration Officer. Signed _John W. Hague_ Master.

Countersigned _____ Officer of Customs and Excise at _____

Date _____

C. No. 149.

Name of Ship: Edinburgh Castle
Steamship Line: Union-Castle Mail S.S. Co. Ltd.
Date of Departure: Sept. 2. 1921
Where Bound: South Africa

NAMES AND DESCRIPTIONS OF BRITISH PASSENGERS EMBARKED AT THE PORT OF Southampton

First Class (cont'd).

(2) Names of Passengers	(3) Last address in the United Kingdom	(5) Port at which Passengers have contracted to land	(6) Profession, Occupation or Calling	(9) Country of Intended Future Permanent Residence
Brought forward				
Higgins, Mrs. L.G.	Inglenook, Harpenden, Herts.	Natal	Doctor	England
Pickin, Mr. & Mrs. A.J.	40 Bell St. & London Wall Bldgs. E.C.	Cape	Civ. Servant	S. Africa
Johnson, M?	11 Foster Lane			
Ochberg, Mr. I.	15 Sexulton St. E.C.	Cape	Merchant	S. Africa

Chapter 4 – REMEMBERING THE ORPHANS LEFT BEHIND

Nobody really knew the number of orphaned children in Eastern Europe in 1921.

The Chief Rabbi of the British Empire, Rabbi Joseph H Hertz declared that 1,000,000 human beings had been butchered and that for three years 3,000,000 persons in the Ukraine had been made 'to pass through the horrors of hell. He said there were something like 600,000 homeless children, 150,000 orphans and 35,000 double orphans in the Ukraine who would die from cold, hunger or disease unless Jewish hearts remained human and came to the rescue."

Mr Zultsman an executive of the Federation of Ukrainian Jews reported that the Jews in Eastern Europe have gone through horrible torture and are still living through terrible times and anguish. There are no less than 600,000 Jewish orphans in Eastern Europe, helpless and hopeless. Of this great number there are, he states, 110,000 Pogrom Orphans.

According to one American investigation, there were at least 300,000 orphans left unsupported.

Besides the group rescued by Isaac Ochberg there was a similar sized group that went to Canada and Palestine. Many others would have emigrated from Eastern Europe in the 1920s and 1930s but there can be no doubt that the majority of those left behind perished in the Holocaust, as you will see below as we examine the history of the various towns and cities from which the Ochberg Orphans were gathered.

BREST-LITOVSK

Brest-Litovski was the first town from which a group of Ochberg Children was selected.

Brest-Litovsk is a fortress city on the river Bug on the border of Belarus (Russia) and Poland. It was once an important trading centre and prominent in the 15th and 16th Centuries when it was part of the Lithuanian ascendancy. It subsequently passed into Polish hands but in the Polish partitions of 1793 it became Russian.

In 1914 the population of the city was about 48 000 of which 70% were Jews. Although Jews did not play a major part in the city's life, mostly being traders, small artisans, inn keepers and the usual occupations that Jews had throughout the Pale of Settlement which was the area of restricted Jewish settlement in the Tsarist Russian Empire.

The war started in August 1914 and for some reason the Russian army drove all the Jews out of Brest-Litovsk in August the following year. The Austrian/German forces occupied the city later that month but they in turn were driven out by the Russians. With all this fighting it was naturally chaotic for the civilian population and many died leaving hundreds of orphans alone and abandoned in the war zones.

Notes (1) Lionel Slier
(2) **From Wikipedia, the free encyclopedia**

The major Peace Treaty between Russia and Germany took place at Brest-Litovsk in January 1917 after the Russian Revolution and Russia withdrew from the war. Brest-Litovsk was part of a large swath of territory that the Germans took from Russia which eventually became Polish. The city became Brzsc and Bugiem. *(1)*

The Germans invaded the Soviet Union in summer 1941, and on June 22, 1941 the fortress and the city was attacked by Nazi Germany at the beginning of the surprise war, codenamed Operation Barbarossa, but held out for six weeks. Nearly all the defenders perished.

On 16 December 1941, a Jewish ghetto was created in the city. Soon afterwards, in January 1942, first underground resistance organisations were formed among Jews in the ghetto. In autumn of 1942 the Germans demanded a large contribution (money, jewellery) from the Jews under the threat of liquidating the ghetto. Despite the significant contribution, the ghetto was liquidated soon afterwards, and most of the Jews were murdered.

Today a Holocaust memorial commemorates over 34,000 Jews of Brest ghetto that were killed in 1941 - 1942. *(2)*

WLODAWA

Although no Jews are known to live in the town today, Wlodawa was over 70% Jewish before WWII and the Holocaust. Situated next to the Sobibór Concentration and Death Camp, Wlodawa's Jews were mostly rounded up and killed by German Nazis in Sobibor or one of its arbeitslagers (workcamps) such as Adampol. On the road to Wlodawa there is a memorial to the Jews from Wlodawa who were killed at Adampol. The handsome, Baroque, Wlodawa Synagogue survives. The Jewish cemetery was demolished by the Germans who used the headstones as road building material. They used the synagogue buildings for military storage. *(2)*

LVOV

L'vov was occupied by Germany from 1941 to 1944. Almost the entire Jewish population was murdered in concentration camps in Lvov and elsewhere. *(2)*

WISŁA (WISWA)

There are no Jewish residents of Dobrzyn and Wisla today with most current-day residents unaware of the rich Jewish history of the town and also of the decimation of the Jewish population in the Nazi genocide. *(2)*

SARNA

Sarna is a village in the administrative district of Gmina Małdyty, within Ostróda County, Warmian-Masurian Voivodeship, in northern Poland. It lies approximately five kilometres north of Małdyty, 32 km north-west of Ostróda, and 53 km west of the regional capital Olsztyn. The village has a population of 30. *(2)*

KOVEL (KOWEL)

In World War II, following the Nazi German invasion of Poland and subsequently, their Operation Barbarossa the Germans murdered 18,000 Jews in Kovel, mostly during August and September of 1942. *(2)*

A Testament of a Jewish Woman from Kowel.
During the months of August and September 1942, thousands of Jews were herded into the synagogue in the town of Kowel, Poland where they were imprisoned until their execution. In their fear and desperation, many of them wrote on the walls of the synagogue using whatever they could; unsharpened pencils, pens and even their own fingernails. Last testaments, letters and declarations were written in Hebrew, Yiddish and Polish. Below is one of the inscriptions that were found. The Germans murdered 18,000 Jews in Kowel.

"Reuven Atlas, know that your wife Gina and your son Imush perished here. Our child wept bitterly. He did not want to die. Go to war and avenge the blood of your wife and your only son. We are dying although we did no wrong. Gina Atlas". (3)

KAMIN-KASHYRSKYI

Memorial at the killing field outside of town reads

*"Here lie about 2600 Jews residents of Kamin-Kashirsky and the vicinity who were murdered by the Germans and their helpers.
27 Av 5702 - 10 August 1942
22 Heshvan 5703 - 2 November 1942
May their souls be bound in the knot of life." (4)*

LUBOML (LUBOMIL)

On 1 October 1942 the Germans, who controlled the town, with the aid of Ukrainian police units rounded up the remaining Jewish inhabitants of Luboml and marched them into the countryside. There the Jews were lined up in front of open pits and shot.

By the time the Soviet Red Army liberated Luboml in 1945, only 51 Jews from Luboml (excluding those who had emigrated before 1939) survived the Holocaust. More than 1,000 died in the mass execution on 1 October 1942. The German liquidation of the town effectively ended a six-century history and presence of Jewish life in Luboml.

Today Luboml is a part of the Republic of the Ukraine but there are no longer any Jews in the town.

ROVNE

On 28 June 1941 Rovne was captured by Nazi Germany, who later established the city as the administrative centre of Reichskommissariat Ukraine. At the time, roughly a half of

Notes
(3) Safira Rapoport (Ed.), Yesterdays and then Tomorrows, Yad Vashem 2002, p. 183 (in the Hebrew edition).   (4) Internet website

Rovne's inhabitants were Jewish; of these, about 23,000 were taken to a pine grove in Sosenki and killed between 6 and the 8 November. A ghetto was established for the remaining 5,000 Jews. In July 1942, its population was sent some 70 kilometres north to Kostopil where they were killed; the ghetto was subsequently liquidated. *(2)*

KOSTOPOL

The town had become a centre for Jewish settlement in the interwar Poland and this continued until World War II, when about 40% (about 4,000) of the population were Jewish. Kostopol became the local administrative centre of Kostopol County in 1925. The town had been joined with Poland after the end of First World War. By the end of the 1920s, there were three timber yards (two of them Jewish owned, one government owned), three plywood factories (Jewish owned), two furniture factories, two glass factories, two agriculture machinery works, three flour mills (two Jewish owned), two oil presses, four tar and turpentine factories and a brick factory operating in Kostopol. In nearby Janowa Dolina, there were granite and basalt quarries, with railway links to Kostopol station. The Polish government built a housing project for the quarry workers.

The Germans occupied Kostopol on 1 July 1941 and immediately there was a pogrom against the local Jews, perpetrated by local Ukrainian nationalists. The Germans progressively degraded the Jews' position and condition, by enforcing the wearing of yellow stars, imposing forced labour and confiscating Jewish property. On 16 August 1941, the Germans rounded up 470 of the most influential Jews in the community and transported them out of Kostopol, where they were all executed. Another 1,400 Jews related to those who had been executed, were arrested on 1 October and also taken away and killed.

A ghetto was established in Kostopol on 5 October 1941. Despite the great over-crowding, there were no epidemics. One hundred Jews, Judenrat members, Jewish Police and key professionals, were exempt and were allowed to live outside the ghetto. The ghetto was liquidated on 25 August 1942. Ukrainian and German police surrounded the ghetto. The ghetto was emptied and the remaining inhabitants were transported to Khotinka, a nearby village, and exterminated upon arrival. A few managed to escape but they were caught by local Ukrainians, returned to the Germans and murdered.

On 24 August, in Kostopol's forced labour camp, 700 Jewish labourers, led by Gedalia Braier, revolted during the daily census. When Brajer shouted "*Hura!*", he started a mass escape attempt. Some reached the nearby forest, but most of them were caught and killed by local Ukrainians. Some survived with the help of Polish villagers and joined Soviet partisan units. Less than ten survived the war.

Kostopol was liberated by the Red Army on 31 January 1944. Only about 270 Kostopol Jews had survived the German occupation, including those who had escaped eastwards before the mass killings. *(2)*

SECTION 2

THE HORRORS IN 'THE PALE OF SETTLEMENT' AND THE HELP GIVEN BY THE JEWISH COMMUNITIES AROUND THE WORLD

THE HORRORS:
This section commences with details of the horrors faced by Jews in the Pale of Settlement. It then tells of the oppression of Jews in Poland and starvation in the Ukraine.

THE HELP:
We start with the enormous help given by the JDC (The American Jewish Joint Distribution Committee) and follow with details of the rescue of Ukrainian Orphans by the Canadian Jewish Community in 1921. Next is the help from the South African Jewish Community and details of The Cape Jewish Orphanage – 1920 Bulletin. We then focus on the Ochberg Orphans and Isaac Ochberg (1878-1937) and conclude with details of his bequests.

Chapter 5 – THE HORRORS FACED BY THE JEWS IN THE PALE OF SETTLEMENT

THE JEWS IN THE EASTERN WAR ZONES
Published by the American Jewish Committee, 1916

Introduction

Of all the people that have suffered deeply from the present war, none have borne a greater burden than the Jews - in physical and economic loss, in moral and spiritual torment.

Jews are today fighting each other in all the armies of Europe. Russia alone has 350,000 Jewish soldiers; Austria has over 50,000; altogether there are one-half million Jews in the ranks of the fighting armies.

The Jews are bearing the brunt of the war's burdens, not only on the field of battle, where they suffer with the rest of the world, but also in their homes, where they have been singled out, by their peculiar geographic, political and economic position, for disaster surpassing that of all others.

When the war broke out, one-half of the Jewish population of the world was trapped in a corner of Eastern Europe that is absolutely shut off from all neutral lands and from the sea. Russian Poland, where over two million Jews lived, is in a salient part. South of it is Galicia, the frontier province of Austria. Here lived another million Jews. Behind Russian Poland are the fifteen Russian provinces, which together with Poland, constitute the *Pale of Jewish Settlement*. Here lived another four million Jews.

Thus seven million Jews, a population exceeding that of Belgium by one million, have borne the brunt of the war. Behind them was Holy Russia, closed to them by the May laws of 1881. In front were hostile Germany and Austria. To the south was unfriendly Rumania. They were overwhelmed where they stood; and over their bodies crossed and recrossed the German armies from the west, the Russian armies from the east and the Austrian armies from the south. True, all the peoples of this area suffered ravage and pillage by the war, but their sufferings were in no degree comparable to those of the Jews. The contending armies found it politic, in a measure, to court the goodwill of the Poles, Ruthenians and other races in this area. These sustained only the necessary and unavoidable hardships of war. But the Jews were friendless, their religion proscribed. In this medieval region all the religious fanaticism of the Russians, the chauvinism of the Poles, combined with the blood lusts liberated in all men by the war - all those fierce hatreds were sluiced into one torrent of passion which overwhelmed the Jews.

Hundreds of thousands were forced from their homes on a day's notice, the more fortunate being packed and shipped as freight - the old, the sick and insane, men, women and children, shuttled from one province to another, side-tracked for days without food or help of any kind - the less fortunate driven into the woods and swamps to die of starvation. Jewish towns were sacked and burned wantonly. Hundreds of Jews were carried off as hostages into Germany, Austria and Russia. Orgies of lust and torture took place in public in the light of day. There are scores of villages where not a single woman was left inviolate. Women, old and young, were stripped and knotted in the public squares. Jews were burned alive in synagogues where they had fled for shelter. Thousands were executed on the flimsiest pretext or from sheer purposeless cruelty.

These Jews, unlike the Belgians, have no England to flee to. The sympathy of the outside world is shut off from them. They have not the consolation of knowing that they are fighting for their own hearths, or even for military glory or in the hope of a possible reward of indemnity. The only thought they cherish is that after the struggle shall be over they may at last achieve those elementary rights denied to no other people, the right to live and move about freely in the land of their birth or adoption, to educate their children, to earn a livelihood, to worship God according to the dictates of their conscience.

Russia

Nearly half of the Jewish population of the world lives in Russia, in the immediate area of active hostilities, congested in cities, which are the first point of attack. The dreadful position of the Jews of Russia in normal times is well known. Forbidden to live outside of the enlarged Ghetto, known as the *Pale of Settlement*; burdened with special taxes; denied even the scant educational privileges enjoyed by the rest of the population; harried by a corrupt police, a hostile government and an unfriendly populace - in brief, economically degraded and politically outlawed - their condition represented the extreme of misery. It was the openly expressed policy of the reactionaries who ruled Russia to solve the Jewish question by ridding the country of the Jews. 'One-third will accept the Greek Church; one-third will emigrate to America; and one-third will die of starvation in Russia' - so ran the cynical saying. Some did abjure their faith, tens of thousands did starve in Russia and hundreds of thousands did emigrate to America.

Loyalty of Russian Jews

Then came the war. The Jews saw therein an opportunity to show the Christian population that in spite of all the persecutions of the past they were ready to begin life anew in a united and regenerated Russia. Thousands of Jewish young men who had been forced to leave Russia to secure the education which their own country denied them, returned voluntarily to colors even though they knew that all hope of preferment and promotion was closed to them. On the field of battle the Jewish soldiers displayed courage and intelligence which won the respect of their fighting comrades and gained for them the much desired cross of St George, granted for distinguished valor in the face of the enemy; while those who remained at home opened and equipped hospitals for wounded soldiers without distinction of race or creed, contributed generously to all public funds, and, in brief, gave themselves and their possessions unsparingly to the Russian cause.

It appeared at first as though the long desired union with the Russian people was about to be realized. But it soon developed that the chains which bound the Jews of Russia to their past could not be broken. Forces which they could not possibly control doomed them to the greatest tragedy in their history. The Pale in which they lived was Polish in origin and population. Poles and Jews were fellow victims of the Russian oppressor; but instead of being united by the common bond of suffering, they were separated by religious and racial differences and above all by dissension deliberately fostered among them by the Russian rulers until it developed into uncontrollable hate.

Russian Atrocities

Immediately before the war the struggle had assumed its bitterest form - that of unrelenting boycott waged against the Jews. When the war broke out the political status of the Poles changed overnight. Both the Russian and the German armies found it politic to cultivate the goodwill of the Polish population. Many Poles seized the opportunity to gratify personal animosity, religious bigotry or chauvinistic mania by denouncing the Jews, now to the one invader and now to the other, as spies and traitors. In Germany the animus of the attacks was to some extent uncovered and the lies refuted. But in Russia they found fertile soil. The Russian military machine had met with defeat at the hands of the Germans. To exonerate themselves in the eyes of their own people the military camarilla eagerly seized the pretext so readily furnished them by the Poles and unloaded the burden of their ill-fortune upon the helpless shoulders of the Jew. Men, women, even children were executed without the shadow of evidence or the formality of a trial. Circumstantial stories of Jewish treachery, invented by the Poles, were accepted as the truth and circulated freely through the Russian press and on the local government bulletin boards; but when official investigation proved those stories false in every particular, the publication of the refutation was discouraged by the censorship. The authorities gave the troops a free hand to loot and ravage, even encouraging them by the publication of orders which officially denounced all Jews as spies and traitors. The result was a series of outrages unprecedented even in Russia. A million Jews were driven from their homes in a state of absolute destitution.

Protest of Liberal Russia

All of the liberal elements of Russia protested against this campaign of extermination, but were powerless in the face of the military Government. Hundreds of municipal bodies, trades and professional organizations, writers, publicists and priests, petitioned the civil government to admit the Jews to human equality or at least suspend its policy of persecution. These memorials, together with the speeches delivered in the Duma, constitute a body of evidence from non-Jewish sources, which must condemn the Russian Government in the eyes of the world.

Galicia

During the ten months of the Russian occupation of Galicia, the Jews of that section suffered even more severely than did the Jews who dwelt in the Russian Pale. For here the Jews were the subjects of the enemy and no pretext was needed for their maltreatment. The Ruthenians and Poles who occupied the land were friendly to Russia, which promised them independence and power. But Russia could expect nothing from the Jews of Galicia, for they were already in the possessions of rights and liberties not enjoyed by the Jews of Russia, and the weight of the Russian invasion fell upon them mercilessly. Here thousands of Russian Jewish soldiers were forced to give up their lives in an attempt to impose on free Jews of Galicia the servitude from which they themselves so ardently longed to escape in Russia. They were forced to witness the desecration by their Russian companions-in-arms of synagogues, the outrage of Jewish women and the massacre of innocent and helpless civilians of their own faith.

Rumania

Though Rumania is not yet a belligerent, some of the Jews of that country have been vitally affected by the war. In July of 1915, the Ministry of the Interior issued a general order expelling the Jews of the towns near the Austro-Hungarian frontier into the interior. Though this order was later alleged to have been designed to prevent the operation of Jewish grain speculators from Bukowina, many Jews who had resided in the border towns for generations were summarily expelled.

This action of the Government was bitterly criticized by the liberal press and a memorial addressed to the King by the League of Native-born Jews, and the order was finally revoked.

Whether the present Balkan situation may or may not result in the entrance of Rumania among the belligerent nations, there is no doubt that upon the termination of hostilities the question of Rumania's treatment of the Jews should be reopened.

Palestine

At the outbreak of the war Palestine contained, according to reliable estimates, about 100,000 Jews, some of whom were economically independent agriculturists, but the great majority of whom were aged pilgrims dependent upon their relatives and the goodwill offerings of their pious co-religionists in Europe. The war cut them off completely from both the markets of Europe and from their relatives and friends; nearly the entire Jewish population was thus left destitute. Their position was further aggravated by the severity with which Turkey, upon her entrance into the war as an ally of the Central Powers, treated the nationals of hostile countries. About 8,000 Jews who declined to become Turkish subjects were either expelled or departed voluntarily.

Jews in Other Belligerent Countries

In all the countries where the Jews have heretofore enjoyed freedom, there has been no special Jewish problem during this war. The Jews have identified themselves completely with the lands of their birth or adoption, and have shared the trials and glories of the peoples among whom their lot was cast.

In England, the Jewish population, according to estimates prepared by Lord Rothschild, furnished more than its share of recruits to the British army, its quota of 17,000 comprising about eight and a half percent of the total Jewish population as compared with six percent furnished by the non-Jewish population. The Lord Chief Justice, Baron Reading, a Jew, mobilized the financial resources of the country and was called upon to head the Anglo-French commission which negotiated the $500,000,000 credit secured in the United States. Lord Rothschild is treasurer of the Red Cross organization. Hon Herbert Samuels is a member of the Coalition cabinet. A Jewish battalion organized by Palestinian fugitives rendered exceptional service to the allies in the Gallipoli Peninsula. Many rewards, including the bestowal of Victoria Crosses and promotions, are listed in the Anglo-Jewish press every week.

In Germany the Jews, although without complete social privileges, have borne their full share of the burdens of war. To Herr Ballin, the head of the mercantile marine, was given the task of organizing the national food supply, and other Jews have been prominently identified with every department of the industrial mobilization of the country. In France and Italy, Austria-Hungary and Turkey, Jews are to be found in the ministerial cabinets, in command of troops in the field, and prominent in charge of the medical service of the armies.

Thus the present war has again demonstrated the great truth that, in times of struggle as in times of peace, the Jews constitute a most valuable asset to those nations that accept them as an integral part of their population and permit them to develop freely, but wherever an autocratic government demoralizes its people by confronting them with the spectacle of an unprotected minority denied all human rights, the government itself feels the reaction and the moral tone of the nation is thereby impaired.

Russia

Russia acquired the great bulk of her Jewish population through the partitions of Poland, from 1773 to 1795. Strongly medieval in outlook and organization as Russia was at that time, she treated the Jews with the exceptional harshness which the medieval principle and policy sanctioned and required. By confining them to those provinces where they happened to live at the time of the partitions, she created a Ghetto greater than any known to the Middle Ages; and by imposing restrictions upon the right to live and travel even within this Ghetto, she has virtually converted it onto a penal settlement, where six million human beings guilty only of adherence to the Jewish faith are compelled to live out their lives in squalor and misery, in constant terror of massacre, subject to the caprice of police officials and a corrupt administration - in short, without legal right or social status.

Only twice within the last century have efforts been made to improve the conditions of the Jews in Russia; and each interval of relief was followed by a period of greater and more cruel repression. The first was during the reign of Alexander the Second; but his assassination in 1881 resulted in the complete domination of Russia by the elements of reaction, which immediately renewed the persecution policy. The 'May laws' of Ignatieff (1882) which enmesh the Jews to this day, were the immediate product of this regime. The second period, a concomitant of the abortive revolution of 1904-5, was followed by a 'pogrom policy' of unprecedented severity which lasted until the outbreak of the present war.

The Pale of Settlement

At the beginning of the war the number of Jews in the Russian Empire was estimated at six million or more, comprising fully half of the total Jewish population of the world. Ninety-five percent of these six million people were confined by law to a limited area of Russia, known as the *Pale of Settlement*, consisting of the fifteen Governments of Western and Southwestern Russia, and the ten Governments of Poland, much of which territory is now under German occupation. In reality, however, residence within the Pale was further restricted to such an extent that territorially the Jews were permitted to live in only one two-thousandth part of the Russian Empire. No Jew was permitted to step outside this Pale unless he belonged to one of a few privileged classes. Some half-privileged Jews might, with effort, obtain special passports for a limited period of residence beyond the Pale; but the great majority could not even secure this privilege for any period whatsoever. A tremendous mass of special restrictive legislation converted the Pale into a kind of prison with six million inmates, guarded by an army of corrupt and brutal jailers.

The Recent Abolition of the Pale

In August 1915, the Council of Ministers issued a decree permitting the Jews of the area affected by the war to move into the interior of Russia. This act has been supposed in some quarters to constitute the virtual abolition of the Pale, this interpretation being chiefly attributable to the extensive publicity given the measure by the Russian government; but the evidence, official and otherwise, clearly indicates that far from being a generous act of a liberal Government toward an oppressed people, it is in reality only a temporary expedient, dictated mainly by military necessity and partly by the need of a foreign loan; it is evident that it was granted grudgingly, with galling limitations which served to emphasize the servile state of the Jews; that it is in practice ignored or evaded at the convenience of the local authorities; and that it has been utilized, if not designed, to mislead the public opinion of the world."

Published by the American Jewish Committee, 1916

JEWS INDIFFERENCE TO WAR AID REBUKED
Louis Marshall Denounces Apathy Toward Suffering of Co-Religionists

MILLIONS IN DIRE DISTRESS
Jacob H Schiff, Meyer London, and Dr Enelow Plead with the Rich to Give

Louis Marshall, speaking at a meeting in Temple Emanuel last night, deplored what he termed the failure of the Jews of America, particularly of New York, to realize the terrible calamity that has overtaken the millions of Jews whose homes are in the eastern theatre of the European war.

The meeting was held in the interest of the American Jewish Relief Committee, of which committee Mr Marshall was President. Besides Mr Marshall Congressman-elect Meyer London, and the Rev Dr H G Enelow of the Temple Emanuel, spoke. Like Mr Marshall, each deplored the fact that the Jews of America have not given the assistance they should to their suffering co-religionists. Further emphasis on the same subject was contained in a letter from Jacob H Schiff, read by Mr Marshall.

'It is discouraging to those who have devoted so much time and energy to this work that there is so small a response from Jews in New York, a city which is so great a Jewish centre. It seems to me that the people are so dazed by the European cataclysm that they are unable to realize that it is their duty to aid those who are suffering through the calamity.

'In the world today there are about 13,000,000 Jews, of whom more than 6,000,000 are in the heart of the war zone; Jews whose lives are at stake and who today are subjected to every manner of suffering and sorrow, and the great American Jewish community is not doing its duty toward these sufferers. In the United Stated there are between 2,000,000 and 3,000,000 Jews, nearly all able to do something and yet, after months of work, we have not raised more than $300,000. In New York there are more than a million Jews, some of them persons of great affluence, but many of them seem to think if they have given a few hundred dollars they have done their duty.

'We hear of pogroms in Russia, in Poland, in Galicia, and we sit indifferent. In Palestine, starvation stalks through the land. Shall we selfishly enjoy ourselves and say we would like to, but cannot help because of hard times, and think that we are doing our duty? No. The time has come for every man and woman and child to do his duty, and we must fulfill that duty quickly or it may be too late in hundreds of thousands of cases'

At this point Mr Marshall read Mr Schiff's letter. Mr Schiff said his own interest in the work was intense, and that it should appeal to every Jew. Private reports he has received, Mr Schiff said, showed conditions in Russia, Palestine, Poland, and Galicia, the frightful nature of which could not be pictured.

He said that the Emanuel congregation is the largest and wealthiest in the United States and hoped that its members would give in proportion to their means. He further suggested a committee to canvass the congregation for a Temple Emanuel fund and said he would contribute. Mr Marshall put the suggestion in the form of a motion which was unanimously carried. Mr Marshall will name the committee soon.

Mr London said this was the 'worst period in Jewish history,' and that the saving of millions of Jewish peoples depended on the generosity of more fortunate Jews of the United States. Dr Enelow emphasised what Mr Marshall had said and added that never before were the Jews of this country confronted with so great a duty."

The New York Times - January 14, 1915

700,000 JEWS IN NEED ON THE EAST WAR FRONT
German Hebrew Relief Association, Striving to succor them, requires more food.

An associated press correspondence from Berlin said, 'of the normal total of about 2,450,000 Jews in Poland, Lithuania, and Courland, 1,770,000 remain, and of that number about 700,000 are in urgent and continuous want. About 455,000 of these are in Poland, and 50,000 of these numbers are persons who are without homes and in particularly distressful circumstances. The number of the needy is increasing from month to month. Opportunities to earn money are few, and thousands who are still living on their savings will, sooner or later, find these exhausted and become dependent on charity.

These estimates appear in the annual report of the German Hebrew Relief Association, which has taken upon itself the work of aiding co-religionists in the occupied districts of the battle line in Russia and Galicia. The sum of 500,000 marks monthly is required to alleviate the distress of the most necessitious of the 700,000 sufferers, and even that sum which is all that the relief association can devote to the work for the next few months, can do little more than keep them from starvation.

"With this sum 225 cities and villages in the occupied districts are being assisted. The Grand Lodge of B'nai B'rith in Germany has had a large share in the relief work, and more than a half million marks has thus far been received from America. Up to date nearly 2,250,000 marks has been paid out of the Hebrew Relief Association for Poland and Lithuania. Funds available have not been sufficient to afford relief to some 10,000 Jews in Courland, where the distress is not so great as in the other districts.

'Those activities have formed but a part of the work of the Relief Association. Quite as important and even more arduous has been its work as an intermediary between the residents of the occupied districts and the outside world. In this department no denominational distinctions were made, Jews and Catholics alike being aided. Chief advantage was taken of this work by relatives and friends in America of the Polish sufferers. About 8,000,000 marks has thus far been received from America for direct transmission, and the relief association handles as many as 100,000 letters monthly to and from America.

'A slight elevation of conditions may come from the recently secured permission of emigration from the occupied districts. Many families have already availed themselves of the permission, most of them going with tickets sent from America."

The New York Times - May 22, 1916

GERMANS LET JEWS DIE
Women And Children In Warsaw Starving To Death

"Through the Intelligence Department of the Mayor's Committee on National Defense, the Provisional Zionist Committee last night made public a letter describing conditions among Jews in Warsaw under German rule. The name of the writer of this letter is not divulged for obvious reasons. The veracity and authenticity of the letter is vouched for by the Zionist Committee, of which Dr Stephen S Wise is chairman and Supreme Court Justice Louis D Brandeis, honorary chairman. The letter says in part: 'Death from starvation is a real fact. It is witnessed here all over, in every street, in every step, in every house. Jewish mothers, mothers of mercy, feel happy to see their nursing babies die; at least they are through with their suffering.

'Our wealthiest people cut off their daughters' hair and sell it to be able to buy the indispensable things like bread for their dying children. Four and five year old children have become so weak they must be carried on their arms like babies. Fathers, should they return from the battlefield will meet of their five and six children they kissed good-by when they left for the war two or probably one or more. How long yet will this suffering last. From where will our help come. A commission has been sent to Switzerland to maintain our soup kitchens, but I doubt the success of their mission. Help us, help us. Awaken America. This is our only hope. Should America not aid us all will be lost."

The New York Times - August 10, 1917

FELIX M WARBURG TELLS SAD PLIGHT OF JEWS
Felix M Warburg Says They Were the Worst Sufferers in War

Felix M Warburg, Chairman of the Joint Distribution Committee of American Funds for Jewish War Sufferers, who returned several days ago from a trip to Europe for that organisation, made public yesterday some of his findings.

'The successive blows of contending armies have all but broken the back of European Jewry,' he said, 'and have reduced to tragically unbelievable poverty, starvation and disease about 6,000,000 souls, or half the Jewish population of the earth.

'The Jewish people throughout Eastern Europe, by sheer accident of geography, have suffered more from the war than any other element of the population. The potential vitality and the capacity for self-help that remains to those people after the last five years is amazing to me.'

The people are deeply moved by the help given them by America, Mr Warburg said, but it would be fatal to lessen the emergency aid now while millions are in tragic need. The $30,000,000 spent by this committee, he said, has fed and clothed more than a million children and it has renewed the hope of five million parents and elders.

'For more than four years,' he said, 'The war on the Eastern front was fought largely in the congested centres of Jewish population. A straight north and south line from Riga, on the Baltic, to Salonica, on the Aegean Sea, will touch every important battle area of the Eastern war zone and every center of Jewish population. After the cataclysm of the last few years it is too much to expect this Jewry to become self-sustaining in a short twelve-month.'

Mr Warburg is concerned over the program soon to be started for the discontinuance of emergency relief. This plan, he said, calls for the formation of a $10,000,000 reconstruction corporation.

'This organisation,' he said, 'would afford facilities for constructive aid to Jews abroad in the way of loans and credit at nominal interest rates. The value of this sort of assistance as a substitute for pure charity is apparent.'

Other relief projects recommended by Mr Warburg include the establishment of an express company to forward money and packages from Jews in this country to relatives and friends abroad; the distribution of $120,000 worth of fuel in sections of Poland where destitution is greatest; the purchase of $300,000 worth of cloth in the bolt whereby unemployed workmen of Poland may get raw material, and a plan to reunite those Jewish families that have relatives in the United States and those who have become separated abroad."

The New York Times - September 29, 1919

The Crucifixion of Jews Must Stop!
By MARTIN H. GLYNN
(Former Governor of the State of N. Y.)

From across the sea six million men and women call to us for help, and eight hundred thousand little children cry for bread.

These children, these men and women are our fellow-members of the human family, with the same claim on life as we, the same susceptibility to the winter's cold, the same propensity to death before the fangs of hunger. Within them reside the illimitable possibilities for the advancement of the human race as naturally would reside in six million human beings. *We may not be their keepers but we ought to be their helpers.*

In the face of death, in the throes of starvation there is no place for mental distinctions of creed, no place for physical differentiations of race. In this catastrophe, when six million human beings are being whirled toward the grave by a cruel and relentless fate, only the most idealistic promptings of human nature should sway the heart and move the hand.

Six million men and women are dying from lack of the necessaries of life; eight hundred thousand children cry for bread. And this fate is upon them through no fault of their own, through no transgression of the laws of God or man; but through the awful tyranny of war and a bigoted lust for Jewish blood.

In this threatened holocaust of human life, forgotten are the niceties of philosophical distinction, forgotten are the differences of historical interpretation; and the determination to help the helpless, to shelter the homeless, to clothe the naked and to feed the hungry becomes a religion at whose altar men of every race can worship and women of every creed can kneel. In this calamity the temporalities of man's fashionings fall away before the eternal verities of life, and we awaken to the fact that from the hands of one God we all come and before the tribunal of one God we all must stand on the day of final reckoning. And when that reckoning comes mere profession of lips will not weigh a pennyweight; but deeds, mere intangible deeds, deeds that dry the tear of sorrow and allay the pain of anguish, deeds that with the spirit of the Good Samaritan pour oil and wine in wounds and find sustenance and shelter for the suffering and the stricken, will outweigh all the stars in the heavens, all the waters in the seas, all the rocks and metals in all the celestian globes that revolve in the firmament around us.

Race is a matter of accident; creed, partly a matter of inheritance, partly a matter of environment, partly one's method of ratiocination; but our physical wants and corporeal needs are implanted

WHITHER?

in all of us by the hand of God, and the man or woman who can, and will not, hear the cry of the starving; who can, and will not, take heed of the wail of the dying; who can, and will not, stretch forth a helping hand to those who sink beneath the waves of adversity is an assassin of nature's finest instincts, a traitor to the cause of the human family and an abjurer of the natural law written upon the tablets of every human heart by the finger of God himself.

And so in the spirit that turned the poor widow's votive offering of copper into silver, and the silver into gold when placed upon God's altar, the people of this country are called upon to sanctify their money by giving $35,000,000 in the name of the humanity of Moses to six million famished men and women.

Six million men and women are dying —eight hundred thousand little children are crying for bread.

And why?

Because of a war to lay Autocracy in the dust and give Democracy the sceptre of the Just.

And in that war for democracy 200,000 Jewish lads from the United States fought beneath the Stars and Stripes. In the 77th Division alone there were 14,000 of them, and in Argonne Forest this division captured 54 German guns. This shows that at Argonne the Jewish boys from the United States fought for democracy as Joshua fought against the Amalekites on the plains of Abraham. In an address on the so-called "Lost Battalion," led by Colonel Whittlesey of Pittsfield, Major-General Alexander shows the fighting stuff these Jewish boys were made of. In some way or another Whittlesey's command was surrounded. They were short of rations. They tried to get word back to the rear telling of their plight. They tried and they tried, but their men never got through. Paralysis and stupefaction and despair were in the air. And when the hour was darkest and all seemed lost, a soldier lad stepped forward, and said to Col. Whittlesey: "I will try to get through." He tried, he was wounded, he had to creep and crawl, but he got through. To-day he wears the Distinguished Service Cross and his name is

ABRAHAM KROTOSHINSKY.

Because of this war for Democracy six million Jewish men and women are starving across the seas; eight hundred thousand Jewish babies are crying for bread.

FIVE MILLION FACE FAMINE IN POLAND
American Jewish Relief and Red Cross Societies Fighting Disease and Hunger
Many Children Stunted
A New Malady Spreading Blindness Among War Refugees - Typhus Toll Is Heavy

Five million people east of the River Bug in the new Poland are at the point of starvation, according to a statement made public yesterday by the American Jewish Relief Committee as a result of investigation by the American Red Cross and the American Jewish Relief Agents. The vast region, from which there has been practically no news in five years, has just been penetrated by the American Red Cross and the American Jewish Relief Committee's representatives.

'The war has left 5,000,000 destitute and stricken Jews in Eastern Europe,' the statement says, 'a number as great as the entire population of New York City, utterly helpless, in many cases sick, in every case hungry and dependent.

'East of the River Bug these people are living in devastated houses, in stalls of old stables, on roofless platforms built for refugee families, one family to a platform, in old freight cars, in holes in the ground, or under the open sky. They are weak from many months of semi-starvation, for they have gone for five years without one square meal. They are still terror-stricken from the war. Their number is being reduced every day by a series of the most terrible epidemics that ever swept any section of the world.

'Typhus, cholera and smallpox are all raging in the territory east of the River Bug. No estimate of the actual number of those smitten with typhus in Poland has yet been compiled, but it probably is greater than in Siberia, where the American Red Cross found 100,000 cases. Dirt and malnutrition are the two great causes of the epidemic of disease.

'All through Poland may be found children of eight or ten years old no larger than youngsters half their age ordinarily are. Two out of three infants do not survive their first year of life. The average child in the territory east of the Bug River has never tasted milk, even mother's milk. American Red Cross investigators say that an abnormal number of children are born blind, because of the malnutrition of their mothers. American Jewish relief investigators discovered a new eye disease that had attacked thousands of children, beginning with constant blinking and ending in total blindness, resulting when long-continued starvation had affected the muscles of the eyes.

In the battle against disease that is going on in the territory east of the Bug River the American Red Cross is fighting the former with medicines and doctors and attempts toward cleanliness, while the American Jewish relief workers have entered the lists against hunger, with soup kitchens and milk stations, and Children's Relief Bureaus, established here and there, all through the vast stretch of territory.

'If all of the people in the territory east of the Bug River could be fed properly at once, disease would soon disappear, doctors in this afflicted region say. If they could replace the rags which they have worn since the beginning of the war with fresh clothing, the epidemics would cease to spread. If their living places could be made habitable and clean, it would no longer be as it is today the most desolate expanse of land in the world. It is toward this end that the two great organisations, one of Gentiles and the other of Jews, are working hand in hand, differences of creed forgotten, in the great practical need that they face."
The New York Times - December 3, 1919

A WORK OF MERCY

Hitherto the Jews have financed their own philanthropies and with a liberality and skill that has been universally recognised. On behalf of those of their religion who are still suffering in the war-ridden districts of Europe they are now for the first time seeking outside aid.

With the fate of Belgium and Serbia it was easy to sympathize. A nation's territory was invaded and its citizens were making a united stand. The Jews have no fatherland, no means of uniting in the common defense. Yet from the outset, wherever the call came, they fought, and fought bravely, for the allied cause. Meantime, in widely scattered lands the folk at home suffered as perhaps those of no other people, and their suffering has in many localities outlasted the war.

In Europe there are today more than 5,000,000 Jews who are starving or on the verge of starvation, and many are in the grip of a virulent typhus epidemic. An appeal has been issued throughout the world. The quota of New York City is $7,500,000. The drive will occupy the week of May 2-9, and will be based wholly upon the principle of sympathy and a common humanity."
The New York Times - April 21, 1920

JEWS ASK PUBLIC TO AID WAR VICTIMS
Non-Sectarian Appeal for $7,500,000 Starts Today with Sermons in All Churches.

POLAND'S WOE APPALLING
Campaign to be Pressed by 10,000 Active Workers, in the Five Boroughs

A famished child upon the auction block, a mother in the foreground pleading for aid, death with outstretched arms lurking near and the legend, 'Shall Death Be the Highest Bidder?

'Such is the pictorial representation of the needs of stricken peoples in the war devastated zones of Central and Eastern Europe which will confront New Yorkers everywhere today. Back of that representation stands an organisation designed to take advantage of every channel to press home to the people of this city the need for contributing toward the $7,500,000 to be raised here this week by the Greater New York Appeal for Jewish War Sufferers.

irrespective of creed, for help. Heretofore the Jews themselves have contributed many, many millions which have been expended by the Joint Distribution Committee through relief agencies of all countries and without regard to the religious beliefs of those in need. This time the burden is too gigantic to be borne by Jews alone.

Millions Racked by War

A pen picture of actual conditions, typical of those in several countries, has been sent to the Campaign Committee by Dr Boris B Bogen of this city, now in Warsaw as head of the First Relief Unit, sent abroad by the Joint Distribution Committee. Dr Bogen writes:

'Hunger, cold, rags, desolation, disease, death - Six million human beings, without food, shelter, clothing or medical treatment in what now are but the wastes of once fair lands, lands ravaged by long years of war or blighted by its consequences!

'That, in a few words, is the actual situation in all those countries that constituted what was known during the great conflict as the Eastern theater of war.

'Words cannot adequately convey nor can any picture be drawn which can bring home to comfortable, affluent, happy New Yorkers, surrounded by their families and friends, riding in their automobiles, enjoying every luxury, the utter, abject, hopeless misery confronting the population of these lands, a population about equal to that of New York City itself.

'If you would try to visualise, to realise the situation, place yourself at the corner of Fifth Avenue and Forty-second Street.

'The once teeming avenue is all but deserted. Gone are the gay equipages, their bejeweled occupants and liveried attendants. No longer are the sidewalks filled with a surging crowd of gaily dressed men and women. The street is all but still. Laughter and lively chatter are heard no more.

'Instead, old men lean for support against the buildings. Mothers, with dying babes tugging vainly at their breasts, sit along the curb. The flower of what was once young manhood and womanhood of the city is not in the picture, for they, by thousands and tens of thousands, lie stricken in the overcrowded hospitals, laid low by the breath of a pestilence.

Too Weak to Cry For Bread

'Little children, with wasted frames and swollen bodies, cling to their mothers' rags, too weak even to cry for bread that is not to be had.

'A bitter wind sweeps the avenue from the north. A man - his tatters cannot be called clothes - his face blue and pinched, looks at you with unseeing eyes. You do not at

This fund is but a tithe of that which must be subscribed in the entire country if disaster to whole peoples is to be averted. The world nature of the calamity which has overtaken men, women and children, deprived not only of life's bare necessities but of all means of rehabilitating themselves without aid from the outside, has led leading Jews of New York and the nation to turn to the public,

first recognise him. It then dawns upon you that you have seen that face before. It is the face of a friend, a man who but a few short months before was well-to-do, a banker, as prosperous, well fed and well dressed as you are now. He reaches out his arms toward you and falls at your feet. You stoop down to lift him up. He is dead! Hunger did it.

'The scene is not exaggerated, not overdrawn. It has its exact counterpart in hundreds of cities, towns and villages throughout Central and Eastern Europe at this very moment. The call comes from one human being to another, from those who have less than nothing to those who have much. It is the call of humanity.

'At no time during the war, in any land, not either in Belgium or Northern France, was there a situation more critical, a need more great, a demand for sacrifice and help more insistent than now comes from Eastern and Central Europe. Both the present and future existence of an entire people are at stake.'

The campaign is receiving the active co-operation and support of Archbishop Patrick J Hayes of the Roman Catholic Diocese, Bishop Luther B Burch of the Episcopal Diocese, Bishop Luther B Wilson, President of the Board of Foreign Missions of the Methodist Episcopal Church; Miss Evangeline Booth, Commander of the Salvation Army.

Members of the Executive Committee include Cleveland H Dodge, Treasurer of the Committee for the Relief in the Near East; President Nicholas Murray Butler of Columbia University, George Gordon Battle, Otto T Bannard, John G Ager, the Rev. Dr David J. Burrell, Robert Grier Cooke, Paul G Cravath, Francis D Gallatin, Charles H Sabin, President of the Guaranty Trust company; former Attorney General George W Wickersham, Judge Joseph F Mulqueen, Judge William H Widhams and Alfred E Marling.

The appeal is to be brought home forcibly to the people of New York in many ways. Today is Church Sunday, and there will be special sermons in the churches of all denominations. The Rev Dr S Parkes Cadman has prepared a model sermon for Protestant churches. Vicar General Joseph F Mooney has written a message to the Roman Catholic churches, and Dr Nathan Stern, rabbi of the West End Synagogue, prepared an appeal to be read to the Jewish congregations.

Children in the public schools, through the co-operation of the Board of Education, are to hear the story of the sufferings of the children in other lands. In theaters, moving-picture houses, clubs, hotels and restaurants, in short wherever people are gathered together, the conditions they are asked to alleviate will be made clear to them.

It is estimated that not fewer than 10,000 active workers have been enlisted in the cause in the five boroughs. The organisation for the campaign has been divided into three parts: The organisation of the trades and industries, so that not a single business or profession in the city has been overlooked; the women's division, embracing 3,000 women workers under the leadership of Mrs I Unterberg, Mrs Samuel C Lampert and Mrs S S Prince, which has divided the city into districts: the women organized the schools and churches and will make a direct appeal to the homes and to the neighborhood storekeepers: the third organisation is that of the boroughs, each borough, Manhattan, the Bronx, Brooklyn, Queens, and Richmond, having a borough organisation."

The New York Times - May 2, 1920

THE JEWISH WAR SUFFERERS

The non-sectarian character of the drive on behalf of the Jewish war sufferers was emphasised in the appeal which marked its formal beginning yesterday. An accompanying letter was signed by Evangeline Booth of the Salvation Army, Bishop Burch, Archbishop Hayes and many other representatives of Christian churches. A statement of the nature of the crisis was prepared by the Rev Dr S Parker Cadman and sent to every Protestant minister in the city to serve as the basis for an announcement from the pulpit. A similar statement for the Catholic churches was sent out by Mgr Joseph F Mooney.

Hitherto the Jews have financed their own charities, and with a liberality and skill that has been universally recognised. The present need transcends the means of any single sect and centers in a catastrophe which threatens the entire world. In Russia and the neighboring countries the Jews have been subjected to a particularly malignant persecution which has not ended with the war. Without any national organisation of their own, they have no central organisation to appeal to. Living in segregated and generally impoverished communities, their misery is cumulative to an extent unknown among other sufferers. It is estimated that more than five million are actually starving or on the verge of starvation, and a virulent typhus epidemic is raging among them and is already spreading among the neighboring populations. Both in intensity and the extent of present suffering and in the menace it holds out for all Europe, the situation is one which directly concerns the public of all races and creeds. The quota of New York City is $7,500,000. On the American Joint Distribution Committee are Professor Harry Fisher of Chicago, Professor Israel Friedlander, Max Pine and Maurice Kass. In their work of distributing food and medical aid through the ghettos of Central Europe they are obliged to proceed without the protection of the Government of the United States which has no diplomatic relations with Soviet Russia. Ample precautions will be taken, however, to make sure that the supplies will be used for the purpose in hand. It is a work of mercy that makes a peculiar appeal to both the hearts and the interests of a common humanity.

The New York Times - May 3, 1920

BRITISH CHIEF RABBI CONDEMNS SILENCE ON POGROMS IN THE UKRAINE

At the second annual conference of the Federation of Ukrainian Jews the Very Rev Joseph H Hertz, Chief Rabbi of the British Empire, called attention to the 'astonishing fact in the moral history of contemporary humanity that one of the blackest pages in the annals of man has just closed, and yet the world knows next to nothing of the unspeakable horrors and infinite crimes perpetrated against the Jewish people.'

Dr Hertz declared that 1,000,000 human beings had been butchered and that for three years 3,000,000 persons in the Ukraine had been made 'to pass through the horrors of hell' and that hardly a word of these facts had appeared in the newspapers.

The voice of the Jewish community, Dr Hertz continued, had not been raised as it should have been, and it was humiliating to find the apathy and callousness with which certain sections of Jewry had faced this disaster. He described in detail some of the crimes that had been committed.

He said that although the pogroms in the Ukraine had ended there were something like 600,000 homeless children, 150,000 orphans and 35,000 double orphans in the Ukraine who would die from cold, hunger, or disease unless Jewish hearts remained human and came to the rescue.

London, January 8, 1922 (Associated Press).

THE MOST TERRIBLE WAR IN THE HISTORY OF MANKIND
Canadian press

The most terrible war in the history of mankind has left nothing behind but destruction, untold suffering, social upheaval, and unrest. No one people who have been torn or affected by this war have suffered more than the Jewish people in the eastern war zone. The soldiery of advancing and receding armies have continually passed over that enormous Jewish population on the borders of Russia, in Poland and in Galicia.

In Russia, in Poland, in Galicia, in Romania, in Palestine, and in Turkey proper, there is a Jewish population of probably not less than eight or nine million. Just think of that mass of people, who have led honest lives, and who have been forced into lives of misery, into death – their men and children murdered, their women ravished, crying out 'From where shall my saviour come?' – crying it without any answer.

The Joint Distribution Committee, the Reimbursing Agency of the Jewish War Relief Committee, is expending more than $2 000 000 a month now to keep alive the Jewish and non-Jewish peoples in these afflicted countries. The ships *Westward Ho* and *Democracy* make continual trips, and for the period ending September 1, 1919 approximately $24 000 000 has already been spent.

This year $35 000 000 is required to sustain the lives of these people, and Canada, always generous, is asked to supply $1 000 000 of this sum.

Huge as the figures seem, the total asked for is less than $6.00 a year per person with which to provide food, clothing, fuel, shelter, medical attention, drugs, and the other necessities of life for these unfortunate people.

Two cents a day to keep alive an old man, woman, or young boy or girl, whose only fault is that they have been born to a life of war suffering, is truly a small sum indeed to ask of a nation whose most frugal citizens must spend at least $500.00 a year for sustenance, clothing and shelter.

The reports of investigators of the Red Cross and other relief agencies show that in Poland hardly a child under five years old remains alive. There are no able-bodied young men – no strong young women. The old, the maimed, the emaciated children [more than 800 000 of these] are entirely dependent upon America and Canada. At best these peoples and millions in the other war-stricken countries can be kept from starvation – they can be kept alive until the industries in the nations are resumed, if this appeal is successful.

Major H T Davis, a member of the Red Cross Commission to Poland, in a letter to Mrs Davis describes the conditions as he actually found them in Poland and this one paragraph from his letter is enough to convince everyone of the urgent need of the appeal in Canada:

'Thousands and thousands of children, old men and women without clothing, warmth or food, and racked by typhus [in some places half of the population is sick] and other diseases. Wanderers by the thousands trying to return to their homes from which they were driven out by Russians or Germans. Starving and dying women and children deliriously crying for bread. Huddled together in synagogues, men and women all too weak to stand up or move about, piteously stretching their hands toward you. And those faces, emaciated, thin, burning eyes, listless, unable to appreciate anything you may say to them, only begging for a piece of bread. In the city of Pinsk I saw hundreds of children, women and inmates of hospitals who did not have a piece of bread for four days. And the bread they are asking for – a filthy mixture of a little flour with bark of trees or leaves, sawdust and God knows what. What do you think of a diet of wild horse-chestnuts for those sick with typhus or of warm water with a little cornmeal mixed with it?' '

For God's sake, let us take pity on these unfortunates', says Nathan Straus, America's foremost philanthropist.

'There never was a better opportunity for the Christian to prove his practical Christianity – and never a better one for the Jew to prove his broad humanity and devotion to the teachings of his fathers, than the opportunity presented in the war zones today,' says Mr Straus. 'One dollar a week is enough to keep alive a person. How many lives will you save? Each one must do his share, his sacred duty. And we can do it without any great effect upon our luxuries, much less our necessities.'

Under-Nourished Children
in the War-Stricken Countries in Central and Eastern Europe BEG FOR BREAD!

SHALL THEY PLEAD IN VAIN?

Canadian Jewish War Relief

Almost a million innocent children have been robbed of their birthright. *They can't remember what milk tastes like.* Here is a situation where race, creed, nationality – nothing counts except humanity. Shall these children plead in vain? No, Canada will respond generously!

In Canada, such minded men as Sir Edmund Walker, Sir William Mulock, Sir Mortimer, B Davis, and a score of others equally as well known are taking an active interest in the appeal and it is hoped that the objective $1 000 000 will be raised without difficulty. Committees are being organised in every city and township in the Dominion and the slogan. 'Humanity knows no creed' typifies the broadness of the appeal.

All funds collected for this relief work are applied directly to the aid of these sufferers by the Joint Distribution Committee. This organisation has its own representatives abroad to see that the money is properly and wisely administered by local committees in the communities to which aid is extended. Nor is this help limited to Jews and it is because those who are non-Jewish in the afflicted areas are beneficiaries, that every man, woman and child in Canada, without regard to creed, is asked to contribute.

HOW RELIEF FUNDS HAVE BEEN DISTRIBUTED BY THE JOINT DISTRIBUTION COMMITTEE

	$
Alexandria	58 904.
Czecho-Slovakia	80 010.
France	7 000.
Galicia	200 000
Greece	156 572
Holland	14 116
Jugo-Slavia	35 000
Palestine	3 194 381
Poland	11 731 392
Roumania	571 273
Serbia	35 850
Siberia	188 187
Turkey and Syria	1 181 574
Spain	18 000
Switzerland and Denmark	11 200
Japan [House in Yokahama]	110 000
Lithuania	150 007
Abyssinia	5 000
Emergency [at discretion Paris Comm]	654 295
Russia	2 932 300
Italy – Verona	4 000
Austria – Refugees in Vienna	932 000
Central Powers	289 442
	$23 812 203

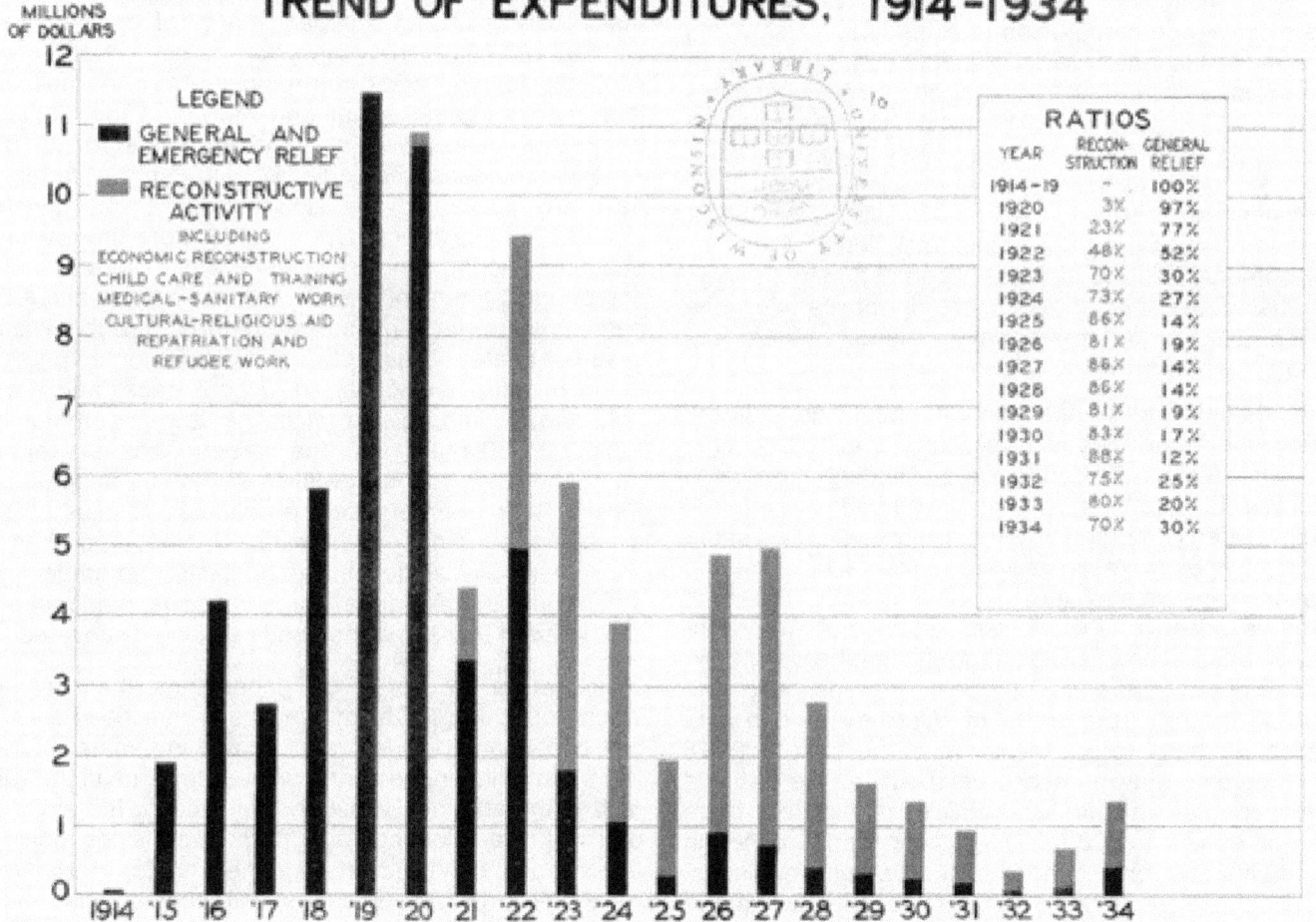

Chapter 6 – JEWISH LIFE IN POLAND

Written by John Cooper in his article
THE WORK OF THE PINSKER ORPHANS RELIEF FUND OF LONDON 1921-1936
Printed with the permission of Jewish Historical Studies

During the 1914-18 War, the German and Austrian armies advanced into Lithuania and large portions of Poland, where one and a half million Jews lived. The anti-Semitic Tsarist regime accused the Jews of collaborating with the Germans and evacuated large numbers of Jews into the interior of Russia or Poland. By 1916 there were 350 000 Jewish exiles living in Russia, and large numbers of Lithuanian Jews residing in Poland, whose presence was resented by Polish nationals. The Polish harvest of 1915 was destroyed, while that of the following year was poor, so that there was widespread starvation in Poland during the War. Essential supplies of food, such as bread, potatoes, and sugar were distributed first to Poles and then to Jews after the War, but during the War when food shortages were more acute the more heavily urbanised Jewish population suffered from worse distress. Isaac Bashevis Singer recalling his childhood in Warsaw wrote that 'for us the winter of 1917 was one continuous fast. We ate only frozen potatoes and farmer cheese. Both typhus and typhoid fever were rampant in Warsaw. Nor was it surprising that they should be so, since people were keeping themselves alive by eating potato peelings and rotten chestnuts'. Because of this privation typhus epidemics raged among Jews in cities like Warsaw and Vilna; and in the latter town the annual death rate among Jews climbed from 20.4 and 22.6 per 1 000 inhabitants before 1914 to 68.2 in 1917, while the birthrate fell precipitously from 1 502 births in 1913 to 489 in 1917. Recent research has indicated that starving women suffer from famine amenorrhea, the cessation of menstruation, a symptom accompanied by temporary bouts of sterility. In all, some 600 000 Jews were deported during the War, often being transported like cattle in boxcars on the Russian railways, and the property looted from them was estimated to be worth 400 million dollars.

Nor did the misfortunes of the Jewish population end here. In 1918 and 1919 there were a series of disturbing anti-Semitic incidents in Eastern Europe. Although the victims were few in numbers, perhaps 100 000 to 120 000 persons, when compared with the millions who died in the Holocaust, they were on a scale unheard of since the Cossack massacres of the mid seventeenth century in Poland, a shock to the western democrats who were trying to build a new, civilised international order and a deep affront to the East European masses, who had found a haven in the cities of Western Europe and America. Perhaps to put the scale of the post 1914-18 War pogroms into better perspective we should remember that in the Chmielnicki massacres three centuries earlier 40 000 to 50 000 Jews had perished in Poland-Lithuania or a quarter of the Jewish population. The worst excesses were perpetrated in 1919 in the Ukraine, where at least 100 000 Jews died, but there were earlier massacres in Poland in the winter of 1918 and the spring of 1919 in which 348 Jews were killed, while attacks on the Jews occurred in some 130 towns and villages. However, Bernard Weinryb has estimated that 'The war and the subsequent pogroms and struggles cost East European Jewry some 500 000 casualties, killed and wounded in the pogroms and on the battlefield, or dead in epidemics'; and in 1922 Dr Lee K Frankel of the Joint voiced a similar opinion, declaring that '350 000 Jews had been killed in at least 2 200 pogroms, and tens of thousands had since died of starvation'.

When the Poles imposed their rule over Eastern Galicia at the end of 1918, they accused the Jews of sympathysing too much with the aspirations of the Ukrainians, who were the dominant minority in the area, and there was a pogrom in Lemberg in which 73 Jews were killed. So carefully was the pogrom organised that when 442 houses in the Jewish quarter were set on fire the water supply to these houses was deliberately cut off. Later as the Polish army pushed the Russian Bolshevik regime out of large areas of Poland, there was a fresh wave of pogroms in the central and northern provinces of Poland with heavy Jewish casualties in the towns of Pinsk, Lida and Vilna.

On 5 April 1919 in Pinsk, units of the Polish army surrounded a meeting at the Zionist headquarters which had been arranged to distribute funds for Passover provisions supplied by the American Food Commission, maliciously accusing the participants of being a secret communist cell. Thirty five of these young Jewish intellectuals, who had been removed from the hall, were later placed against a wall and were machine-gunned to death by Polish soldiers, only the timely intervention of an American officer at the behest of a Jewish girl student the next day prevented the slaughter of a new batch of victims. Among the martyrs of Pinsk were the owners of chemists shops, Hebrew teachers, a bookkeeper and the son of a local bank official. Twenty six women and elderly persons were put in prison, where they were tortured and severely beaten, causing two of the four women prisoners to go insane, one to vanish without trace, and leaving only one woman able to rejoin the Jewish community in Pinsk. On 30 May 1919, the Jewish Chronicle reported that 'About 90 young Jewish men have disappeared in Pinsk. Their whereabouts are unknown. Bodies of Jews are being found daily in the river'. One young orphan girl, who eventually settled in London, still remembers how she heard stories as a child, of Jews being secretly murdered in Pinsk and their bodies being discovered later.

Pinsk was a town of 30 000 inhabitants, the majority of whom were Jews. Chaim Weizmann described Pinsk as 'not a pleasant town to live in ... low lying, malarial, it was like Motol, mud in the spring and autumn, ice in the winter, dust in the summer. When the rains came the lower part of Pinsk was flooded, and from three sides could be approached only in boats. Of the streets, two or three were paved, or rather, covered with cobblestones. As the floods retreated with the approach of summer, a miasmal mist went out of the earth, and after it came a thick dust'.

The condition of the Jews in Poland after the First world War was desperate. In Pinsk 'The Jewish Community has issued an appeal stating that nearly all our coreligionists in the town were starving. Epidemics were raging in most Jewish houses, and large numbers of Jews were dying daily from hunger and infectious diseases'. Otto Schiff, the philanthropist, quoted from a report of the American Joint Distribution Committee in the summer of 1919: 'In Poland the suffering is intense. There are children's institutions without a morsel of food, and there are hospitals unused because of the lack of doctors and nurses and of medicines, although there is an enormous lot of disease. A great percentage of people have been kept alive on soup made of water, potatoes, and a little salt'. In Vilna there was no bread for eight weeks but 'In the smaller towns between Vilna and Warsaw, mainly inhabited by Jews, such as Pinsk, the conditions are much worse. The agricultural communities are mostly Christian and people have some food, but in the little towns where people get their livelihood by trade with the farmers the situation is different. People are not allowed to go from place to place, and hence have no food at all. They are actually living from soup made from poison ivy. Our representatives... cried like children when they came face to face with this terrible condition of starvation and typhus. In the children's institutions visited, the children looked like skeletons'.

We know that this description of the catastrophic conditions in Poland is not exaggerated, as they are matched by the recollections of a lady, who became an orphan during the War. At the beginning of the War, the father, mother and six young children, including one boy and five girls were taken by the German army that invaded Pinsk to barracks near Danzig (Gadansk). Here because of the inadequate rations and the insanitary conditions, Mrs A contracted typhoid fever and after being separated from her children for a few days, they were suddenly informed that she was dead; their father could not give them much comfort, as the men were housed in a separate section of the barracks. Later the family was transferred to a camp in a small shtetl called Vishkave in the Warsaw region, where they remained for most of the War years. Here the conditions were again bad, partly because of the Allied blockade which caused an acute food shortage, and the family subsisted on meager rations of bread and water. The baby daughter, who was one year old, died of hunger; some time later, the children thought that their father was lying asleep in bed, when he too had perished from lack of food, lack of clothing and lack of adequate heating in the severe winter. At the end of the War, the four little girls were sent back to Pinsk, their leader being a 12 year old girl, but found that the family home had been destroyed. As a result, they sought shelter in a nearby synagogue, where they at least had the comforting warmth of a stove and kindly men and women brought them soup and food. All their aunts in Pinsk had vanished in the upheavals of the War and were never heard of again, although they had a dim recollection of another aunt, who had settled in London.

When the representatives of the orphanage called at the synagogue, they were overheard to say with reference to the four little sisters: 'We have hundreds of children waiting to go into the orphanage. We have to pick out the worst ones.' The warden and cantor pleaded with them to save all the children, to which the representatives replied, 'We can take the two younger ones. They are half dead anyway' -- a phrase said with a shrug implying that even these favoured ones might not survive.

In Britain and the United States, the Jews from Eastern Europe were angered by the persecution of their brethren in Poland and the Ukraine. In Britain for the first time there were joint protest meetings on 26 June 1919, in which East European immigrants and members of the Anglo-Jewish establishment marched side by side from the East End to the West End to a meeting in the Queen's Hall, organised jointly by the Anglo-Jewish Association and the Board of Deputies. The scenes were unprecedented in Anglo-Jewish history with 100 000 to 120 000 persons participating in the protest demonstration. In the East End 'Shops and factories were closed, but the synagogues were open from early in the morning, and were filled with praying and fasting congregations of men and women. In many instances the 'day of mourning' was observed more strictly than Yom Kippur. 'Certain establishments that are open on Rosh Hashana were closed last Thursday' reported the *Jewish Chronicle*. Further, throughout London 'At hundreds upon hundreds of Jewish homes, a token of mourning was noticeable by the blinds of the houses being closely drawn throughout the day'. Huge gatherings were held at the People's Palace in Mile End and the Pavilion Theatre in the Whitechapel Road, while the meeting in the Queen's Hall was graced by Lord Rothschild, the Chief Rabbi, Dr Hertz, Dr Weizmann, Zangwill, and Herman Landau, the City patron of the Jews Temporary Shelter. Yet in contrast to the situation in 1882, the Lord Mayor of London influenced by Foreign Office pressure had refused to sponsor the latter meeting which was ostracised by the Gentile political and intellectual elite; and as Zangwill said in rebuke, English public figures, 'with few exceptions, even her great religious leaders, sit still in silence while Jewish blood is flowing.....' In New York 400 000 persons took part in protest demonstrations, including ex-soldiers with banners. As a result of world-wide Jewish pressure, a British Parliamentary Commission of Enquiry headed by Sir Stuart Samuel, MP arrived in Poland in September 1919, staying there for three months, and Congress dispatched a similar roving commission; the activities of these bodies checked the more blatant persecution of the Jews, which eased but never ceased.

Emergency conditions returned to Pinsk when the Bolshevik army captured the town for a second time for a two months period, 26 July to 26 September 1920. Business and commerce came to a standstill, while the supply of funds from the Joint was abruptly halted and Jewish institutions did not know if they could continue. The Bolshevik commissars requisitioned houses, goods and furniture and people went hungry for bread. Even worse sufferings were to befall the Jews of Pinsk when the White Guard under the control of Bulak Balakhovich seized the town from 26 to 29 September 1920, acting as an advance unit of the returning Polish forces. On the first night of their capture of the town, the White Guard ransacked Pinsk killing four to five Jews but more Jewish inhabitants of Pinsk and its surrounding towns were robbed, raped and murdered by these reactionary brigands during the next two days. Normal conditions did not return to Pinsk until the Peace of Riga in March 1921.

After the War, the commercial boycott of the Jews in Poland was enforced with fresh vigour being fostered by an ultra-nationalist press. The provincial authorities tried to oust the Jews from certain trades that they had developed, by discriminating against Jewish dealers in bread, hides, petroleum and salt. Jews were squeezed out of the bureaucracy, Jewish doctors found it difficult to obtain employment in hospitals, as did Jewish teachers in schools. On a visit to Poland in 1923, J Cohen Lask described conditions in the shtetl of Kolo. 'The Jews in the streets and markets are like skeletons. They have lost both their courage and vitality. The Jewish shops, too, are empty. There is a government monopoly of certain goods such as sugar and tobacco, and these are supplied exclusively to Christian traders. Then again, there are a number of agitators who, either by argument or by force, prevent customers from entering shops owned by Jews'. He reported, however, that in Lodz, the Manchester of Poland, and in Warsaw and Vilna conditions were better for Jews than in the smaller towns. He was of the opinion that 'The population, and particularly the Jewish population..... are dressed very poorly, many of them being almost in rags, and in a large number of cases their spirit would seem to have been broken by their hardships.' It was estimated that in the 1920s about 80 per cent of the Polish Jewish population lived in conditions of poverty, particularly artisans, village and street peddlers, porters and carters, whose horsedrawn vehicles were replaced by competitors with motor transport. On Cracow it was reported that 'Famished apprentices faint from hunger at their work....' The Board of Deputies were informed '.... that they were up against a condition of things in Poland at the present time which was unprecedented in Jewish history... They had to deal with pogroms and burnings and robberies, but they had never had to encounter a problem of this kind, which was a sort of creeping paralysis which was coming over the whole of Polish Jewry and which was caused by the economic condition of the country'. Dr Rich, a Polish Jewish leader, declared that 'The staple industries of the country, which had formerly been almost entirely in the hands of the Jews, were now monopolised by the state ... No Jewish worker was given work in those state-owned factories. The impending withdrawal of the liquor licences from Jews would deprive 30 000 Jewish families of their last means of livelihood'. So too, the world depression in the 1920s brought a higher rate of unemployment to Jewish workers, as the Polish workers in the state owned industries were somewhat cushioned against a downturn in the trade cycle.

Jewish soup kitchen during the first World War

Chapter 7 – STARVATION IN THE UKRAINE

MAN-MADE FAMINE IN SOVIET UKRAINE 1921-1923
Written by Dr Roman Serbyn

Much has been written in recent years about the man-made famine that ravaged Ukraine in 1932-1933 and caused the deaths of 7 million to 10 million people. This is in stark contrast to the largely ignored famine of 1921-1923 - the first of three famines that Ukraine's population has suffered under the Soviet Communist regime, and a famine that, contrary to popular belief, was not caused by drought and crop failures, but by the policies of the Soviet state.

What follows on the next few pages of The Ukrainian Weekly is a pull-out section about the 1921-1923 famine, featuring an article prepared and illustrations collected by Dr Roman Serbyn, professor of Russian and East European history at the University of Quebec in Montreal.

Grain requisition and export - not drought and poor harvest - were the real causes of the first great famine in Soviet Ukraine which occurred in 1921-1923. This is borne out by Western and Soviet documents alike.

The famine was concentrated in the rich grain-growing provinces of southern Ukraine, an area inhabited by about a third of the republic's 26 million citizens. It affected both the rural and the urban population. Most of the victims were Ukrainians; national minorities like Germans, Jews and Russians also suffered. Between the fall of 1921 and the spring of 1923, 1.5 million to 2 million people died of starvation and accompanying epidemics.

Saving this population would have required no more than half a million tons of grain or equivalent foodstuffs per year. During the two years of the famine, the Bolshevik government took from Ukrainian peasants many times that amount. Most of the confiscated grain was shipped abroad: the first year to Russia, and the second to Russia and the West. Ukraine was also obliged to send additional "voluntary" famine relief to the Volga, and to feed some 2 million people who came from Russia as refugees, soldiers and administrators.

At the time of the famine, many witnesses recorded the tragedy, and some of them even hinted at its criminal nature. But the passage of time dulled the memory of succeeding generations, and subsequent publications dealing with Ukraine and the Soviet Union said little of substance about this particular disaster. More surprisingly, the Ukrainian community itself has preserved but a vague memory of these events. Today most Ukrainians would be hard-pressed to explain why the famine had broken out, why it lasted so long and what was done to overcome it.

Famine and Epidemics

The High Commissariat of Dr Fridtj of Nansen was a Geneva-based international organization devoted to famine and refugee relief work. In his capacity as Dr. Nansen's representative, Captain Vidkun Quisling toured Ukraine in early 1922, and filed some of the best informed and most detailed reports on the famine. On 25 February after inspecting the province of Zaporizhzhia, Quisling wired:

"The situation is terrible. Local official statistics show that of the province's 1,288,000 inhabitants, 900,000 are without food. This number will certainly grow by 200,000 before the end of April. Sixty percent of the famished are children. Public resources are exhausted and public institutions can provide only 10,000 rations daily."

Two days later he reported: "the situation in the province of Katerynoslav is just as bad...At this time it is estimated that 520,000 persons are without food, including 200,000 children. By the end of May there will be 730,000."

In mid-March, Quisling found that "in the province of Mykolayiv, about 700,000 persons, or half of the population, is without food. It is estimated that by the end of March the number will rise to 800,000, and by the end of April to 1 million... 40 to 50 percent of the starving children die...The situation is particularly bad in the city of Kherson and the surrounding district, where many villages have died out and remain desolate." By the fall of the same year, the city of Kherson was reduced to one-quarter of its normal population.

Quisling's most complete report, titled "Famine Situation in Ukraine," was written in March and published by the High Commissariat in April 1922. It gives a detailed account of the famine conditions in the five provinces completely overcome by starvation: Odessa, Mykolayiv, Katerynoslav, Zaporizhzhia and Donetske; it also describes the affected districts of three other provinces; Kremenchuk, Poltava and Kharkiv. A dozen photographs of famine victims and a map of the famine regions accompany the document. The report faults the Soviet government for not recognizing the famine in time and criticizes the regime for doing so little about it afterwards. It concludes that unless help comes quickly, the number of the starving will reach 7 million by the summer.

Weakened by malnutrition, the population of southern Ukraine easily fell prey to contagious diseases. In October of 1921, Volga refugees brought typhus and cholera to Ukraine, and in the next month the whole country was swept by epidemics. The epidemics continued, on and off, throughout the whole period of the famine. Although no complete statistics are available on deaths from diseases, we know that epidemic cases were recorded by the hundreds of thousands and that their mortality rate was very high.

The prime victims of the famine and the epidemics were children. They also were the main targets for kidnappings and cannibalism. A million children had been orphaned by wars and the famine, and they had to fend for themselves as best they could since neither the state nor state-controlled charitable organisations could care for them in any significant way. These children known as "bezprytulni," continued to pose serious social problems during the 1920s. Hordes of these children succumbed to starvation and disease; others resorted to petty crime.

Still others became wanderers. They flocked to railway stations and rode freight cars in search of food and shelter.

Ukrainian railway stations became the main gathering centers for people fleeing the famine. Refugees lived for weeks in dilapidated wagons, waiting for a chance to board a train that would take them away. Penniless, they fought for space on wagon rooftops. In the winter, many train riders died of cold and exposure. Suzanne Ferriere, assistant secretary general of the International Save the Children Fund, visiting Poltava in 1922, was told that in that city 400 frozen children were removed from the train on two particularly cold days.

Mortality was so high during the famine that the corpses could not be buried fast enough. For days and weeks they lay in morgues and cemeteries, or simply where they fell. Many cadavers were devoured by hungry animals, and there were cases of starving people being reduced to anthropophagy.

Uniqueness of Ukrainian Famine

Simultaneously with Ukraine, the Russian Soviet Federated Socialist Republic (RSFSR) experienced a major famine along the Volga valley, in the northern Caucasus and the Crimea

It was the Volga disaster that attracted particular attention and became well-publicized. It later provided the focal point for the study of what is described by history books as "the Russian famine of 1921-1922."

In 1921, and again in 1922, southern Ukraine was subjected to a terrible drought. Harvests fell to between 10 and 25 percent of the normal crop yield, and in some cases the crop failure was complete. In spite of this, Ukraine as a whole had enough food to feed every one of its inhabitants. The crops in the northern part of the country generally were good, and there were still some reserves from previous years. To overcome the crisis in Ukraine it would have been sufficient to prevent grain from leaving the country and to organize food distribution in the south. Had the Soviet government of Ukraine taken these steps - simple measures which any national government worthy of the name would not hesitate to take - there would have been no famine at all.

While famine ravaged the southern provinces of Ukraine, the Kharkiv government did virtually nothing to alleviate it. Instead it was very actively involved in organising famine relief for Russia.

Throughout the whole period, the starving areas of Ukraine were taxed, and forced to provide 'voluntary" aid for Russia. This amounted to criminal behavior on the part of the Bolshevik authorities and astounded foreign observers.

"Up to the time the American Relief Administration (ARA) began its activities (January 1922)," wrote H H Fisher, a former ARA worker, "neither the central government at Moscow nor the Ukrainian at Kharkiv had made any serious move to relieve the famine in the south [ie Ukraine]. In fact, the only relief activity which went on in Ukraine, from the summer of 1921 to the spring of 1922, was the collection, for shipment to the distant Volga, of foodstuffs, for lack of which people along the Black Sea were dying."

"...not before the 11th of January of this year," wrote Quisling in the March 1922 report quoted above, "could the gubernia of Donets stop their obligatory relief work for the Volga district and begin to take care with all their forces of their own famine problem, at a time when already more than every tenth person in the Donets was without bread. In the beginning of March of this year, you could still see, in the famine stricken gubernia of Mykolayiv, placards with: 'Working masses of Mykolayiv, to the rescue of the starving Volga district!' The gubernia of Mykolayiv itself had at the same time 700,000 starving people, about half the population."

It was only in the beginning of 1922 that the Kharkiv government made a half-hearted effort to organize famine relief for the starving Ukrainian population. Meagre financial aid was allocated to the Sovietized Ukrainian Red Cross and the recently formed Pomhol (Famine Relief Committee). These organizations could not help even 10 percent of the starving Ukrainian population, as their main duty continued to be famine relief for Russia. Starving Ukrainians had to look for help elsewhere than to "their own" government. This aid eventually came from the West.

Foreign Relief

In July of 1921, anguished cries pierced the air, begging the West to "save starving Russia." Tikhon, patriarch of the Russian Orthodox Church, wrote to the Pope and the heads of other Churches; the prominent Russian writer Maxim Gorky addressed Western intellectuals; George Chicherin, as commissar for external affairs, sent a message to the heads of states; and Lenin appealed to the proletariat of the world. This campaign received an immediate response. States, Churches and charitable organizations offered to supply food, medicine and clothing.

The most significant aid, by virtue of its size and quality, was that provided by the American Relief Administration, headed by Herbert Hoover, secretary of commerce in the Harding administration. At the height of its activities, in the summer of 1922, ARA fed 10 million people in the RSFSR and another 2 million in Ukraine. It also provided medical supplies and clothing.

The Soviet authorities begged the West to send aid to Russia, but interfered with its delivery to Ukraine, at least at first. Although as early as August 1921, the West knew from Soviet sources about the catastrophic conditions in Ukraine, Soviet representatives either denied that there was starvation in the country or played down its importance. Moscow insisted that all aid go to the Volga and assured the West that Ukraine could take care of itself and even help Russia. Not being eager to assume more financial burdens, the West found it convenient to ignore the Ukrainian disaster, even if it meant letting the country starve.

The situation improved at the end of the year when the American Jewish community decided to send massive help to starving brethren in the Soviet republics. The American Jewish Joint Distribution Committee put pressure on the ARA to organize distribution centers in Ukraine for the food parcels sent by American Jews to their friends and relatives living there. The "Joint" (as it was commonly known) also wanted the ARA to investigate the famine situation in Ukraine, since it was getting alarming news from Ukrainian Jewry. The ARA succeeded in persuading the Soviets to allow a delegation to visit Ukraine in December of 1921. The result was the Hutchinson-Golder report and a separate agreement signed by the ARA and Soviet Ukraine, which led to the extension of American aid to Ukraine.

Help came to Ukraine in two forms; food and clothing parcels and soup kitchens.

Since the fall of 1921, food parcels could be bought by private individuals and organizations in the West and sent through relief organizations to designated parties in the Soviet republics. Most of these parcels, costing $10 each and capable of feeding one person for one month, were bought in the United States and distributed by the ARA in Ukraine.

A small number of parcels were bought by Ukrainians. ARA records show that on 5 July 1922, the Rev. Basil Kusiw of Bloomfield, N J, paid $200 on behalf of the Ukrainian Relief Committee for food parcels to be distributed equally among five Kiev institutions: the (Shevchenko?) Scientific Society, the Ukrainian Academy of Sciences, the National Ukrainian Theatre, the Medical Academy and the Ukrainian Institute of Popular Education. Three weeks later, the Ukrainian Relief Committee of Newark, N J, bought $500 worth of food for general distribution by the Ukrainian Red Cross in Kiev. But the Ukrainian American aid channeled through the ARA was insignificant when compared with the millions of dollars spent by the American Jewish community for Ukrainian Jewry.

Of much more significance for the Ukrainian population were the soup kitchens. These mass feeding stations began to be organized in May of 1922. By the summer of that year, the ARA was feeding about 1 million children and another million adults. Dining halls were also set up by various religious organizations, agencies of the Red Cross, and the international network of the Save the Children Fund. Representatives of the American and Canadian Mennonite communities were particularly active among the German Mennonite colonies set up on the former lands of the Zaporozhian Sich.

While the responsibility for organizing the American famine relief in Ukraine fell to the ARA, the actual costs of the soup kitchens were underwritten by the Joint. By the time the ARA decided to intervene in the Ukrainian famine, its own resources had been committed to the Volga relief. At this point the Joint offered to help finance famine relief in the Ukraine, on condition that the kitchens be set up in predominantly Jewish districts and that they carry Yiddish signs acknowledging the support of the Jewish organizations that sponsored them. The ARA was delighted by Joint's offer and only insisted that the kitchens be made accessible to all, regardless of religious or ethnic background. This was agreed upon and a wide network of soup kitchens was set up in Ukraine, frequented mostly by Jews but benefiting hundreds of thousands of non-Jews as well. Later on, Hoover even suggested that the Joint take over and run the operations in Ukraine by itself, but after some hesitation, the Joint declined the proposition.

Soup Kitchen a common sight – courtesy Brian Fine's Website

Chapter 8 – THE HELP GIVEN BY THE JDC
(THE AMERICAN JEWISH JOINT DISTRIBUTION COMMITTEE)

This chapter has been compiled from information and photos kindly supplied by Solly Kaplinski, Misha Mitsel and Lisa Margolin of the JDC

Since 1914, the American Jewish Joint Distribution Committee (JDC) has acted on behalf of North America's Jewish communities and others to fulfil the principle that "Kol Yisrael Arevim Zeh L'Zeh"—all Jews are responsible for one another. JDC is dedicated to serving the needs of Jews throughout the world, particularly where their lives as Jews are threatened or made more difficult.

From 1919 to 1921, JDC raised $33.4 million toward relief programs for well over a million impoverished and starving Jews in Europe as well as reconstructive aid to rebuild community institutions. It promoted economic development in Palestine, cared for war orphans and at-risk children there and in Eastern Europe, established Agro-Joint in the Soviet Union, and helped European Jews regain their economic footing.

In the Ukraine the JDC worked together with the American Relief Administration (ARA) where the Chief of Operations was Col Wm R Grove. While funds raised by the JDC were collected by Jews from Jews and for Jews in the Ukraine (and in other of JDC's operations) help was given on a non- sectarian basis.

EXTRACTS FROM COL GROVE'S REPORT TO HERBERT HOOVER ON FEEDING PROGRAMS IN THE UKRAINE

"An arrangement was made in New York on 9 March 1922, for a joint operation by the American Relief Administration (ARA) and the Jewish Joint Distribution Committee (JDC) to provide sufficient food for a maximum of 800,000 children and 400,000 adults - the maximum to be reached by 15 July. The adult program was carried out with the corn and corn grits from the Congressional Appropriation, but about 80% of the child-feeding was financed by the Joint Distribution Committee and the remaining 20%, as well as the medical program, were borne by the ARA, the administration of the whole to be strictly non-sectarian.

"It was also decided to include the larger cities outside of the famine area in the distribution of food as the refugees and patients in hospitals and other institutions in those cities were in many cases in a deplorable condition.

The first regular meeting to discuss affairs connected with the child-feeding program in the Ukraine was held in Kharkov early in April 1922 and attended by representatives of the Ukrainian Red Cross, the Ukrainian Co-operative Union, the Ukrainian Central Relief committee, the Nansen Organisation and Mr George P Harrington of the American Relief Administration. At this meeting, figures showing the population, the number of the starving, and the number to be fed by the government, were discussed.

"We have been unable to secure any reasonably accurate figures as to the percentage of starving people. This is not surprising when we consider the important facts involved. There is a difference between hunger and starvation, but the line is hard to fix. A family starving today gets a food package and is well fed for a month. Some districts estimate too high while others have such poor statistics that their estimates have proven lower than their actual wants. This is true of some of the extreme southern districts. In some of the non-famine districts it was found in March that there were many starving people, as certain sections in the southern parts of these districts had poor crops, and the people had no money to buy food.

"In some cities, such as Kherson, the people were dying in March at a rate which would have wiped the city out in one and one-half years.

"The best evidence we have as to starvation figures is that there were in the Ukraine on 31 July no known cases approaching starvation. It is evident, therefore, that the 1,923,435 persons being fed by the ARA on that date cover the real needy and those figures might be used as a maximum of starving people for the Ukraine. In fact, we were feeding hundreds of thousands who were at that time ready to go on the undernourished rather than the starvation list, but if the ARA food had not arrived these and many others would have starved, for the food we imported not only enabled these to survive, but released the food they would have consumed, thus making it possible for others to live.

Figures at that time given by the central government of the Ukraine were as follows:

		Starving			Government Intended to Feed			Remaining		
Districts	Population	Child	Adult	Total	Child	Adult	Total	Child	Adult	Total
Odessa	1 951	225	150	375				225	150	375
Nikolaiev	1 422	220	300	520	12	9	21	208	291	499
Zaporojsh	1 128	384	509	893	34	26	60	350	483	833
Ekaterinoslav	1 779	319	447	766	22	16	38	297	431	728
Donetz	3 112	402	279	681	28	20	48	374	259	633
Total	**9 392**	**1550**	**1685**	**3235**	**96**	**71**	**167**	**1454**	**1614**	**3068**

ESTIMATE OF STARVING CHILDREN AND ADULTS, AND NUMBER THE GOVERNMENT PROPOSED TO FEED FROM ITS OWN RESOURCES (These figures are in 1,000s)

Organisation

"It was originally planned to feed a maximum of 100,000 children in the Ukraine, but when the joint ARA-JDC movement was inaugurated, and it was decided to increase the number, it became necessary to divide the Ukraine into further sub-divisions than those already used for food remittance work, so that each of the five famine districts was made a separate unit for child and adult feeding purposes, and as rapidly as they became available the personnel to start work was assigned. The personnel was increased until a total of 39, including the nine medical relief men, was reached.

Supervision and Control of the Feeding

"The feeding in the Ukraine has been under the supervision of the various sub-district supervisors and has varied with the available facilities and the temperament and ability variously constituted, but always with a view to continuing ARA control of the food until consumed. In the cities the Pelidist system of physical examination for children has been used and in many cities physical examination of adults has also been made to determine the most needy. In the rural districts, as a rule no examinations have been practicable or necessary as the most needy cases there can be reached without the danger of playing favorites. Control has been maintained by the use of a large number of Russian inspectors whose work was in turn checked by the ARA representatives as far as practicable. The general instructions given from the start were that no technicalities were to interfere with getting the hungry person and the food together at the earliest possible moment. Refinements were to be made at a later date, but the organisation of the work required the attention of the personnel to such an extent that the time for many of the refinements never came.

Effects of Child-Feeding

"The effects in a real starvation area of a ration such as the ARA has given in Russia are tremendous. In the city of Odessa, where prior to receipt of ARA food the situation was as bad as could well be imagined, the improvement within 30 days was very marked. In one kitchen visited on May 22nd, out of a total of 1,100 children there were about 100 cases of the typical starvation class; five weeks later in going through that same kitchen not one child was found that would be called anything but undernourished. Another very noticeable effect of the ARA feeding was the lively and cheerful attitude of the children after having been fed a month, as compared with their quiet demeanor before. In April Odessa was a desolate city with noiseless children; in July the streets were filled with lively youngsters playing and shouting and crying 'Arah' whenever an ARA automobile would pass. It is from the children that we get the spontaneous recognition of relief work, as they know nothing of politics and no amount of propaganda can convince them that their best friend is not the one that feeds them.

Rations

"The ration for adults in the Ukraine was one Russian pound (9/10 English pound) of corn grits per day per person. It was issued dry, no kitchens being operated for adults except special kitchens for students in Odessa and Ekaterinoslav. The ration was 780 calories for each child and the menu was varied daily, the following being a sample for a week:

Sunday - Maize gruel, cocoa, bread
Monday - Maize grits, bread
Tuesday - Dumplings, cocoa
Wednesday - Maize grits, bread
Thursday - Maize pudding, cocoa , bread
Friday - Bread, pudding, bread
Saturday - Maize gruel, bread

The maize gruel is made up of sugar, milk, corn grits and a small portion of salt. The maize grits consist of corn grits, fats and salt. The dumplings are made up of sugar, flour, fats and salt. The components of the maize pudding are sugar, milk, corn grits and a little salt. Sugar, flour and fats are the commodities used in the preparation of bread pudding. The child ration was given in kitchens to those between three and fifteen years, inclusive. Nursing and expectant mothers were also fed.

Conclusion

"It is not believed that any deaths from starvation occurred in the Ukraine after 15 July. If so, they were isolated cases where the starving were not brought to the attention of any of our personnel. We had difficulty in some of the cities, even after we were feeding the full number of known starving people, to get at all of the cases.

Occasionally a family would be found where the attention of the children had not been directed to an ARA kitchen. This seems impossible with so many kitchens operating in every city of the famine district, but it is nevertheless true and shows to what extent demoralisation exists. For instance, a family was recently found in Odessa where there were three children not eating at ARA kitchens and yet in a deplorable state. The father was dead, the mother lying sick, and none of the people in the house had taken the trouble to send these children to an ARA kitchen. The mother, when asked why they did not give them any attention, stated that the children were so dirty that she felt the neighbours were afraid to have anything to do with them for fear of getting disease from them. This is, of course, an isolated case.

"There is a very general feeling of appreciation of our work among the masses, this feeling being tempered only by the dread of the ARA's withdrawal and the attendant fear of the coming winter, when both fuel and food are predicted so short that the population of the cities fear great suffering, if not actual death, from these causes.

"It can be fairly said that the work of the ARA in the Ukraine in 1922 has left on the mass of people a very fine impression. It has been repeatedly told us by natives that they do not understand how a country 5,000 miles away could take such an interest in people not of their own blood, as to send so much food to them without cost. For some time they had a lingering suspicion that at the bottom of each sack of flour they would find an advertisement of somebody's superior seed wheat or

People wait for a meal at a soup kitchen in Odessa. Ukraine. c.1923
Photos courtesy of American Jewish Joint Distribution Committee

Trade school, students working at the cabinet making workshop. Pinsk, Poland. c. 1923

propaganda of some character; but as the weeks went by and the children were restored to health and no demon appeared, they began to appreciate the fact that we were here only to help. The result is that among the masses, and the villagers there is a great appreciation of the general work of the ARA.

"Since it became widely known that the Joint Distribution Committee financed the Ukrainian program on a non-sectarian basis, much favorable comment has also been received as to this humanitarian contribution, but it is too early to say what effect, if any, it will have on the relations heretofore existing between the Jews and Russians in certain sections of the Ukraine. Like all similar movements, however, it must have a permanently beneficial effect in the minds of the large majority of people who are capable of appreciating such magnanimous action. A contributing influence in improving this relationship was the very able manner in which Dr Boris D Bogen conducted his work in the Ukraine for the Joint Distribution Committee. The nature of the operation required close contact with the district of Ukraine and the various sub-district supervisors, as well as the government representatives and a large number of Russian people. The broad-minded viewpoint of Dr Bogen left a fine impression on all with whom he came in contact"

Dr Boris Bogen. Russia, 1924

EXTRACTS FROM DR BOGEN'S LETTERS

Kiev, 13 April 1922

"In the early morning Col Grove and myself spent a little time at the railroad station where the refugees were concentrated. There were thousands of them all huddled in a large dark hall lying on the bare floor, moaning, picking vermin and suffering. There was a man with a terribly sickly child telling us how for months he was trying to get back to Riasan, but he had no money and the child was ill. There was a group of women - they were sitting on their ragged belongings, they had no place to go, they arrived in Kiev looking for food. There was a boy of about 14 years of age moaning and pitifully begging for a piece of bread. At the time of our visit the refugees were moved from one room to another so as to clean up the place and take away the sick and the dead and there in the corner a woman was arguing in a frenzy with a soldier not to touch the sick or perhaps dead man lying near her. Oh! This was a horrible scene. The air was foul, the people were covered with vermin, sick, miserable, dilapidated humanity.

"We followed up this investigation by visiting the home of refugee children, a kind of a hospital conducted by the government for the children of the famine district. At that particular time there were about 150 children there, all sick, some with typhus, dysentery and other diseases. The doctor in charge is Miss Brylowski. She pleaded for the sake of the poor children. They were all hungry she said. They receive nothing but bread and occasional supplies of other commodities.

"It was pitiful to see how the children huddled under the blankets. They have nothing else on their bodies. They are in bad need of clothing and linen. The place was clean but exceedingly cold.

"We visited also the refugee feeding stations, a horrible place. Here were men, women and children all waiting in vain for food and occupying their time in picking off the vermin. The lady in charge explained to us that they have tried to build a disinfecting plant and in fact she showed us the place where they had already begun the construction but the amounts required for this undertaking were so large that it had to be given up.

"We then visited the concentration shelter for refugees where they are taken care of for fourteen consecutive days. This was a nightmare of horror. The stories we heard there were enough to drive a person insane. There were all human beings, men, women and children of various classes huddled together in as small a place as possible (for the entire building could not be heated for lack of fuel) hungry, ragged, eaten up by vermin, without any hope and with an expression in their faces and eyes of utter despair.

"We went over the entire refugee situation with a lady physician, a representative of the government. She explained to us that the situation is becoming more and more serious for Kiev is one of the centers to which the refugees are attracted, that the city is already saturated with all that it can absorb, that the government was compelled to establish restriction points so as not to admit any more refugees, that the death rate is appalling and that epidemics are continually raging throughout the entire district. In this case the death was attributed to dysentery but on investigation it was diagnosed as a mild case of cholera undoubtedly due to starvation.

"There is no question in my mind that this situation is the most acute case of mass suffering due to neglect and want that I ever witnessed. It represents only a sample of the situation to be found in the other cities where refugees are concentrated. This condition cannot be permitted to continue without at least every possible effort made to meet the situation.

"I am telling you as I feel just coming from the field where I mingled with and talked to the people. Their faces haunt me, their voices ring in my ear and my heart bleeds because I know that among the thousands here there are many who are just as good as you and I.

"In this connection I want to tell you of the visit we made to a special hospital for children, the head of which is Dr Balaban. This was formerly a hospital modern in every respect. At the present time the entire equipment is dilapidated. There are about 400 children in this hospital. It was a blessing to see the good use that they made of the ARA blankets and shawls, the only things that keep them warm. Dr Balaban showed to us two examples of child starvation; one an actual skeleton and the other swollen with hunger. She explained to us that very few survive, especially in the winter. The department of infants was especially appalling. They had no milk in the place and the food that they get is not fit for children. They employ a large number of wet nurses but the latter cannot feed the children because they are not sufficiently nourished. The food they receive is absolutely insufficient and besides, imagine children suffering from dysentery, typhus, scarlatina and diptheria fed on black bread and a limited amount of lard.

Prosburov, 17 April 1922

Then we were taken to an infant home with 45 beds. This is an international institution for children of all nationalities. This institution was in the most horrible condition that I ever saw - dirty, very badly equipped, the children emaciated and in general it produced a most appalling impression.

"Next to that we visited the hospital with 200 patients, one of the worst institutions of this kind that I ever saw - no bedding, no blankets, dirty, unhygienic, no bathing or disinfecting facilities (while they have the equipment they have not the wood).

"This was only a prelude to an institution that they showed us in connection with the work for the refugee children. Imagine 194 little men and women huddled in rags on the floor without clothes to cover their bodies; they cannot leave the house for lack of clothes. They cannot move for lack of room; all of them looking emaciated and undernourished, some of them like skeletons. This was a horrible sight to behold. We were especially impressed with the terrible restraint that could be felt in the conduct of these children. They showed a kind of a fear in their eyes, they were almost motionless. I am especially picturing eight or ten children grouped in a corner on the floor throwing at us the most pitiful look. Upon further inquiry we found that these children came from the famine district; that because of lack of clothing, they cannot leave the rooms and as there are only two or three rooms designated for them they have no place to move around.

"I spoke to the matron and she informed me that the reason the children are in this shape is because they are suffering from long hunger and that even the feeding that they receive now is not sufficient and that it does not do them much good when they cannot move about.

"These children have no beds to speak of or blankets or any other thing on which to lie down and are practically speaking leading an animal existence. We were so strongly impressed with the critical situation that I was tempted at once to make arrangements to provide some clothing for the children but upon inquiry we found that it would be exceedingly difficult and very expensive.

"After discussing the matter with Col Grove we decided that we should send a telegram asking for an emergency appropriation of at least $50,000 worth of clothing and linen for children. This is a very insignificant sum but it will at least give us a chance to satisfy here and there some of the children who will perish on account of neglect and want. I hope that this request will be granted without delay."

Odessa, 21 April 1922

Ódessa is the most dismal town that we have so far visited. As soon as we arrived we could notice that the town is in desperate condition. There were very few people on the streets and in their walk and look we could see that they are disheartened and distressed.

"Everywhere I heard horrible stories of the raving disease and starvation death. The population of Odessa is about 500,000 of whom 60% are Jewish. The mortality rate per day is estimated as 500; about 110 bodies are daily picked up on the streets. In going through the various districts we saw a number of bodies which were not as yet picked up for burial. The recent order is that these bodies must be removed immediately but unfortunately the number are so great that even with this rule in effect it is difficult to keep up with the number. In the outskirts of the city some of the bodies have been devoured by stray dogs.

"We visited yesterday the City Hospital, an institution with a capacity of 2,000. There are only 300 patients there. The administration cannot accept any more because of a lack of food. In going through the wards we saw little children and men and women; all of them pleaded and prayed for bread. They did not get any allowance for the past four days. Many of the children were in the last stages of starvation. This was the most trying experience that I ever had. Col Grove and I decided that we cannot wait until the organisation is completed and we sent $50 worth of foodstuffs to this institution; this was done by buying an 'Internal Sale' with money that I had. I have written a letter to the Superintendent that this was a gift of the Joint Distribution Committee. Naturally, this is a very small proposition; the children in the other institutions are in the same deplorable state. Col Grove is trying very hard to start the feeding immediately.

People share a meal at a communal soup kitchen. Kharkov, Ukraine. c.1923. JDC was the largest single donor to ARA food programs in the Soviet Union during a widespread, prolonged famine. In the Ukraine alone, their contributions helped nearly two million Jews survive.

THE MIRACLE OF EKATERINASLAV
By Benjamin Pepper

When I expressed my willingness to go to the Ukraine, Mr Rosenberg begged me to keep a diary. I did so for the first ten days in Ekaterinaslav, but our hours of work were such that I could not keep it up and I therefore must write this account from memory. I left London on 7 April 1922 as an ARA man appointed by Colonel Grove, with Mr Benjamin Blattner, JDC accountant, Mr Frank L Price, a publicity man of the ARA, and two Englishmen employed as accountants by the ARA. I travelled via Ostend to Berlin and then to Riga where we obtained the necessary Russian visas permitting entrance into Russia. From Riga we went by train to Moscow (then a three day trip for what now takes a day and a half). Moscow had a drab, rundown appearance, but the only indications of famine were the many beggars on the street. On the day of my arrival, I received my inoculations against typhoid, paratyphoid and cholera and left the following day for the Ukraine. My first stop was at Charkov where I waited for Col Grove and Dr Bogen to arrive and assign me to my work. There I got my initiation into the horror of famine.

On my arrival in Charkov, it became necessary to pass through the main waiting room of the railroad station which is a room about one half the size of the main floor of the Grand Central Station. The floor of this room was literally covered with people, old and young - men, women, children, infants - all starving and a number already dead. At least 30 dead bodies were being removed daily from this station. To get out of the station I had to pick my way over these bodies of human beings lying there dying of starvation. Charkov was not in the famine area, it was a railroad center and these people were refugees from the famine districts who had gathered at all the various railroad centers throughout the Ukraine in such numbers that the Government had no place to put them, no means of feeding them nor any possibility of coping with the situation in any way and these gathering points were centers of pestilence and death.

After several days in Charkov, Col Grove and Dr Bogen arrived from their trip of inspection through the Ukraine. I received my instructions from them and departed for Ekaterinaslav, arriving there on the 28th of April. Ekaterinaslav, about 300 miles south of Charkov, is a city of 175,000 inhabitants, 76% of them Jews. At the railroad station I was met by the ARA district supervisor, Mr Thomas Barringer, who took me through the city to the ARA headquarters. The impression I gathered was that of a dead city. The street along which we rode was the famous Ekaterinenskai Prospect - a broad avenue wider than Fifth Avenue, four miles long in a straight line, with a once beautiful alley of acacias down the centre. But where there once was grass there was now bare dirt and where many a tree had formerly stood there was now a stump. Many of the buildings on either side were in ruins for there had been much fighting there during the war and revolution. Other buildings were boarded up and through the gaping broken windows, one saw empty wrecks of what had been stores and shops.

The ARA headquarters were located near the edge of the city on the Novo Dworanskai. Practically every building on this street excepting the one assigned to us had been damaged, although many a family still found shelter in these roofless, ruined, windowless homes. The building we had was a three storey, solid, cement and brick building about 50 by 50 feet and here the ARA had several months previously opened offices for the distribution of the $10 food package which it sold in America. The main floor and basement of this building were used for the clerical work and distribution warehouse of the food package work, the second floor was used for sleeping quarters and on the third floor we now prepared to organise the non-sectarian child feeding division.

My very first day at Ekaterinaslav had one most important meeting. I wish I could do justice to Dr Boris Chanis. Dr Chanis is a leader among the Jews and indeed among all the people in Ekaterinaslav, possessing the respect and admiration as well as the trust and confidence of all people with whom he came into contact. He is a man of about 35 years of age, ill of an incurable disease, frequently suffering intense pain, and yet devoting his time and his life unstintingly to the cause of helping his fellowmen. With us he devoted all his time to relief work and took barely enough pay to sustain life himself. His unselfishness and self-sacrifice combined with his keen mind and unflagging energy were a guide and an inspiration to us in our work. Upon meeting him I realised that he was a man who could and would be of immense service to us in our work and I immediately arranged with him to go on a trip of inspection the following day to some of the Jewish children's homes in the city of Ekaterinaslav, and on this next day I received my first picture of what the famine meant in the children's homes.

The home we first visited containing 50 children was quite near the ARA headquarters, a small two storey cement and brick house considerably dismantled, windows broken and lacking the ordinary facilities of sanitation. It was a dreary looking place without even the simplest equipment. There was not a single knife or fork for the children though that was unimportant, as they had nothing to eat with knives or forks, the diet at that time consisting almost entirely of a very watery soup and some indigestible black bread. Most of the children were in rags and some were actually stark naked. They were little tots, none older than 14 and most of them between seven and ten - all Jewish children. Due to the fact that they had already received some food from the JDC food packages, they had not had any deaths within the preceding month, though before that they had suffered severely from starvation. But the food packages had not gone a very long way in maintaining more than existence. The children were emaciated, some of them unbelievably thin and gaunt with skin drawn tight over the jaws and cheek bones and with deep sunken eyes, so that their faces looked like skeleton heads. They had a frown on their faces with deep vertical creases between their eyebrows which I later learned was the typical frown of starvation. Their skin was a sort of mottled brown which I later learned was also a sign of starvation. There were a few who had been through even more extreme stages of starvation, for their stomachs were bloated and swollen and one or two were even swollen about the joints of the legs and feet. These youngsters slept three and even four together in tiny cribs without mattresses at all or with mattresses made of coarse sacking stuffed with stiff straw. The two women in charge of this children's home were deeply ashamed for the condition of the house which it was obvious they could do nothing to prevent.

When I first came to Ekaterinaslav, one could find on the streets every day persons who crept wearily into some corner never to rise again. Beggars met one at every turn. I remember particularly one Jewish family, a mother with three weeping children lying on the sidewalk at one of the more busy corners. Another case that I shall never forget I saw at one of our kitchens in company with Dr Chanis. It was a woman with a tiny infant in her arms. The child seemed to me to be not more than six months old but what attracted our attention was its sunken, wrinkled face which was that of a man of 75. That child was four years old! In all the terrible time of revolution, banditry, bloodshed and famine, the mother had kept this child alive, but no more than that. She had had so little nourishment to give it that she had been unable to do more than maintain the spark of life, but the child, unable to grow, at the end of four years was still an infant in arms.

The first few days were spent at the ARA office getting acquainted with the problems and working out the details of the child feeding work with Mr Barringer, the ARA supervisor. The program which we were to carry out involved the feeding of 200,000 children and 150,000 adults in the district of Ekaterinaslav, a territory about 300 miles long and 150 miles wide. This district contained in addition to Ekaterinaslav itself, the smaller cities of Alexandria, Krivoi, Rog, Nikopol, Sinelnico, Povlograd etc. Fortunately for us, the railroad system in our district was very well laid out for our purposes, so that we were able to depend almost entirely upon the railroads for getting food to the various distributing points which we established throughout the district. From these distributing points the food was conveyed to the little villages and towns scattered over the district by the farmers of the villages who came with their little wagons and small cossack ponies or ox carts in long trains from all directions.

We had warehouses in all the cities that I mentioned above and Russian representatives appointed to supervise the management of the warehouse and the organisation of kitchens and distribution of food in the area surrounding each one of these points. This organisation, of course, was entirely Russian. For the whole Ekaterinaslav district we had only three Americans in the child feeding work and one additional American for the food package work - four Americans in all. I am not going into detail about our organisation, but am trying to give only a broad idea of the work in one district. By the 15th of May we were actually feeding 12,000 children, by the 30th of May 40,000 and at the height of the work on 1 August, we were feeding 210,000 children and 150,000 adults.

The child feeding and adult feeding work was entirely non-sectarian and conducted according to the principle of greatest need, which principle the ARA and JDC men worked out and carried through in entire accord. The child feeding was done entirely through kitchens or through giving food to institutions. In the entire Ekaterinaslav district there were 311 kitchens, in the city of Ekaterinaslav there were 22 kitchens. The houses for these kitchens were provided by the local governments and were also equipped by them with large kettles, pails and tin dishes. The children who came to the kitchens received one meal a day of about 670 calories food value. The food consisted of gruel of oatmeal grits, cocoa with evaporated milk, sugar, some fats and a quarter pound of white bread daily. I remember well the opening of the first kitchen at Ekaterinaslav on the Potiomkinskaia during the first week in May. This kitchen accommodated about 400 children. The preceding week the local committee of representative citizens living in this area had been busy selecting the children who should be fed and when the work was done word had gone forth that the kitchen was to be opened. From early morning the fortunate children with little mugs in their hands began gathering about the door while hundreds of others who had not been selected for feeding stood about hoping that something would happen so that they might also be admitted. It is impossible for anyone who has not seen it to picture these long lines and rows of thin, tragic faces and forms with their look of expectation as they waited there for the doors to open. One of the curious features of our feeding was that hungry as the children were, for a long time it was impossible to get them to drink the cocoa. They had never seen it in their lives, they did not know what it was and they were quite afraid of it. But after they had once acquired the taste they could not get enough of it. The feeding in the institutions was conducted in the same way as in kitchens directly under our control with regard to the menu and amount of calories per meal. We printed circulars showing the rations for each day and the ration per child allowed so that the only difference between the feeding in institutions and kitchens was that in one case we directly controlled the work, while in the other case we merely exercised a supervisory function. Wherever possible we used existing institutions.

The difficulties we had to contend with were of various sorts. On 30 June we were feeding 90,000 children which was up to schedule. Then suddenly the food ceased coming in and we were unable to expand our program as required. Daily messages to Odessa brought no response and Mr Barringer and I were frantic. In the first week in July Col Grove happened to come through Ekaterinaslav on a tour of inspection, we informed him that our program of expansion had stopped and we were in actual immediate danger of having to close our kitchens due to the fact that our food reserves were being exhausted. Col Gove was astonished. He said that he himself had signed the order for additional shipments and that he would investigate this matter instantly on his arrival in Odessa. There, as I later learned, he discovered that some clerk through whose hands our order had passed had decided that our warehouse space in Ekaterinalsav, which he had never seen, was not sufficient to accommodate the supplies ordered and that he had better hold up this requisition. He had therefore filed it away. It was through such occurrences that each day contained its drama. The food started to come in immediately after Col Grove reached Odessa and you may imagine the sigh of relief and delight which Mr Barringer and I heaved when the telephone call came from the railroad station that the trains had come in. Within 36 hours, 75 carloads arrived and the day was saved.

I ought to touch on one more matter and that is the adult feeding, particularly in the country districts rather than in the city. There originally had been no intention of feeding adults in the Ukraine, but investigation showed that the feeding of children was not sufficient to meet the problem of famine in this area and that unless something was done to save the adults, tremendous numbers of them would die and that furthermore the peasants in the villages had become so weakened from lack of food that it was highly probable that a large part of the harvest would be lost due to the fact that they were unable to harvest the crop. Therefore, upon very short notice, we organised our adult feeding work. This was done through the same agencies as our child feeding, but the food was not distributed cooked each day, but a two weeks' supply of uncooked corn grits was given out at once to each adult entitled to help. The object of this was to enable the peasant to remain at work in the field without the necessity of interruption, a long tramp to some kitchen and back each day. The importance of this adult feeding cannot be measured. I have had representatives of a number of villages come to me after the harvest and tell me with tears in their eyes that our food came at the time of most extreme need as though in answer to their prayers and that without it they and their village would have been unable to save the harvest upon which depended not only their lives, but the lives of all the city workers.

The recuperative power of a human being is marvelous. One would have supposed that to save these haggard, skeleton-like children that I saw when I first arrived in Ekaterinsalav would have required years of careful feeding, yet it took no more than two months. The change which took place in Ekaterinaslav in that brief time was unbelievable. Where once the streets had been filled with beggars, without any other act than the opening of the ARA kitchens, these beggars disappeared from the streets as though some great hand had swept them away. Where one saw previously thin, pale little children with no strength in their limbs, with no laughter in their eyes, two months later these creatures were gone and in their place were merry, rosy-cheeked, happy youngsters. It is this unbelievable transformation particularly among the children due to no other factor than our feeding which I shall always look back upon as something akin to a miracle..

Awaiting the opening of a JDC Soup Kitchen Ekaterinoslav Ukraine, 1921.
Courtesy of American Jewish Joint Distribution Committee

Chapter 9 – THE RESCUE OF UKRAINIAN ORPHANS BY THE CANADIAN JEWISH COMMUNITY IN 1921.

At the same time that Isaac Ochberg, the President of the Cape Jewish Orphanage and the representative of the South African Jewish Community was gathering the orphans to be brought out to South Africa there was a very similar scheme being carried out by the Canadian Jewish Community.

While the ship carrying the South African children arrived in Cape Town on 19 September 1921 the children arrived in Canada about three weeks earlier.

THE RESCUE OF UKRAINIAN ORPHANS
Courtesy Janice Rosen, Archives Director, Canadian Jewish Congress Charities Committee National Archives. Extracted from the books "THE JEW IN CANADA" compiled and edited by Arthur Daniel Hart and "Lillian And Archie Freiman Biographies" by Bernard Figler.

It was in the summer of 1920 that the pitiable condition of the Jewish child population of Ukrainia first came to the attention of Canadian Jewry in a direct and authoritative way. Professor Elie Heifetz of Ukrainia came to America in July of that year with a description of suffering and tragedy that would have seemed unbelievable had it not been fully substantiated.

There were more than 137,000 Jewish children in the Ukraine orphaned by the war, he reported, children of tender age practically living wild and semi-barbarous lives, without homes or means of obtaining regular sustenance beyond their own puny resources, which were mainly the garbage lots of Ukrainian towns and villages. When this course failed to provide for them they tried to assuage the pangs of hunger by eating such edible wild roots and herbs as were left in a territory that had been sadly ravaged by war and post-war excesses. It was felt that aid for these orphans was an imperative duty of the Jews of the American continent who had known nothing of such terrible privation.

While seeking relief supplies for Ukrainia through the People's Relief Committee of New York, Professor Heifetz had conceived a plan to rehabilitate many of the orphans by their emigration to America where they would be placed in foster homes. The United States laws, however, were not favourable to such immigration. He then turned to Canada in the hope that his scheme might be successfully carried out here.

A meeting was convened for this purpose in Montreal on 11 July 1920 presided by Lyon Cohen, president of the Canadian Jewish Congress. A Committee was appointed to examine the proposed plan. It became evident at the outset that the task was a huge one, requiring the active interest and support of all Canadian Jewry. It involved a campaign for a large sum of money for relief of the children in Europe; obtaining permission of the Canadian Government to admit a number of the children; finding

Some of the Orphans – 1921

reliable foster homes for their adoption; dispatching competent persons to Europe to select the children; preparing them for the trip and accompanying them to Canada.

A national committee would have to be set up, headed by a prominent personality. Everyone agreed that the ideal person as leader of this undertaking was Lillian Freiman.

Four days later she was visited by a committee consisting of Professor Heifetz, Harry Hershman, representing the People's Relief Committee and Mrs Anna Selick of Toronto. The Committee placed before her all the facts in their possession regarding the Ukrainian orphans.

If there was anything calculated to stir her fullest sympathy it was a story of children in distress, particularly orphans. She promptly pledged herself to the pressing cause. She wasted no time getting matters started and arranged a conference with F C Blair, secretary of the Department of Immigration and Colonisation, attended by herself, Professor Heifetz and Hershman.

She explained to Mr Blair the urgent problem and asked permission, for the admission of 1,000 orphans from Ukrainia, to be adopted into Canadian Jewish homes. The department felt that the immigration of 1,000 children might be too big a problem to handle and therefore consented to the entry of only 200, as an initial experiment. Further numbers might be approved if the admission of the first 200 was made in a manner satisfactory to the Department of Immigration.

It was stipulated that the children must be in good health; not over 12 years of age; complete arrangements for their reception and adoption had to be made in advance of their arrival; a proper organisation had to be formed to execute the project. These conditions were immediately agreed to by Mrs Freiman and her colleagues.

On 8 August Louis Zucker, president of the Peoples' Relief Committee, and Professor Heifetz met with Mrs Freiman in Ottawa and went into further plans for the work and decided to appeal on Rosh Hashana for Canadian Jewry's support. The following day a conference was held in Montreal, attended by delegates representing more than 100 organisations. They formally named Mrs Freiman as Dominion President of the Ukrainian Orphans Committee, and Professor Heifetz, director. The following committee was appointed to direct the appeal in Montreal: Lyon Cohen, Rabbi H Cohen, Leon Meltzer, S D Cohen, Louis Zucker, Lionel Coviensky and Harry Barsky.

Mrs Freiman issued a stirring message to Rabbis and presidents of Synagogues throughout the Dominion, asking them to address their congregations on Rosh Hashana on the plight of the Jewish orphans in Ukrainia. Meetings were held with leaders of communities. Professor Heifetz addressed gatherings in Winnipeg and a conference in Saskatoon of delegates from western cities. A J Freiman spoke at two large meetings in Montreal, one of them in Prince Arthur Hall, at which great enthusiasm was aroused for the undertaking.

It was necessary to take steps to win the interest and support of Jews in all parts of the country. It was decided to convene a Dominion-wide conference. On 1 October 1920, telegrams, bearing the signatures of Lillian Freiman and Professor Heifetz, were sent to leaders of communities from coast to coast, inviting them to a conference in Chateau Laurier, Ottawa, 6 to 8 October. The telegrams read in part:

"Jewish hearts all over Canada have been deeply stirred by authentic accounts of suffering of these Jewish orphans and everywhere great enthusiasm prevails for our plans to rescue and bring some here for adoption in homes where they will be given the love and care they now so pitiably lack. May we not have your co-operation in this noble undertaking?"

This was one of the most momentous gatherings of its kind ever held by Canadian Jewry. Mrs Freiman presided. Delegates were present from many parts of the country. Present also were S W Jacobs K C, MP; Solomon Lowenstein and Charles Zunser, representing the orphans branch of the Jewish Joint Distribution Committee of America and Reuben Brainin, noted Hebrew author and journalist. Harold Fisher, mayor of Ottawa, welcomed the delegates and F C Blair, Secretary of the Department of Immigration, explained the Department's attitude and promised all possible co-operation and assistance.

The Conference adopted the official name of the Jewish War Orphans Committee of Canada; elected Lillian Freiman, National President, and her husband Chairman of the Executive Committee, and an Executive which included Lyon Cohen, D S Freidman, Dr C J Gross, Lionel Coviensky, H Wolofsky, L Zucker, H Hershman, Nathan Sloves and representatives of a large number of communities. The Conference decided also to conduct a campaign for funds on 26-28 December 1920.

On Lillian Freiman's invitation, Mrs Arthur Meighen, wife of the Prime Minister of Canada, accepted the office of Honorary President of the Committee. Lady Davis, Lady Borden and Mrs Mark Workman became Honorary Vice-Presidents.

Her Excellency the Duchess of Devonshire, wife of the Governor General, was apprised by Mrs Freiman of the proposed undertaking and replied: "Under your leadership the scheme will be carefully worked out and will prove a very successful one" and desired to be kept informed of the progress of the Committee for the adoption of the first 200 orphans.

An executive office was opened in Ottawa with Sam Berger as secretary. Under the personal supervision of Mrs Freiman an extensive publicity campaign was planned and quantities of literature dealing with the orphans' situation in Ukrainia were sent out.

The Executive decided that it was of the utmost importance that a prominent person tour the country to explain the urgency of the undertaking, organise local committees and receive applications for adoption of orphans. They urged Lillian Freiman to undertake such a tour herself.

Early in November 1920, she set out, accompanied by Miss Ida Seigler of Montreal, editor of the Canadian Jewish Chronicle, to visit the leading cities from Halifax to Vancouver. They did not spare themselves. Mrs Freiman delivered scores of addresses, met delegations in every community, and assisted in the organisation of numerous local committees.

Many applications for adoption were received. These were turned over to the local committees for investigation so that the orphans would be assigned only to homes offering the right sort of care and assurance for their future. Many individuals and organisations also undertook to contribute annually $200 per child for the maintenance of orphans in their respective European countries.

Groups of women everywhere began to sew garments for the little ones. The hearts of mothers were filled with pity at the thought of thousands of boys and girls, like their own, wandering the streets of Ukrainian towns and villages, footsore, ragged and hungry. Enthusiasm was the greater as it became known that no other country had attempted the actual bringing of orphans from Ukrainia. Hadassah Chapters, B'nai B'rith Lodges, local councils of Jewish women, Synagogue Ladies Auxiliaries, were all co-operating in the work.

On her return from the four-week trip she said: "Canada's Jews are ready to open their homes to these children from Eastern Europe. We have received over 1,500 applications for adoption of children. The idea of financial adoption on the same plan as that carried out on behalf of the French and Belgian orphans is meeting with enthusiastic response. The little colony of Edenbridge, with 22 Jewish families has applied for adoption of 22 children."

Nor did she content herself with routine checking of the applications but personally investigated, as far as geographically possible, the prospective homes for the children, for she was worried lest any child 'of hers' may *chalila* be placed in the wrong home and not receive the proper care and upbringing.

The campaign that followed in December raised nearly $100,000, in addition to donations of large quantities of children's clothing, which were shipped abroad. Boys and girls were also urged to make sacrifices from their penny banks for the purchase of clothing and shoes for their less fortunate brothers and sisters in Ukrainia.

Non-Jews as well supported the cause, for through the very generous publicity given by the general press the sad plight of helpless children touched Christian hearts too. Thus, in Yarmouth, Nova Scotia, the mayor J M Walker, was treasurer and another prominent Christian, K Kilty, was an active member of the campaign committee.

SELECTION OF THE ORPHANS

In the meantime, the National Committee for War Orphans decided to send a delegation, or unit, to Europe to select the children, ascertain that they were in good physical health and otherwise comply with the requirements of the Canadian Immigration authorities, and to bring them to Canada.

There was unexpected delay in dispatching the unit to Ukrainia. It was hoped that its members would sail in November 1920, but Professor Heifetz, who was to head the unit, being a subject of Soviet Russia, could not obtain the documents indispensable to pass unhindered through different European countries. It was found necessary therefore to appoint a new director in the person of Gregory Sanders of Montreal. He was to be accompanied by Harry Hershman of Montreal, as assistant director, Dr Joseph Leavitt, Montreal, as medical director and William Farrar, Hamilton, director of transportation.

William Farrar, a non-Jew, and former alderman of Hamilton, was a popular figure with the Hamilton Jewish Community. For many years he had taken an active interest in Jewish affairs and even attended synagogue services frequently, especially on the High Holy Days. Mr Farrar was also an enthusiastic Zionist and attended the Eleventh Zionist convention held in Toronto 23-26 December 1910. At this Convention president Clarence I de Sola submitted a resolution to create a Land Fund to

Harry Hershman with some of the Orphans

Purchase land in Palestine. When the resolution was adopted de Sola and Treasurer A A Levin led with the first contributions and were immediately followed by Alderman Farrar!

When the committee learned that Mr Farrar would like nothing better than to serve as a member of the unit his appointment was unanimously approved for he was a prominent business man and organiser, with special knowledge of transportation problems. [It was characteristic of Mr Farrar that he later reimbursed the committee all the money spent on his transportation and maintenance while with the unit.]

In December Mr and Mrs Freiman and Mr Sanders went to New York where they were assured the facilities of the Joint Distribution Committee in Europe, including personnel, records, offices, warehouses, automobiles, etc.

Some contributors expressed the wish that relief be also extended to orphans in the part of Ukrainia under Soviet rule. The delegation had learned, however, in New York, that it would not be practical to enter Soviet territory. It was therefore determined to concentrate the work of the committee in Polish Ukrainia where the situation was perhaps more acute. As a matter of fact, however, many of the orphans that were rescued came from towns and villages in Soviet Ukrainia from which they had fled in terror following pogroms against the Jewish inhabitants.

On 2 February 1921, a conference was held in Montreal confirming the necessary change in plans, and arrangements were rushed for the departure of the unit to Europe. Unfortunately they suffered another setback when the wife of Gregory Sanders became seriously ill and he was obliged to resign as director and was replaced by Mr Hershman. The Department of External Affairs in Canada facilitated the task of the committee by issuing special documents, in English and French, requesting the co-operation of governments abroad. As all three members of the unit were British subjects the necessary passports and visas were speedily procured.

The entire Canadian Jewish community followed with quickened interest the departure of the unit on 5 February 1921 on the White Star liner 'Cedric'. Applications for adoption continued to flow to the Dominion headquarters at Ottawa where G Garrow-Greene, private secretary to Mr and Mrs Freiman, was the new executive Secretary. The applications, after careful scrutiny, were classified according to sexes and ages of the children desired, to facilitate the work of selection by the unit in Europe. Care was taken to distribute the children among as many communities as possible.

Upon arrival in Europe the unit met with Jewish leaders in Paris, Vienna and Warsaw. Considerable time was spent preparing in advance for the movement of the children to be selected, following conferences with the Polish Ministry of Foreign Affairs in regard to passports and with the Polish Ministry of Transportation to assure an adequate supply of railroad cars.

Although they had been prepared for very tragic conditions, the members of the unit were shocked to discover the indescribable plight of the war and pogrom sufferers in the small cities and villages of Polish Ukrainia. Writing from Warsaw, on 17 March 1921, Mr Farrar said "The Jews in Ukrainia have been in Hell. Young girls come here with the most heartrending stories. I am made sad from morning until night."

After completing the preliminary work in Warsaw, the unit proceeded on its way, reaching Rovno, which had been selected as the base for activity, on 3 April. It was the glorious hopeful season of spring, but alas, such a spring in Poland. How the thoughts of each member of the unit must have turned toward Canada, where the springs come year after year under happy circumstances. Spring meant nothing of what it had in Canada, to these Canadians in Poland. True, here and there, the trees were green with budding foliage, and the ground had splotches of grass, but there was so much of desolation that the signs of spring became insignificant. Trees everywhere gaunt and charred, met their gaze, trees that seemed to speak of war and pillage, and upheaval; and most indelibly impressive of all, was a population which faced the picture of utter hopelessness and misery. Women clutching their skirts, their eyes darting hither and thither were filled with the fear that experience had taught them to have. And the children! What horrible mute stories the faces of the little ones told. They did not need to speak. Children of perhaps four or five with features of aged persons, eyes sunken, cheeks nothing but skin and bone, bodies almost mere skeletons. Surely, thought these missionaries of humanitarianism, this was the saddest spot on earth.

There was no lack of children for the unit to examine. Thousands had been registered by the representatives of the Joint Distribution Committee, and the fortunate ones accommodated in the three homes that had been established in Rovno. But there were also many others living in sheds and in the open, for space in the homes was limited. Did they want to go to Canada? The excitement, and the anxiety to be chosen which prevailed amongst the children of Rovno, stirred pangs of pity in the hearts of each member of the unit, for sad though it was to decide that way, very few, if any of the children first examined were fit to pass the physical and mental tests. With the valuable co-operation of the agents of the Joint distribution Committee, the unit set to work. The memory of the week that followed their arrival in Rovno will probably never be erased from their minds. Over 1,000 children were examined by Dr Leavitt and he found only 46 whom he thought might be of the standard required. The pale thin faces of the little ones, the eyes which mirrored years of intense suffering, almost unnerved the doctor. Over 8,000 children had to be examined eventually before the number brought to Canada was selected. Three children who came before the doctor were all that remained of a happy family of 15 members. All the others had been killed or had died of diseases brought on by wounds and hunger. One of the three was a cripple, and so the Jewish community of Rovno refused to allow the other two to be taken, as it was felt that they would likely be the sole means of support of the crippled child in later years. In a letter which he wrote to Mr Freiman from Rovno on 7 April, Mr Hershman said, "We examined children from the Felstin district, and out of 80, found only 15 to comply with our regulations. Most of the others are in a very poor physical state, some of them maimed and crippled from the effects of pogroms they were in." In this letter, Mr Hershman expressed the belief that it would take from two to three months longer to pick out the required number of children. And then, in a later letter, he wrote:

"Children born in the Ukraine from three to six years ago could not survive, especially if they had become orphans at the ages of one or two years. Those who survived are the fortunate ones whose parents were spared, and only superhuman sacrifices on the part of the parents saved them."

By 21 April, Hershman cabled that the unit had already selected 60 children, between the ages of four and 12. As people in Canada were becoming impatient for the arrival of the children, the Ottawa headquarters cabled on 25 April to send the first party of children as soon as possible.

The unit in the meantime was meeting with tremendous difficulties. First, there were no suitable houses in Rovno where to place the children after they had been selected. There had been delay in the arrival of the cases of clothing, and the greatest difficulty of all was the absolute lack of official records relating to the birth of the children. This, of course, was vitally essential.

The parents of the children were dead; official records had been destroyed in the pogroms. Hershman had to make dozens of visits here and there, interviewing old residents who had known the parents of the orphans. In this way a sufficient record was built up and, when completed, the documents of origin were certified by the local rabbinate. One can appreciate the quandary of the unit in this respect as, for example, 55 of the children chosen were from the district of Novgorod, Wolinsk, which had been burned and pogromed no fewer than 15 times and records of vital statistics had been completely destroyed.

With the shortage of railroad cars following the war, the unit encountered further difficulty when different governments refused to allow their equipment to pass beyond their respective frontiers. During all this time the people of Canada were chafing a little at the protracted delay in the consummation of the undertaking, it being naturally hard for them to understand why it was taking so long to collect the children.

On 20 May 1921, Freiman cabled Hershman instructing him that, as conditions in Canada necessitated quick conclusion of the project, the number of children to be brought to Canada should be reduced to 150, instead of the original 200. One of the reasons that forced the committee to this decision was that most of the children found eligible for emigration were older than desired by adoptive families. Hershman had reported that there were few children under six years of age who had survived, whilst 70 per cent of the applications for adoption were for children under six.

As news arrived from the unit, and was conveyed by bulletins to all the local committees most of the applicants consented to accept children older than originally stipulated. A further cable was sent to Hershman instructing the unit to endeavour to finish its work by 15 June. At last the first party of orphans was ready for departure. They left Rovno on 14 June, in the words of Hershman "to the greatest joy of the children and the grief of the population."

There were 51 boys and girls in the first party. In two days they reached Vienna where they were comfortably housed. Here Farrar taught them some of the simple words of the English language and described to them in an interesting manner Canada, Canadians and Canadian customs, all of which, needless to say, increased the eagerness of the children to come here.

It was decided to gather all the children in Antwerp until the date of sailing. Finally, after the lapse of another month, the rest of the children had been selected, all obstacles surmounted and passports and visas secured. A cable was dispatched to Ottawa to purchase steamship transportation. All the children reached Antwerp on 6 August, just three days before the date of sailing of the *SS Scandinavian*.

SHE LEAVES FOR EUROPE

When word was received in Canada of the readiness of the children for the sea voyage Mrs Freiman prepared to leave for Europe in order to take charge of the orphans and accompany them to Canada. Before embarking she said: "I hope to be able to minimise the terrors of the voyage for the little ones and prepare them for the new and strange life they may expect to come to in their new Canadian homes."

She was accompanied by her cousin, Mrs Asher Pierce, of Montreal, who was a member of the Executive committee. Mrs Pierce was deeply interested in Child Welfare, being actively connected with the Children's Memorial Hospital and was also a board member of a number of communal organisations. Both were travelling at their own expense and both had applied for the adoption of orphans. They sailed for Southampton on 17 July.

Mrs Freiman's coming to Antwerp had a two-fold purpose: firstly, to become acquainted with the children before they were placed with their adoptive parents and secondly, to supervise carefully and unhurriedly their distribution to the various homes, and make certain, as far as possible, that each child will be assigned to the proper home.

The children were all well clothed and in good appearance, especially when compared with other European children. But when "mama" Freiman examined them with her motherly eye, she was not happy with the way they were dressed as "they lacked individuality". And she decided that they must have different clothes. She explained:

"It is true, as they say, that a diamond sparkles even when in the mire, but how much more beautiful is it when placed in a proper setting?"

She left at once for Paris where she purchased new and appropriate clothes for each according to age and physical build.

She examined each child and said: "This little girl has dark hair and dark complexion and needs this kind of dress and coat; this one has blond hair and rosy complexion" and so on for each one. This is the "mama" motif in the title "Mama Freiman" given her.

Hershman later told the moving story.

"I can still see vividly the unforgettable scenes, scenes of joy and tears, an ocean of tears, that followed Mrs Freiman's first meeting with her children. The great joy that shone from her smiling face and the flow of tears that stemmed from her eyes in pain over the fate of the 150 destitute and friendless orphans who now surrounded her and looked up to her as to a guardian angel, their Mama Freiman, and tears of joy that she had lived to see the fruit of her untiring work.

"Friday evening following her arrival, the children were seated at long tables, at the hotel where they were staying, with many leading persons of the Antwerp Jewish community. Mrs Freiman had brought with her the 'Loving Cup' presented to her by the Orphans Committee at the Conference held in Ottawa. At that time she had taken an oath not to make use of this gift until she had seen the children. And here she had lived to this great moment to see around her these children. Tonight she will for the first time use this cup and she honoured me by asking me to chant the Kiddush.

"The Loving Cup is a massive silver cup, with two handles. It is now filled with wine, provided by the Antwerp Jews, and is quite heavy and I have a 'job' to hold it high while pronouncing the Kiddush. But still more difficult than holding the cup is my struggle with the 'ivre', but thanks to the festive atmosphere, or perhaps by the grace of my forefathers, I successfully pronounced the entire Kiddush and handed the cup to Mrs Freiman.

"She then carried the cup to each child to taste from the Kiddush, and from her eyes flowed a stream of tears that nearly fell into the cup, but through the tears we could see her great nachas that she derived from this experience."

"PLEASE DON'T LEAVE ME BEHIND!"

In Antwerp, before the children were to be examined medically, Mrs Freiman washed and combed them and wept all the time like a child.

Suddenly another obstacle arose, with an outbreak of a skin infection, preventing several children from sailing with the group. The Jewish community of Antwerp undertook to accommodate and care for the stricken children till they were well enough for a subsequent journey across the Atlantic.

The turn to be medically examined came for a sweet-faced little girl whose golden curls and fair skin made her look like a typical 'Anglo-Saxon. Through a blow of some sort one of her nails had turned black. The examiners, who were unreasonably severe, refused to allow her to go on board unless the nail was removed on the spot.

As the ship was ready to sail at any moment this meant that there would be no time to administer an anaesthetic. Mrs Freiman was afraid to allow the child to undergo such torture and both she and Hershman were greatly agitated at the thought of leaving her behind.

The little girl, perceiving their agitation and seeing that something was amiss, begged them to tell her what it was. No one had the heart to tell her. Finally, Mrs Freiman told her, in her Yiddish, and the child, throwing her arms around her, cried out:

"Let them cut off my whole hand, but please don't leave me behind."

She went through the operation like a brick and as soon as it was over she rushed out to her friends and boasted, "It hardly hurt me at all," while the long-repressed tears ran down her cheeks.

THEY SAIL

They now feverishly prepared for the ocean voyage; the racket with each one's packing, the big 'garden party' in the beautiful garden of Antwerp's Jewish leader, Mr Unterman, the parting with the children who must remain for a second boat, and finally they are aboard the SS Scandinavian with the first group of 108 children, in the ages of 2½ to 12. It is 19 August 1921 and they are on their way to Canada!

One can imagine the hearts of the little ones beating more rapidly as their thoughts centred on the land of promise to which they were bound at last.

Each child had an outfit of clothing and shoes, and fastened to each little jacket and blouse was a tag on which the identity of the child was inscribed. The steamship officials had made special preparations to ensure a comfortable and pleasant voyage, including a kitchen for kosher food. During the voyage Mrs Freiman and Mrs Pierce worked with the members of the unit in classifying the children for adoption so as to avoid delay in the assignment of the children on arrival at Quebec, the port of debarkation. Four special nurses had been engaged in Europe to accompany the children and attend to their wants.

CHILDREN DISAPPEAR

The trip is smooth, no storms, no fog. The children are well and happy and "mama" Freiman with them. But "mama" Freiman also has much "trouble", because it is difficult to keep them together. The older ones are constantly disappearing, led by their eagerness to examine the big ship, while the younger vanish in thin air The reason for this is that many of them are so charming "Chainevdig" that the passengers of first and second class "kidnap" them and amuse themselves with them and shower them with attention and presents. The little ones were having a taste of the human kindness which awaited them in Canada.

One of the most popular children on the boat was a five-year old little girl, Yochele, a lovely child, with big fascinating dark eyes and exceptional brightness. Yochele also sang very beautifully Yiddish folk-songs. Time and time again she "disappeared" into the captain's or purser's cabin where a number of passengers are gathered and feed her with sweets and coax her to sing again and again. Far from shy, Yochele obliges with "Kukuriku Hundele" and other songs.

On the last day of the voyage they were sailing up the St Lawrence. Early morning Mrs Freiman was already on deck, around her a number of the older children who shower her with questions; "What place is this we are passing now? When will we arrive in Ottawa? And where is Montreal? And will Mr Freiman be at the ship when we arrive? They wanted so much to meet Mr Freiman!

Mrs Freiman struggles to speak to the children in Yiddish in reply to their questions, but her Yiddish is rather imperfect and the children have fun hearing her speak and smile secretly. One would suspect that the children deliberately ask her all these questions just to hear her speak Yiddish. They delight not only with what she tells them but with her entire attitude towards them. Because she does not reply to a question just to dispose of it but embraces the questioner and with the gentlest motherly love gives her reply, no matter how childish the question.

ARRIVED!

The *Scandinavian* approached Quebec in the evening of Friday, 20 August. What excitement prevailed! The children spent the last few hours on the boat scurrying around, packing their little valises, their "baggage" consisting of many little keepsakes, toys, dolls and playthings given them by sympathetic Jewish persons of Vienna, Dresden, and Cologne where the children had passed through. And every few minutes they rushed to the side of the boat to gaze in wonderment at the twinkling lights on the shore.

Before landing in Quebec they were examined again and each child, terrified that he or she might be refused admission, begged: "Please, doctor, dear man, let me pass, do not keep me back."

A little boy whose eyes showed great terror was detained as not normal but was quickly released when Mrs Freiman threw herself at the doctor like a tigress and said that she will fight to her last breath for the child, who was well and healthy but was terrified of anyone in uniform. Whilst the youngster was kept a few hours under observation the rest of the children became frightened and did not want to go anywhere without their little pal. His little sister broke into such sobbing that they had to take her to her little brother, and she remained with him till he was released.

Once they were all assembled the children asked if they had to be examined again before landing and when they were told that there will be no more examinations they began to jump and sing and weep and kiss each other and hugged Mrs Freiman and Hershman.

THEY LAND!

It was Saturday morning. A steady rain was coming down. On the dock was gathered the entire Quebec Jewish community and members of the committee who had come from several cities. From Ottawa came A J Freiman and from Montreal, Horace R Cohen, Asher Pierce, Mrs H Wolofsky and D S Friedman.

The children were lined up on deck in neat rows, with the younger ones in the front. At a signal from Mrs Freiman they began to sing the "Hatikvah" and there was not a dry eye in the crowd assembled on the dock. They followed with "O Canada" and sang the national anthem with such fervor, like a prayer to God, to bless the land that gave them a home and freed them from fear and death.

A Quebec newspaper described this scene:
"Over a hundred little Jewish orphans from Ukrainia, bereft of parents, relatives and homes by the cruel fortunes of war and by the barbarous pogroms on defenceless people, which are one fruit of the still seething political conditions of Central Europe, landed from the ocean liner, *SS Scandinavian*, when she docked here Saturday morning. When they trod the soil of Old Quebec and saw the comforting Union Jack, flying in the breeze from the citadel, they sang "God Save the King."

The gangplank was lowered and the first to board the ship was A J Freiman. After embracing his wife he greeted the members of the Commission.

Then Lillian Freiman went over to the children and returned, leading by the hand a little girl of 11, with blue eyes and black hair.

"Archie", she said smilingly to her husband, "this is our new daughter."

Freiman bent down and kissed the child and asked her in Yiddish "What is your name, my dear?"

"Gitel" she timidly replied.

The community had arranged a reception and repast for the children in the community hall, some distance from the dock. On account of the Sabbath, however, the children refused to drive from the immigration quarters to the hall. They formed into a procession, each child carrying a tiny Union Jack, with knapsack on the back, and marched in the rain through the principal streets of the city.

Louis Lazarovitz, president of the community, presided at the reception. Mrs Lazarovitz greeted the children and their guardians in Yiddish, and Miss Rachel Smiley read an address of welcome to Mrs Freiman, in English. Speeches were also delivered by Mrs Freiman, A J Freiman, Farrar, D S Freidman and Hershman.

Mrs Freiman was too overcome by her recent experiences and by the constant watch she had kept over her little charges to be able to say very much. "I only wish", she said, "that every Jewish woman in this country had had the privilege we've had of being thrown into contact with these wonderful children. If they had, then I am sure there wouldn't be a Jewish home in Canada that wouldn't be clamouring for a little orphan. They will make splendid Canadian citizens, and above all, they will be loyal Jews. Those of us who have been so fortunate as to be allowed to adopt these children have been given a great privilege as well as a great responsibility. God grant that we may bring to the task the understanding, the sympathy, the helpfulness and the mother love that these little ones so sorely need."

As some of the speakers made reference to the great Jewish tragedy that had occurred in Europe, adults and children began to weep. It seemed for a moment as if it was Yom Kippur. A representative of the "Keneder Adler" then reminded the children that this Sabbath being "Shabbos Nachamu" – the Sabbath following Tisha B'Av – it was not a time for weeping but to comfort each other and to forget the past. The world was before them. Many of them will become the future Jewish leaders in Canada. They were the future Lillian Freimans and the Hershmans.

THE PARTING

That evening the children were embarked on their final destinations, Saint John, Montreal, Ottawa, Toronto, Winnipeg, care being taken to keep brothers and sisters together for adoption in the same communities.

A member of the committee related: "Those who did not witness how the children parted from each other and from Mrs Freiman and Hershman do not know the meaning of a shudder, have no concept of catastrophe."

The terrible experiences of the children had bound them together as one family and when the moment of parting came one saw the most tragic scene one can imagine. They fell on each other's neck and sobbed and sobbed. There were loving embraces, murmured endearments and promises to write.

When the moment came to part from Mrs Freiman and Hershman many adults had to leave the hall, so moving was the scene.

Each child fell on her neck and sobbed and begged her: "Darling mother, where are you sending me?" Will you come to see me?" Not once but ten times they turned back from the door and ran back to her and Hershman to bid them again farewell. Mrs Freiman's eyes were swollen, her face drawn from the worry and strain. Like a statue she stood there, hugging each child and sobbing quietly, and it seemed that in this weeping one heard a curse against those who brought such a terrible tragedy upon Jewish life.

Gently the children were separated and taken to the railway station where they were made comfortable in their berths. They were escorted to their various destinations: by Mrs Freiman, to Montreal and Ottawa; by Hershman to Toronto; by Myer Budovitch, to Saint John; and by Miss Hattie Silverman to Winnipeg.

On their arrival in Montreal a large crowd awaited them at the station. The children noticed that several persons held copies of the *Jewish Daily Eagle* which carried photographs of Mrs Freiman and Hershman. They began to plead that each be given a copy of the newspaper. A bundle of papers was soon brought and distributed among them.

One little girl sat quietly on a bench staring at the photographs and suddenly broke into heartrending sobbing and began hysterically to kiss the photographs. Many adults were moved to tears and Mrs Freiman embraced the child, and herself began to weep and could not calm herself for many minutes.

The parting farewells were repeated as Mrs Freiman had to leave for Ottawa a half hour before the children destined for Toronto and she had to bid each one goodbye. One little boy held onto her neck and refused to let go. He kept crying "I will not leave you, you are my mother, the best mother in the world and Mr Hershman is my dear father. I cannot live without you both …"

Returning to Ottawa, the Freimans also brought with them two young girls, one of them adopted by Lillian Freiman's parents.

FURTHER ARRIVALS

Less than two weeks later, though still fatigued from her ordeal, Mrs Freiman went to Rimouski where she boarded a ship bringing another 24 children who had been obliged to remain over in Antwerp. On this journey too she was accompanied by Hershman.

The ship arrived in Quebec on 3 September and was met by Mr Freiman, Mrs Asher Pierce and many others. Sixteen more children arrived on 24 September, one on 6 December and one on 24 January 1922.

The children became quickly accustomed to Canadian life and many of them showed intelligence and musical talent. A few months after her return Lillian Freiman boasted that her adopted daughter, Gladys, "speaks excellent English and has become a thorough Canadian, knowing more about the Queen's birthday than many of her Ontario-born associates."

Though Canada had received these few Jewish orphans of the Ukraine, thousands of orphans remaining in Europe were maintained by the charity of world Jewry. In Canada appeals were held from time to time to raise funds for this purpose. When a campaign on a larger scale was planned in 1925 it was but natural for people to turn to Lillian Freiman and H Hershman, whose names represented the highest concern for these orphans, to assume the leadership.

A campaign for $50,000 was launched under her chairmanship. Dr Leo Motzkin, Dr Oscar Cohn and Rabbi Dr Eisenstadt came to Canada as delegates of the World Relief Organisation to describe the plight of thousands of Jewish orphans in Ukraine.

In August 1925 the 'Conference Universelle Juive de Secours' of Paris nominated her one of three world representatives on the honorary committee of the first general congress for the children, which was convoked that month by the Save the Children Fund, International Union, in Geneva, Switzerland. The Congress discussed the problem of orphans and widows left by the war, measures for the increase and tightening of safeguards for uprooted women and children, as well as questions of charity.

The Conference elected her one of the Honorary Vice-Presidents of the Organisation. The award came in appreciation for her work on behalf of the Ukrainian orphans.

MICHAEL G PIERCE - ONE OF THE CHILDREN

The writer was curious to know if Mrs Asher Pierce, who had accompanied Mrs Freiman, had also adopted a child. He asked this question of her son, Sidney D Pierce, Deputy High Commissioner of Canada in London, England, and former Canadian Ambassador to Mexico.

"Yes," wrote Mr Pierce, "my mother did adopt a son, my brother Michael."

'Michel-Moshe' was a blond, blue-eyed boy of ten when he came to Canada.

"I was brought up by my grandmother", Michael told the writer, "after both my parents passed away. I do not know why I was so lucky to be chosen to be brought to Canada. My grandmother was reluctant to let me go. When, at the last minute, she finally consented, I had to run to catch up with the other children, who were already departing from our village.

"On board ship Mrs Freiman and Mrs Pierce were always together. Dr Leavitt was busy running around treating the children who were seasick. I was not seasick. I believe I knew on the boat that Mrs Pierce was adopting me. I remember that Mr Pierce was at the boat when we arrived in Quebec and that we motored to Montreal. Sidney took to me at once and always took care of me, like a brother. Often, when I came home late, he waited up for me and scolded me.

"I recall that my parents' name was 'Glatter' and to this day I write my name 'Michael G Pierce'.

"Asher and Ella [Vineberg] Pierce were wonderful parents to me, but I have lost them both, in one year. Mr Pierce passed away on 18 May 1936 and Mrs Pierce on 31 December 1936."

Michael served six years in the Canadian Army, in the Second World War, spending three years overseas.

Note
There is only one known case where siblings went to South Africa and Canada.
Rivka Kailer was one of the Ochberg Orphans while her sister Zippe (Celia) was part of the group that went to Canada.

The Polish Ukrainian Orphans brought out to Canada – Harry Hershman is the man with the beard holding a child

Chapter 10 – THE HELP OF THE SOUTH AFRICAN JEWISH COMMUNITY

Orphans in the Ukraine and Poland were helped in three ways through the generosity of the South African Jewish Community
- *They were maintained and cared for in their towns of residence in the Ukraine and Poland,*
- *Some were transported to Palestine and maintained there; the group taken to Palestine by Israel Belkind to Kfar Yeladim (Children's village).*
- *Some were brought to South Africa and maintained there; Ochberg's Orphans who were placed in the care of the South African Jewish Orphanage (Arcadia) and the Cape Jewish Orphanage (Oranjia).*

SOUTH AFRICAN JEWRY
Extract from THE JEWS IN SOUTH AFRICA Edited by Gustav Saron and Louis Hotz. Printed in 1955

"This may help to explain how South African Jewry has acquired the characteristics which distinguish it as a group. It has a world-wide reputation for liberality towards those of its co-religionists who are in need, and for staunch support of the Zionist movement. It is also recognised as a well-organised and relatively united community.

Being largely descendants of Lithuanian Jewry, South African Jews are a fairly homogeneous group, unlike those of the United States of America. They have inherited some of the qualities of the *Litvaks* - their warm-heartedness and generosity, their practical-mindedness, a strong feeling of Jewish solidarity, and a love of learning combined with a somewhat critical attitude to religious traditions, their religion being often more of the head than of the heart.

Enterprising and hard-working, they have been able to take advantage of the opportunities offered by a new and developing country."

THE JEWISH WAR VICTIMS' FUND
This article, kindly sent in by Ron Lapid, was first published in the The South African Jewish Year Book 1929 and it comes with a note "We are indebted to Mr A Cousin of Johannesburg for much of the information contained in this article."

The Relief Fund for Jewish War Victims of British and Allied Nations and Palestinian Jews, popularly known as the Jewish War Victims Fund, was established at Johannesburg on 27 January 1915, as a result of a meeting of representatives of Jewish organisations. Forty three Jewish institutions were represented at the meeting by 76 delegates. The resolution creating the organisation established the principle that the Fund should be administered and supervised by the South African Jewish Board of Deputies, and that the President, Treasurer and Secretary of the Board should fill these respective offices of the Fund. Mr Bernard Alexander, President of the Board, was the first Chairman and held the position for the following ten years.

The inaugural meeting was successful only after several ineffectual attempts had been made, and to the United Hebrew Polish Society of Johannesburg belongs the credit for its persistence in inducing the SA Jewish Board of Deputies to take the lead in this very necessary relief movement. Mr A Couzin, of Johannesburg, was originally responsible in large measure for the activities of the United Hebrew Polish Society in respect of this scheme.

Almost simultaneously with the establishment of the Fund in Johannesburg, organisations with similar objects sprang into existence in Cape Town, Port Elizabeth, Kimberley, Bloemfontein, East London, Durban and Bulawayo.

Although there was no actual affiliation, there was close co-operation between the various organisations, and there was no overlapping of territory or activities.

At the outset the funds collected were allocated as follows: 65 per cent to Russia, Poland and Lithuania, 20 per cent to Palestine, 10 per cent to Alexandria for the relief of refugees there, and 5 per cent to Belgium.

Later, when the needs for Alexandria and Belgium became less urgent, this extra 15 per cent was added to the Russian, Polish and Lithuanian allocation. Branches of the parent organisation were established in every village and town, committees were formed, regular monthly collections instituted and functions and entertainments on a colossal scale were organised in augmentation of the Fund.

By 31 March 1916, £24,000 had been collected and forwarded to responsible committees in the stricken areas.

By 30 May 1917, the Fund issued its first printed audited Revenue and Expenditure Accounts for the period 25 February 1915 to 31 March 1917.

The accounts make very interesting reading.

From the inception of the fund to 31 March 1916, the sum of £24,072 15s 1d was collected, and for the next succeeding 12 months the sum of £27,386 6s 6d was collected, making a grand total of £51,459 1s 7d. Of this amount £44,193 14s was sent to Russia and Poland, £5,313 to Palestine, £380 to Belgium and £90 to Alexandria.

The entire cost of collecting administering and despatching this large amount was £423 11s 9d, of which the major portion was spent in postage, printing and bank charges. Salaries amounted to the very modest sum of £355. This must surely be a record for economical and efficient management. The audited accounts are signed by B Alexander, President; I M Goodman, Hon Treasurer; P Cowen, General Secretary; and M Abrahams, Registered Public Accountant, Auditor.

In November 1920, it was announced that the Transvaal Fund had reached £129,843.

Owing to slackening off in the activities of many of the branches, on the initiation of the Doornfontein Branch, a Conference of War Victims Fund Branches was held in Johannesburg, and the connection of the Board of Deputies with the Fund ceased.

But the Conference resulted in a wonderful revival of activities. At the time of the Conference it was reported that 28,000 garments had been collected and shipped overseas for distribution in the war ravaged areas, and in the two years following the Conference an additional £76,604 was collected.

Cape Town

It is of interest at this point to record the progress of the sister fund in the City of Cape Town. The Cape Relief Fund for Jewish War and Pogrom Victims was established in December 1914. The territory over which the Fund had jurisdiction was the Cape Province, excluding Kimberley and district, Port Elizabeth and district, East London and district, and after the first two years, Paarl and district. These centres each had their own organisation and despatched their collections direct to the London Committee.

From December 1914, to 31 December 1920 the sum of £77,835 18s 5d was collected at a total cost of £1,220 3s 10d, truly a remarkable achievement, and a striking proof of self-sacrificing labours on the part of a comparatively small band of workers.

During these six years of the existence of the Fund, the following gentlemen held office: Chairman, Mr Morris Alexander; Vice-chairman, Rabbi M CH Mirvish, Hon Treasurers, Rev B Strod, Dr S E Kark, Mr A Brodie and Mr J Gitlin; Hon Secretaries, J Mirvish, I M Goodman, J Gesundheit and B Chideckel.

The following is a summary of the amount remitted to:

Russia	£39,000 0 0
Roumania	1,000 0 0
Poland and Eastern Europe	19,300 0 0
Palestine	12,150 4 0
Lithuania	2,000 0 0
Salonika	1,000 0 0
Hebrew Schools in the Palestinian Colonies	500 0 0
Russo-Jewish Prisoners of War	400 0 0
Relief of Persian Jews	300 0 0
Students at Basle	50 0 0
Vienna	300 0 0
	£76,000 4 0

In 1919 and 1920, 22,500 garments were collected and sent to Warsaw for distribution to the various stricken areas.

The Fund underwent several changes of name before it became finally merged into the *United South African Jewish Relief Reconstruction and Orphans Fund*. Its first designation was *The Cape Russo-Jewish War Relief Fund*, then *The Relief Fund for Jewish War Victims of British and Allied Nations and Palestinian Jews*, and in 1920 to *The Cape Relief Fund for Jewish War and Pogrom Victims*.

Kfar Yeladim

To the Cape Fund belongs the credit for having formulated the scheme for the establishment of an Orphan Colony in Palestine, which eventually became what is now known as Kfar Yeladim.

In addition to the organisations established in Johannesburg and Cape Town, active committees existed at Kimberley, Port Elizabeth, East London, Durban, Bloemfontein and Rhodesia.

Various attempts were made on the initiative of the Johannesburg Fund to bring the various organisations together, pool their resources, co-ordinate their activities, and generally unite for the good of the common objective. Following much correspondence with the various organisations occupied in similar work throughout South Africa, a Conference of all interested organisations was held in Bloemfontein in August 1922.

At this Conference, *The United South African Jewish Relief Reconstruction and Orphans Fund* came into existence, with headquarters at Johannesburg. All branches of the Transvaal movement and all centres in South Africa affiliated, with the exception of Port Elizabeth and Roodepoort.

Fate of War Orphans

For some time prior to the Bloemfontein Conference the question of the war orphans had agitated the minds of many of the workers, and several of the branches had forwarded resolutions and recommendations on the subject. While most of the workers felt that something should be done specifically for the war and pogrom orphans, there existed three distinct schools of thought on the subject:

(a) That the orphans should be maintained and cared for at their present towns of residence.
(b) That a number should be transported to Palestine and maintained there.
(c) That a number should be brought to South Africa and maintained here.

Eventually all three schemes were in part adopted.

With regard to (a), South African Jewry maintained 2,250 orphans through the agency of the Central Relief Committee in Paris, at the following centres:

1.	Kherson	800 children	(by the United Fund)
2.	Odessa	500 "	(by the United Fund)
3.	Odessa	150 "	(by the Cape Jewish Orphanage)
4.	Tiraspol	300 "	(by the Cape Fund)
5.	Berezovka	100 "	(by Wynberg, CP)
6.	Lvovo	200 "	(by the Cape Fund)
7.	Lvovo	100 "	(by Krugersdorp)
8.	Otchakoff	100 "	(by Pretoria)

The children received food, clothing and medical attendance. In addition to this the United Fund equipped and maintained three hospitals under the control of OZE for a considerable period.

Chaluzim Assisted

The United Fund also remitted relief for the Chaluzim, to the Habin Bureau for Jewish War Sufferers in the Far East, to the Russian Jewish Students' Society in Switzerland, to Jewish sufferers in Japan from earthquake, to Jewish refugees in Romania, to the OZE to the ORT to refugees in Germany, and wherever else an appeal from suffering Jewry emanated.

In November 1922, an appeal was issued by the United Fund for clothing and within a short while 60,000 garments were collected and were carried rail free by the South African Railways and freight free by the Union Castle Steamship Co. The United Fund appointed Mr I Ochberg, of Cape Town as its delegate in the Ukraine, and right worthily did he carry out his mission in the field of relief work.

With regard to (b), after protracted negotiations with the Palestine Orphans' Committee of the American Joint Distribution Committee, and the Waad Leumi, of Palestine, it was ascertained that Russia would not permit the transportation of any more orphans beyond its borders.

The Children's Colony

It, however, transpired that a Mr Belkind had brought to Palestine about 120 children from the Ukraine, and through various causes had found himself stranded with the children. Mr S Hillman, who was at this time on a visit to Palestine, investigated the position on behalf of the United Fund. Eventually the United South African Fund took over 86 of the Belkind children, and 44 children maintained by Durban, making a total of 130, obtained land from the Jewish National Fund in Balfouria erected buildings at an approximate cost of £12,000 and formed a children's colony at Givat Hamoreh.

The United Fund guaranteed the maintenance of the children for five years. Mr Richard Feldman of Johannesburg, while on a visit to Palestine, did yeoman service at the children's colony. The colony is now known as Kfar Yeladim, and on the closing down of the Relief Fund was handed over to the South African Zionist Federation to be maintained as a children's colony in the name of South African Jewry.

The Local Orphans

The third activity (c) remains to be dealt with.

In Cape Town and in Johannesburg there was a strong body of public opinion in favour of bringing out to South Africa war pogrom orphans principally with a view to their being adopted. The Cape Relief Fund fathered the movement at the Cape, but the scheme was eventually taken over by the Cape Jewish Orphanage. In the Transvaal the idea was taken up with much enthusiasm.

Mr I Ochberg, President of the Cape Jewish Orphanage proceeded to Europe and, at the request of the Committee of the Cape Jewish Orphanage and the Johannesburg Committee, brought with him from the Ukraine about 180 children. About half the number remained at the Cape Jewish Orphanage, and the other half were handed over to Johannesburg.

An arrangement was come to between the Relief Fund and the South African Jewish Orphanage in Johannesburg whereby the Relief Fund allotted £12,500 to the Orphanage to assist them in the purchase of their present building (*Villa Arcadia*). The Johannesburg children therefore became the charges of the Jewish Community of the Transvaal, just as the children at the Cape came under the care and protection of the Cape Jewish Community.

At the Cape an additional building was erected and the advent of the children for a time revived the activities of the United Fund in Johannesburg and brought largely increased funds to the Cape Jewish Orphanage.

Total Amount Collected

At the outbreak of the World War, the Jewish population of South Arica was about 55,000. In 1921 the official figures give 62,000. The Transvaal Fund up to the time of the amalgamation in 1922 collected £206,347 and the Cape about £100,000 making a total of £306,347. In the two years following amalgamation the United Fund collected £55,580 and the nett results of three fetes held in Johannesburg were £24,600. This brings the total up to £386,527. The total amounts collected by the Committees at Durban, Port Elizabeth, Bloemfontein, Kimberley, East London, Bulawayo and Salisbury in all probability exceed £100,000.

It can with all safety be stated that South Africa raised upwards of £500,000 for Jewish relief in the war and pogrom-stricken areas. Thus the relief funds subscribed by South African Jewry averaged over £9 per head of its Jewish population, a record which is hard to believe has been equalled by any other Jewish population in the world.

Chapter 11 – THE CAPE JEWISH ORPHANAGE – 1920 BULLETIN

THE CAPE JEWISH ORPHANAGE

REPORT AND BALANCE SHEET
For the period ending 30 April 1920

Office Bearers (1919-1920)

President:	Isaac Ochberg, Esq
Vice President:	J Kadish, Esq
Hon Treasurer:	J B Shacksnovis, Esq
Chairlady:	Mrs H Stodel
Vice Chairlady:	Mrs A Leve
Hon Treasurer (Clothing Guild):	Mrs Henry Harris

COMMITTEE:
- Mr O Basson
- Mr C Baker
- Mr A Benson
- Mr A Friedlander
- Mr J Frank
- Mr S Goldstein
- Mr E Goldsmith
- Mr L Gradner
- Mr H Harris
- Mr H Kadish
- Mr M Lentin
- Mr I Mauerberger
- Mr L Raphaely
- Mr S Sachs
- Mr D Shargey
- Mr R Weinberg

LADIES' GENERAL AND HOUSE COMMITTEE
- Mrs I Barnett
- Miss L Blumeneau
- Mrs N Friedlander
- Mrs B Hill
- Mrs B Jacobs
- Mrs M Lentin
- Mrs I Ochberg
- Mrs A Silbert
- Mrs L Schrire
- Mrs J B Shacksnovis
- Mrs W Stern
- Mrs T Velenski
- Mrs R Weinberg

TRUSTEES:
- Mr Adv M Alexander, KC, MLA
- R Herman Esq

DELEGATES:
- Mr W Satusky: Woodstock & Salt River Hebrew Cong.
- Mr N Emdin: Muizenberg & Kalk Bay Hebrew Cong.
- Mr M Wisnekowitz: Paarl Hebrew Congregation
- Mr S Marcus: Stellenbosh Hebrew Congregation
- Mr L Goldberg: Worcester Hebrew Congregation
- Mr L Rosenzweig: Robertson Hebrew Congregation

HON OFFICERS:

Ise Levy Esq	*Hon Auditor*
Messrs C & A Friedlander	*Hon Solicitors*
Dr S E Kark	*Hon Medical Adviser*
S Sachs Esq	*Hon Chemist*
S Koonin Esq	*Hon Dentist*
Messrs Winer & Baigel	*Hon Hairdressers*

STAFF:

Mrs D Levin	*Matron*
Miss R Cohen	*Assistant Matron*
Miss R Tieger	*Secretary*
Mr Sandrusier	*Authorised Collector*

REPORT OF THE CAPE JEWISH ORPHANAGE

Ladies and Gentlemen

After the full and comprehensive report submitted by your Executive to the general body of members on the 28th December, 1920, your General Committee decided, in order to save expense, to publish for submission a short report only, together with the necessary financial statement up to the end of April, 1920 at the forthcoming General Meeting. As to the general working of the Home, we have to report that all members of the staff fulfilled their duties to the entire satisfaction of the Management. The health of the children has been everything that can be desired; the educational progress of the children has been favourably commented upon by all who have had the pleasure of noticing the splendid progress they have made both in secular and religious instruction and we can say with confidence, that the good name already established by the Cape Jewish Orphanage has been very much enhanced, not only in the Province of the Cape but throughout the whole of South Africa. It is therefore with feelings of pride and pleasure, that we have to report these pleasant facts in the hope that all members, donors and sympathisers will experience satisfaction in the thought, that they have been the means of the Holy work being carried out successfully and that they will also in the future endeavour by every possible means to strengthen and support our Institution which may be termed the premier charity of the Cape Province.

The number of children in the Home at present is 52.

The Board of Management here wish to place on record their heartiest thanks to all the Honorary Officers for the valuable services they are rendering to the Home.

The most important and outstanding matter we have pleasure to record, is the decision of your Committee and the General Body of Members to bring from the Pogrom Areas in Eastern Europe a number of orphaned children and provide accommodation for some of them in our Home and for others to obtain a Home for them with some private members of the Community. After the appalling trials experienced by the Jewish population in common with their non-Jewish fellow countrymen during the World War, in which they bore more than their part of sacrifice and sorrow and of hopes for a happier future, however an even more terrible storm burst upon them in the shape of a new war – a war of extermination exclusively against them – a war of Pogroms. During the past two years the most thickly populated centres of Jewish life in Eastern Europe have been swept by an endless succession of these terrible pogroms, and as a result, official reports state that many Jewish Communities in the Pogrom Areas have been entirely wiped out.

Most terrible disasters and cruelties were inflicted, and the agonies and sufferings of our Nation in the terrible Pogrom areas are not paralleled in the two thousand years history of our people. The inhuman hordes, with no other thought but to kill, dishonour and exterminate the Jewish Communities, have destroyed Jewish homes and maltreated and murdered their peaceable and innocent inmates with a fury and beastiality which defy description. Everywhere men and women, the old and the young, the aged, infirm and the helpless were outraged, burnt and buried alive; every Jewish house either a ruin or a wailing place. One of the results of these terrible happenings has been that over 400 000 children are left parentless, homeless, naked and hungry, wandering in the woods, forests and streets of Eastern Europe. Never in the history of the Jewish Nation has the Pogrom Monster inflicted such terrible atrocities. What torrents of blood and rivers of tears has he made to flow! How many victims has he deprived of life? It is with this spectacle before us that we, as an Institution for Jewish orphans, decided on the holy task of saving at least a few of the many thousands of Jewish children from what may be rightly described as a 'Hell on Earth'. What greater charity is there than to save human life, and more particularly so when the saving of such human life means the saving of innocent, helpless, hungry and starving children? Your President and Treasurer decided to bring home to the Jews of South Africa the duty they owe to their Nation, by making a strenuous effort to gather together £50 000 to assist in carrying out the noble work of saving some of the Jewish orphans in the Pogrom Areas of Eastern Europe. A tour was arranged and the following itinerary was duly completed:- Bloemfontein, Bredasdorp, Brandfort, Caledon, Claremont, East London, Hermanus, Kroonstad, Maitland, Malmesbury, Muizenberg, Oudtshoorn, Observatory, Paarl, Port Elizabeth, Simonstown, Stellenbosch, The Strand, Woodstock and Wynberg. As a result of this tour a magnificent sum was promised.

One thing your President and Treasurer can say, that they found the Jewish hearts most responsive to the appeal for this particular charity and wherever they addressed meetings they were received with true national enthusiasm and the response which followed was one which you would rightly expect from the 'Rachmonim bnei Rachmonim'. The only regret that has to be recorded is that owing to certain circumstances the tour undertaken by your President and Treasurer could not be completed, and as a consequence many important centres which should have been visited were omitted; but there is every hope that in the near future these places too will receive a visit, and we trust that the appeals there will be as successful as in the other centres. So much has been completed. Now as to the future – we earnestly appeal to every Jewish man and woman in South Africa who has not yet been approached for a contribution towards the Fund to save poor innocent Jewish Orphans to answer the heart-rending cry of these little ones in Eastern Europe. If each and every Jew would approach the subject from a personal point of view, and look upon this matter as if their own little children were homeless and helpless amidst a band of ruffians and human beasts and then ask themselves the question, what would be their duty towards these helpless little ones. Once we are able to realise the terrible agonies of these hungry and naked children roaming about in thousands, without a glimmer of hope in their innocent little lives, we shall then out of sheer gratitude to God who has preserved us for our children, decide that not only must we give in the ordinary way, but we must make the great sacrifice which the Father of Orphans demands from us. In this way, and in this way only can we justify our Judaism and display the true Maccabean spirit which has been the means of keeping our Nation alive during the last two thousand years of massacres, persecutions, and hopeless and helpless wanderings. Realising this, we again and again earnestly appeal to the Jewish hearts of South Africa and feel confident that a liberal response will be made to the heartrending cry of these poor orphans, and that unstinted support will be given to the Management of the Orphanage to carry out in full the noble task they have set themselves. Yes, even today a cry of panic and distress reaches us from large tracts of the Ukraine and other Pogrom areas, and it is our bounden duty to answer that cry in a practical manner. We specially appeal to all our Jewish men and women in South Africa to do all in their power to make the adoption scheme a complete success by taking one or more children into their private homes or elsewhere. In this way, and in this way only, will it be possible to save thousands of these poor little orphans. The Management will be pleased to receive applications for adoption as soon as possible, so as to give our President an indication as to the number of orphans that will be absorbed under the adoption scheme.

As a preliminary we have already started to build a suitable Home to accommodate the poor orphans on their arrival in Cape Town. Our many subscribers, donors and sympathisers will be gratified to learn that your President, Mr Isaac Ochberg, offered to the General Committee to go to Europe at his own expense to bring the first batch of these children; your Committee accepted your President's offer, and he has already booked to leave early in March for Europe. We wish him Godspeed on his mission of mercy, and may the Almighty bless and protect him and bring him and the orphans safely back to us. Further you will realise the enormous task of transporting about 100 orphans from Eastern Europe to South Africa over continents and oceans. All this needs *money* and the Jews of South Africa will appreciate that during the next 12 months or two years they must strain their hearts, nerves and sinews and make every endeavour to rescue as many of these orphans as possible and to make necessary provision for them, so that they will receive the care and protection they so richly deserve.

Finally, we feel it our duty to make special reference to extracts from correspondence that has passed between your President and Dr Jochelman, President of the Federation of Ukrainian Jews, London, in connection with the Pogrom orphan scheme.

The thanks of the Jewish Community are due to the Government of the Union of South Africa for their response in giving us permission to bring as many Pogrom orphans as we may desire to this country. We feel certain that this concession given by the Government to the Jews will rebound to the credit of the Government of South Africa for in years after they will find that these poor homeless and helpless little boys and girls will rank among the best citizens in South Africa.

The 'Cape Times and 'Argus' deserve our best thanks for granting us advertising space free of charge in their valuable papers, and we feel that the Management of these papers have, by their liberal response to the cause of the orphans, accomplished a very good and noble work. In mentioning the above papers we must not fail to thank the 'Zionist Record' for the assistance given us by way of free advertisements in connection with the Pogrom Orphan Appeal.

In the preparation of the advertising notices your Committee received valuable assistance from Messrs C J Sibbet, W M Redford, H F Grapes and C Sims, and to these gentlemen, we tender our sincerest thanks for the valuable honorary work they rendered to the cause. Likewise are our thanks due to the African Theatres Trust for displaying slides on their screens in their places of amusements free of charge.

As the work of our Home is rapidly increasing from day to day the Committee trusts that many willing helpers in the Community will come forward and assist in the noble task of ministering to the wants of those who are entitled to our care, affection and protection.

FOR THE BOARD OF MANAGEMENT
ISAAC OCHBERG (President)
J KADISH (Vice President)
J B SHACKSNOVIS (Hon Treasurer)

Extract of letter from Mr Isaac Ochberg, Cape Town to Dr D Jochelman, London

Dr D Jochelman
26a Soho Square
London W 1

Dear Sir

From the 'Jewish Chronicle" I noticed that you are Chairman of a Committee formed to collect funds in aid of War and Pogrom sufferers in the Ukraine, and I therefore take the liberty of addressing you.

It is stated that in many towns in the Ukraine there are hundreds of Jewish children left orphans, whose parents have been murdered during the Pogroms. I do not think that the assistance of money alone can give the help required for these unfortunate children, as I presume they have practically no one to look after them.

South Africa has been living through some fairly prosperous times during the last few years and the feelings here amongst the Jewish Community are very sympathetic towards the unfortunate members of our nation who have recently suffered from Pogroms etc in the Ukraine and elsewhere, and I feel that, if necessary, the sympathy of our Jewish people out here could be enlisted to support a scheme which would enable us to bring to this country a number of Jewish orphans, say between 200-300, who would receive here proper support and education, etc that would be necessary to bring them up to be good Jews and citizens, and I should be glad to hear from you on the subject so that I could put the matter more fully before the leading members of our Community.

Yours truly

(Signed) ISAAC OCHBERG

Extract of letter from Mr A M KAIZER, Secretary of the Federation of the Ukrainian Jews to Mr Isaac Ochberg

Isaac Ochberg, Esq   30 June 1920
Cape Town

Dear Sir

Dr D Jochelman has handed me your letter of the 11th inst addressed to him, receipt of which I beg to acknowledge.

The proposition made by you regarding the Jewish orphans of the Pogrom sufferers is received by my Committee with great satisfaction, and Dr Jochelman himself thinks that this is just the kind of work most needed at the present time.

He considers it would be a great thing in itself to take 200-300 Jewish children from the Ukraine to South Africa, but that the main point is that such a proposition, if carried out, will give an impulse to relief work amongst the larger Jewish communities on the other side of the Atlantic, possibly resulting in their bringing over thousands of Jewish orphans. The plan indicated by you will receive the full support of my Committee.

Yours faithfully

(Signed) A M KAIZER

Extract of letter from S Goldenberg Esq, Hon Sec Federation of Ukrainian Jews, to Mr Isaac Ochberg

Isaac Ochberg Ewq   27 November 1920
President Cape Jewish Orphanage

It will certainly be a splendid piece of constructive work if finally South African Jewry will have brought out, two thousand children and be responsible for their upbringing.

We note the various conditions you make with reference to the age and health and sexes of the children, who are to go to South Africa, and of course these instructions will be carefully studied when the time arrives for their consideration.

(Signed) S GOLDENBERG   Hon Secretary

200 orphans and a man called Isaac Ochberg

ZARA JACKSON

IT WAS billed in the What's On column of the *Jewish Report* as "A great event in Jewish history - the pogrom orphans". The presentation at Our Parents Home gave the audience at the United Zionist Luncheon Club infinitely more than the title suggested.

It breathed life into historical background of the times, the 1920s, post-war economically depressed Europe.

Not only did it deal with those conditions which had left so many Jewish orphans in the area, "The Pale of Settlement", totally abandoned, hungry, sick, completely deprived of any assistance as parents had disappeared, but it gave us insight into so many fascinating details depicting the fragility of the "peaceful" times in Europe preceding the outbreak of the 1914-1918 World War.

What is the relevance of this to the situation of Jewish orphans in Eastern Europe?

The war had caused a great deal of problems for the Jews - murders, rape, looting, were taking place everywhere.

In South Africa the Jews looked on in horror at what was happening in Eastern Europe. A few received messages from Europe describing the death and destruction that had taken place.

The war had been followed by widespread pogroms and then came the flu epidemic just after the war which killed as many people again as had died in the war.

There were thousands of orphaned children, hungry, sick and dying. The South African Jews were asking themselves whether there was not something that could be done.

At least try and rescue the children who had been fortunate to survive this ghastly tragedy that had almost eradicated the millions living in "The Pale".

The saying "Some are born great, some have greatness thrust upon them", applies to Isaac Ochberg, president of the Oranjia Jewish Orphanage in Cape Town. Ochberg had come to South Africa from the Ukraine in 1895. He knew the area well and of course spoke the language.

He was now a wealthy businessman with many successful financial interests. He was a compassionate man and did not remain impervious to the plight of his fellow Jews.

In 1921 Ochberg contacted the Federation of Ukrainian Jews in London to get advice from them. They promised to assist him. Ochberg then went to see Gen Jannie Smuts who had become prime minister in 1919 to ask permission to bring Jewish orphans to South Africa.

He told Ochberg he could only bring 200 children to this country, subject to certain conditions. (This was a sad comment on the inhumanity and lack of compassion of the Smuts government of the time.)

The conditions were stipulated as follows:

1. The children had to be proper orphans. Those with even one parent still alive could not be taken.
2. Siblings were not to be separated. If for some reason one did not qualify then the other had to be left behind as well.
3. No children with physical disabilities were to come, nor any sick or retarded children.
4. Sixteen was the age limit for any child.
5. The Jewish community had to bear the cost of bringing the children out to South Africa and they were also to be responsible for their upkeep here. The government was not to be involved in any expense whatsoever.

Ochberg, the dynamic philanthropist, immediately launched a "Pogrom Orphans Fund" and soon he had collected fifteen thousand pounds. Many non-Jews also contributed.

Although there was generally great enthusiasm among the Jews for the effort, there were many dissenting voices in the Jewish media.

There were fears that "because of the post-war economic depression in South Africa, bringing Jewish orphans to this country would jeopardise the Jewish position here," according to an editorial in the SA Jewish Chronicle.

Ochberg was undaunted by all these dissenting voices. He set off for London where he organised the papers needed to go to Poland and the Ukraine. Poland was in a shambles after the war but Ochberg went to orphanages and shuls looking for children.

He had the heartbreaking task of choosing which children to take and which to leave behind. He found children that were hungry, weak, dirty and traumatised.

Although Ochberg's health suffered by being on this compassionate mission, he stated: "I feel that no sacrifice can be too great for any Jew, if some of those unfortunate children of our race can be helped."

Eventually, Ochberg chose the 200 children. A boat took them first to England. Ochberg and the children left Southampton on the Union Castle liner, the Edinburgh Castle. Although he and his wife travelled first class, he spent most of his time with the children and plied them with candy and biscuits. The children adored him and called him Daddy Ochberg.

After a three week voyage, the ship arrived in Cape Town on September 21 to a tumultuous, even hysterical welcome from Cape Towns Jews, who had flocked to the docks to meet the children.

The children were taken to Oranjia Jewish Orphanage but it was so crowded that 87 had to be sent to Johannesburg where the Jewish Board of Deputies had acquired the Phillips property known as "Villa Arcadia" and this was converted into an orphanage.

And what of Ochberg? In 1937 he took desperately ill with stomach cancer while in England, returned to South Africa, but died at sea. His body was brought back to South Africa. He was 56 years old.

On his tombstone in Cape Town is written: "He was a good South African and a great Jew.".

Nora Favish was introduced to the audience at Our Parents Home. This added a moving, emotional personal note to the presentation as Nora is the widow of one of the Ochberg orphans - she married Mannie Favish, who had come to South Africa at the age of eight with his sister Rose who was 10.

He was adopted by Israel and Shaina Favish of Benoni, where he received his schooling and studied law through the University of South Africa. He practised as an attorney in Benoni until his death in 1994.

Nora Favish has published a book written by Rose's (his sister) and Mannie's biological mother, Feiga Mirel Shamis in Palestine.

Nora decided to publish it as a legacy for Rose and Mannie's children, and posterity.

(Primary source of research - article by Jonathan Boiskin I "Jewish Affairs" 1994).

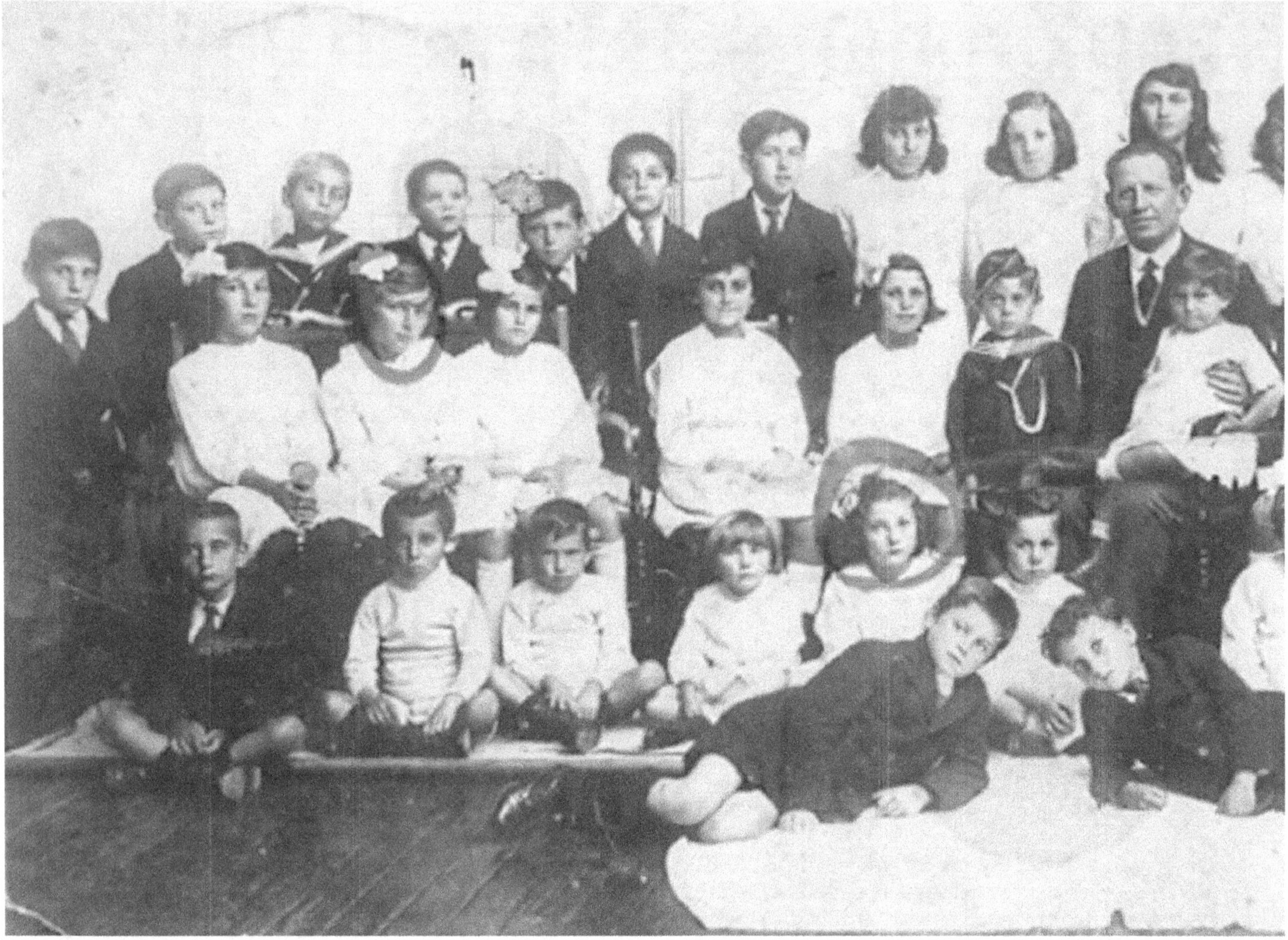

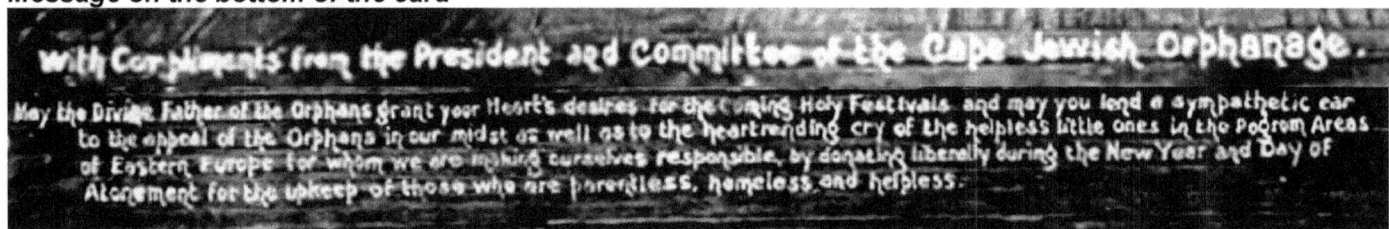

1920 Group photo of the children at the Cape Jewish Orphanage (over two pages)

Message on the bottom of the card

With Compliments from the President and Committee of the Cape Jewish Orphanage.
May the Divine Father of the Orphans grant your Heart's desires for the coming Holy Festivals and may you lend a sympathetic ear to the appeal of the Orphans in our midst as well as to the heartrending cry of the helpless little ones in the Pogrom Areas of Eastern Europe for whom we are making ourselves responsible, by donating liberally during the New Year and Day of Atonement for the upkeep of those who are parentless, homeless and helpless.

With Compliments from the President and Committee of the Cape Jewish Orphanage.

May the Divine Father of the Orphans grant your Heart's desires for the coming Holy Festivals and may you lend a sympathetic ear to the appeal of the Orphans in our midst as well as the heartrending cry of the helpless little ones in the Pogrom Areas of Eastern Europe for whom we are making ourselves responsible, by donating liberally during the New Year and Day of Atonement for the upkeep of those who are parentless, homeless and helpless.

This photo was sent in by Ron Lapid who writes,

"A group photo that was sent as a postcard to the family. It is date marked 10th September 1920.
The girl in front who has been circled is my mother Nancy. The girl second from the left in the middle row is Fanny, and Tilly is on the right hand side of the same row."
Isaac Ochberg sits in the middle holding a little girl

1920 Group photo of the children at the Cape Jewish Orphanage (over two pages)

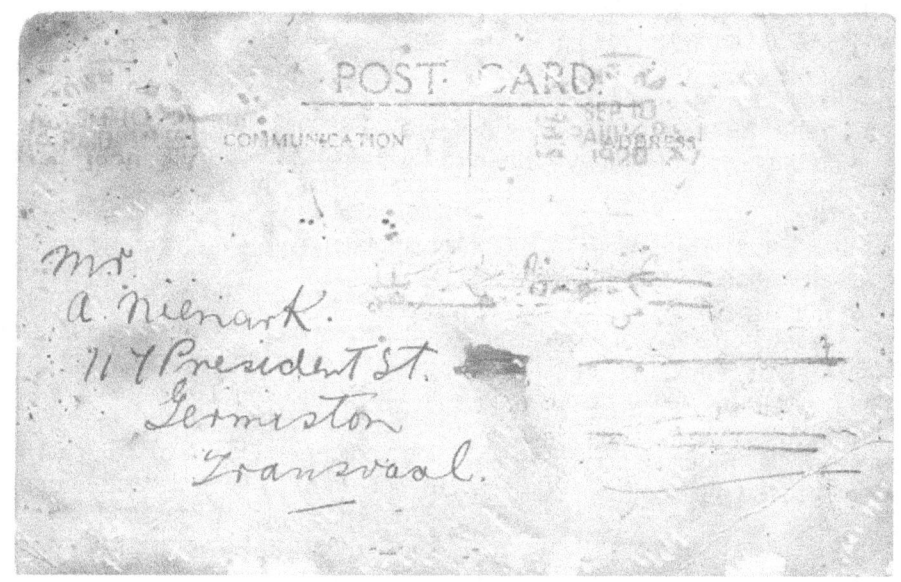

The reverse side of the group photo
It is date marked 10th September 1920 and the stamp says "Paid 1/2 penny".

Chapter 12 – THE OCHBERG ORPHANS

THE OCHBERG ORPHANS
Written by Bennie Penzik and David Solly Sandler - from The Pinsker Orphans

The Ochberg Orphans, also known as the 'Pogrom Orphans' or the 'Ukraine War and Pogrom Orphans,' were a group of 181 Jewish orphans, rescued in 1921 by Isaac Ochberg, the representative of the South African Jewish Community, from the multiple horrors facing Jews in the 'Pale of Settlement' and transported to South Africa.

These horrors commenced in 1914 with WWI and the forced relocation of Jews by the Russians. This was followed by the Spanish Influenza epidemic, pogroms committed by advancing and retreating troops, starvation induced by Soviet policy and the diseases that accompany hunger and cold added to the extremely harsh living conditions that continued well into the 1920s.

The Jewish communities around the world were shocked by the news of the horrors of war, the pogroms and starvation and disease suffered by Jews in the 'Pale of Settlement.' Especially horrific were accounts of wholesale rape, extortion and slaughter of their brethren by Polish, Ukrainian and Belarus nationalistic armies and the Red and White (Cossack) Russian troops.

Among the world Jewish communities committed to assisting their brethren, The South Africans arranged the rescue and relocation of a group of 181 orphans to South Africa, supported other groups transported to Palestine and sent aid to various orphanages within the Pale.

In 1921, the Canadian Jewish Community likewise transported a group of children to Canada and in 1922, a group of about 60 children were transported to Palestine by Israel Belkind. The Pinsk Orphans Relief Fund of London transported 19 children in 1924 and 35 in 1926 to London. The Jewish communities of many other European countries sent aid.

The American Joint Distribution Committee (JDC), although unable to physically relocate children due to immigration restrictions in the USA, raised millions of dollars. Together with the American Relief Administration, the JDC fed almost 2,000,000 Ukrainians by setting up soup kitchens and feeding programs. Aid was provided also to farmers by introducing new seeds and tractors. Man-made famine, created by the requisitioning of grain to the Volga by the Soviets, caused the deaths of millions of Ukrainians.

Jews world-wide were appalled and shocked by the horrors. In London, on 26 June 1919, protest meetings involving up to 120,000 people took place. In New York, a demonstration, that included war veterans bearing banners, numbered some 400,000.

No one will really know how many hundreds of thousands of Jews perished from cold, hunger and disease, or were

Isaac Ochberg, born in Uman, Russia on 31 May 1879, died on the Pretoria Castle on 11 December 1937. He was buried in Cape Town on 13 December 1937.

"He never refused to support a worthy cause; on the contrary, his creed was that since he had been enabled to achieve success in his own enterprises, he had a moral duty to help those less fortunate."

systematically tortured, murdered and raped by nationalistic troops, marauding bands of Cossacks and others. Alas, this period is now a largely forgotten part of Jewish history, a period covered up by the Soviets and completely overshadowed by the Holocaust.

Isaac Ochberg, a self-made, wealthy individual and Chairman of the Cape Jewish Orphanage, travelled to London, where he secured the help of the kind offices of the JDC and their personnel. He then went on to Warsaw and secured the help of Panya Engel, who took care of the children Ochberg selected and gathered, orphans mainly from existing Jewish Orphanages. He travelled to Brest, Dematchewo, Wlodowa, Pinsk, Rovna, Livov, Sarna, Wisna, Kowel, Karmin-Kashish, Pniwna, Lubomil and Shask.

In Pinsk Isaac Ochberg met Alter Bobrow, an Analytical Chemist, who, together with Zionist friends, had helped establish three orphanages in Pinsk in 1917, having returned there on leave and finding the city devastated from battles between the Russians and Germans. Alter took care of the children and was also their teacher. In

Alter Obrov- later caller Alexander Bobrow

1921 he was presented with three exercise books of letters from pupils and colleagues who remained behind after he left as an assistant to Ochberg, accompanying him to South Africa and taking care of the orphans.

Isaac Ochberg had permission from the Smuts Government to bring out 200 children provided they were healthy, double orphans, not over 14 years old and siblings were not to be separated. He selected the children mainly from existing orphanages supported by the JDC where official records of the orphans had beencollected. The children were, therefore, relatively healthy and this proved to be a very wise move as conditions were so bad that the Canadian group headed by Harry Hershman, who similarly had permission to take 200 healthy orphans to Canada, examined over 8,000 children in Rovna but could not find 200 healthy children whose official records were available. Neither could they find children under three years old who were suitable for adoption.

When a total of 233 children had been gathered in Warsaw, nine group passport photos were taken. Later, when 37 of the children ran away, their faces and names were simply crossed out on the passport.

The largest group of 44 children came from Pinsk and they also had travel documents issued by the Magistrate in Pinsk. The other larger groups were 26 children from Brest-Litovsk, 18 from Stanislav, 16 from Lemberg, 15 from Wlodawa and 9 from Kowel.

Isaac Ochberg apparently bent many of the rules set by the Smuts Government. Many children had siblings left behind, one or two had a living parent, some of the girls, over the age of 14, were brought out as nurses and children's ages were reduced, perhaps to make them more appealing to prospective adopters.

The children were transported by rail in cattle trucks to Gdansk (Danzig) where they boarded SS Baltara bound for London. In London they were hosted by Federation of Ukrainian Jews and then boarded the *Edinburgh Castle* bound for Cape Town arriving there on 21 September 1921. Half of these Ochberg Orphans, on arrival in South Africa, were placed in the care of the Cape Jewish Orphanage (later known as Oranjia) while the rest were sent to Johannesburg to be cared for by the South African Jewish Orphanage (later known as Arcadia).

Group Passport Three

Prospective adopters were interviewed and many of thechildren were placed in their care with mixed outcomes. On Sundays, prospective parents would visit the orphanages in order to view and select children.

The Cape Town Jewish Community accepted the children much more warmly, simply because 'Daddy Ochberg' was chairman of the Orphanage and visited 'his children' regularly. The older girls were each taught a trade and found employment by the Jewish Community and there was a 'Ladies Section' in Cape Town and a hostel in Johannesburg where they lived until they were married. Well-meaning committees saw it as their responsibility to marry off the girls and considered that their duty had ended when their charges were placed in the bonds of holy matrimony. Grand weddings were organised and dowries provided.

Isaac Ochberg visited the Ukraine again in 1923 and delivered aid to the oppressed and poor Jews living under the Soviets. He was a delegate of South Africa at the 1932 World Zionist Congress in Basle and on 11 December 1937, he died at sea and was buried in Cape Town a few days later. He bequeathed the largest sum ever made by an individual to the JNF in Palestine and a lesser sum to the Hebrew University. The bequest was used by the JNF to redeem an area of land in the Hills of Ephraim named the 'Isaac Ochberg Tract' which today encompasses Kibbutz Daliah and Kibbutz Gal'ed

Some of the children were traumatised by the horrors they had witnessed and endured, facts that their life stories clearly reveal. At least two children became violent as adults, two are known to have committed suicide, some had recurring nightmares as adults while others, no doubt, bore their memories in silence and did not share their histories with their children.

A few succumbed to TB or other diseases at a young age and some suffered from malnutrition which restricted their growth. Most, however, prospered in the fullness of time and exhibited the ability, endurance and stoicism to cope with the ups and downs of the new life that their adopted country provided.

Today the estimated 3,000 descendants of the original Ochberg Orphans may be found living in numerous countries around the world where many of the South African Jewish population are now dispersed.

Bennie Penzik, the son of two Ochberg Orphans and initiator of an active committee in Israel, persuaded the JNF to honour the memory of Isaac Ochberg and the Ochberg Orphans with the creation of a Memorial Site in 2011, replete with an impressive stone monument to the man and a rocky mound embedded with ceramic plaques in the name of each orphan child. The venue is the newly established park at Ramat Menashe with a panoramic view of the Isaac Ochberg Tract. This will no doubt be a place of pilgrimage for future generations of descendants and a 'must see' tourist attraction for all visitors to Israel.

Isaac Ochberg monument unveiled by Bennie Penzik

Plaques for each Ochberg Orphan at Ramat Menash.   Photos courtesy Anne Brest

Chapter 13 – ISAAC OCHBERG (1878-1937)

ISAAC OCHBERG *Extract from article by Jonathan Boiskin "Jewish Affairs" 1994*

Isaac Ochberg, the eldest son of Aaron and Sarah Ochberg, was born in 1878 in Uman, a small town in the Ukraine. His father Aaron had gone to South Africa in 1893 and Isaac followed him in 1895 at the early age of fifteen, making the trip alone. Several years later he established himself as one of Cape Town's leading entrepreneurs. Interestingly enough his success had in part been owing to his ventures in buying ships; on this account, the *Cape Argus* described him as the 'plucky shipowner'. Important purchases of property had also given Ochberg a high standing in the business community. Moreover, as the *Jewish Relief News* reported, his communal work had been of equal importance. He was a leading member of a number of charitable institutions in Cape Town and his special interest lay in making helpless children happy. His many business and family obligations did not by any means preclude him from participating fully in communal affairs, particularly Jewish ones.

Isaac Ochberg

He worked for the Helping Hand Society, the Jewish Orphanage, the Old Age Home, the *Dorshei Zion* Society, and was an active member of the New Hebrew Congregation of which he was subsequently elected vice- president.

Isaac and his wife Pauline (Polly)

He was also an executive member of the South African Jewish Board of Deputies and an enthusiastic believer in Freemasonry.

In her book *This Was a Man,* Bertha Epstein maintains that Ochberg was eventually recognised as one of the foremost social workers in South Africa, becoming associated in an important capacity with every Jewish organisation or institution in this country and with many overseas. He never refused to support a worthy cause; on the contrary, his creed was that since he had been enabled to achieve success in his own enterprises, he had a moral duty to help those less fortunate.

One of Ochberg's most significant achievements was the evacuation of the pogrom orphans to South Africa. At his own expense, he travelled to that part of the Ukraine which had been overrun by bandits and brought back with him 200 orphans. His burning desire, however, was to see how his fellow Jews in the heart of the Ukraine were faring. After great difficulty he succeeded in getting permission to re-enter the country and was placed in charge of a special delegation appointed by the World Relief Conference, which sent through him shipments of foodstuffs, medical stores, clothing parcels and money. Becky Greenberg, herself an Ochberg Orphan, recalls that: *Isaac was a honey, he was like a father to us. There was no difference from one child to another, every child was a darling, everyone was lovely and everyone he patted. He was just wonderful.*

Isaac Ochberg was a man of heart and courage who always stood ready to proffer help whenever, wherever and to whomever it was needed.

Standing: Louis Melmed, Boris Crasnow, Polly Ochberg, and Leopold Davidowitz. Seated: Fay Ochberg, Joe Ochberg, Sara Ochberg, Isaac and Rose Ochberg. In Front: Bertha Ochberg,

TRACT NAMED FOR ISAAC OCHBERG
First printed in the Palestine Post 25 June 1943

A tract of land in the Hills of Ephraim was formally named yesterday in honour of the testator of the funds which made its acquisition possible, the late Mr Isaac Ochberg of Cape Town, who was President of the local Zionist Organisation and a member of the Executive of the Board of Deputies.

He left the largest bequest known to Palestine from which the Jewish National Fund and the Hebrew University have each benefited by about £90,000 while further sums are expected from the estate.

In the centre of what will later become a civic square in Daliah, one of the settlements on the Tract, a 25 metre long pergola of stone pillars flanked by two 15 metre wings has been built on which a copper plaque bears the legend:

Erected in memory of the late Isaac Ochberg of Cape Town, through whose munificence the land of the Isaac Ochberg Tract was redeemed through the Jewish National Fund 1880-1937.

A pool has been constructed in front of the colonnade which will be surrounded with flower beds. In unveiling this memorial, Dr A Granovsky, Managing Director of the JNF paid a warm tribute to the far sighted munificence of the donor who had taken a deep interest in the National Home and who loved Jewish youth. He had himself rescued pogrom orphans after the last war and bequeathed sums for Zionist youth education. On the Tract which at present comprises 9,000 dumans will arise several villages of which one will bear the name of the testator. He said that the testator was typical of the finest Zionist community - South Africa.

Prof Volcany spoke on behalf of the Hebrew University of their high appreciation of Mr Ochberg's bequest. The mukhtar of Daliah describing its progress said that they had proved that even from hard rugged terrain without irrigation they could get successful results. The luncheon fare represented their first fruits. He added that a research laboratory for hill farming be established in the Ephraim Hills. The proceedings concluded with the singing of 'Hatikvah'.

A JEWISH NUFFIELD by David Dainow
First printed in the Palestine Post 25 June 1943

As reported above a tract of land in the Hills of Ephraim was named yesterday in honour of the late Isaac Ochberg, of Cape Town.

I knew Isaac Ochberg for over 25 years before he passed away in 1937. I had been on a relief mission to Poland just after the end of the last war when I came across a man engaged on a mission of mercy. His project was to collect a few hundred orphaned children from the pogrom areas in the Ukraine and bring them to South Africa. The difficulties of the task were enormous. I had the privilege of helping him. Finally the group of children was safely transported to the welcome shores of South Africa, where the children were placed in two orphanages. Within the first year, nearly 50 per cent of the orphans had been adopted by Jewish families and were brought up as their own children.

Isaac Ochberg came to South Africa as a poor immigrant and by dint of hard work, determination and a keen business sense, was able to attain great wealth. He was always, however, a very simple person and genuinely concerned in the poor and afflicted among his people. He gave generously during his lifetime. When his young daughter of 17 died suddenly some years ago in Cape Town, he gave an amount of £10,000 in her memory to the Hebrew University - an institution in which he was particularly interested.

It might well be said that Isaac Ochberg never knew the full total of his wealth. He had many interests, and bookkeeping and accounting were not his main concern. I believe he thought he was worth about a quarter-million pounds and that always seemed to be a burden to him. In the realisation of his properties and holdings since his death, the executors found that they had to deal with a fortune approximately three-quarters of a million pounds. After certain personal and public benefactions in South Africa and England, the bulk of his estate will finally go to Palestine - some hundred thousand pounds to the Jewish National Fund, and a similar amount to the Hebrew University, being among the fixed endowments. It will be the largest individual benefaction for the Holy Land in modern history.

Isaac Ochberg on the left, a delegate of South Africa at the World Zionist Congress Basle ~1932
Ochberg, Phili, Poliansky, Abrahams, and J Zukerman

Isaac Ochberg was buried in Cape Town on 13 December 1937
Articles courtesy Peter Stange.

Chapter 14 - THE BEQUESTS OF ISAAC OCHBERG

Man of Vision. Isaac Ochberg circa 1935

DETAILS OF THE BEQUESTS OF ISAAC OCHBERG
Extracted from This Was a Man
Written by Bertha I Epstein, Isaac Ochberg's daughter, in 1974.

Isaac has obviously worked out most meticulously and with great deliberation how he could distribute his estate for the greatest benefit to the greatest number of people. Some of the bequests were quite astonishing. Having made ample provisions for his immediate family, all his other relatives, friends and employees, the charitable bequests were as follows, bearing in mind the enormous difference in the value of money then.

1. £25,000 to the Isaac Ochberg Palestine Fund (established under another, separate, clause of his Will).
2. £10,000 to the Cape Jewish Orphanage for permanent investment as a trust fund, the interest to be used for the higher education of the children at the orphanage.
3. £10,000 to the University of Cape Town, the income to provide a scholarship or scholarships, on condition that there be no differentiation between the students by reason of colour, creed, or race. (N.B. It must be noted here that he specified that should this policy ever be changed, the £10,000 would then devolve upon the Isaac Ochberg Palestine Fund).
4. £10,000 to the Hebrew University situation on Mount Scopus, the interest to provide scholarships for Jewish students at the University.
5. £5,000 pounds to be invested and the interest used for the most capable Jewish applicants from Cape Town and its suburbs for higher education over the matriculation standard.
6. £1 000 to the Cape Jewish Orphanage.
7. £500 to the Cape Town Jewish Board of Guardians to be distributed amongst the Jewish poor of Cape Town.
8. £1 000 to the same institution, the income to be distributed amongst the Jewish poor every year on May 31st (the date of his birth).
9. £500 to the Jewish Helping Hand Society.
10. £500 to the Jewish Old Aged Home.
11. £1,000 to the Jewish Hebrew Schools.
12. £500 *each* to the New Somerset Hospital, the old Somerset Hospital for non-Whites, the Child Life Protection Society, the Community Chest, the Old Hebrew Congregation to be used for the redemption of the building bond, the New Hebrew Congregation for the same, the Constitution Street Synagogue for the same.
13. £250 each to the Jewish Sick Relief Society and the Free Dispensary for the Poor.
14. £2,000 to the Dorshei Zion Society to redeem their bond.
15. £500 to be used for the purpose of spreading among the Jewish young generation in South Africa, the ideal of Zionism, and the importance of Jewish Settlement in Palestine.
16. £1,000 to be divided between persons or institutions that deserve support whom I may have omitted to mention by name.
17. £2,500 to be used in a large town in Palestine in the manner best calculated to be for the benefit of Jews from the point of view of health and physical culture.
18. £5,000 to the Corporation of the City of Cape Town for the use of the young generation from the point of view of health and physical culture.
19. £3,000 on trust for the benefit of colonial-born Coloured children of Cape Town and the suburbs to be used for the purpose of providing a recreation ground where the most population of the Coloured people live, or for a hall for Coloured people to be used for recreation, social meetings and/or entertainment.

20. £10,000 in trust, the income to be used to provide dowries, wedding gifts, or gifts to girls in distress, preference to be given to orphan girls brought from the Ukraine, orphans in "Oranjia" or "Arcadia", and any poor Jewish girl from Cape Town and suburbs.
21. £100 to the Salvation Army.
22. £100 to the Italian consul to be sent to Genoa, Italy, for distribution among the poor there.

He directed that the selection of candidates for bursaries and other purposes of education, be made from poor and deserving persons of promise, it being his wish to afford opportunities to the young people whose means would not otherwise permit them to proceed with their education. He also specified that during the period of realization of the estate all persons, institutions etc. should receive, should they desire it, interest at current rates, on the amount allotted to them, and if not used, to be added to the bequests at the time of payment.

This was very important, as it took the executors seven years to wind up the estate, and it meant that all the beneficiaries could immediately receive some payments.

Finally, and this was the crux of the will, after the persons and charities enumerated individually had been paid out of the four-fifths of the residue of the estate, the balance of the four-fifths was to be divided between the Isaac Ochberg Palestine Fund and the Hebrew University of Jerusalem, in the latter case for lectureships, scholarships, etc. etc. at the discretion of the University Council.

It is extremely difficult to say in exact figures what the actual amounts received by the Isaac Ochberg Palestine Fund will be, due to the fact that certain trust capital has still to be paid to them after the death of the present beneficiaries, and also because there has been such an enormous difference in the value of money since Isaac died. At the time of his death the amount allotted to the Isaac Ochberg Palestine Fund, the Hebrew University and the other charities was almost £500,000 which today is worth many times that amount.

I must explain about Clause 22 – the amount left for distribution in Genoa, Italy. For a long period my Father carried on a very profitable business in derelict ships and scrap-iron. The main market at that time was Italy, and Genoa was the port from which he operated. He obviously felt that this was some way of showing his appreciation of the money he had made through this particular sphere of his activities. It strikes me as quite remarkable that he remembered them after so many years had elapsed.

That all these endowments and bequests have done the work for which they were intended there is no doubt whatsoever, and I myself have seen much of it come to fruition. There must by now be many thousands of people who have benefitted by his generosity and thoughtfulness and have reason to bless his memory. If ever a human being has earned peace and repose in the after-life, he has.

I hope I will be forgiven if I say that Isaac was, in my opinion, the type of man born once in a generation. His magnificent service to the cause of humanity will long continue to be a fragrant memory to those who have benefitted by his munificence, and to those who will still continue to do so for many, many years. Generations have been influenced by his work, and many have followed his example.

For such as he are the salt of the earth, and there could be no higher praise than that.
Verily, as it is inscribed on his tombstone:
"He was a good South African and a great Jew".

Bertha Epstein later wrote:

All the different education trusts, bursaries, and scholarships have functioned uninterrupted. Hundreds of boys and girls, now successful members of their chosen professions, would have languished in obscurity if not for the financial assistance we were able to give them from his bequest.

The "Dowry Fund" (see No. 20 of list), as it has become known, has been most gratifyingly justified. We have been in the position to assist hundreds of girls with their trousseaux, their weddings, their education, or just plain help with money when they were in need of it. Girls of poor circumstances or broken homes unable to receive the necessary assistance from parents or family have come to us, and we have not turned one away empty-handed. We have tried to meet every conceivable request that can reasonably be included within the terms of the will.

Girls who would otherwise go penniless to their marriage are now able to have a tiny nest-egg of their own to bolster their morale. Many girls have been assisted with a University or other education so that they could become self-supporting. There are teachers, doctors, etc. who owe their well-being to the "Dowry Fund".

THE BEQUESTS TO THE HEBREW UNIVERSITY AND TO THE JNF/KKL.
Bertha Epstein wrote:

Nobody could have envisaged, least of all my own parents, that their visit to Palestine in 1926 would intimately affect my life forty-four years later. But that is what happened.

Stemming from that visit of theirs came first of all the Ruth Ochberg Chair of Agriculture in 1936, then the endowments to the Hebrew University on Mouth Scopus, and the creation of the Isaac Ochberg Tract in 1937.

Ruth Ochberg Chair of Agriculture built in 1936, and the endowments to the Hebrew University on Mount Scopus.

New premises at Rehovoth in course of construction, Ruth Ochberg Chair of Agriculture

The Wing of Hebrew University of Jerusalem

Kibbutz Dalia and Kibbutz Galed on the Isaac Ochberg Tract and monuments to Isaac Ochberg

Kibbutz Dalia and Kibbutz Galed were established on the Ochberg Tract of land and below are photos of the pergola and plaque erected to honour Isaac Ochberg.

Mrs Bertha Epstein unveiling the memorial plaque at the Hebrew University in Jerusalem

Dalia Memorial Pergola when erected

The plaque commemorating Isaac Ochberg - 2010 Kibbutz Dalia

In the Jerusalem Post the next day the report of the unveiling was headed "Scopus wing built – twenty two years later". It said, inter alia, "Yesterday's ceremony brought the story to a proud conclusion as the wing housing the Law Faculty's library, and two of its research institutes, those for Jewish Law, Legislative research and Comparative Law, were duly names in honour of Isaac and Pauline Ochberg".

Legacy in Stone. The official unveiling of the plaque honouring Isaac Ochberg in the 1930s, relocated in 2011 to the Isaac Ochberg Memorial Park, at Ramat Menashe near Kibbutz Ein Hashofet.
The inscription "This tract of land has been redeemed by the Jewish National Fund in memory of Yizchak Ochberg of South Africa" is in English and Hebrew

Field of Dreams
On land redeemed through the generosity of Isaac Ochberg, the fields of Kibbutz Dalia being cultivated in the 1940s

Even Yizchak, a memorial of hewn stone

"Daddy Ochberg". Isaac Ochberg at the time he rescued the orphans in 1921

Section 3
The Pinsker Orphans

This section tells of the three Pinsk Orphanages established by Alter Bobrow and his comrades and of the 44 orphans selected from these orphanages by Isaac Ochberg to go to South Africa.

It was from the three Pinsk orphanages and other similarly established orphanages that Isaac Ochberg selected children to go to South Africa. These orphanages were supported by the American Jewish Joint Distribution Committee

Alter Bobrow assisted Isaac Ochberg and accompanied him to take care of the children on their journey to South Africa.

When he left Pinsk he received over 100 letters in Hebrew and Yiddish from the children and his colleagues left behind

The story of the Pinsker Orphans is more fully told in the *The Pinsker Orphans* book that includes the translation of all the letters.

Chapter 15 – THE FORTY FOUR OCHBERG ORPHANS SELECTED FROM THE THREE PINSK ORPHANAGES

Of the 181 Ochberg Orphans, 44 children, the largest group, came from the three Pinsk Orphanages while 26 children came from Brest-Litovsk, 18 from Stanislav, 16 from Lemberg, 15 from Wlodawa and nine from Kowel.

The stories of 130 of the 177 children (including 31 of the Pinsk children) are recorded in the book 'The Ochberg Orphans and the Horrors From Whence They Came'.

Here are photos of the Pinsk children and brief details extracted from that book.

PINSK TRAVEL DOCUMENTS

The children that came from Pinsk had in fact two travel documents; the group passport with the group photo and list and there was an individual affidavit issued by the Pinsk Magistrate with an individual photo which stated;

"NUMBER XX
Affidavit Issued by the Magistrate of the Town of Pinsk on July 6, 1921.
The Magistrate of Pinsk states that XXXXXXXXXXX, of XXXX years, whose photograph is attached, and is an orphan without parents, who resides in the Orphanage, is to depart for Africa with Caretaker OCHBERG.

Stamped and Sealed by two secretaries of the Magistrate of the Town of Pinsk."

The affidavits grant permission for the child to be placed in the care of Mr Ochberg for the journey to South Africa.

The Affidavits were written in Polish. Pinsk was actually located in White Russia, an area ceded to Poland in 1918, but then returned to Russia later.

The photos in this chapter are from the abovementioned affadavit.

ABO SHLEMA AND LEIBL ELSTEIN

The father, Matoth Elstein, was killed by the Denikin in 1919 (27 Shevat) in Kiev. The mother, Rifka Yentel, died of hunger in 1920 (27 Tamus) after living in very difficult circumstances. The children were left without any support.

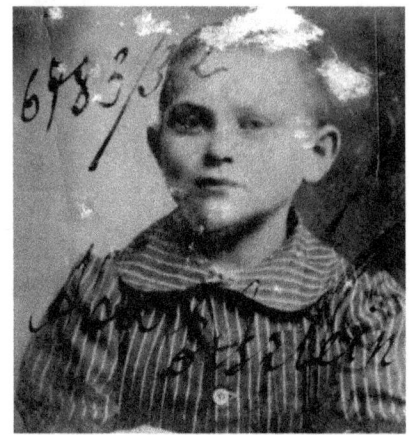
Abo Elstein

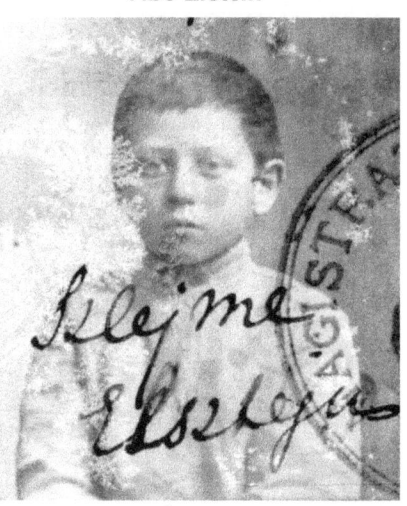
Shlema Elstein

Leibl Elstein

SHMUEL GARBUZ
Written by Lawrence I Garbus

My grandfather, Shmuel, was the youngest child of his parents, Shimon Yehuda and Shifra Garbuz. He had seven older siblings, of which only two others, who also had left Europe, ultimately survived the Holocaust. His mother died while he was very young and his father passed away by the time he reached the age of about 10. His older siblings were unable to care for him so he was put into an orphanage. He hated Pinsk and so, even as a young boy, he dreamed of leaving Poland.

My grandfather's recollections of Pinsk were of harsh conditions and oppressive anti-Semitism. He would often recall the cold and hunger that he endured as a child, and often commented that hunger is a personal experience that can never be described. The persistent acts of violence against the Jews of Pinsk were ingrained in my grandfather's memory - whether it be of a religious Jew's beard being hacked off with a bayonet, or the local constable's son (who died when he fell through some ice) who used his late father's position to terrorize the local Jewish population. This convinced my grandfather early in his life that there was little future for Jews in Poland.

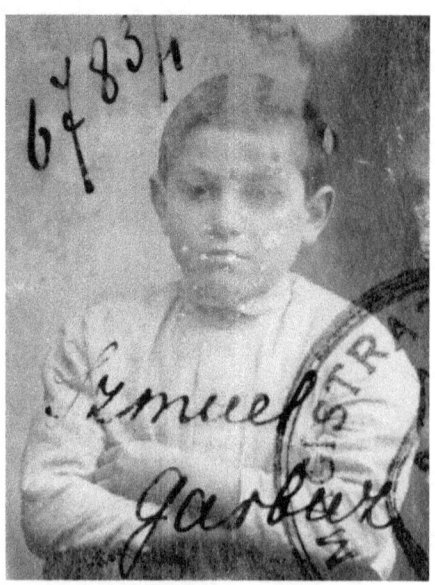
Shmuel Garbuz

JOCHEVET, BRAINDEL AND SHEINE-ROCHEL GESUNTERMAN

The parents, Moshe and Freidel, died of starvation during the War

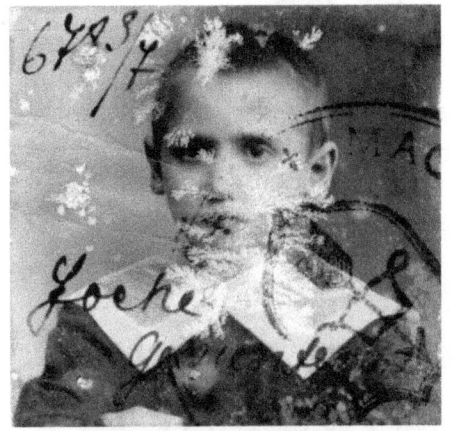
Jochevet Gesunterman

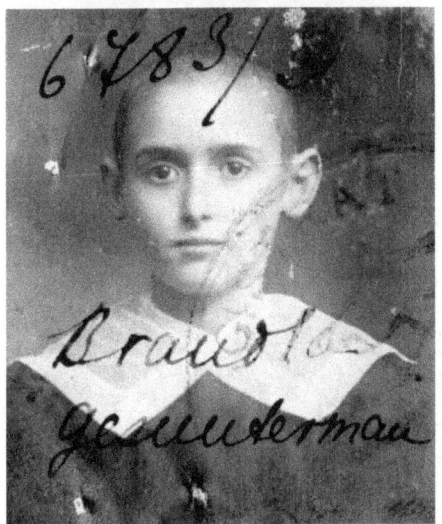
Braindel Gesunterman

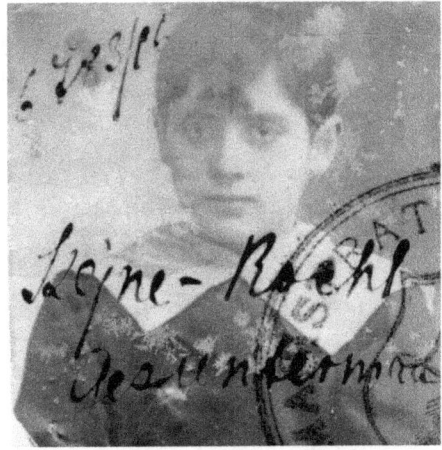
Sjeine-Rochel Gesunterman

My grandmother's sister, Janie Oddes (Sheine-Rochel Gesunterman) relates the following image. She said that on returning from hiding in the forest during a particularly cruel and vicious pogrom, the three sisters came out of hiding and looked down onto their village and saw the most beautiful sight—there was pink snow falling all around, transforming their shtetl into a surrealistic, pink, wonderland. It was only on closer inspection that they realized what in fact they were seeing.

It was the blood soaked feathers of the *perinehs* that the Jews had been sleeping or cowering under when the Cossacks attacked them, slashing through their bed coverings and massacred so many of them. Till the day she died, my aunt never wore red and white mixed together.

Written by Lauren Snitcher

ABRAHAM AND CHANA GORENSTEYN

The father, Chaim, died when he was taken to government work. The mother, Eidel, died of typhoid having lived through hunger and need.

The death of the parents left Avram and his younger sister Chana (Connie) as young orphans, destitute, starving and I cannot even begin to imagine how lonely and scared the two young children must have been to find themselves in the precarious predicament that they were in.

Abe and Connie spoke Hebrew, Yiddish and some Russian.

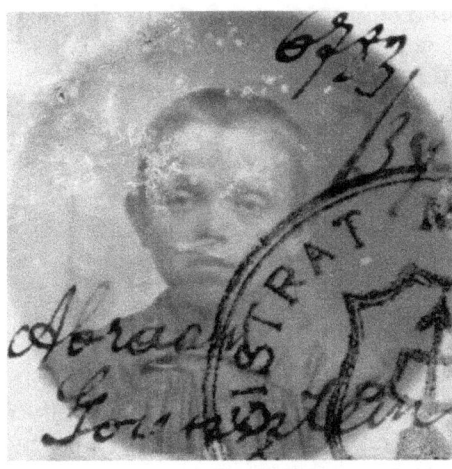
Abraham Gorensteyn

Chana Gorensteyn

Thanks to Isaac Ochberg's endeavours, Avram and Connie won the ultimate jackpot and were saved from certain death if not from the anti Semitism in Eastern Europe at the time, then later from Nazism.
Written by Charles Levitt

ISSER GERMAN

No contact made with descendants

Not listed as an Ochberg Orphan but we have his photo stamped by the Pinsk Magistrate

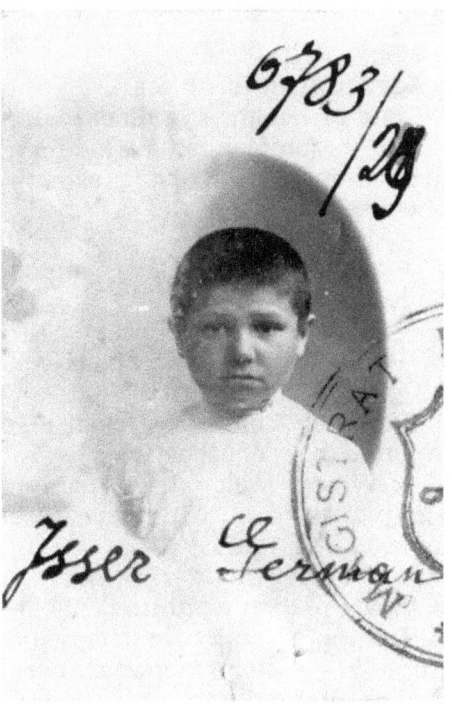
Isser German

CHASHE, ISAAC AND BENJAMIN HELMAN

The father Yoel was murdered in a pogrom by the Bolshevist bands. When they demanded money, and not having to give, they took him out of the house and 30 paces from the house they shot him and took everything out of the house.

When 21 year old Rachel followed to retrieve the father and the things, they brutally hit her, raped her, cut off her fingers and murdered her.

The family all escaped into the forest.

QUESTIONNAIRE AS REQUIRED BY THE JDC FOR FULL ORPHANS:

English translation below and original in Yiddish on the right

Yochanan Binyamin and Chasha Hellman

1. Name: 1)Chanan   2) Aysik (crossed) 3)Binyamin and 4) Chasha
2. Surname: Helman
3. Father's name: Yoel 45
4. Mother's name and maiden name: Chaya Valavelsky 43 years
5. Sex:
6. Age: 10 years and 8 years
7. State of health: Eye disease, heart complaints, lung-complaints, head and skin diseases, etc.
   Healthy
8. Place of birth: place, circuit, district.
   Lubashov (Circuit Pinsk)
9. Place where the child was assigned: Lubashov
10. Address before the child was admitted to: Lubashov
11. What was the parents occupation: Business of grocery wares
12. Were they poor, rich, average (estimate of their worth): Middle
13. Did the parents own immovable property (house, granary/barn, garden, orchard, land, etc.) If yes, who is looking after it now:
   Own house
14. Relatives (brothers, sisters, uncles, aunts, and further relatives) Does the child have the exact address of any of them: Mother, brother sister. The mother is sick and poor and cannot take care of the children. The brother is 12 years the sister is 12 years. The family lived rich and respectable. The children have a doctor, an uncle in Russia by the Bolshevist.
15. Who has legal authority over the child: The mother
16. Is this person agreeable that the child be taken away to another country, to be adopted or to be brought up in a Jewish environment, institution there: Yes
17. Is the child itself inclined to leave his present home and to travel to a faraway country: Yes
18. Can the child read:Yiddish, Hebrew, other languages? Yes
19. Can the child write:Yiddish, Hebrew, other languages? Yes
20. Can the child *daven*? Yes
21. Has the child attended a general folkshul, a Jewish school, *kheyder*, Talmud Torah, etc. and for how long: Yes
22. Has the child learnt a specific trade, with whom, where, and how long: No

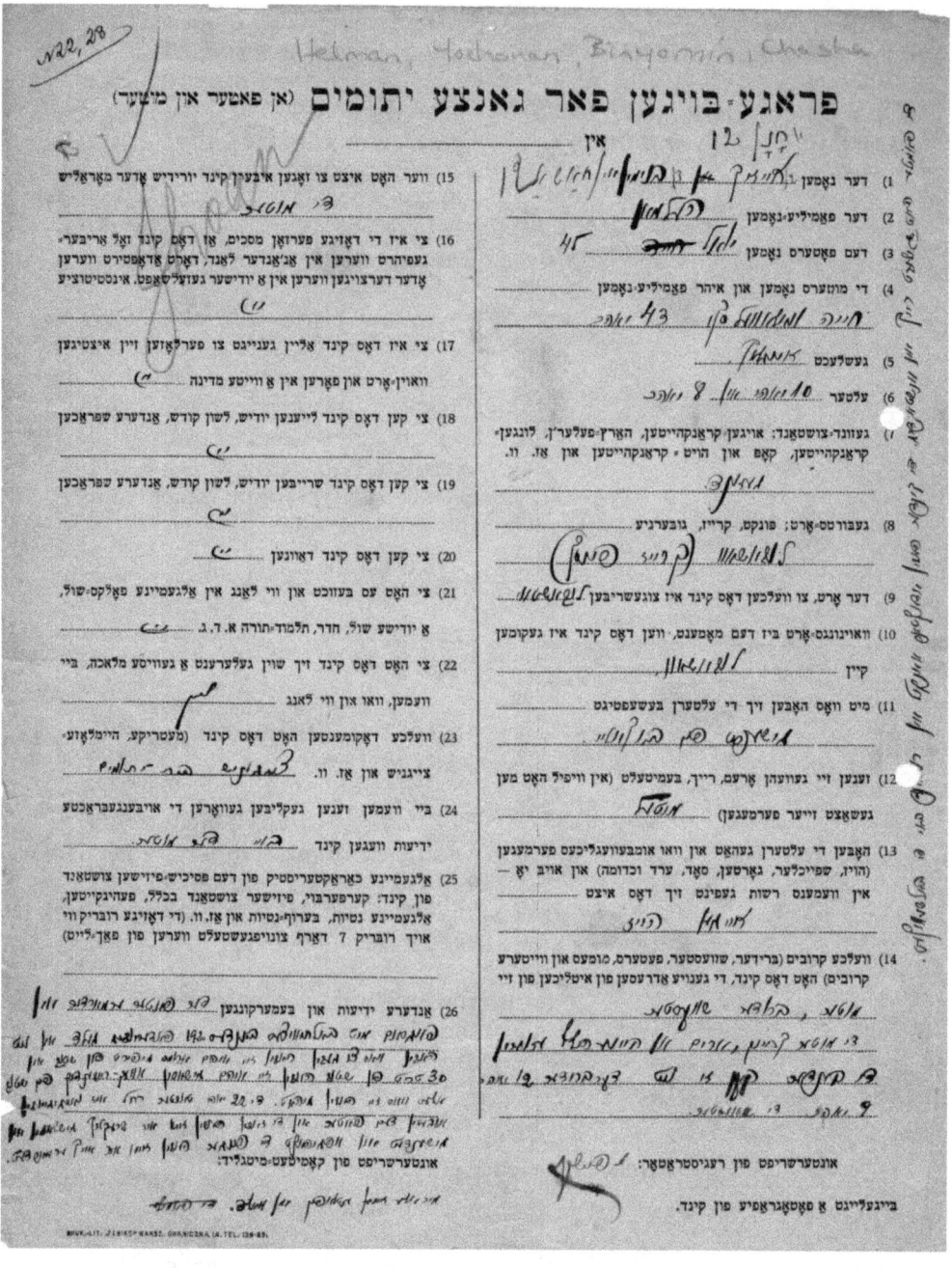

23. What certificates does the child have (matric, school leaving certificate etc.):

Registry of birth, School Testimonies, Certificates, Certificates from the Orphanage

24. From whom is the information about the child obtained: The mother

25. General psychological-physical condition of the child: build, general physical condition, abilities, general inclinations, vocational leanings etc. (this section as well as section 7 should be filled in by trades people:
 None written

Benjamin Helman

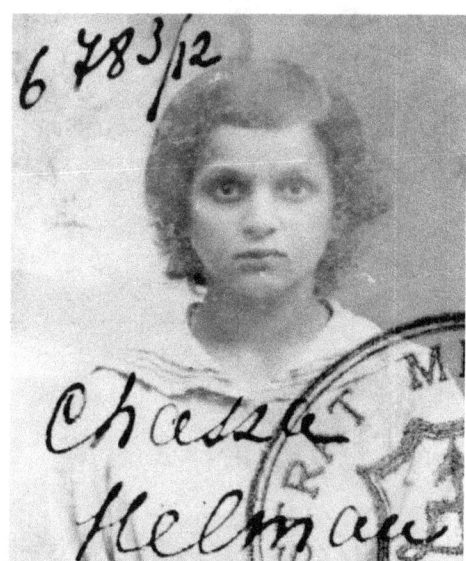
Chashe Helman

Isaac Helman

GOLDE, MORDEHE AND SHACHNA KAHAN

Golde Kahan, aged 17 was from Pinsk.
Both her parents Tevye and Sarah died during the war having experienced many pogroms.

She was left after having lost a large family.

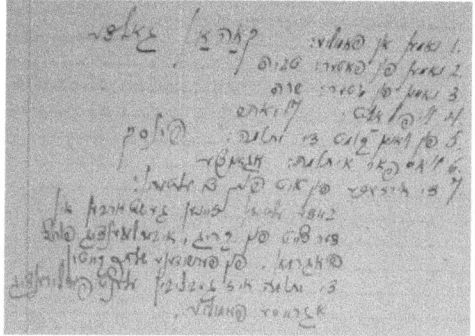
Copy of the entry in the register at Oranjia - The Cape Jewish Orphanage

Contact was made neither with Golde's descendants nor Mordehe's or Shachna's whose photos appear below and we don't know if they are siblings or even related.

Shachna Kahan

Mordehe Kahan

FREIDL AND LIVIA JOFFE

The Joffe Family moved from Latvia to Pinsk after the father, Moshe deserted the Russian Army to avoid the Russia-Japanese war. Later at the time of WW1 he was rounded up by the Germans for forced labour and died from typhus leaving the mother Mariasha and her three daughters, Sarah, Freda (Freidl) and Sylvia (Livia) to fend for themselves.

While Freda and Sylvia went to South Africa with Isaac Ochberg, Mariasha their Mother and Sarah, their older sister remained behind and it is believed perished, in the Holocaust.

Freidel (Freda) Joffe

Cywje (Sylvia) Joffe

ZLATA KNUBOVIZ

Zlata Knubovis

Zlata Knuboviz, aged 12 was born in Pinsk. Her father Beril died in Argentine. The mother, Gitil, survived pogroms and hardships and died of hunger.

The child developed well in bitter circumstances and is a credit to the home.

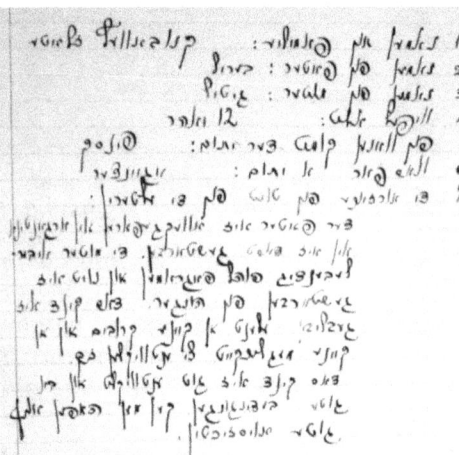

Copy of the entry in the register at Oranjia - The Cape Jewish Orphanage

No contact made with descendants

CHAIM, PASHA AND SARA LEVIN

Their father was Shmariyu and their mother Chana. Nothing else is known of their parents.

Chaim Levin

Pasha Levin

Sara Levin

HERSCHEL LIDVENITZKY

Our father Herschel Lidvenitsky (later Harry Lidvin) was born on 23 May 1908 in Pinsk. His parents were Gershon Lidvenitsky and Leah Foeterman, who was born in Russia.

We don't know if there were any other siblings or what happened to his parents.

Our father never spoke and would not speak about his life in Eastern Europe. The only thing we remember is that he told us about the Soup Kitchens. He said he stood for hours in the lines, in order to receive some food.

At that time we, as kids, did not realise that we would in later life, want to find out or know more about his life in those early days. He died so young at 49 years old when we were only 17 and 12 years old.

All we know is that he landed up in an Orphanage in Pinsk and was part of the group of children selected by Isaac Ochberg that was brought to South Africa in 1921 and placed in the care of Arcadia - The South African Jewish Orphanage

His gratitude to Isaac Ochberg was indescribable.

Written by Laurane (Lidven) Klingman and Anita Lidven

Herschel Lidvenitsky

SARA MARGOLIN

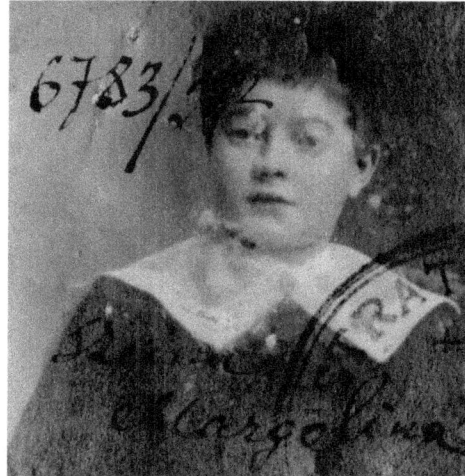

Sara Margolin

Sara Margolin, aged nine, was born in Pinsk.

Her father, Abraham, died from typhoid fever in 1917.

Her mother, Trume, died from typhoid fever in 1918.

The older brother was killed by the Belochowitz in Pinsk in 1920.

The child was left with no relations whatsoever.

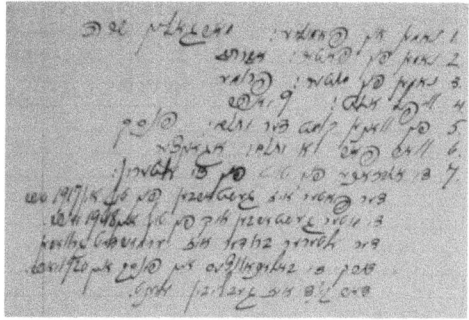

Copy of the entry in the register at Oranjia - The Cape Jewish Orphanage

No contact made with descendants

SALOMON OCHSTEIN

No contact made with descendants

No photos or further information available

CHONON, NACHMAN AND SZYMON MIGDALOWICZ

The parents, Schuel and Chana, have suffered through the Poles and the Belachowitz and after being starved for a considerable time they have both died of typhoid fever.

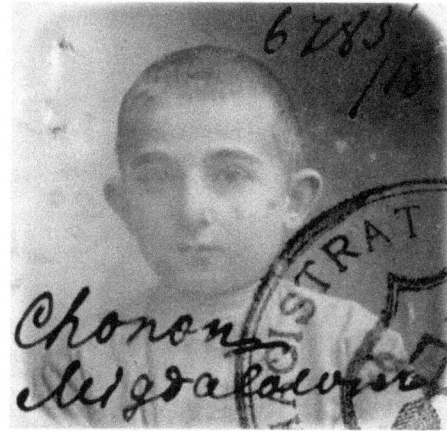

Chonon Migdalowicz

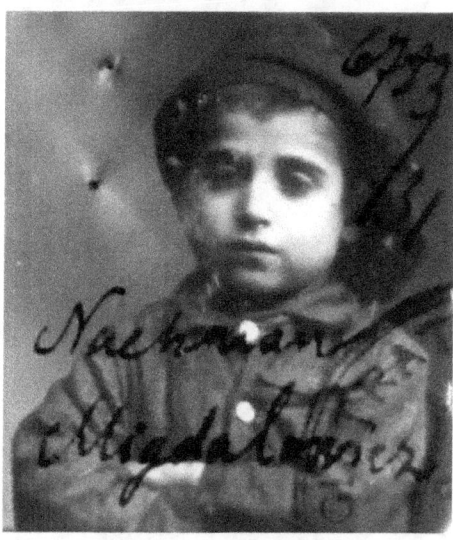

Nachman Migdalowicz

There were four brothers. Chonon, Nachman and Szymon, who came to South Africa with Isaac Ochberg, and an older brother who joined the Russian Army.

My Dad said he was born in Pinsk and the story he told me, was that they walked through forests for a few days, only moving at night, to hide from the White Russians or Cossacks, until they got to Pinsk. The children were under-clothed, and had rags on their feet for shoes. After some time, the children were put in an orphanage, as my Grandfather could not manage them.
Written by Cecil Migdal

YSER AND SZEPSEL PERECHODNIK

Both parents have lived through many pogroms and other difficulties.

They have died from starvation..

DWORA, MEISH, ZLATA, FAYWEL AND FEYGA PINSKY

The father, Aharon was a carpenter who died of hunger and the struggle to survive.

The mother, Yenta, died from the Balachovitches, she contracted syphilis from being raped by them. The children had nowhere to go.

Faywel Pinska

Yser Perechodnik

Dwora Pinska

Fegel Pinska

Szepsel Perechodnik

Zlata Pinska

Meish Pinska - see also page 135

ABRAM AND CHAIM REICHMAN

Listed as from Turow but with travel documents from the Pinsk Magistrate.

Abram Reichman

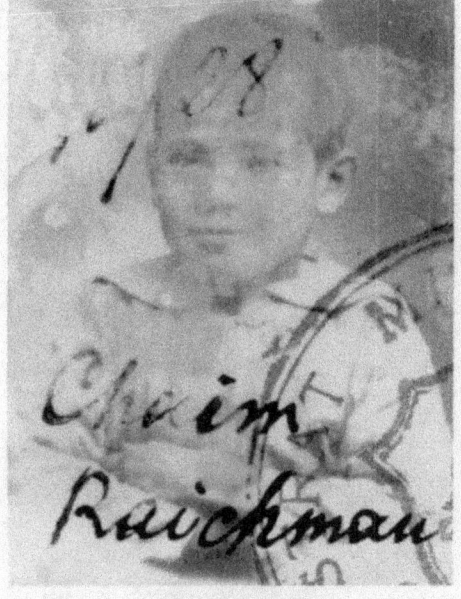

Chaim Reichman

Contact was made with the descendants only after the completion of The Ochberg Orphans book and their life story is recorded in chapter 15.

ARON, FAIWEL AND SHOLEM RUCHOCKI

The parents, Selig and Bashe, had no means for livelihood and were eating grass and potatoe peel. The children were hunger stricken.

Aron and Faiwel Ruchocki

Sholem Ruchocki

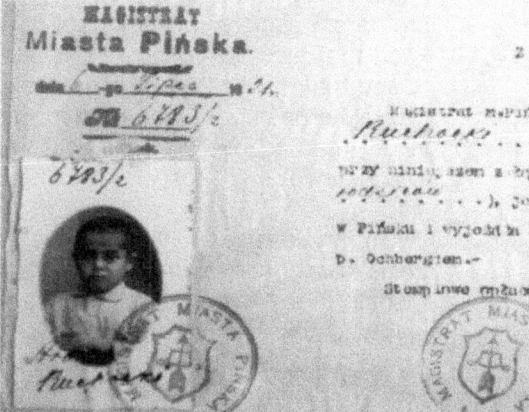

Pinsk Travel Document of Aron Ruchocki

Pinsk Travel Document of Faiwel Ruchocki

ZLATA AND SIMA SAMURINA

Both of the parents, David and Esther, died of stavation having witnessed many pogroms.

Zlata Samurina

Sima Samurina

HERSH, ISAAC AND CHASKEL SHTEINER

My late father Hersh (Harry) and his late brothers Isaac (Isadore) and Chaskel (Charles) were Ochberg Orphans.

Harry was born in Libshei, Poland on 13 April 1909.

His parents were Boruch and Brocha (nee Barenboim) Steiner. On his mother's side of the family, his grandparents were Naomi and Zvi Hersh Barenboim and the names of his father's parents are unknown.

After his father was shot one Saturday morning when he was going to Shul, his mother took him and his brothers to her sister, Bashe's family. Chaya, the sister of the three boys, did not go with as she was waiting to tell her husband. Chaya's husband was in the army (presume in the resistance).

The journey in the snow was too much for Brocha and she died from pneumonia. Before she died she made Harry promise to look after his brothers. Luckily he managed to keep that promise to her. He waited to see that his brothers were married before he decided it was time for him to get married. He was also the last to pass away.

While my dad was working at his uncle's farm, somebody came rushing to tell him that someone was going to take his brothers to South Africa. Needless to say Harry ran to see what this was all about.

The rest is history.
Written by Audrey Rubin (nee Steiner)

Letters written by Chaya from Pinsk to her three younger brothers in Arcadia (The South African Jewish Orphanage) are in chapter 46

The entry in the register kept at The South African Jewish Orphanage (later called Arcadia) shows Hersh aged 12, Isaac seven and Chaskel five. While all boys went up to Arcadia, Isaac and Chaskel were initially "detained in Cape Town".

Hersh Shteiner

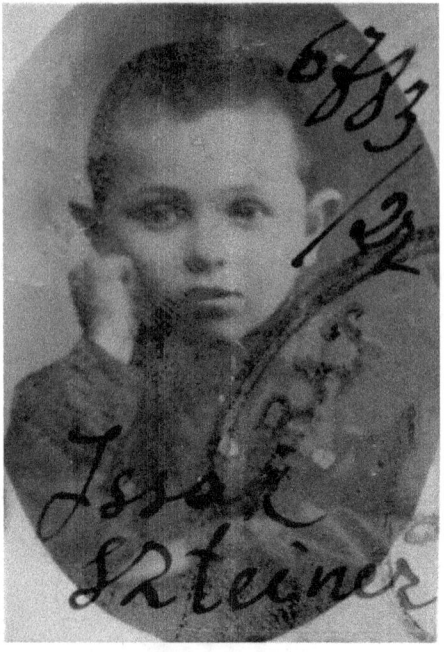

Isaac Shteiner

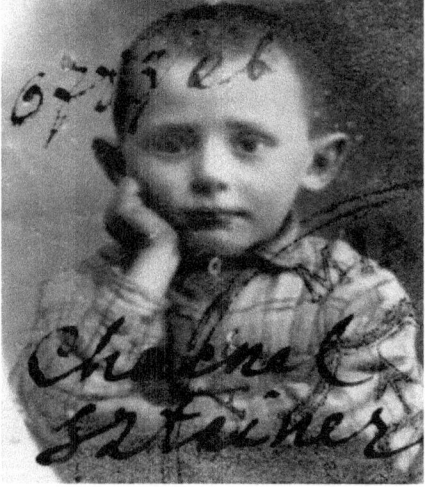

Chaskel Shteiner

IDENTITY AND TRAVEL PERMITS OF THE OCHBERG ORPHANS FROM PINSK

While all the Ochberg Orphans, including those from Pinsk, travelled on a group passport, all of the children from Pinsk also had an additional indentity or travel document.

Most of these were issued by the Magistrate of Pinsk, as per the examples on page 81, however, a few were issued with the document below, from the County (The Third) Orphanage in the City of Pinsk

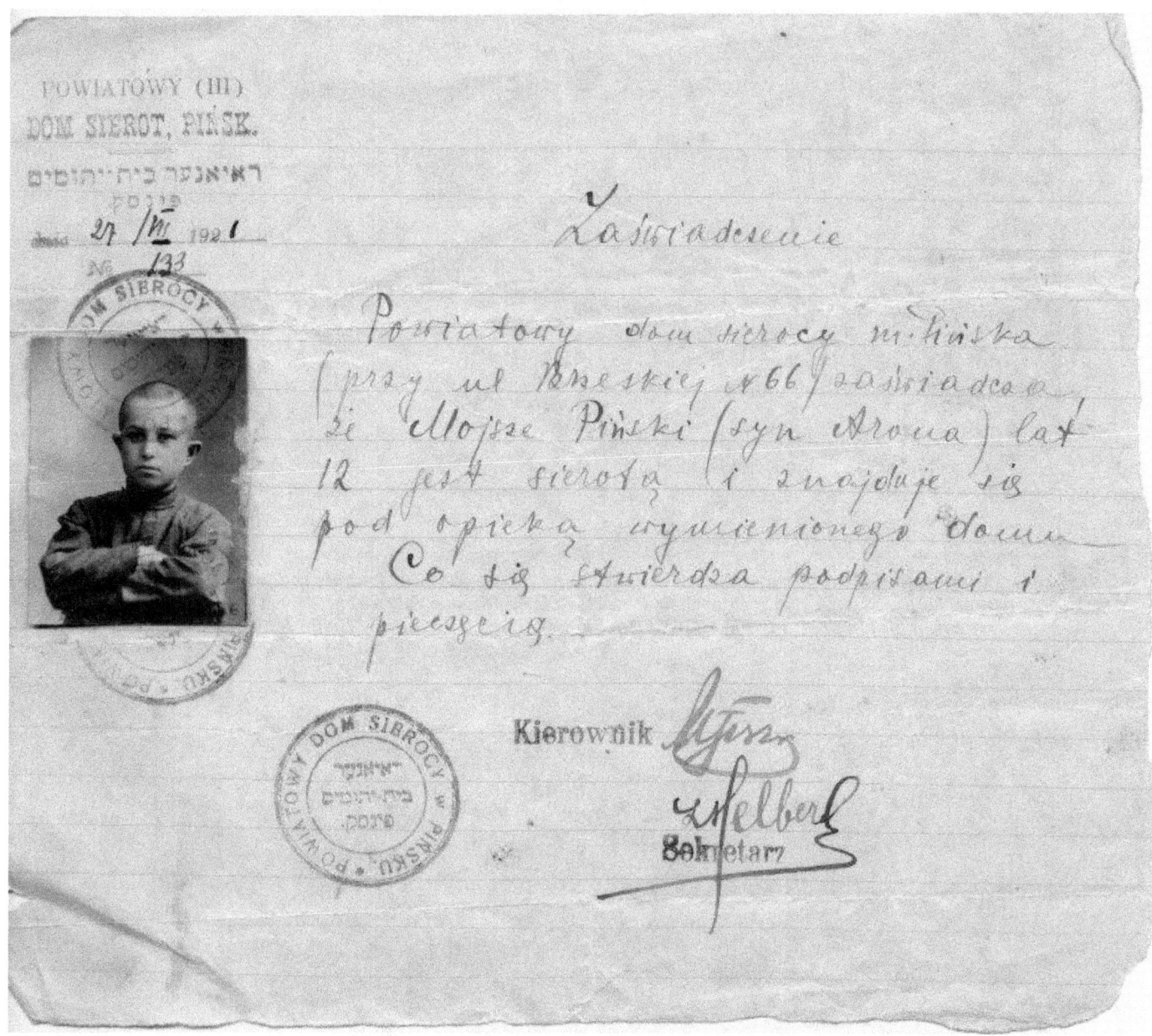

This document written in Polish was sent in by Bennie Penzik and translated by Jack Goldfarb as follows

County (III)
Orphanage, Pinsk
June 27, 1921

Statement

The County Orphanage of the City of Pinsk (66 Brzeska Street) states that Mojsze Pinski (the son of Aron) aged 12 is an orphan and is under the care of the above-named house, which is confirmed with signatures and seal.

Director (*Signature illegible*)

Seal: County Orphanage
In the City of Pinsk

Secretary: Zifelberg

GROUP PHOTO OF OCHBERG ORPHANS IN PINSK - PRIOR TO DEPARTURE - JULY 1921

קינדער פון די בתי יתומים איינגעארדנטע פון דער יודישער קהלה אין פאסט א ט /אמריקע/ פארן אפפאר פון פינסק.

Children from the Orphanages who were settled by the Jewish Community in Cape Town Africa.
Prior from their departure from Pinsk - July 1921
From album presented in 1934 to Regina Rabtsevich - courtesy Bella Velikovskaya

Pinsk Ochberg Orphans prior to their departure - Pinsk July 1921 -. courtesy UCT

Children from the Pinsker Orphanages who were settled by the Jewish Community in South Africa
Ochbera Orphans from Pinsk prior to their departure from Pinsk - July 1921 - left hand side of photo

Children from the Pinsker Orphanages who were settled by the Jewish Community in South Africa
Ochberg Orphans from Pinsk prior to their departure from Pinsk - July 1921 - right hand side of photo

Chapter 16 – ALTER BOBROW AND THE PINSK ORPHANS

PINSK ORPHANS 1917-1921
Written by Liebe Klug

In 1893 a son was born to Yachna Obrov and Leib Obrov in Pinsk. He was named Tzadk-Zander, but was never called by that name. The children born before him had died, either in childbirth or infancy. Instead he was known as Alter, the old one, in that way hoping that he would live to be an old man. In fact he died one week short of his 90th birthday. Members of the family and close friends, always called him 'Alter'. In later years he was known in the family as 'Alec', but only on official terms 'Alexander', the English translation of Tzadek-Zander.

So Alter led the life of a Jewish child in Pinsk in the designated Pale of Settlement. He went to cheder, and to Shul, and when he was older to the Yeshiva. His father Leib, made a living by dealing in futures. Not futures on the stock market as we know it, but futures of the apple crop. Jews were not permitted to own land, so he did the next best thing. Every winter he visited the neighbouring peasant and did a deal with him. He would guess what the apple crop would yield, and offered him a price for the entire crop. In this way he would take a gamble on the possible worms that might enter the apples, a late frost that would kill off the blossom, a high wind that would shake the young immature apples from the trees, or any other misfortune that would ruin his 'futures'. If there was a late frost, Alter and his brother Itzik, would sleep in the orchard and burn smoke pots to keep the frost off the delicate blossoms.

Father Leib though, was also forward thinking in other ways. Alter was devoted to his Yeshiva learning, and it was clear that he was a good and committed scholar. Father Leib wanted his son to have a secular education, to go to Real Schule, a high school, and maybe get a profession at the University in Vilna. He was a far seeing man, and also wanted his son to be freed from the constraints of living in the Pale of Settlement, with its restrictions on movement, land ownership and occupations. A Jew who had a university degree, could get a passport that enabled him to travel and work anywhere.

Alter's father took him out of the Yeshiva and sent him to the Real Schule. Alter was heartbroken. To be enrolled in the Real Schule meant attending on Saturday, the Sabbath, and to Alter, Saturday was the holy day of prayer and contemplation in the synagogue. It was a real wrench for him to leave the Yeshiva, his teachers and his friends.

As a Jew there was a numerus clausus of 5% allowed to enter the university, so Jewish pupils had to achieve even higher grades than the general population. In the event Alter was accepted and studied to become an Analytical chemist. He never spoke about his student days, but was proud of his achievement. As an old man, sorting out papers, he showed me with pride his final degree marks. He achieved 5 for every subject. Every subject was marked out of 5, and that was the highest mark attainable. Now as an Analytical Chemist with a

Alexander (Alter) Bobrow –
"His surname was originally "Obrov" But I suppose that the pronunciation became Abrov. Later when papers for travel were issued, there was a mistake, and the name was written as "Bobrov". So to avoid confusion the papers were issued as Obrov-Bobrov! When my father reached Cape Town he dropped "Obrov". So his name became "Bobrow", as did his mother and family."

passport, he was allowed to move outside the Pale of Settlement, and took a job on a large sugar estate, where beet was grown. What seemed to stay in his mind, when he did talk about it, was the fact that he was allocated his own serf. As a socialist that was repugnant to him. The serf had to look after his every need, and what upset him was that the serf insisted on taking off his boots and cleaning them each night.

Alter went home regularly to his family and his friends in Pinsk. In 1917, the Great War raged, and Pinsk being a border town, received the brunt of the troop movements back and forth. Germans, White Russian troops, Red Army Troops, devastating and laying waste towns, villages, farms On this particular visit, he saw that amongst the rubble of what were streets of houses, were wandering young children, without food or shelter, or care. The orphans of the ravages of war. He belonged to a Zionist Socialist Group, and when they met together, suggested and persuaded them to give up their jobs and work together to rescue the children.

So it was. This small group went from street to street collecting the children. There was at first no coherent plan of what to do. However, the children were hungry, so they started a soup kitchen, no doubt helped with supplies from the Jews in the town. It fast became clear that the children had nowhere to go, no clothes, no roof over their heads. There was no going back. A disused Old Aged Home was taken over, and beds from a derelict hospital commandeered. The first Orphanage was formed. Within a few months there were three orphanages in the Pinsk area alone. All funded by the community, and staffed by voluntary workers.

Then there was the next step. What to do with the children during the day? Start a school of course. Not only the children of the orphanage went to the school, children of the town also joined. This is a story I heard from a cousin of Alter's, now living in Hamilton, Canada. She was an old lady then by the time I met her, and had been a much younger cousin. She remembers being very upset in the class, because when my father (who was teaching) asked a question of the class, and she put up her hand to give the answer, he never chose her. Eventually she complained to him. His answer was that she had a mother and a father, so she had no need to be noticed, and given a chance to speak. But for these children who had lost everything, to be noticed by the teacher had great importance.

The ongoing daily care was undertaken by the team of friends, who had collected the children and set up the functioning orphanage. The costs were probably met by the pockets of the Jews of Pinsk. A most important contributor and mainstay was the Jewish American Joint Distribution Committee. It was set up by Henry Morgenthau (later to be chief Secretary to the Treasury in the US) to provide help and rescue to Jews all over the world.

When crisis struck, as it did in the form of an epidemic of typhoid, the children were nursed by those self same rescuers. This story comes from one of the group, Rachel Bramson one of the group of friends, that emigrated to Israel, and who we met on one of our visits there.

There was a typhoid epidemic in the orphanage. We all worked together for weeks, nursing the children ourselves, and had had no time off for weeks. At that time I was engaged to be married, and as a result of the illness had not seen him for quite a long time. I asked your father - Alter, for permission to leave for a few hours. He was outraged and said to me. 'You ask to go out at a time like this!!! How can you!!' Of course I never left the building. He himself nursed the children for weeks, with not even time to go home to sleep. There were no extra beds, so he used to catnap on two chairs put together, and he was quite a tall man. Eventually, Alter caught typhoid and went home to be nursed by his mother. The children were quite upset by his absence. So, we devised a plan. We took them in groups to his mother's house, put a step ladder up against the wall, he was in an attic room, and one by one the children went up to give him a little wave, and he waved back. Having seen so much death, many of them saw their parents killed before their eyes, that to have a surrogate father figure disappear must have disturbed them greatly.

Eventually Alter came back. The children were overjoyed. He took up his mandolin, and played. They formed a circle round him and danced, calling out 'Alter Alter Alter' as they skipped and hopped round him'.

Alter Bobrow gave an interview for the 50th Anniversary of the Cape Jewish Orphanage - Oranjia.

'So many children were found that soon we were obliged to set up three orphanages. At first Pinsk was isolated by the fighting, and we were thrown almost solely on our own resources. We had neither beds, bedding, nor clothes. I remember our using flour bags to make aprons and other garments for the boys and girls. At one time in the course of my duties, I had to walk through the streets in which shells were bursting. Balachou a notorious Ukrainian fanatic descended on the city with his gangs and the pogroms raged for nearly a week.'

When order was restored, supplies began to arrive, first from the Juedischer Hilfsverein u Berlin, and then from the Joint Distribution Committee, including cocoa, condensed milk, cooking oil and milk. The entire area was in a state of furor. Rival armies were fighting for control, the Red Army against the Whites, as well as Allied contingents and unorganised guerilla bands. Law and order had broken down, transportation came to an end. The condition of Jews which had never been good, deteriorated even more. Famine, as well as diseases followed over most of the area. Pogroms were reported almost daily. The question arose - what to do to help the orphaned children?

By 1921 the Cape Jewish Orphanage was set up and functioning. The committee had heard of the plight of the Jewish Orphans in the Pale of Settlement and decided to help.

Contact was made with Dr Jochelman, President of the Federation of Ukrainian Jews in Britain offering help. The Prime Minister of South Africa, General J C Smuts and Mr Patrick Duncan, Minister of the Interior agreed to allow any children permission to land in South Africa. Isaac Ochberg proposed that the Cape Jewish orphanage be responsible for bringing the children out and taking care of them. A South African Relief Fund for Jewish War victims was already in operation and in less than a week £25 000 was pledged and a larger amount in due course was raised.

Isaac Ochberg offered to go to Europe to make the arrangements and to bring the children back to Cape town. He proceeded from town to town Minsk, Pinsk, Stanislav, Lodz, Lemberg, and Wlodowa.... The conditions in the area were dire, with pogroms an almost daily event. The children and their carers relied for their survival on the American Joint Jewish Committee.

The difficulty would be how to choose 200 children from amongst the several thousand being cared for in the orphanages. Only full orphans, that is those that had lost both parents were selected, and those who were healthy in mind and body. The selection was made in consultation with the Principal and Matron of each orphanage.

Alter Bobrow, was asked to accompany the children and stay for six months in Oranjia, as the orphanage in Cape town was named, with the children to help them to settle in. The children were issued with group passports with group photographs of 20-30 children.

I never heard of the journey directly from my father, but knew from bits and pieces that emerged from other people. They travelled first to Warsaw, where all the children from the different orphanages were collected, and then on to Danzig, where they boarded a boat to England. In London there was a shelter for any travelling Jews, who were immigrating to other countries. There the children waited until they embarked on the *Edinburgh Castle* in September 1921.

Many many years later, in Cape Town in 1968 where I was visiting for the funeral of my mother, I had a surprising graphic account of the journey to Danzig. It was high summer, and to cool off, it was customary to walk in the evening on a promenade by the sea, in a suburb of Cape Town called Sea Point. I was walking with my father. Due to the vagaries of immigration officials, his name was now Bobrow, Alexander. Still though called by his family, Alter, and the young members of the family, Uncle Alex. A man came up to us and said 'You don't remember me do you?' My father shook his head. 'I am one of the orphans who you saved in Pinsk, and brought to South Africa.' Then he went on: 'I well remember the journey from Pinsk. The train stopped at the little stations. The Jews had heard of the children from the orphanages and that they were being taken to South Africa. At each stop we were met with fruit and food and flowers. You Mr Bobrov, got down from the train with the children, and your mandolin. Together with those that greeted us, we sang and danced together with them, led by your mandolin.' He took my father's hand and shook it warmly, and went on his walk.

Over the years, I did hear a little of the journey on the *Edinburgh Castle*. My father had 60 of the children in his care. Twenty two from the orphanage in Pinsk that he and friends had started. Some had been severely traumatised by their experiences, having seen their parents killed before their eyes. Now having to cope with new circumstances and the unknown. There were many times when he brought children beset by nightmares, into his cabin and looked after them through the night.

The children were met by a warm and welcoming reception at Cape Town docks. For Alexander Bobrow, having once seen and lived in Cape Town there was no going back to Pinsk. Although he could not practice as an Analytical Chemist and could not afford to retake the South African examinations. When his contract with the orphanage expired, he lived in a little shack by the sea in a hamlet called Bakoven (it still exists) and grew his own fruit and vegetables. For a small sum he looked after a spastic child. He was always considerate to his parents and family in Pinsk and sent money regularly, which they saved. In 1934, they were able, with the money saved and his intervention, join him in Cape Town. His father had unfortunately died in 1929.

There was another consequence of Alter's arrival in Cape Town. The policy in Oranjia, was not only to educate the orphan children, but also provide them with the means with which to earn a living when they were old enough to leave. To this end my mother Annie Gamsu (always called Channa, by close friends and members of the family) was employed to teach the girls dressmaking. One of her pupils was a beautiful 18 year old called Golda, with whom my mother became very friendly. She had been one of the orphans found and rescued by my father. Golda introduced my parents to each other, and five years later they were married. Golda was a bridesmaid, and the wedding photo is on the wall of my house.

Extract from "An Episode in the History of the Cape Jewish Orphanage" Written by Jonathan Boiskin

Ochberg had managed to secure helpers; a teacher named Alexander Bobrow, Boris Glasman and his wife, and a Miss Bettman.

Alexander Bobrow, one of Ochberg's helpers, was originally an Analytical Chemist in a sugar factory, but the war had turned him to social work in 1916, and he began to help the Jewish refugees in Pinsk. 'So many children were found,' Bobrow recorded, 'that we soon were obliged to set up three separate orphanages. At first Pinsk was isolated by the fighting and we were thrown almost solely on our own resources. We had neither beds, bedding, nor clothes. I remember using flour bags to make aprons and other garments for the boys and girls.'

Typhus broke out in one of these orphanages, and at one stage Bobrow, in the course of his duties, was compelled to walk through streets in which shells were exploding. Balachou, the notorious Ukrainian fanatic, descended on the city with his gangs and the pogroms they instigated raged for nearly a week. As order was restored, supplies began to arrive.

From the notes of Linda Press Wulf who interviewed Fanny Lockitch (Feyga Schrier)

In charge of *the Pinsk* orphanage was a giant of the Ochberg story, Mr Bobrow, who had been sent by Jewish organizations to Pinsk to help Jewish refugees in 1916, giving up his career as an Analytical Chemist in a sugar factory. He was put in charge of three orphanages in Pinsk working with virtually no beds, bedding, food, clothes, or coal. At one point they made large aprons and other garments out of flour bags. A German Jewish welfare organization and then the Joint Distribution Committee were eventually able to send some supplies; cocoa, condensed milk, cooking oil.

When Mr. Ochberg finally gathered his 200 orphans, having spent three hazardous months travelling "through almost every village in the Polish Ukraine and Galicia, etc," Mr Bobrow accompanied him in taking care of the orphans on the way to South Africa, and he remained in South Africa for many years.

Isaac Ochberg didn't know all the languages there. Although the First World War was over and the Russian Revolution was over, the fighting went on and the forests were infested with bandits and he went into the deep forests. He didn't know where he was going and believe me, if we did not get together and notice all that and we said to daddy Ochberg, you are not going that way, and we begged the people that were helping him to engage somebody who knew the languages and we engaged a man. His name was Bobrov. He spoke seven different languages, seven languages spoken in Russia. He died in England at the age of 89 years.

He left from here to England afterwards. He used to play the ukelele, I'll never forget it, to us to sleep on the boat because a lot of the children used to get sea sick so that's how he used to get us to sleep.

LETTERS FROM ORPHANS AND COLLEAGUES LEFT BEHIND IN THE PINSK ORPHANAGES

Liebe Klug has exercise books, given to her father, from the three Pinsk Orphanages from which Ochberg Orphans were selected. These are exercise books with messages from the children and colleagues left behind.

These booklets are very special as many of the children would have perished in the Holocaust just 20 years later. Here are some of the letters.

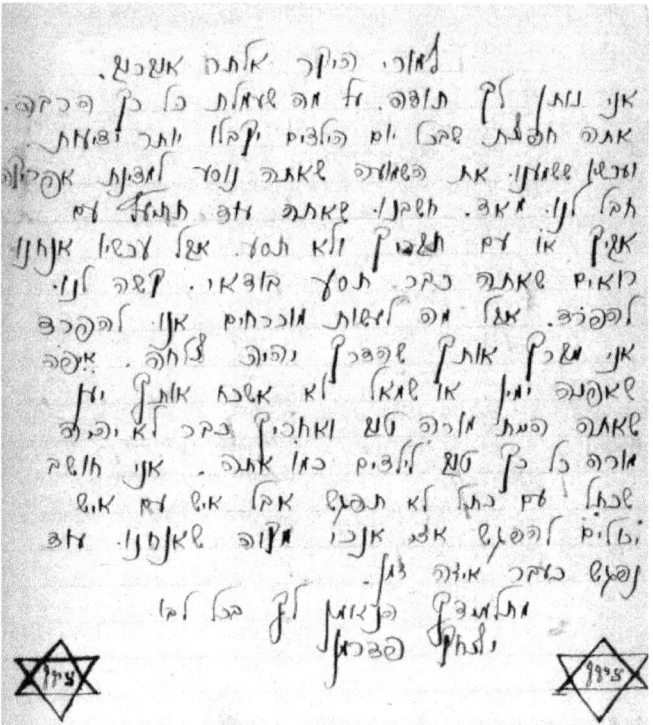

To my dear teacher Alter Abrov

I give my thanks to you for working so hard. You always wanted the children to acquire more and more knowledge every day and now we have heard that you are going to Africa. We are very sorry. We thought that you might still discuss things with your father and friends and would not go. But now we know for sure that you are going away.

It is difficult to say goodbye but what can we do – we have to say goodbye. I bless you and wish you a good trip.

Wherever I shall turn to the right or to the left, I will never forget you and will never find a teacher as good as you.
I think that one wall with another wall will never meet. But one person with another person has a chance to meet. So I hope that one day we shall meet.

Yours faithfully [with all my heart]
Student Itzhak Federman

HAVE COURAGE BE STRONG FREEDOM LIVE

To the teacher A Abrov who's going to Africa with our brothers and sisters   Cheers cheers cheers

A farewell from the Hashomer Hatsair Movement in Pinsk

The Second Orphanage Rosenberg

Translated by Danny Lasker

To the teacher Abrov

Dear Teacher, it is impossible to express in simple words the feeling I have in my heart while writing this letter.

I send you my greatest thanks and gratitude for taking an interest in our children.

As I am writing this letter I wish I had wings and could fly with you to far away Africa.

Dear teacher, you are aware of our bitter situation. Your face will always be in front of my eyes and your words will – like pearls – ring in my ears. May you live a long life. I wish you a good and blessed journey and I wish and hope that you will always be a father to unhappy orphans.
From me   Yehudith Wurman

Honourable teacher and best head master, when you were here with us we knew we had someone to care for us. But now when the time has come and you are saying goodbye to all our children you can imagine, dear headmaster, how horrible we feel in our heart. We feel even worse than before we first came to the orphanage.

We know well who established the orphanage. First G-d, then you together with Mr Goldsman. It is well known that no one was interested in the fate of the miserable suffering orphans. But G-d had pity on the poor lonely souls and sent two angels from heaven to help the unhappy orphans. It was a terrible time; no person wanted to go out into the street, the frost burnt like fire, the winds were howling and no one had pity on our orphans. Only two men had pity on us. They brought us back to life.

The streets were dangerous, bullets were flying over head and few people came to the orphanage, but the teachers Mr Abrov and Mr Goldsman were fearless, they ran around in an effort to bring something to put in the mouths of the unhappy orphans in order to save them from hunger and keep their poor souls alive.

We are deeply grateful for everything you have done for us. We wish you a good trip and everything you wish for yourself.

Before we were taken into the orphanage we were swimming in deep water with no shore in sight no one had pity on us only two men, Mr Abrov and Mr Holsman and saved us from death.

And now the day has come when we have to say goodbye you can quite well imagine how terrible we feel. If we had a problem we came for advice to our best friend but now that you depart we feel so terribly sad and so bitter.

We trust that when you arrive safely to your destination you will plead for us. We wish you a good trip and arrive safely, in good health.

Remember us
from me Ceril Supoznik
To our most faithful headmaster
Alten Abrov
5 July 1921

Translated by Rifka Gabbay

In remembrance. To my friend and teacher. I wish you a successful journey. I express to you from the depths of my heart the wish that you should reach the goal that you strive for in good health and happiness.

Now, teacher, you are going away from us, but we remain like a ship without a rudder. You were our total comfort when our hearts were filled with great pain and when the teacher used to come to us we felt that you were our own father. From your good comforting words which you used to say to us, and also the happiness which you used to give us, in order to quieten us.

Now we don't know in what sort of situation we will be.
Most certainly, if you were still to remain, you would comfort the unhappy orphans who don't have anyone to turn to.

Now there has come such a bitter time for us, when they are sending us out of the orphanage, and where should we go?

We are swimming in the middle of the water and we can't reach the side.

We beg that you shouldn't forget us wherever you may be.

We thank you very much, dear teacher, that you protected us till now. If not for you, and America, long may they live, we would have perished long ago.

Now I end my writing.
Stay well and have a successful journey.
From me
Basha Rochel Levitan - 5 July 1921

Translated by Bella Golubchik

A letter to the teacher Abrov

Dear Teacher

Before you started to teach, everything was strange for me; the benches, the walls, the tables, the blackboard, even the teachers were a strange phenomena for me. But when I started to learn, I began to see the beauty, the joy and the sense of all things. I began to understand what a teacher is and to give respect and love to you.

Now you are going, my dear kind teacher, to a faraway country and it is difficult for me because of my closeness to you.

I am sure you will remember us boys and girls who spent happy times with you at school and you will remember me, your pupil who respects you very much

Nehamia Hetzler

We won't forget you our kind teacher Alter Abrov

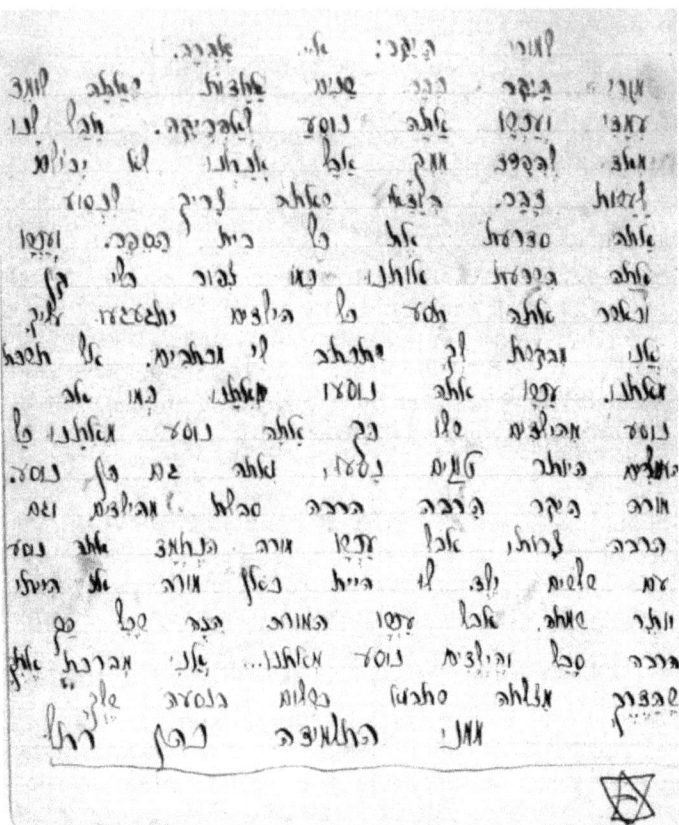

To my dear teacher A Abrov

Dear Teacher

You have taught us for many years and now you are going away to Africa. We are really sorry to say goodbye to you, but that is how it is. We can't change things. You have to leave. You, who have established the whole school, you are leaving us. We feel like a bird without a nest. All the children will miss you very much.

Please write to us and don't forget us. You are going away and we feel as if a father is leaving his children.

The good teachers have left and now you are also going.

Dear teacher you have suffered a lot from the children. You had a lot of trouble and now you are going together with 30 children.

If you stayed here I would be much happier and now the teacher who suffered so much from the children is going away.

I wish you a good trip and a safe arrival at your destination.

From me, your student

Rachel Cohen

Translated by Rifka Gabbay

OBITUARY OF ALEXANDER (ALTER) BOBROW

HE BROUGHT 160 ORPHANS TO SOUTH AFRICA
Zionist Record and South African Jewish Chronicle
Friday September 23 1983
From Dr Aaron Klug, Cambridge, England (1)

Alexander Bobrow, who died n Bournemouth recently, a week before his 90th birthday, was well known in Jewish educational circles in South Africa, but perhaps the greatest contribution he made to the community was his work to rescue children orphaned and abandoned in Bylorussia in the turmoils of the First World War and the Russian Revolution.

Bobrow was born in Pinsk in 1893, and after studying at a yeshivah, received a Russian University education, from which he graduated in 1915, as an industrial chemist and worked outside the Pale of Settlement in his profession. Returning to Pinsk in 1917 he he found starvation and typhoid epidemics and homeless children living in ruins. He took the initiative with a few friends to gather up the orphans and to open up a home in a disused Talmud Torah, where they could be sheltered, given whatever food could be found, and eventually educated.

By 1919 there were three orphanages with 500 children and aid began to come in from the American Joint Distribution Committee. Since the prospects for the orphans were bleak, the JDC sought to provide homes for them in other countries, notably America, England and Palestine (as it was).

In 1921, Alexander Bobrow took a party of 160 children, to South Africa, of whom half went to Cape Town and half to Johannesburg, where a new orphanage was established.

After the children were settled, Bobrow continued in the field of Hebrew education, and eventually became principal of various Hebrew Schools in the Witwatersrand, before returning to Cape Town in 1942. Here, he and his wife, formerly Annie Gamsu, as principal and matron, built up the first Jewish Boarding School, largely for children from the small Jewish Communities of the country districts.

After his wife's death in 1968, Mr Bobrow went to England to live with his only daughter, Liebe Klug, in Cambridge.

On his blindness, he moved in 1975 to the Dolly Ross home in Bournemouth of the Jewish blind society where he became a leading figure. He bore his disability with stoicism, cheered the sick, gave impromptu concerts on his mandolin, officiated at Sabbath services and led the singing at Sederim. Only 10 days before his death he organised and conducted a Yom Ha'Altzmaut ceremony.

Mr Bobrow was a many faceted man. He had a knowledge of Hebrew and Russian literature, and a love for Yiddish, which led him to become a founder-member of the South African Cultural Federation to whose monthly magazine 'Dorem Afrika' he contributed translations of Bialik and Pushkin. He translated Russian poems into telling English and WB Yeats into Russian and Yiddish.

Although by background a Maskil he was by temperament a Chosid, full of optimism which combined with a natural authority made him a leader who devoted his talents to the service of his fellow man.

Note 1
Sir Aaron Klug OM HonFRMS PRS (born 11 August 1926) is a Lithuanian-born British chemist and married Liebe, the daughter of Alter Bobrow. Aaron was the winner of Nobel prize in chemistry in 1982.

Copy of the news cutting that is retyped in full above

Chapter 17 – THE THREE PINSK ORPHANAGES

This chapter is copied from the website set up by Brian Fine www.ochbergorphans.com with his permission. Brian's father Jack Feinschmidt, was an Ochberg Orphan. I understand that most of the information in this chapter is from Liebe Klug, Alexander Bobrow's Daughter.

Alexander (Alter) Bobrow, a true hero of the Jewish People, established three orphanages in Pinsk and it was from these orphanages that Isaac Ochberg selected some of the children that he brought out to South Africa.

The Chief Rabbi of the British Empire declared:
" 1,000,000 human beings had been butchered and that for three years 3,000,000 persons in the Ukraine had been made 'to pass through the horrors of hell.' He said there were something like 600,000 homeless children, 150,000 orphans and 35,000 double orphans in the Ukraine who would die from cold, hunger or disease unless Jewish hearts remained human and came to the rescue."

PINSK 1917.

The year was 1917. The towns of the Pale of Settlement suffered from repeated incursions of White Russia Troops and Red Russia forces and was now occupied by the German army. Pinsk was cut off from the outside world.

Alexander Bobrow, known to friends as Alter was returning home to visit his family in Pinsk from the sugar estate where he worked as an analytical Chemist.

As he travelled nearer to his home town he could see far and wide, how streets, homes and buildings had been razed to the ground. In the rubble he could see little figures moving, sitting or lying. Not trusting what he saw, he got down from the bus and walked through the devastation to his home.

ESTABLISHING THREE ORPHANAGES

Alter belonged to a Poale Zion Group and on his initiative, and at his insistence and with his example, they all left their jobs to help.

Their big task was to walk from place to place and area to area, literally collecting children one by one from the wreckage which was their homes. Many had seen their parents, and in some cases, their entire families killed before their eyes.

Alexander Bobrow with a group of orphans

Once they were all assembled, it was obvious that without exception the children were starving. With the generous help of the townspeople, a soup kitchen was started, to feed the children. Once regularly fed the next question was what to do with them? The answer was, to start a school.

The next question, where could the children sleep? Back in the rubble of their homes? No, of course not. The group commandeered a disused Old Aged Home and found beds in an empty hospital. The building was cleaned and disinfected. The first Pinsk Orphanage received their children

Within two years there were three orphanages in Pinsk alone. You see, the story of the Ochberg Orphans, is not complete. There is another story, an earlier story. Most of these stories came to me from either orphans or their saviours as I think of them. My father was Alter Bobrow, and he rarely talked of this remarkable endeavour. However many of the Poale Zion Group made Aliyah to Israel. One Rachel Bramsonrecca recalled the dedication of this group, and said that it was the spiritually strong leaders that were able to keep them all relational. They literally parented the children.

TYPHOID

They fed the children, clothed them, taught them and nursed them when an epidemic of Typhoid struck the area. Alter was there night and day. He never left the building and napped on two chairs put together. There were no free beds.

Eventually he succumbed to the illness and went home to be nursed by his mother.

The children were devastated and they panicked that he might die as did their parents. So a plan was devised. All the children, with a step ladder went to Alter's family's home. His bedroom was in the attic. Then one by one each child climbed the ladder to peep in at the window where Alter lay in bed. To each one he waved. The children were reassured that Alter, as they called him, was alive.

When Alter returned, the children were overjoyed and showed it by making a circle and dancing around him singing Alter, Alter, Alter. And he, as was his way played the mandolin to them as they danced and sang together.

THE JOURNEY

Events then took an unexpanded turn and Alter was asked to accompany the children selected by Isaac Ochberg to go to South Africa.

In fact, the Orphanages Committee would only allow the children to leave if Alter accompanied them. Of course no one wanted him to leave; not his family, not the children or his colleagues. Notwithstanding their pleading he decided to go to Cape Town with the chosen children.

The children who were not chosen to go to South Africa with him, expressed their feelings in notes and drawings in three black school exercise books.

A MEETING ON THE SEA POINT PROMENADE
Written by Liebe Klug, Alexander Bobrow's Daughter

Many years ago, when I was on a visit to Cape Town following the death of my mother, my father and I were walking one evening on the Sea Point promenade.

A middle aged man came up to us and said. "You don't know me do you'?" My father said that he had no idea who he was.

I will quote you what this man said. "I was one of the orphans you saved, and I was one of the children chosen to go to Cape Town."

"I will never forget that journey. We were travelling by train to Danzig. The train stopped at stations on the way. At each station we were greeted by the Jews of the town with food and flowers. We the children got down from the train. Alter took his mandolin and together with the townspeople we all sang and danced together on the platform."

Whether this is the exact picture of the events we will never know. But what remains in this man's memory is that the journey was made a joyous one for the children.

POST CARD ALTER WROTE TO HIS PARENTS THE NIGHT BEFORE HE LEFT PINSK.

My dearest parents,

Forgive me if I have caused you heart break. I am not responsible that my thoughts are not your thoughts.
Do not worry that I am going away. I am travelling. on a great and important mission. I hope that I will still have the possibility to repay you for all the good things that you have done for me.
Have no regrets over your son, who is devoted to you with his whole heart.

Alter

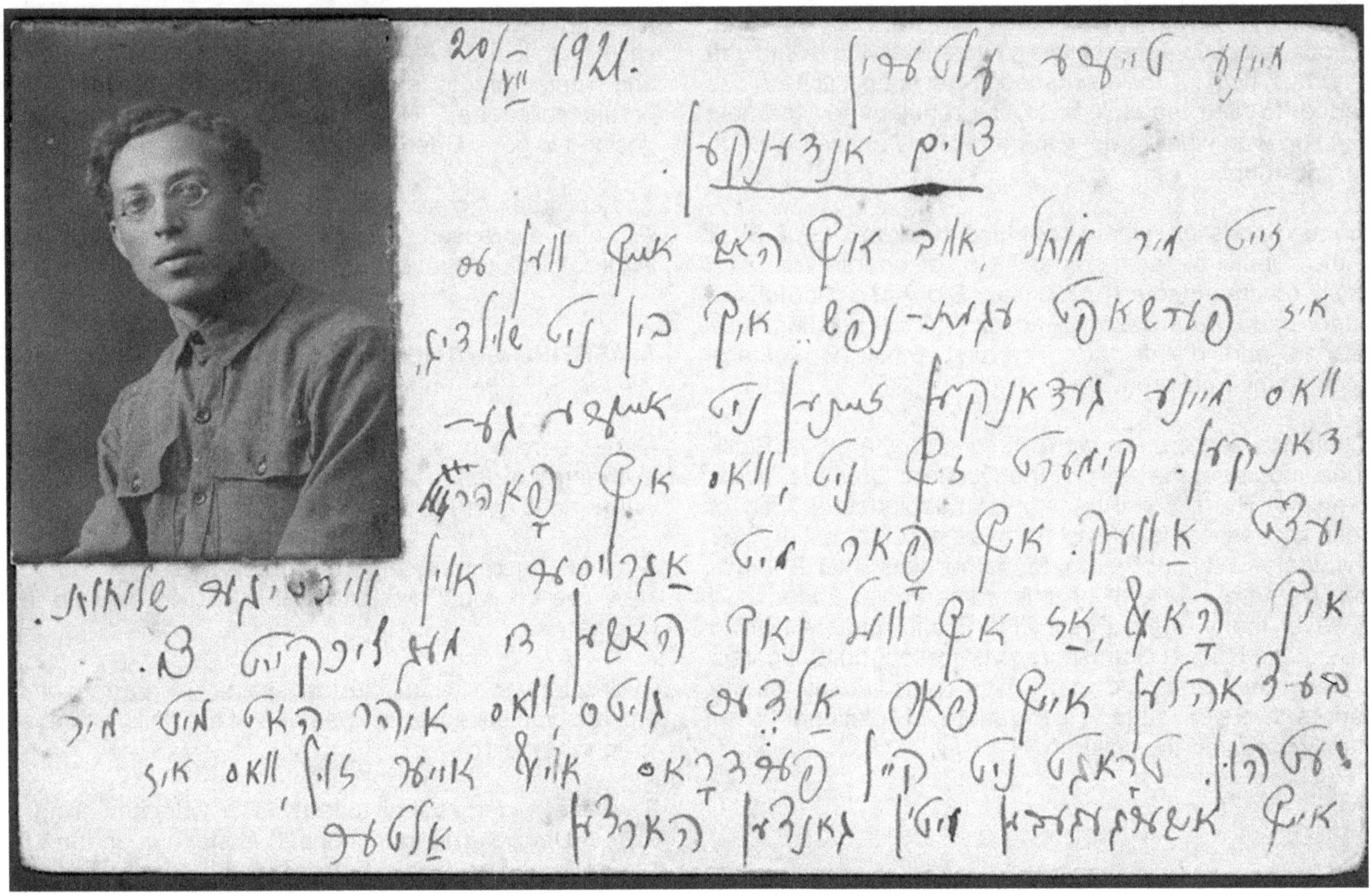

Alter wrote this farewell postcard to his parents the night before he left Pinsk,.

TWO OF THE LETTERS FROM THE EXERCISE BOOKS WRITTEN TO ALTER BY THE CHILDREN WHO REMAINED BEHIND.

Postcard from Shaska Dawidowsky

To Teacher Abrav –

Dearest teacher in memory

In the last days before your travel away you brought all the orphans together. You don't know what an impression you made on us. God knows when we will see you again. When you are gone what will happen to us?

You have taken us out of the water and now we are back in the water.

Dear teacher you have been like a teacher and Father for two years that you were with us.

We have thrived like a plant and now we only hope that we will continue to thrive.

I wish you 'lucky' safe trip from me.

**Shaska Dawidowsky
Year 1921**

Postcard from Zeta Dawidowsky

I'm writing in 'memory' (souvenir) to you.

Teacher I hope you travel in peace, but dear teacher I'm writing to say I'm sorry you are going.

You are like a Father but you have also built the school and the orphanage and you are also our teacher.

I know you have not slept or often not eaten for our sake.

How hard it was to separate from our teacher and 'benevolent' Father.

Sorry that you are leaving, but what can we do?

We will not forget you in all our days. I can't write as well as my learning is not enough. I'm sorry.

But dear teacher and Principal Mr Abrav whom I love more than ever.

**From me Zeta Davidowsky
In the Year 1921**

The letters were written in Yiddish and Hebrew and have been translated by octogenarian Old Arc Boys; the late Eli Zagoria, an artist of Perth and Michael Perry Kotzen an actor of Sydney.

Chapter 18 – REMEMBERING THE PINSKER ORPHANS LEFT BEHIND

PINSK

Pinsk, was the town in which Alexander Bobrow and his Zionist socialist friends established three orphanages and it is the second major town from which Isaac Ochberg collected 44 children.

Pinsk is the capital of Pinsk Oblast, Belorussian SSR. Originally, in the sixteenth century, it was a Russian-Orthodox town and capital of a semi-independent principality

The Jewish population was 17,513 in 1921, 75% of the town's population. In the town there was a clash between Hasidism and Mitnaggedim from the early eighteenth century onwards and it became a transit centre for trade between south-western Russia and the Baltic ports. *(1)*

In April 1919, at the beginning of the Polish-Soviet War, 35 Jews from Pinsk were murdered by Polish soldiers, in an incident known as the Pinsk massacre. The Poles suspected them of being Bolshevik collaborators. This event created a diplomatic incident that was noted at the Versailles Conference.

Pinsk became part of Poland in 1920 after the Polish-Soviet War and was occupied by the Soviet Union in 1939. At this time, the city's population was over 90% Jewish.

Until the Second World War and the Holocaust, like many other cities in Europe, Pinsk had a significant Jewish population: according to Russian census of 1897, out of the total population of 28,400, Jews constituted 21,100 (so around 74% percent), making it one of the most Jewish cities in the Eastern Europe.

From 1941 to 1944, Pinsk was under Nazi Germany. In 1939, the population of Pinsk totalled 30,000, of whom 27,000 were Jews. Most of them were killed in late October 1942, after their deportation by the Nazis from the Pinsk ghetto. Ten thousand were murdered in one day. Since the collapse of the Soviet Union in 1991 Pinsk has belonged to the Republic of Belarus.

The names listed on the right hand side of this page were translated by Eli Zagoria from the names listed below in Yiddish on the back of the photo of the children on page 99. Names marked ? are not clear.

(1) Gloria Sandak-Lewin, the daughter of Simon Sandak-Lewin, in her poem about her father "My Father's House" has the above definition of Pinsk in the notes to her poem. Her source was Enc. Jud., 'Pinsk', by Mordekhai Nadav; and Everyman's Judaica, ed. Wigoder. P. 480.

Following is a list of the children left behind in two of the three orphanages established by Alexander (Alter) Bobrow and his comrades in Pinsk.

THE CHILDREN FROM PINSK ORPHANAGE ONE

**In remembrance of the children of Orphanage One, who are travelling to Africa.
Stamped: Beys Yesoymim, (Orphanage) Pinsk.**

Mindel Merzel	Bracha Trushkin	Dvorah Lev
Bashe Rachel?	Sarah Trushkin	Fasha Lev.
Lichtan	Trina? Dan?	Miryam Knovits
Shmuel Lichtan	Feigal Tsarl	Moshe Dubovsky
? Elman Yosef	Leah Rufershtein	Chana Rivka Litvin
? Mental Frozinski	Rania Levin	? Safanznik
Mordechai Levin	Lev Debranshka	Rachel Safanznik
	Malka Litvin	Chana Lichtinson
	Fridel Kagan	Dina Kaplan
	Ruzi Kmshtein	Yochbad Kantsfleski
	Ginl Zavodinkov	Yitshak Gunzer
	? Rubara?	Rashke Rubin
	Chava Fridel	Fellta Feldman
	Klempert	Nata Shulman
	Leah Dorfman	Rosa Tshiz
	Rafel Dorfman	Toybel Safolznik
	Bashra Rubinshtein	Dvorah Dolinki
	Abraham ?	Chana Lichton
	Bashe? ?	Miriam Epstein
	Gushagot Shabat?	Shindel Golshmit?
	? Shabat?	Zlata ?
	? Shabat?	Gitel ?
		Chaya Gute ?

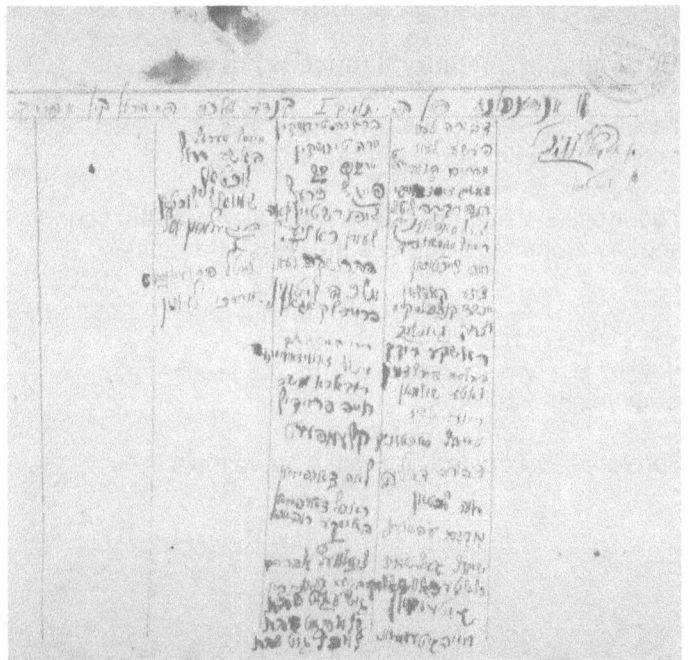

*Children and staff from Pinsk Orphanage One
-see names on prior page*

*Children and staff from Pinsk Orphanage Two - Photo taken in 1921 or prior
On the back of this photo is a list of all the children - see pages 64 and 65
-see list following*

THE CHILDREN FROM PINSK ORPHANAGE TWO

In remembrance.
For the Children who are being adopted (taken) to Cape Town, Africa.
From the management, employees and children of Orphanage Two, Pinsk.

Rivka ?	Leibel Lamish	1	Moshe Avizonshtein	Asher Kantor	Asher Bantshik
Yacov	Hene Lubashavsky	2	Nachum Avizonshtein	Yacov Leviton	Gershon Luria
David Rubin	Mirle Mailin	3	Motil Eizenberg	Asher Mashal	Genia Luria
Yente Rubin	Elke Melamed	4	Leah Izluk	Dov Silberman	Izik Friedman
? Shteinberg	Tova Migdalovits	5	Sheindol Aranov	Necham Borman	Harshel Friedman
	Moshe Faladavonik	6	Chaim Bammel	Michael Relznesi	Regina Rabinomit
	Chashar Fagelevits	7	Feigel Bammel	Avigdor Gotlieb	Malkia Rubin
	Gdala Epshtein	8	Shachar Bregman	Eliezer Kagan	Torpak
	Galda Epshtein	9	Hershil Bregman	Yakov Tomsky	Liodzinsky
	Chaim Sheme Pinsker	10	Baruch Bregman	Daniel Tarantsa	Yosef Feldman
	Otke Pinsker	11	Kalman Bergman	Benzalel Beliak	Yacob Telman
	Nechama Portnoy	12	Label Belozavski	Luby Lidvinsky	Yacob Helshtein
	Yehudit Fikman	13	Hillel Bakaltovich	Dov Portnoy	
	Rubin Fikman	14	Nramia Basalitz	Yehuda Gelfond	Personal
	? Fazitsky	15	Moshe Grets	Shmuel Chaim Gorbooz	Shevach Kantor
	? Fazitsky	16	Esther Grets	Vair Dorfman	Nechama Helper
	Piltchik	17	Rachel Grooshka	Chira Levin	Breshge Gefy
	Itshak Abraham Fritman	18	Feivish Dalinka	Arye Tsifarshtein	Toybe Kosol
	? Plotnik	19	Masha Dllaron	Arye Zuberman	Shepshge Bragton
	Miriam Tsoofershtein	20	Fina Haltsman	Aharon Ruchalnki	Tina Rubin
	Seindil Tsoofershtein	21	Mile Vegman	Sara Zuberman	Tina Zil
	Itshak Tsoofershtein	22	Leah Vaks	Fesh Bashevits	Rachel Koosk
	Arye Tsoofershtein	23	Zisl Vonik	Zlota Knorvats	Sarah Raskot
	Toybel Tsoofershtein	24	Chana Dingman	Golda Libshovsky	Aharon Kaperplinski
	Chava Tsnovats	25	Malka Zilberman	Henia Shifon	?
	Leibel Kushner	26	Chaya Rimski	Rivka Bokliar	?
	Aharon Mosel Klempert	27	Chana Toranda	Yehudit Varman	
	Shmuel Katsenelson	28	Rivka Teitelbaum	Nechama Portnoy	
	Elke Katsenelson	29	Chaim Torkin	Chaya Yerlansky	
	Sarah Cosmonisim	30	Fruma Yerlinkski	Henia Kagan	
	Gishel Koodnats	31	Chaya Menasha		
	Nechama Kole ?	32	Moshe Lydrok		
	Bashke Knoosolnits	33	Mendel Tsutski		
	Abraham Knoosolnits	34	Tsat Liberman	Harosh: P. Kantor	
			Fridol Liberman	The Headmaster	
			Yosel Liberman		

The names listed were translated by Eli Zagoria from the names listed below in Yiddish on the back of the photo of the children on the next page.
Names Items marked ? are not clear.

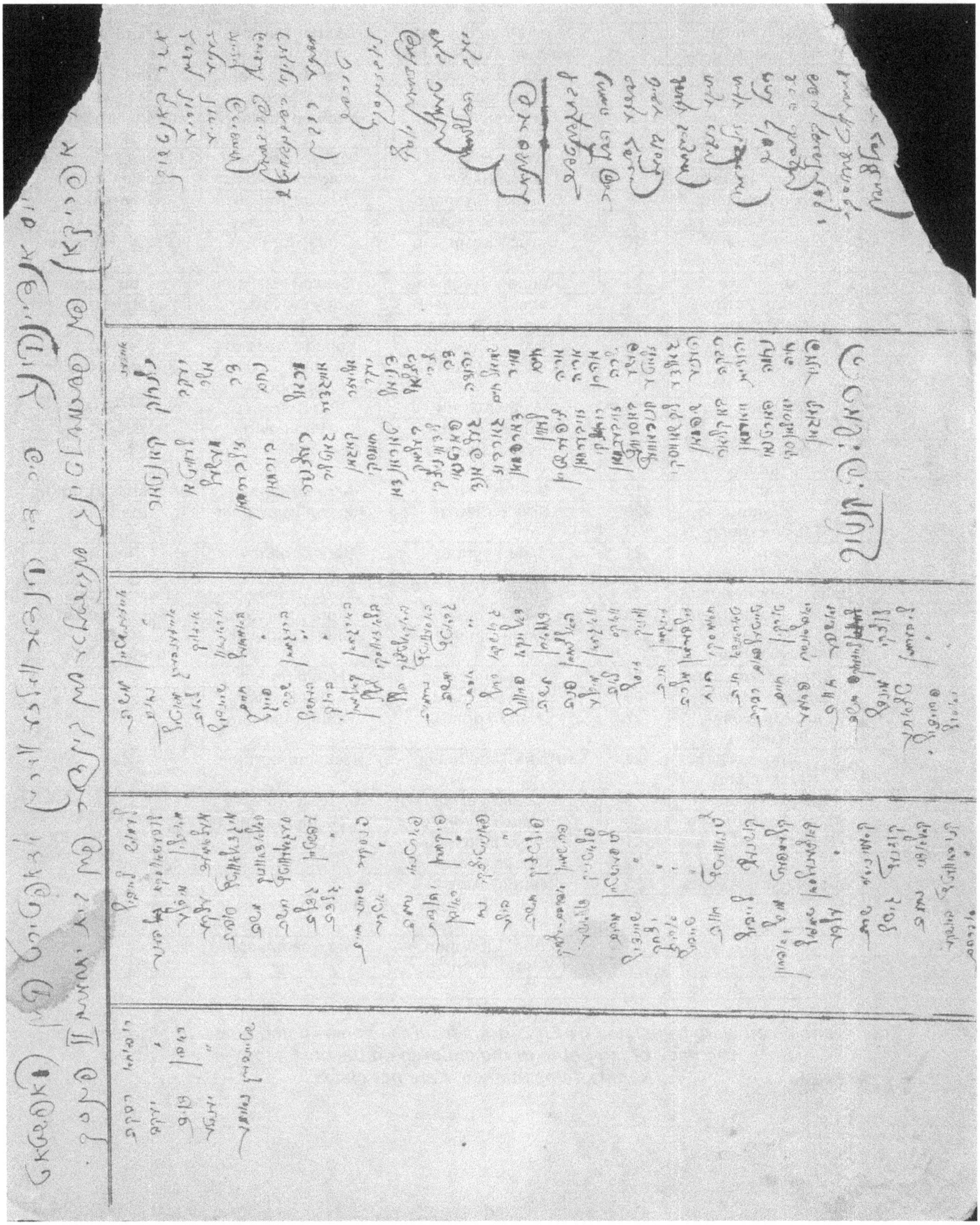

Children and staff from one of the Pinsk Orphanages

SECTION 4

THE PINSKER ORPHAN RELIEF FUND OF LONDON

This section commences with
the history of the three Pinsk Orphanages
and the history of the Fund.

It tells of the support given by the Fund to
the three Pinsk Orphanages and of
the 19 children who in 1924 and the 34 children in 1926
were brought to London for adoption.

This section was written by John Cooper in his article
THE WORK OF THE PINSKER ORPHANS
RELIEF FUND OF LONDON 1921-1936.
It is printed with the permission of Jewish Historical Studies.
Documents and translations are courtesy of John Cooper

Chapter 19 – THE JEWISH ORPHANAGES IN PINSK

***Written by John Cooper in his article* THE WORK OF THE PINSKER ORPHANS RELIEF FUND OF LONDON 1921-1936** *Printed with the permission of Jewish Historical Studies*

After the 1912-18 War, Eklyohu Holtzman, a wealthy businessman, opened the first Jewish orphanage in Pinsk, utilising an old school building, but his initial efforts were supplemented by philanthropists who established two more orphanages. One was an institution founded by the Bundists which soon collapsed, the other was an orphanage also known as the Rayoner Orphanage which had an intake of children from the villages and small towns surrounding Pinsk. When the Bundists closed their orphanage, some of the children were sent to the Rayoner Orphanage, where they had to sleep on the floor for a time, as there was a shortage of beds. By 1923 only the first orphanage founded by Holtzman with a Zionist and moderately religious orientation remained in being. Holtzman was ably assisted by Zeev Lev, who had formerly been a bank clerk, but who had gradually worked his way up to the position of secretary of the orphanage; and earlier by Aaron Dubrovsky, a brilliant teacher and a cultured individual, who was also a notable platform orator. He had already achieved some success in the Tarbut school movement in Russia which was secular in outlook but Zionist in orientation and which used Hebrew as its language of instruction. Dubrovsky was a successful manager of the orphanage, where he coped with the perpetual crisis in its finances by drastically curtailing the number of children under its care. We can best see this shrinkage in numbers from a return compiled by the Joint in October 1921 which gave as 408 the number of children in orphanages in Pinsk, but group photographs of the children taken in 1924 and 1926 show that their numbers had dropped to 79 and 84 children respectively. Owing to the shortage of accommodation, most of the youngest children aged between one and six years could not be taken into the orphanage, but these children were boarded out with the poorer Jewish families in Pinsk, where according to the orphanage staff, they acquired bad habits which could not be corrected later.

How did the children come to enter the orphanages in Pinsk? We know something of the individual circumstances of the families both from the accounts of the former orphans and there is also a series of short biographical sketches of certain children which have survived. One family from Pinsk was totally disrupted by the War. The father, who was a blacksmith, joined a labour detachment and was ordered to cut down trees for the Russian army and died prematurely, causing his wife to die in turn, of a broken heart. A son, who was conscripted into the Russian army at the age of 15 years, was badly frozen in a campaign and had both legs amputated which resulted in his early death. Of the five children who survived, the eldest girl brought up her younger sisters, although she later died of tuberculosis, and the three youngest children entered the orphanage. This was a common pattern. The father was killed or reported missing during the War, the mother was unable to manage on her own and swiftly succumbed herself, after which the children were taken into the orphanage. This is also why Friedel and Aaron Kalmpert and the Dorfman children entered the orphanage. Let us now take a different example; that of the F Family from the shtetl of Lelin which was near to Pinsk. Originally there were five children, but one boy died of influenza following an outbreak of a serious strain of the disease after the War. A little while later his parents died in a typhus epidemic in 1920. For two years their grandfather struggled to bring up the four surviving children before he entrusted them to the care of the orphanage; moreover, so undermined was the health of these other children by the War and the post-War deprivations that two of them eventually contracted tuberculosis, dying as young adults. We also have knowledge of other cases where the children were admitted into the orphanage, after their parents died prematurely of disease. We have a report that not only the parents of Mordechai and Chaya Zucker died of typhus during the War, but that both parents of Moshe Lev had passed away in hospital, possibly from a similar infectious outbreak. The death of parents from starvation was another factor that propelled their children into the orphanage. In the case of the Piekov family it is mentioned that both the father and mother died of hunger, while in the case of another family it is recounted that the father died suddenly when coming out of Court and that the mother perished from hunger.

On 18 July 1923, the secretary of the Holtzman orphanage wrote to the Pinsker Relief organisation in London a letter which fully explains the parlous financial state of the orphanage. This letter is important as it outlines the main sources of its financial support and shows how much of its expenditure was earmarked for necessities like food and clothing. The background to the letter is the French occupation of the Ruhr, the industrial centre of Germany, at the beginning of 1923, the collapse of the German economy, and the hyper-inflation which blazed throughout Eastern Europe.

'We confirm herewith the receipt of the £50 which we received from your Relief Centre', wrote Ze'ev Lev. 'This money we have spent specifically on food. It is not a pleasant task to tell you news like we are passing on to you now about the level of our newly created difficult financial position due to the upheaval caused by the new foreign currency boom. In May our monthly budget reached $700 or 105 million marks ... 15% of our budget we receive from your Relief Centre and the American one. The remaining 35% equalling 12 million marks and certainly not the cost of the additional increases. As we have indicated to you, the receipts from the Joint also do not cover their normal 50% contribution, and now as declared by the Joint, the Joint will only remain active till the 1st of January! Such luck we have! We cannot recover from the War situation.... In order to escape from the situation it is absolutely necessary to buy up products for the next three months - August, September, October. For this purpose, it would be easiest if you were to subsidise us with a once only subsidy of £100 for the next three months... If you could obtain this... from your landslayt, please request from them as well something towards the winter and for the children to have shoes made, also socks and for some children dresses and suits.'

THE LETTER FROM THE JEWISH ORPHANAGES IN PINSK to THE PINSKER ORPHANS RELIEF FUND IN LONDON - 18 July 1923

Honoured Gentlemen

We confirm herewith the receipt of the £50 which we received from your Relief Centre. This money we have spent specifically on food. It is not a pleasant task to tell you news like we are passing on to you now, about the level of our newly created difficult financial position, due to the upheaval caused by the new [foreign] currency boom. From a distance you are certainly aware, that we are now living through a difficult situation in general, so in private life one rides with the book, but a community institution cannot in any way cover the budget. In May our monthly budget reached $700 - about 35 million marks and in June $700 or 105 millions. We obtained our requirements in marks - 50% we receive from the Joint in marks according to the budget drawn up a month ago, ie when it was supposed to cost 35 million, but then the true reality arrives and supersedes so that June costs 105 millions. This raises the question of an increase from the Joint, they discuss the increases for such a long time, when will they stop? This is how it unexpectedly happened that our deficits and rather poor prospects have been created. This means that the Joint still owes us the increase of 5 million marks from the previous month which had then a value of $100 - so even if the Joint were to repay us the 5m marks now it would only amount to $33. 15% we receive from your Relief centre and the American one. The remaining 35% we have to obtain ourselves. In May this reached a figure of 12 million and at today's rate 40 million marks. Despite our greatest efforts we could not have covered the normal 35% - 12 million and certainly not the cost of the additional increases. As we have indicated to you, the receipts from the Joint also do not cover their normal 50% [contribution] and now as declared by the Joint, the Joint will only remain active till 1 January! Such luck we have! We cannot recover from the war situation. All other projects and hopes encounter the rises and the falls, obstacles of such a kind we have never previously seen nor heard. In order to escape from the situation it is absolutely necessary to buy up products for the next three months August September October. For this purpose, it would be the easiest if you were to subsidise us with a once-only subsidy of £100 for the next three months. Perhaps you would be in a position to lend us such a sum? If you could obtain this in the course of the coming three months, from your compatriots, please request from them as well something towards the winter and for the children who need to have shoes made, for socks and for some children for dresses and suits. Please convene your committee and they should turn yet again to your compatriots about the once-only subsidy, for food and clothes. Please pass on to your compatriots our heartfelt thanks for their devotion and willingness to lead the children to a goal. Please let us also know what happened to the project to take the 30 children over and what you decided.

In expectation of your answer, I remain respectfully yours,

R Rabinowits
On behalf of the Centre
Signed by: The Manager

Stamped by the Secretary the Central Administration of the Jewish Orphanage

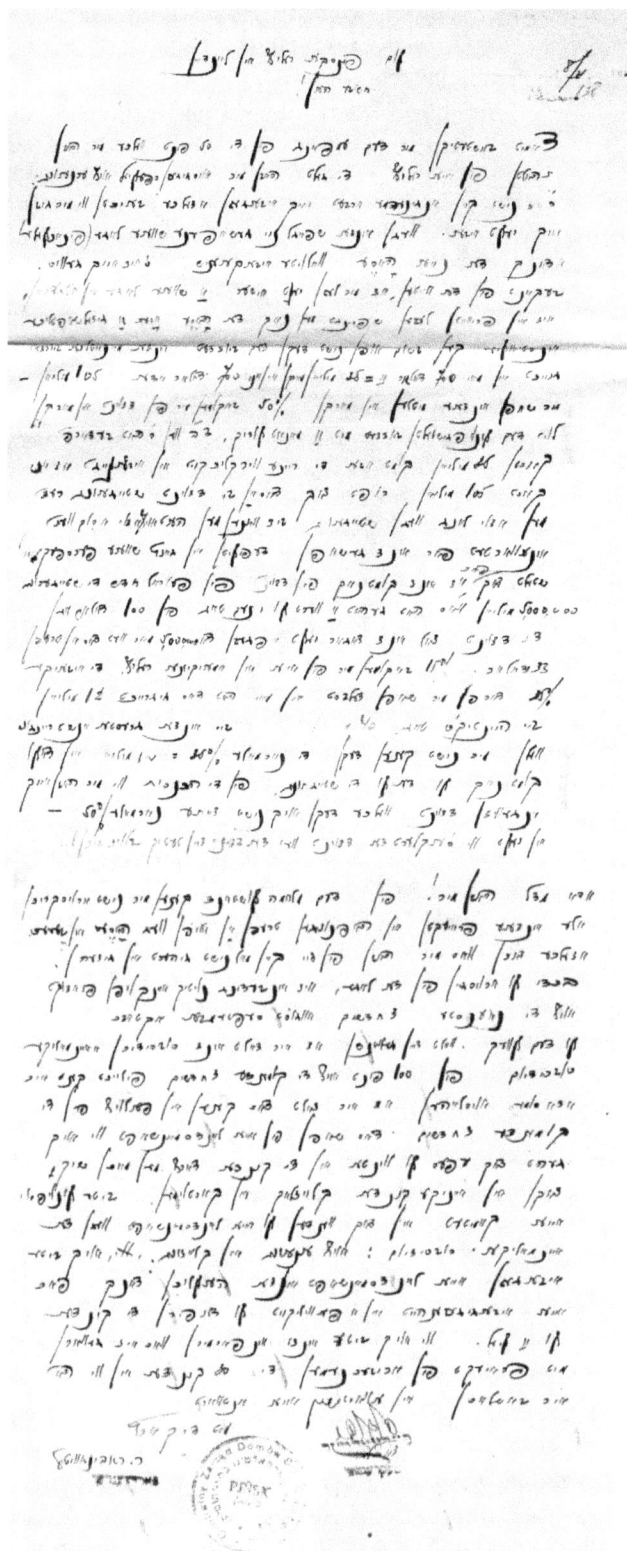

Letter in Yiddish above and translation opposite

courtesy John Cooper

***THE WEEK OF HELP FOR THE ORPHANS APPEAL TO ALL THE BUSINESS PEOPLE OF PINSK AND ITS SURROUNDINGS** The critical position of the orphanage in Pinsk from the present moment when the support from America fails to get through and it causes a danger for the further existence of the orphanages where 300 orphans are being supported where parents perished during the war. Call upon us to fulfill a citizens obligation and each one should help to the extent of their ability to alleviate this distress. For this purpose was organised the orphans week in Pinsk and to you Jewish business people we turn to you for your help to fulfill your obligations for the orphans.*

After the expulsion of the Bolsheviks from Pinsk, the Joint used their funds to feed 300 refugees, and opened a soup kitchen where between 2 400 and 1 000 children were fed daily until the middle of 1921, when such aid was suspended; and the Joint's efforts were concentrated on ensuring the well-being of the orphans.

Between 1920 and 1928 it has been estimated that the Joint expended $2 388 000 on childcare in Poland. Sometimes financial aid from America failed to reach the orphanages in Pinsk, causing a danger to their existence. This crisis was met by an appeal to the business people of Pinsk and its surroundings. One undated broadsheet, published in 1922 or 1923, mentioned that 'For this purpose orphans' week, the raising of emergency funds, was organised in Pinsk and to you Jewish business people we turn for your help to fulfill your obligations towards the orphans'. There was also a group of wealthy Jewish ladies who regularly visited the children in the orphanage. Later the committee in charge of the orphanage promoted concerts to raise money, while the children from the orphanage under adult direction participated in shows in the town's Yiddish theatre for this purpose. One lady remembers forming part of a human pyramid in a gymnastic display and playing the mandolin as part of this entertainment.

The children in the Holtzman orphanage were expected to look after their rooms and had to clean and polish the wooden floors. One of the girls recalls that there were 26 beds in her dormitory. Like the bulk of the Jewish population in Poland, the children in the orphanages were badly fed and clothed. In the Holtzman orphanage the children were given four slices of bread without butter in the morning which they were supposed to eke out for the whole day, but because of hunger some of them ate everything for breakfast. Otherwise they had to subsist on vegetable soup twice a day. There was no fish or meat. Another lady remembers that the diet at the Rayoner orphanage was more wholesome and varied. For breakfast the children were handed a slice of black bread with margarine. After school at 2.30 pm they lunched on barley soup with a bone, if they were lucky, but with no meat or potatoes, while at 6.30 pm they ate an evening meal, consisting of herring, black bread and tea. On Friday night, they dined on Chalah, a small piece of meat and potato. On the Sabbath for lunch they ate a vegetable cholent without meat. She also recollects that the diet was more sparse at the Holtzman establishment, to which she was later transferred. This lady remembers being frequently hungry in the orphanage and the joy of participating in special expeditions to the orchards in the summer, when she could eat as much fruit as she liked. A gentleman has recounted that the children in one orphanage were so hungry that a few of them raided the dustbins rummaging for scraps of food, but unfortunately three or four of the children contracted typhus or dysentery as a result of this foraging and died. A report of the Joint in January 1922 confirms the essential accuracy of these memories, emphasising the lack of food, heating and clothing in these institutions apart from certain exceptional cases, and describing the children as being filthy and lousy and as subsisting mostly on tea and bread. Conditions in the Holtzman orphanage slowly improved in the 1920s but were always spartan. The children ate all their meals with spoons, and when one girl was provided with a knife and fork in Danzig on her way to Britain, she did not know how to use them. Nor was American aid always properly employed. One lady recalls that the tinned salmon was mixed in their soup and that the cooks were completely baffled by the dehydrated food. Certain more fortunate children visited relatives in Pinsk on the Sabbath, where they would be regaled with tasty morsels or more nutritious food, while others had friends or relatives on the staff of the orphanage who gave them extra portions of food.

At first the clothing of the children in the orphanage was very shoddy. The girls in one orphanage wore dresses made out of sacks; aprons provided by the Red Cross were unstitched and also utilised. Then parcels of clothes with such luxuries as pyjamas and toothbrushes started to arrive from America and Britain; and Mrs Katrinsky, a dressmaker attached to the Holtzman orphanage, whose father had been killed by the Bolsheviks, altered the garments to enable them to fit the individual children. After a few years, the dressmaker made a uniform brown dress for the girls, and each Passover the children were given a new outfit. During the winter the children wore boots, when walking through some of the muddy unpaved streets of Pinsk, widely renowned for its mud, Pinsker blotter, but in the summer the children went about barefooted, although a year before some of them left for England the orphan children were supplied with sandals.

The majority of the children attended Jewish schools, where the language of instruction was either Hebrew or Yiddish, but a few of the brighter children were found places in a Polish gymnasium. One lady remembers that her classmates at the gymnasium were the daughters of the Polish gentry. At one of the Jewish schools, the children were taught everything in Hebrew, including arithmetic and even did their physical training exercises in Ivrit, while they were only given the most meagre instruction in Polish. Whereas the girls received no religious education and synagogue attendance in the Holtzman orphanage was not compulsory, the boys in the orphanage were taught the rudiments of Judaism in a Talmud torah, a religious school usually reserved for orphans, and one of the pupils Leibel Mattos was commended because of his ability of learning a page of Talmud at the age of ten years. After they reached 14 or 15, the children were given a training in a trade, the boys being taught tailoring and shoe-making, although there was one boy who was apprenticed as a locksmith, and the girls were taught dressmaking and millinery, but a few girls no doubt found positions in domestic service. Many of the young men and women were eager to learn and supplemented their education by attending evening classes. Sometimes the children were permitted to stroll in the market square in their free time and look at the shops, sometimes kindly members of the committee supervising the orphanage took them for walks along the banks of the river that ran through the town. At Chanuka and Purim there were concerts arranged for the children in the orphanage; perhaps it was on one such occasion that the famous Cantor Serota from Warsaw sang to the children in the orphanage. As a special treat the children were taken to see a film entitled 'the Ten commandments' with Yiddish sub-titles. When one of the girls was ill, she remembers that she was sent to a convalescent home in the mountains, where the children bathed in the nude as was the Polish custom.

The medical treatment available for the children in the orphanage was inadequate, as there were no dispensaries or doctors willing to treat Jews in Pinsk in 1921. The distinguished journalist Brailsford speaking in 1919 said that when the Jewish doctor in the Pinsk and Brest-Litovsk area died, the Jewish population was devoid of modern medical assistance, as the Polish doctors refused to treat Jews; and a little later when another Jewish doctor opened a surgery in Pinsk, after fleeing from the Bolsheviks, he died after a few months and no replacement could be found. In 1921 and 1922 there were reports that the children in the orphanages were affected by scarlet fever, diptheria and typhus, and in April 1926 it was estimated that 15 per cent of the 150 000 Jewish school children in Poland showed symptoms of tuberculosis with 75 000 cases being registered among the total Polish Jewish population in 1925. Treatment for tuberculosis was rudimentary, but one girl recalls that the cook used to prepare chicken dishes for her sister, who had contracted tuberculosis, and lived in an isolation unit. When the Rayoner orphanage was closed in 1922, children with skin diseases such as scurvy and favus were separated from the other children in the Holtzman orphanage and treated there. One orphanage boasted outhouses with vapour baths which the children utilised once every three months. Otherwise the children were attended to by a male feltsher, a healer practicing folk cures as opposed to Western medical techniques, when they were ill. One lady remembers that the feltsher used to give the girls the traditional bunkas treatment for bronchitis, in which the patients had to lie down while small glasses with lighted candles were placed on their backs, nonetheless, the heat treatment proved to be an effective remedy. Apart from this, the children just stayed in their beds if they were ill, and one girl recovered from an attack of rheumatic fever in this way, without any special medical attention. In June 1922 the committee administering the orphanage, when prodded by the Joint, agreed to provide medical treatment for the children, and although it is known that the Joint implemented an effective health program throughout Poland for the Jewish population, the actual details of the local measures in Pinsk are unknown.

Anti-Semitism in Poland never abated in the inter-War period. In 1922 there was a riot in Minsk in which four Jews were killed and six were wounded, arising out of a ritual murder accusation; and rioting also occurred in the towns of Radom, Vilna, Olsham and Mlava, while blood libel allegations were made against the Jews in Warsaw, Lodz and Vilna. Again in 1923 there were anti-Jewish disturbances in Lemberg and Cracow. In Pinsk a lady recalls a hail of stones banging against the shutters on the windows of her orphanage at Passover. Another lady has recounted that an anti-Semitic group burst into the Holtzman orphanage one evening and entered her dormitory, whereupon one of the teachers asked them to go away, as there were only children in the orphanage.

Chapter 20 – THE PINSKER ORPHANS RELIEF FUND OF LONDON

Written by John Cooper in his article THE WORK OF THE PINSKER ORPHANS RELIEF FUND OF LONDON 1921-1936 Printed with the permission of Jewish Historical Studies

The Pinsker Relief Fund was established by Pinsker Landsleit who had long settled in the East End of London in 1922 with the aim of assisting the orphans in Pinsk. These immigrants, who had settled in London, had detailed knowledge of the tribulations that had recently befallen their kinsmen and friends in Pinsk from two good sources. Four young orphan girls were brought to England in 1921 by their aunt Mrs Franks, a dynamic lady, who told anyone who would listen about the cold and hunger endured by the orphans in Pinsk. Another family, the Zilbermans, whose favoured son had been killed in the Pinsk pogrom of 1919, went to live in Brighton, although they later moved to London where they had relatives; and actively participated in the work of the Fund. After its inception the society failed to flourish and remained few in numbers, as many Pinsker Landsleit were not convinced that it had a useful function to fulfill. What galvanised the society into action was a disastrous fire in Pinsk, probably in the autumn of 1922. The re-industrial shtetlekh and villages in Poland, where many of the buildings were constructed of wood, were frequently ravaged by fires, after which the resultant destitution impelled the young and vigorous sections of the population to leave. Among the Abraham Isenberg papers is a letter of appeal which from internal evidence appears to date from 1922. 'In the name of the Pinsker Relief Fund of London, we come to you with a special warm request', it began, 'that you should be so kind as to ask your congregants tomorrow before the Kol Nidre that they should come to help the Pinsker citizens who have lost all their belongings in a fire. You have surely heard of the great calamity which has happened in the Jewish town of Pinsk. Thousands of families have lost their homes and remained without their livelihood and without a roof over their heads'.

The appeal ended by stating that if anyone had any old clothing to spare for these unfortunate inhabitants they should inform the Jews Temporary Shelter and that arrangements would be made by the fund to collect it from their homes. By March 1922, and perhaps earlier, money was being sent to Pinsk by the Pinsker Relief Fund, as it then styled itself. 'My dear friend', wrote Israel Feldman the Pinsker to Abraham Isenberg, 'I left in your synagogue a postal receipt for the £40 which I sent over to Pinsk the same day for the orphanage. Wishing you a Happy New Year'. There is also in existence a receipt dated 6 July 1921 for the sum of one pound eighteen shillings given by Saul Lourie to Mr Pushkin being the freight charges for sending two boxes of clothes to Pinsk. Clearly the original name of the London organisation and the widespread impoverishment of the inhabitants of Pinsk in 1921 and 1922 indicate that at first the London Fund carried out general relief work and did not devote itself exclusively to the needs of the orphans.

Partly because the finances of the orphanage were always teetering on the brink of disaster, partly because of the squeezing of Jews out of the labour market in Pinsk, the heads of the Holtzman orphanage were determined to reduce the number of children under their care and to settle some of them overseas.

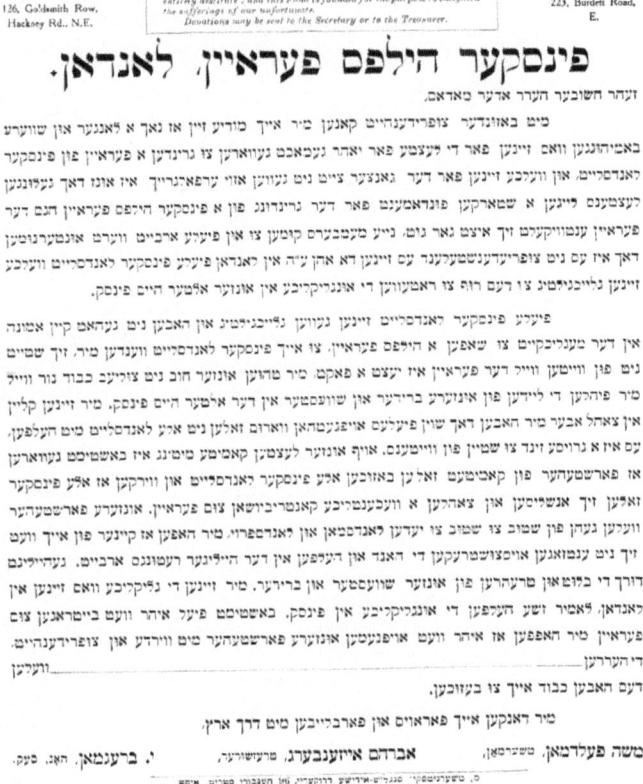

Appeal in Yiddish from the Pinsker Relief Society to Landsleit in London - Circa 1922 - with translation below

PINSKER RELIEF FUND, LONDON   Circa 1922
Honorary Secretary I Bregman 126 Goldsmith Row, Hackney Road, N E
Treasurer Abraham Isenberg 223 Burdett Road E

We appeal to every Pinsker and the suburbs. The position in that place is horrible. There are hundreds of Orphans without Fathers and Mothers entirely destitute; and this Fund is founded for the purpose to enlighten the sufferings of our unfortunates.

Donations may be sent to the Secretary or to the Treasurer.

With great satisfaction, we can inform you that after long and much trouble which we had in establishing a Pinsker Relief Society. It was not successful in the beginning. Still we managed to put up a foundation, to establish a Pinsker Relief Society.

Many Pinsker Landsleit did not believe in the Society. Therefore, we appeal to you to do something for our brothers and sisters in the old home (alte heim) of

Pinsk. We are small in number but we have achieved much. Why should not all landsleit help together with us. It is a great sin to stand by.

At our last committee meeting it has been decided we should visit all Pinsker landsleit and encourage them to register with us in order to donate a weekly contribution to the society. Our representatives will go from house to house to each landsman . We hope that nobody will refuse to put out a helping hand and help in this holy work. Sanctified by the blood and tears of our brothers and sisters we are the lucky ones who live in London. Let us help the unfortunate ones. You should please decide how much you will contribute for the Society.

We hope that you will accept our delegate with cordiality

Moshe Feldman Chairman
Abraham Isenberg Treasurer
I Bregman Honorary Secretary

In the summer of 1923 Ze'ev Lev wrote to the London committee to ascertain whether or not they had reached a decision on the project to bring over a group of 30 orphans to England. The children in the orphanage were offered the choice of settling in Britain or South Africa, where perhaps the largest batch of children were dispatched. One lady when faced with the prospect of travelling to South Africa was frightened, having only the haziest of notions of conditions in that country; and remembers telling the orphanage staff: 'They are cannibals. I do not want to go there'. Despite the fact that the Hebrew speaking school which some of the children in the orphanage attended had a strong Zionist orientation, despite the fact that certain children in the orphanage belonged to a Zionist youth movement and enthusiastically drilled in a khaki uniform, none of the children went as pioneers directly from the orphanage to Palestine. However, some of the ex-orphans migrated to Israel as adults, one lady journeying there by way of Siberia and Tashkent in the 1930s. In the early 1920s a group of ten to 12 children from the Holtzman orphanage travelled to Warsaw in preparation for their journey to Palestine, but because of a factional dispute between different Zionist parties, the orphans from Pinsk were weeded out as politically unsound by being asked deliberately difficult questions and reluctantly returned to the orphanage. There was also a steady trickle of children to the United States, where they were brought over by relatives on an individual basis, but surprisingly the Pinsker landsmanshaft in the United States did not sponsor the mass movement of orphans. However, a party of 70 orphan girls from other parts of Europe were stranded for a time in a hostel near to Southampton, when the United States government tightened its immigration restrictions.

Incidentally an analysis of the residents of the Jews Temporary Shelter situated in the East End for the period from 6 November 1919 until 1 August 1920 reveals 12 persons out of a total of 1883 arrivals, whose place of origin was Pinsk, but all 12 had as their ultimate destination the United States; they were mainly mothers travelling with their children.

ABRAHAM ISENBERG 1874-1955

Abraham Isenberg the founder and the first Treasurer of the Pinsker Orphans Relief Fund

Abraham Loss (Isenberg) was born in Motel, a small shtetl near Pinsk in Belarus in 1874, where he was brought up by his grandfather Michael, as his mother abandoned her three children after the premature death of her husband. Michael Loss was a chicken farmer, who lived to 105 in full retention of his faculties.

Abraham's elder brother Solomon was conscripted in the Tsarist army. A tough personality , Solomon rose to the rank of sergeant but he advised his brother that he would find the conditions in the army too rough; so he told him to flee over the frontier and evade military service which he did with a false passport under the surname of Isenberg which he adopted when he migrated to Britain as a young man.

He settled in the East End and stayed with a Mrs Kitsberg, who was probably a landsman, seeking work as a builder and cabinet maker, for which he had received some training. In February 1897, at the age of 23 he married Esther Globerman then aged 22, who was also born in Motel. Before marriage she worked as a feller in a tailoring establishment.

Abraham Isenberg abandoned work as a carpenter and after his marriage opened a newsagent's shop in Dorset Square London, not far from Baker Street. When his eldest son Isaac set up a successful business as a trouser maker, Abraham Isenberg joined his son in the enterprise.

He was a member of the Machzikei Hadath Synagogue, but on one occasion when he tried to address the congregants on the subject of Zionism he was ejected from the platform. Dejected by the attitude of the management of the shul, he joined a small synagogue attached to the Redman's Row Talmud Torah, presided over by the Rev J.K. Goldbloom, a prominent Zionist; here the atmosphere was much more congenial. During 1925 and for a time thereafter he served as the vice-chairman of the London Mizrachi Council, of which Sir Stuart Samuel, the brother of Herbert Samuel was chairman. If he had been born in Britain, Abraham Isenberg liked to muse, he would have carved out a career as a politician devoted to public service. For the rest of his life, he remained idealistic and a trifle unworldly. In 1921 with a group of landsmen from Pinsk and the surrounding area he formed the Pinkser Orphans Relief Fund of London to bring over children orphaned and uprooted by the First World War, as he so empathized with the plight of these children.

The founder and the first Treasurer of the Pinsker Orphans Relief Fund was Abraham Isenberg, who was a modern orthodox businessman, a Zionist, a man imbued with vision but somewhat unworldly. A man of similar stamp was David Solomons, who at first helped his wife in her corset making business, but he later established D Solomons and Sons to import Palestinian products such as lokshen and mazzah from Zelavensky, now Aviv, halva and sweets from Lieber and Co, and other goods from Lemonstein and Shulman, now Elite, at a meagre profit. He was an avid reader of the works of Sholom Aleichem and Sholom Asch, and likewise a keen Zionist. Mr Niditch was the owner of a sawmill and a man renowned for his charitable acts, although he was not very religious. Mr Pushkin was a master tailor, and in his youth he had been a member of the Bund, the Jewish labour movement in Pinsk, and when the Tsar was overthrown he attended a big rally in the Albert Hall in support of Kerensky, but he was not so involved in the work of the committee as his wife and young son, a mere schoolboy, who was prevailed upon to serve as honorary secretary. Another more active member of the committee was Mr Pomerantz, an itinerant bookseller, and it was such men as these who gave the society a progressive ethos. There were other solid citizens like Mr H Vysove, a traditionalist furrier, who served as joint vice-chairman of the society with Mr Solomons.

Not surprisingly women also sat on the committee of the Pinsker society participating in its work on equal terms with the men, and there were 11 such female members of the committee, perhaps the most formidable being Mrs Marsha Pushkin. Women in their traditional roles as folk healers, feltsherkehs, leaders of less knowledgeable women in prayers in the synagogues, firzogerin, letter writers for their illiterate sisters, interrupters of the Reading of the Law to redress communal wrongs had wielded considerable power in the shtetlekh, quite apart from the prestige accruing from their economic activities; and the immigrant women who had settled in the East End adhered to many of these traditional modes of conduct. But after the First World War Jewish women enjoyed an enhanced status both in Poland and Britain, by annexing fresh fields of activity; the Pinsker society was one such area, but other women in London busied themselves with helping their relatives in Poland to surmount the new immigration regulations and their family circle acted as a clearing house for this legal information. Even among the Jews in the East End, the new sexually emancipated women aroused anxieties, but real anxieties as opposed to the fear of a female demon or Lilith, as can be glimpsed in the lines of a Yiddish song sung by a young girl at a concert given by the Pinsker orphans in the people's Palace in 1926.

Heint untzer damen	Today our women
Ze pitzen sich	They paint themselves
Un schmiren sich	And smear themselves
Un drein sich arum	And whirl themselves around
Mit yinger lattes	With young fellows

Flyer advertising the concert
'Here you can buy tickets for the show. 50 orphan children will play at the People's Palace on Thursday 10 June'

The Pinsker society then was run by a group of small businessmen assisted by their wives and a sprinkling of working class men and women, utterly distinctive in character from the upper middle class Anglo-Jewish elite, who administered the communal charitable institutions. For instance, Mrs Yetta Franks whose husband was a presser, was one of the outstanding women committee members. Among the most dynamic and affluent families in the East End were those of the money-lenders, and it was from their ranks that the intellectuals of the Anglo-Jewish community eventually came. Abraham Isenberg persuaded Moshe Feldman, a travel agent and money changer, and a member of one such family with marked upward social mobility, to become the chairman of the Pinsker Relief Fund at its inception. Although his wealth could not equal that of the patrons of the Jews Temporary Shelter, such men as Herman Landau and Ernest Schiff, Moshe Feldman's family was better established and a step above the other Pinsker committee members in social standing. After a year or two, there was a personality and policy clash in the leadership of the organisation, perhaps exacerbated by some class friction, from which Abraham Isenberg emerged as the victor; and after a reshuffle of the leadership of the society, it changed its name to the Pinsker Orphans Relief Fund in 1924 which seems to indicate a clarification of its aims. By 1922 the immediate post-War work of rehabilitation had been completed in Pinsk and both the Joint and the Pinsker Fund now concentrated their efforts in trying to secure the well-being of the orphans. Abraham Isenberg was very friendly with Israel Feldman Senior, an old-fashioned gentleman dressed in a frock-coat, who still retained close personal ties to many families in Pinsk, as is borne out in the correspondence from the leading Pinsk orphanage; he has been described as being 'humane, wise and pleasant'; he was known as Israel Feldman the Pinsker, to distinguish him from his nephew Dr Israel Feldman. To Abraham Isenberg's chagrin, he failed to enlist the support of Dayan Asher Feldman for the aims of the society, despite hints at one stage of the sympathy of the London Beth Din for the work of the organisation, as the Dayan refused to have anything to do with the Pinsker Fund and tried to distance himself from foreign East European Jewish immigrants. So too, the Anglo-Jewish elite who controlled the Jews Temporary Shelter, kept their social distance from the committee of the Pinsker Society; and it is somewhat astonishing to find at one and the same time, that while none of them deigned to become patrons of the Pinsker Society and its existence is ignored in the minutes of the Shelter, there was close co-operation between the officials of the Shelter and the Pinsker Fund. For instance the official address of the Pinsker Society on its headed notepaper was that of the Shelter at 82 Leman Street Whitechapel, the secretary of the Shelter made all the arrangements with the shipping company in 1926 for the orphans to travel to England, from time to time clothes were collected and stored at the Shelter for the Pinsker Fund, and as a token of their appreciation for this assistance the committee of the Pinsker Fund made a presentation of £6-3-0 to the officers of the Shelter. On 14 October 1926, Mr Mundy, the secretary, wrote to Abraham Isenberg, stating that 'Mr Otto Schiff likewise thanks you most sincerely for your kind promise to try and make members for the shelter at the General Meeting of the Pinsker Relief Fund'; perhaps yet another illustration of the lack of direct contact between officers of the two bodies.

Nonetheless, the ever conciliatory Israel Feldman Senior secured the patronage of his own son, Dr William Moses Feldman, who consented to serve as a vice-president of the society in 1924 together with Saul Lourie, and Dr George Helperin, a banker. Dr Feldman was a general practitioner in the East end and a consultant paediatrician at an annexe of the London Hospital; he was a truly remarkable personality, who wrote on biomathematics and child development in general and specifically on the Jewish child, even contributing a Yiddish manual on the rearing of children. Saul Lourie was a businessman connected with the Lurias, a wealthy family of industrialists owning forests and a matchbox factory in Pinsk, and built up one of the biggest plywood companies in Britain. Despite his business activities, his position of vice-president was not that of a sinecure and correspondence survives to show that he was busily engaged in forwarding money to Pinsk on many occasions. For instance, on 11 November 1925 he noted: 'Received from Mr Isenberg the sum of Twenty Pounds (£20) to be remitted to the orphan House in Pinsk'. When Abraham Isenberg became chairman of the Pinsker Fund in 1924, the policy of settling orphans from Pinsk in England was pursued with fresh energy and determination; and surely the changes in the composition of the committee of the Fund which allowed this policy to come to the fore were not coincidental.

The committee of the Pinsker Relief Fund decided in 1922 that certain of its members should visit Pinsker Landsleit in London in order to request them to make regular weekly contributions; the society 'was not successful in the beginning', but its membership rose from 202 in April 1925 to 408 in October 1926. The secretary of the Pinsker society was Leopold Davidoff, who worked part-time for a variety of Jewish organisations including friendly societies, and who was an extremely busy man, dashing along to appointments at 9.00 pm in the evening with Mr Isenberg. In the 1920s, there was no such thing as cheque book charity among the new immigrants with donations being solicited by appeals through the post. One of the most important personages in charitable organisations was the collector, who trudged from house to house in the East End to collect the weekly contributions. The first honorary secretary of the Fund Mr I Bregman wrote to Abraham Isenberg on 22 June 1922 declaring that having prevailed upon to accept the position of collector, he just could not do this job which was too onerous and which would interfere with his making a livelihood for his family. In the financial year April 1925 until October 1926, the collector Mr Morgenstern, remembered as being 'a jolly, fat man', was paid commission of £48-17-3 by the Pinsker Fund, while the money he had spent in fares of £5-0-9 was also repaid. Henry Solomons as a young man recalls that his father kept a Pinsker charity box in his home.

From the balance sheet of the Pinsker Society for the period 15 April 1925 until 1 October 1926, we can see how the income of the society totalling £655-8-3 was collected. Members contributed £22-9-11, the bulk of which must have been amassed through the efforts of the collector. Also leading members of the society, such as Mr Israel Feldman, Mr Datlow and Mr Polatnick, collected money at simchas, weddings and engagements, raising £109-6-0 in this way. It is noteworthy that one woman Mrs Caplan, a member of the committee, raised £5-18-6 by these means. The Committee, for instance, wrote on 16 June 1922 to Mr Frankel that 'Mr Isenberg and Mr Feldman our honoured committee members who were instructed to be present at your simcha will convey to you all our best wishes. Naturally with your kind permission we shall make an appeal for the Pinsker orphans knowing that your celebration will be attended by many Pinsker Landsleit... We hope and we expect from you Mr Frankel, that not only will you allow our delegates to make a collection, but you yourself will participate in this collection which will be successful'. There was also a yearly ball at Monickendams which together with an auction raised £141-2-10. This ball with mixed dancing shows how quickly the former immigrants from Pinsk were assimilating to Anglo-Jewish norms. On 19 June 1926, 50 of the orphan children who had been brought to London from Pinsk, provided entertainment at the People's Palace, giving a concert which boosted the funds of the society by another £108-10-3.

On 23 August 1923 Ze'ev Lev, the secretary of the Holtzman orphanage, wrote a letter to the London Pinsker society, enclosing the names of 31 children and four adults, who wished to settle in England. Most of the adults were associated with the administration of the orphanage but because of the depressed economy in Pinsk and the endemic anti-Semitism which engendered psychological malaise they were eager to find a place of refuge in this country. (see the detailed letters with translations in chapter 24) The unease and anxiety of the staff of the Holtzman orphanage, when coupled with its strained financial resources, explains why they were so keen to dispatch large groups of orphans to another country. The majority of the children who were selected for adoption overseas were orphans who had no relatives or friends in Pinsk, while others had poor relatives who could do little to assist them. When the children were given a choice of settling in England or South Africa, some decided to go to the country where a friend from the orphanage had settled earlier. The women associated with the Pinsker Fund played a vital role in placing the orphans in new homes in London. The daughter of Mrs Marsha Pushkin remembers going with her mother on visits to families in the East End, not all of whom had connections with Pinsk, to plead with them to adopt an orphan; and how difficult it was to find enough families willing to open their homes to these children. Photographs of the children which had been taken in Pinsk were handed to prospective parents to stimulate their interest and to encourage them to take an orphan into their home. Mrs Pushkin was one of the dominant figures on the committee of the Pinsker Society, and devoted much effort not only to ensuring the well-being of the orphans but was active in a Bikkur Cholim Society, often visiting the sick, and was involved in an organisation which collected dowries for poor brides. Another lady, who placed a number of the children in homes was Mrs Frumkin, the wife of the wine merchant.

The first group of 19 children came to Britain in 1924, followed by a second larger group of 34 orphans in 1926. As far as the first batch of children is concerned, a photograph taken on board the ship on which they were travelling is still extant, while the medical cards of the second group of children have also survived, so that we know that these figures are accurate and that a total of 53 children were assisted by the Pinsker Society in finding homes in this country. On the first occasion the children were accompanied by staff from the orphanage on the train to Danzig (Gdansk), where they boarded a ship for England. At Danzig the children had to go through a cleansing station to make certain that they were not carrying lice and they were also vaccinated; the medical cards of the children clearly show that these procedures were complied with. As all the immigrants' underwear was destroyed in Danzig because of the risk of the presence of lice and their outer clothing was poor by West European standards anyway, additional clothing had to be provided for the children after their arrival in Britain.

Danzig 9 April 1926 - Vaccination Certificate

Henry Solomons as a young boy remembers seeing the arrival of the orphan girls in 1924 at the London Docks with shaven heads, but one of these young girls has admitted that they wore hats in an attempt to hide this.

The bulk of the money for the passages on the ship in 1926 was advanced to the London committee by the secretary of the Jews Temporary Shelter, although it was promptly repaid. From the documentary evidence that survives, it appears that it cost £184-2-7 to bring the 34 orphans from Pinsk to London on 13 April 1926 or approximately £5-8-0 per head. Whereas the ships passages cost in all £181-15-0, the cost of hiring two motor vans was £1-8-0 and luggage expenses were 11 shillings, while such incidental expenses as cables totalled another 8/7^d.

The children from the orphanage were adopted by their prospective families before they left Pinsk, and after a brief rest were met on arrival by their adoptive parents at the Jews Temporary Shelter. It should be noted that we use the term 'adoption' in its loose sense, as there was no legal process for adopting children in this country until the *Adoption of Children Act* in 1926. One lady vividly recalls how she was introduced to her new family by an older girl from the orphanage. 'Das is dyr Mama, ge zu er un zug Mama. 'this is your mother, go to her and say mother', after which she was given a banana which she did not know how to eat.

Both the orphan children and their adoptive parents came from varying backgrounds, and the children were often placed with particular parents because of a supposed

The first group of 19 children who came to Britain in 1924
Photo sent in by Adam Rose

affinity based on nothing more than the fleeting attraction of a child's photograph. Certain families with whom the orphans were at first boarded were not suitable. The first family one young girl stayed with had neither the room nor the financial resources to keep her and she was left to sleep on a settee. Soon she moved to another family, but they were equally unsatisfactory, as they could not speak Yiddish and she had to sleep in the back room of a dry-cleaning shop, where she was terrified by the presence of a guard dog. She was saved by the good offices of a lady from the Pinsker Society, probably Mrs Pushkin, who travelled with her to Brighton and placed her with a more congenial family.

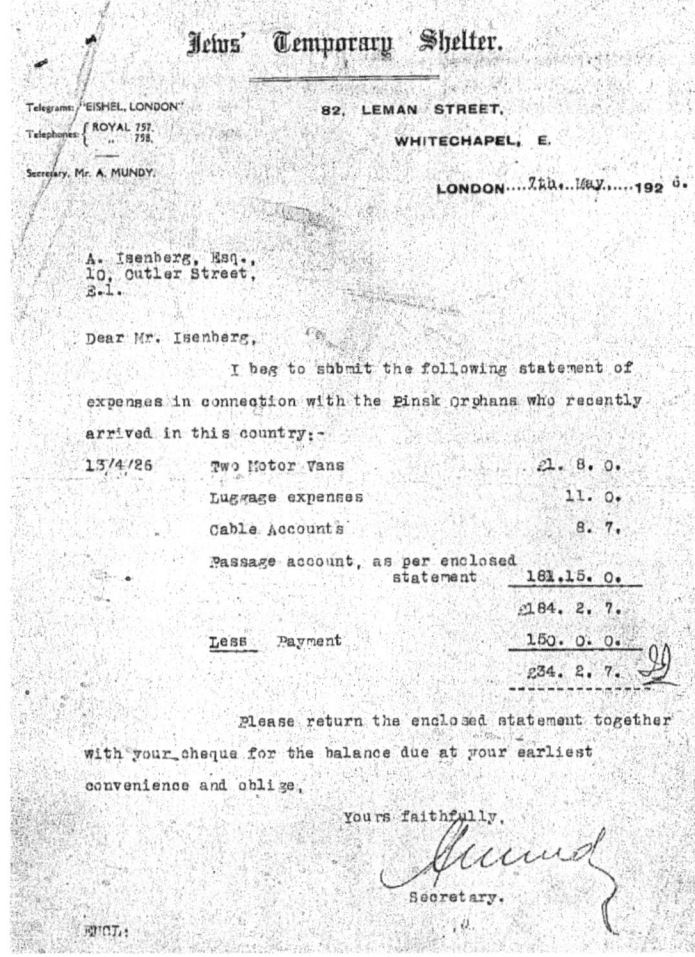

Invoice from Jews Temporary Shelter for costs of passage and other costs 13 April 1926

Yet in other cases the adoptive parents had no children of their own and treated the children who had been entrusted to them as if they were their own children. One young girl was brought up by a childless couple and to this day does not know her original surname or have any detailed knowledge about her real parents. Another adoptive father was so attentive to the girl whom he had invited into his home, that this created friction between his wife and their adoptive daughter, particularly when he requested the young girl to rub talcum powder on his feet and back after he took a bath. His wife became extremely jealous and if the daughter failed to return home by midnight when she was 20, her mother ensured that she was locked out for the night and that she had to spend the night in a friend's home.

The children went to school in England, where they rapidly acquired the rudiments of English, and the girls learned various trades such as dressmaking and millinery. Not all the orphans' lives had happy endings; one boy died from tuberculosis, despite the efforts of his adoptive parents to save him; one of the orphan girls intermarried; one orphan boy was deported to Poland amid mutual recrimination, accusations of theft on the one side and exploitation on the other. Although Abraham Isenberg interceded with Attlee and George Lansbury, the boy was still deported. Nonetheless, many of the orphan children and the associated families who emigrated with them from Pinsk prospered in England and the second generation can boast of a number of successful businessmen, a lawyer, a television producer and two professors.

Sadly there was a personality clash in the committee of the Pinsker Society in 1926 and a power struggle ensued, led by a group of members who had been trounced in the election at the annual general meeting, but who were supported by the secretary Leopold Davidoff. In a letter of resignation which was sent to the Yiddish press, Abraham Isenberg drew attention to the fact that 'in Pinsk there are still left many orphans.... who also wish to be adopted in good Jewish homes in London; and held out the hope of 'saving them'; the orphans and arranging for them to come to London; but the dissensions within the Pinsker society had so weakened it, that unfortunately no more orphans were rescued from Pinsk. Yet this was not the whole story, as the organisation was also riven by important differences over policy.

The adoptive parents had invested both emotionally and financially in the children they had taken under their wing; they did not want them to mix with the other children from Pinsk but they wanted their children to start a new life, undisturbed by the sweet and painful memories of Pinsk. The opposing faction in the Pinsker society held that the children should retain their corporate identity by forming a special Pinsker orphans group. The story was leaked to the Yiddish press, where it briefly became front page news and provoked a scandal.

Although the Pinsker Society lingered on into the 1930s, its leading members assumed the role of an after-care committee, watching over the welfare of their proteges and assisting one girl financially when she studied millinery. In the mid 1930s the Young Pinsker society was still active and dances were held, while parcels of clothes were dispatched to Pinsk; there was also an attempt made in 1928 to raise funds for building an extension to the orphanage to house the infants.

Eliyohu Holtzman and Ze'ev Lev were really caring individuals, who came on a visit to England before the Second World War to find out how their former charges were adjusting to life in this country; tragically both men perished in the Holocaust. However, as the orphans from Pinsk married and moved out of the East End, they gradually lost touch with each other, a process accelerated by the War; and a heroic story was forgotten.

Chapter 21 – MORE ABOUT THE PINSKER ORPHAN RELIEF FUND

All documents and translations courtesy John Cooper

PINSKER ORPHANS AID SOCIETY
The Jewish Times 21 September 1928

News cutting with translation below

A society who looks after the orphans had, after a big gathering, decided to enlarge the present building of the orphanage which is not large enough to take in all the orphans who had to be provided with a home and the necessary education.

An important question is now that not having sufficient space in the house, many children will be homeless until a home will be found for them. Up to 400 children placed in the orphanage are provided with shelter, food, clothing and education from the age of one until 16 years.

A great many of them cannot be taken in owing to a shortage of space. Owing to financial emergencies not all of them can be taken into the orphanage. Very young children cannot be accommodated until they reach the age of six years. Owing to this situation the very young children are being cared for in poor private homes and the society cannot keep them under surveillance to ensure that they are having a motherly upbringing. The children are brought up in an unsatisfactory manner which they bring with them when they arrive in the orphanage. They have to be under special care.

Taking account of these orphans, the orphanage is obliged to make a good home for the children. Therefore, it is necessary to make an effort to enlarge the orphanage and make a place for the younger children who are being cared for in poor private homes, in order to bring up a healthy Jewish generation.

We live at a critical moment owing to that the committee is hampered by the summer months [holiday times] and are unable to provide the sums of money which is required. The care of the orphan children is not a question of pity, but it is a sacred duty of every Jew to take part in this action of building and fulfilling their duty to the orphan children. When you care for your own children, don't forget the orphans. Everybody should remember and help the committee of the orphans to find them a home in the name of the committee.

L Davidoff Secretary

THE PINSKER RELIEF FUND

The Jewish Post
Friday, 14 September 1928
News cutting with translation

The society for Orphans Care, after a meeting, decided to enlarge the present building of the orphanage which is not capable of taking any more children to give them a good home and the necessary upbringing.

The question is very important for the children who are not supplied with a good home and proper upbringing. The question is very important because there is a scarcity of accommodation which causes many children to wander about until some place is found for them. Therefore we had to decide to come together in the near future and deal with this responsibility for this undertaking. Up until the present day, there exists in the orphanage such conditions which cannot be fulfilled or the necessary requirements and the result is that it makes a bad impression on the children. Up to 400 children are cared for in the orphanage with living accommodation to feed them and clothe them and to teach them a trade. The orphans are aged from one year until 16.

A large part of them cannot be taken into the present building owing to the shortage of space. Also being short of funds, the little children need suitable nurses. The orphanage at the present time cares for the children with accommodation from six years until 16 years old and the age group from one to six years are being boarded with private families who are being paid and when they reach the age of six years, they are taken over by the orphanage.

It is necessary to express the difficulties which exist when small children are being boarded out with poor people and the society [from orphanage] has not got the proper facilities for looking after them [inspecting].

The children should be properly brought up and owing to this, the children are brought up with bad habits until they can join the orphanage when they are six years old when it is very difficult to bring them back to a better upbringing.

In view of the previous request, it is necessary to start to extend the building to be able to take in more children and also take better care of the children who are scattered among poor families. We are now at a critical moment that we cannot care enough for the above mentioned children and we find it very difficult to support the 400 children who require a great sum of money. Therefore, we appeal to you to help us in this responsible action. It is a duty for everybody to help us in this noble action. Don't forget the children whose parents perished during the war.

PINSKER ORPHANS RELIEVE FUND LONDON COMMITTEE Notice of Members meeting 1926

Dear Sir or Madam

You are cordially invited to take part in the yearly members meeting which will be held on Sabbath evening 5 Cheshvan / 16 October 1926 at 7 o'clock punctually at Canon's Street Synagogue Commercial Road, East London.

Agenda

1. To read and pass the balance sheet
2. Auditors report
3. Yearly report of the committee's work
4. To discuss our future work for the benefit of the orphans
5. Election of honorary officers and committee

The following are the Honorary officers and committee

Hon President - Dr Feldman
Hon Vice-President - Dr G Halperin
Mr Saul Lourie
Chairman A Isenberg
Collector Mr Morgenstern

Committee names

1. Mr and Mrs Silverman
2. Mr and Mrs Pushkin
3. Mr and Mrs Melenik
4. Mr and Mrs Daniels
5. Mr and Mrs Nyclots
6. Mr and Mrs Cantin
7. Mr Davidoff
8. Mr Franks
9. Mr Gold
10. Mr Caplin
11. Mr Blumenfarb
12. Mr Shofer
13. Mr Segal
14. Mr Lewis
15. Mr Kisberg
16. Mr Shapiro
17. Mr Dentser
18. Mr D Handman
19. Mr I Pomeranth
20. Mr R Klein
21. Mr A Polatnick
22. Mr H Frankel
23. Mr A Stoksky
24. Mr M Goodman
25. Mr a Shwuther
26. Mr I Feldman
27. Mr S Columboutch
28. Mr A Calphen
29. Mr M Vossotsky
30. Mr A Kinn
31. Mr M Drusen

The committee appeals to you to influence your relatives and friends to become members and fulfill a mitzvah to care for orphans.

Signed by **Isenberg Chairman**
              Davidoff Secretary

Other information

Page 2	Income of	£655- 8-3
Page 3	Expenditure	£616-14-3
	Balance	£38-14-0

There were 204 members at 15 April 1925 and at 1 October 1926 another 202 members giving a total of 408 members

Notice of 1926 Members meeting - page one - in Yiddish with translation on left hand side

Page 4

1. The purpose of the organisation is to support the necessities of the orphanage in Pinsk.
2. To bring the orphans into good homes and a decent upbringing.
3. The committee thanks you for your help which you have given up until now to support the orphanage. With your support there have been brought over two groups of 55 orphan children, supplied with good homes and decent upbringing. As it is already known to you, your help and your work has been critical for this holy purpose which you helped to accomplish and you have seen for yourself the living witnesses who have been saved with your help from the awfully bad angels and who have been given over here to noble good hearted fathers and mothers who we can testify are giving these children the best upbringing, like real good parents would have done.

There has been accomplished a very great thing. The further work to carry on depends on you. It is necessary to ensure the existence of the orphanage and to bring over and bring up some more orphans that they should be productive members of the society. Support an evening for this holy purpose. Fulfill your obligation also in the future for the orphan children.

Notice of 1926 Members meeting - page two - in Yiddish with translation on prior page

THE APPEAL AFTER THE FIRE IN 1922

'In the name of the Pinsker Relief Fund of London, we come to you with a special warm request', it began, 'that you should be so kind as to ask your congregants tomorrow before the Kol Nidre that they should come to help the Pinsker citizens who have lost all their belongings in a fire. You have surely heard of the great calamity which has happened in the Jewish town of Pinsk. Thousands of families have lost their homes and remained without their livelihood and without a roof over their heads'.

The appeal ended by stating that if anyone had any old clothing to spare for these unfortunate inhabitants they should inform the Jews Temporary Shelter and that arrangements would be made by the fund to collect it from their homes.

PINSKER RELIEF SOCIETY TO LANDSLEIT IN LONDON Circa 1922

To the President

In the name of the Pinsker Relief society, we come to you with a special warm request that you should be so good to ask your congregants tomorrow before Kol Nidre that they should come to help the Pinsker citizens who have lost all their belongings in a fire. You have surely heard of the great calamity which happened in the Jewish town of Pinsk. Thousands of families have lost their homes and remained without their livelihood and without a roof over their head. Help is very urgent. We are not asking for any money. We only want from you old clothing and everybody should give as much as they can. You have only to send a postcard to us at the Jewish Shelter, 82 Lemon street and we will collect from them in order to save you the trouble of sending it to the shelter. The London Beth Din is interested in this help.

We hope that our appeal will find a warm response.

Yours faithfully

Moshe Feldman - Chairman
A Sellwing - Treasurer
I Feldman - Secretary

Letter from the Pinsker Relief Society to Landsleit in London
Circa 1922 - Signed by Moshe Feldman - Chairman, A Sellwing - Treasurer and I Feldman - Secretary

In this chapter copies of all documents and translations thereof are courtesy John Cooper

Chapter 22 – ABOUT THE CHILDREN

All documents and translations courtesy John Cooper

LETTER FROM THE JEWISH ORPHANAGES IN PINSK TO THE PINSKER RELIEF FUND IN LONDON 20 August 1923

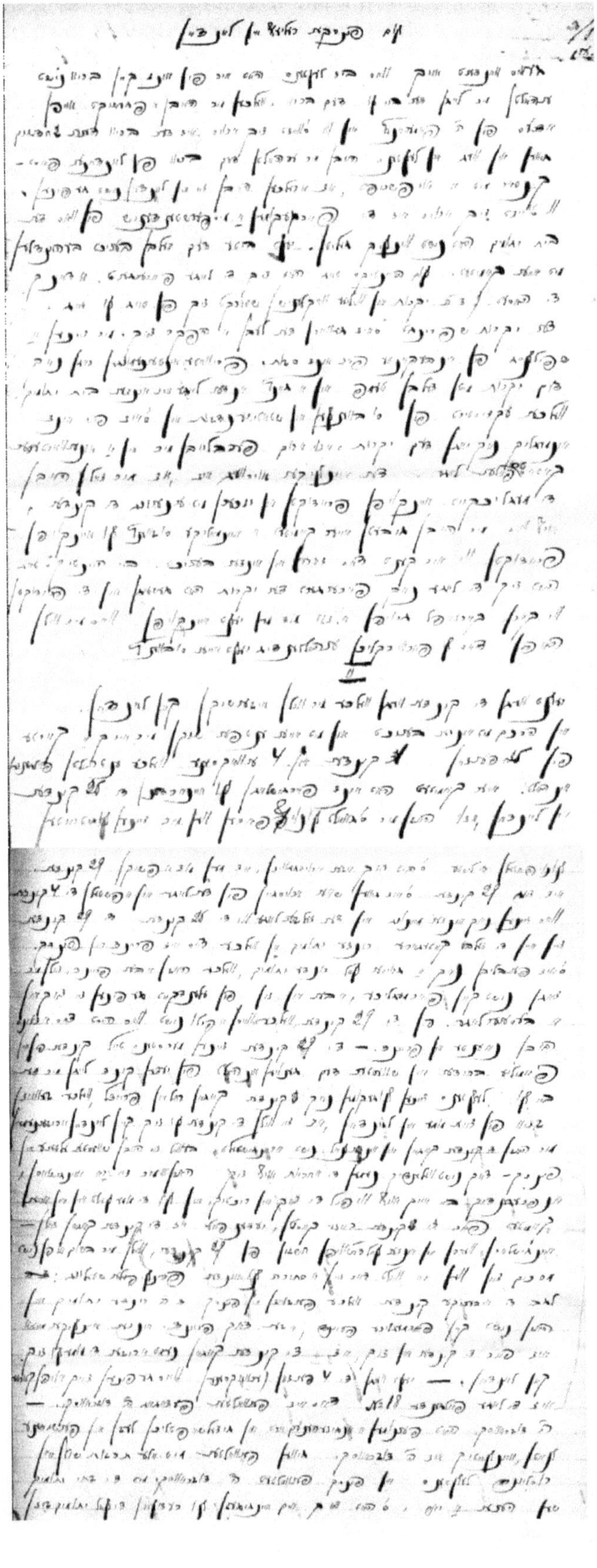

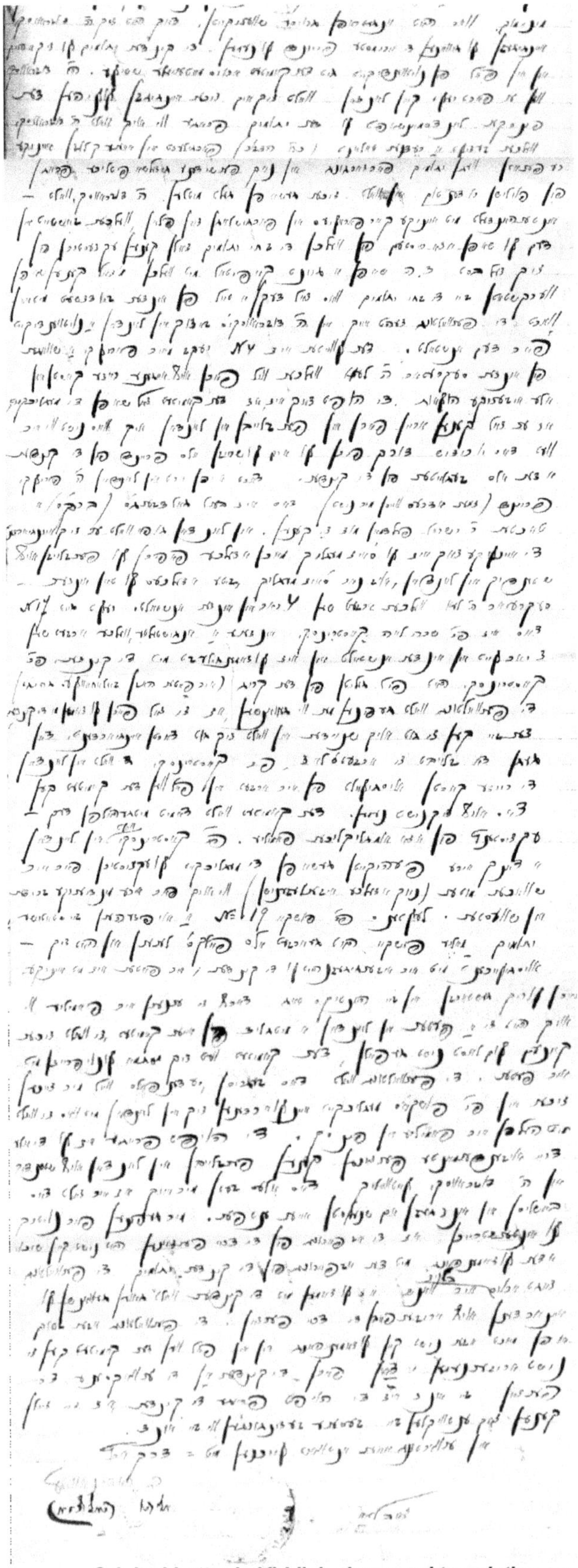

Original Letter in Yiddish above and translation on following page   courtesy John Cooper

Surely you wonder why you did not hear from us for such a long time. We enclose herewith a letter from Mr Pomeranth. Their letter took more than two months to reach us. Recently we had a letter from the London Post Office who said that such a letter was not found. Apparently there was some misunderstanding from which the orphanage suffered.

Now we ask you to deal with this matter through your committee. The position got much worse owing to the staggering inflation. Due to things that are unknown to us. Private undertakings still manage to beat the inflation and to keep pace with the expenses of the orphanage. It would help if we had the opportunity of buying food products and for this we would suggest that you let us have a bigger sum of money for this purpose.

Now, about the children whom we want to send over to London with your consent. We send herewith a list of 35 persons. Thirty one children and four adults. Your committee suggested to bring over 25 children to London. But after making up the list we found that we had to send 29 children. It was difficult for us not to include the four remaining children in the same category as they are orphans who have no friends or relations in Pinsk.

Apart from them, there are still more orphans who do have some friends or relations, but they are poor and cannot do anything for them. The two children Rochel and Friedel Kagan, have an aunt in London, who is prepared to care for them. The aunt is also prepared to pay their travelling expenses.

About the four adults who are on the list, the position is as follows:

One is a manager and a pedagogue, Aaron Dubrovsky. This Mr Dubrovsky was very well known as a social worker. He was connected with the Tarbuth Schools in Russia. In Pinsk he was the manager of the orphanages for more than one year. During the time he was in the orphanage he managed to reduce the number of orphans. Mr Dubrovsky is a very good public speaker and we hope that he will let you know in London the position of the orphans and we trust that he will advise you to establish a society (landsmanschaft) to make orphanage self-supporting or to have a regular income.

The second man, no 4 on list, Yakov Mect Poritsky. A brother-in-law of our secretary Mr Lowe; one who wants to go on his own travelling expenses. The only thing that he wants is that the committee should help him to get in London and to remain in London. I don't know whether you will be able to achieve this. I don't know the legal point of view, but write to him about obtaining permission to stay in London. He can be described as a relative of the children or as the supervisor of them. We don't know the addresses of these two people, that is the daughters of Berel Goldberg. Israel Feldman knows them probably in London. Israel Feldman may be able to help you in the arrangements for them to remain in London.

Secretary M (Ze-ev) Lev was secretary for four years in our establishment.

Then there is a lady by the name of Sarah Leah Katrusky who is employed by us in our establishment for the last three years and knows how to go about with the children. Mrs Katrusky went through a difficult time during the war. Her father was killed by the Bolsheviks. The society would be very grateful if she could come to London together with the children. She is also a good dressmaker. Here she would remain unemployed. She would undertake to refund her travelling expenses. Mrs Katrusky would also undertake to support her old mother through her earnings in London and also her brothers and sister who remain in Russia.

Frai Pushker 19 on list, is a manageress in the orphanage. Molly Pushker was a teacher and now very devoted to the children. Her father died a few years ago and now she is the only one to care for the family. She has an uncle in London who is a member of your committee. We trust that the committee will speak to her uncle in order to bring her over to London. We are sure that she will be able to establish herself and help her family.

We trust that the committee will be able to bring these persons over to London and we would ask you to be so kind and to let us know by return if the committee will be successful in their undertaking. If these three persons mentioned above are unable to make this journey, then the children will go without them. We mainly care for the children.

They should be brought over and get established here in London.

We await your early reply.
Yours faithfully
Ze-ev Lev – Secretary
R Rainovitch
Elilyahu Holtzman

INFORMATION CONCERNING EACH CHILD FROM THE PINSK ORPHANAGE   20 August 1923
See original letter in Yiddish below

1. Esther 15 years old and David 11 years old - Sherman/Sheckman

The father and mother died in Russia in the year of the war. Esther learns dressmaking. David learnt in Talmud Torah. Jolly children. Esther learns well at work and she wants to study. She knows her position. David is a boy who does not understand languages yet.

2. Sholmo 17 years old and Leibel (boy) 10 years old Mattos

The name of the father is Esreal Mattos. The mother died before the war, the father during the war. The father found it impossible to care for the four children, he was not in the position. They were taken in the orphanage. The older two children are grown up and working. The younger children are of good character. Leib is a good boy; a diligent scholar. He is learning a *daff* of Gomorah already.

3. Chaim Fotman 17 years
The father and mother died in Russia. Chaim learns tailoring. He is a good worker and wants to work. He enjoys his trade.

4. Yakov Poritsky (see letter above)

5. Sholmo also 17 years old. Yakov 12 years old - Ziniuk
The father died suddenly when he came out from Court. He was a shoemaker. Israel Feldman must remember it. The mother died from hunger in Poland. The children were taken to Beth Shlmo, another orphanage. He learnt tailoring. He is interested in culture. He is a member of a club. Yakov learnt in Talmud Torah. He is a very naive child.

6. Friedel 15 years old. Aaron 12 years old - Klampert
Orphans. The father went to war ten years ago and has not returned yet. The children do not remember their father. The mother died soon after from a broken heart. Friedel learns dressmaking and is a clever child who knows how to talk. The boy Aaron is 12 years old and he is a mischievous boy. He does not know anything yet. He only knows that he wants to make mischief.

7. Leah Dorfman 15 years old
The father was lost in the war. The mother died in Poland. The family of the children took them to the orphanage. The older, Leah is learning to be a dressmaker. She learns the trade very well and in the evening she goes to lessons. She is a clever girl. The youngest two children are for the time living in the orphanage.

8. Yocheved (girl) Kniplech 15 years old
The father got killed in peace time. The mother died. Yocheved finished school and is a very good scholar. She is also learning dressmaking. She is also very studious. Yocheved is very intelligent and she will reach a high standard. She is also a beautiful girl and she has a good character.

9. Michal Pickov 17 years old. An orphan
The father and mother died of hunger. Michal learnt tailoring. He hopes to be a great man, like Eddison, but he is not very intelligent, but he still wants to learn and to earn money. He also goes to evening classes to learn.

10. Moshe Waxman 15 years old
He learns to be a locksmith. The father and mother died of hunger during the war. Moshe has good qualities, is a handsome boy but he needs to be looked after. He is very mischievous and would not take to learning a trade.

11. 12. Rachel/ Rochel 18 years old   Friedel 16 years Kagan
Both orphans. They have a sister in Pinsk. We have written about the children in the letter above but the committee will have to decide whether their aunt in London will take them over to London.

13. Michal (boy) Rickner 15 years old
Learns shoemaking. Their father died in peace time and was a workman in the time of war. The only survivor of the family. The boy is gifted. If you talk to him you feel as if you are talking to someone who has lived through the tragedy of the war.

14. Pesel (girl) Kashitsky 17 years old
The parents died in Russia. She is a clever and pretty girl; she is learning diligently. The father died during the war on the battlefield.

15. 17. Batya 16 years old – Shmuel 9 years – Luchtan
Their father was a builder in peacetime and he died in the war. The father and mother died in Poland. Batya learns dressmaking. In the evenings she goes to classes. Shmuel learns in Talmud Torah.

16. 24. Chaya 8 years Chana 14 years – Gitelman
Chaya learns in the school and Chana Gitelman learnt dressmaking. In peacetime they lived in a village near Pinsk. In the war they became ruined. The parents died and the children were taken to an orphanage. They too have an aunt in London. They too are good children and very diligent.

20. 32. Gitel 9 years old and Zelata (girls) 17 years – David Davidsky
They are very gifted children. They are attending a school. Zelata is learning millinery. Their father in peacetime was a blacksmith. He died in the time of the war. The children were taken into an orphanage. They have an older sister, but the doctor never allowed her to go.

22. Holelke [child] Buchalshuk 8 years old   The child learns in Talmud Torah. A clever boy. The parents died in Poland. He does not remember anybody.

29. 31. Mordechai 10 years old and Machya (girl) 14 years old Zucker
The father and mother died in Pinsk. Anybody who remembers the beadle Mordechai and Reb Eliezer Moshe of Blessed Memory, these are his grandchildren. The parents were shopkeepers in peacetime. The parents died in war from the disease of typhus.

Mordechai is learning – a clever boy, but very naughty. It is necessary to look after him. Chaya is a quiet girl. She is learning to work and she also attends an evening class.

26. 33. Sholem 8 years old. Marsha [Menam] Fredkoff 10 years old.
The parents died in the war. The children do not remember them. They are poor children who have nobody. They are gifted and learning beautiful and they learn very well in school.

37. Moshke Lev 12 years old.
Learns in Talmud Torah. A child who has suffered. The father and mother died in hospital. The youngster learns very well. He is a quiet child and has a good character.

The biography of each child who is orphaned during the war, whose ages may not be correct according to the magistrate's records. This is taken from our books. According to our records. If you want to correct ages make an application to the magistrate to obtain the correct ages of the children. It is important for us you should get acquainted with the family and their occupation, to see if he [the child] is gifted. We have made efforts to get their information.

Original Letter in Yiddish above and translation on prior page courtesy John Cooper

LETTER FROM THE PINSKER RELIEF FUND IN LONDON 22 June 1926

Letter and list opposite with translations below

Dear Friend Mr Isenberg

I herewith send you the list of Names and Addresses of the people who took in the 34 children who were recently sent over.

A few weeks ago I asked each of them to get ready the children's old clothes for collection. I hope you will not have to wait too long for the parcels.

At the meeting on Sunday night we discussed the continuation of the work of the fund.

Wishing you a successful trip

Yours

SURNAMES AND ADDRESSES OF PEOPLE WHO TOOK IN THE 34 CHILDREN IN 1926

1 Harris Shlach 130 Kenen Street E 1
2 Kaplan 31 West Arbor Street
3 Filterman 438 Mayland Ride E1
4 Polsker 40 Lower Chapman Street E1
5 Rodintatz 87 Warden Street E1
6 Geldman 32 Chapman Street
7 Collecter Laman Street
8 Cohen 26 Parkland Street
9 Cohen 56 Artillary Lane
10 Gleider 11 Russel Street
11 Leder Kramer 5 Cameron Place Nelson Street
12 Chaiken 7 Cameron Place
13 Kritz 67 Hamstead ??
14 Palashuk 3 North Place Barkston Street
15 Moskowitzer 272 Curwitch Street
16 Gold 144 Cannen Street Ride
17 Reiden 28 Patterson Street
18 Silverstein 26 Bridgeport Place St Ride
19 Canton 126 Clarence Ride E5
20 Feigel
21 Telfer 79 Sandringham Ride Dalstone E8
22 Sarner 153 Emerse Ride Walk N16
23 Arterman 88 Queen ?? Walk N16
24 Cohen 52 Hero Ride W2
25 Epstein 11 ?? ?? ??
26 Yankelowitz 1 West Street Golders W1
27 Weitman 380 Edgeware Ride N2
28 Goldstein 380 Edgeware Ride N2
29 Lever 98 Rodham Street Calgton Ride, Apton Manor
30 Aronowitz 51 Clairemont Ride Satend
31 Anfung 228 Main Ride E 17
32 Gilwater 11a ?? ?? ??
33 Richman 55 Chatham Ride Satend
34 Feldman 6 Church Lane

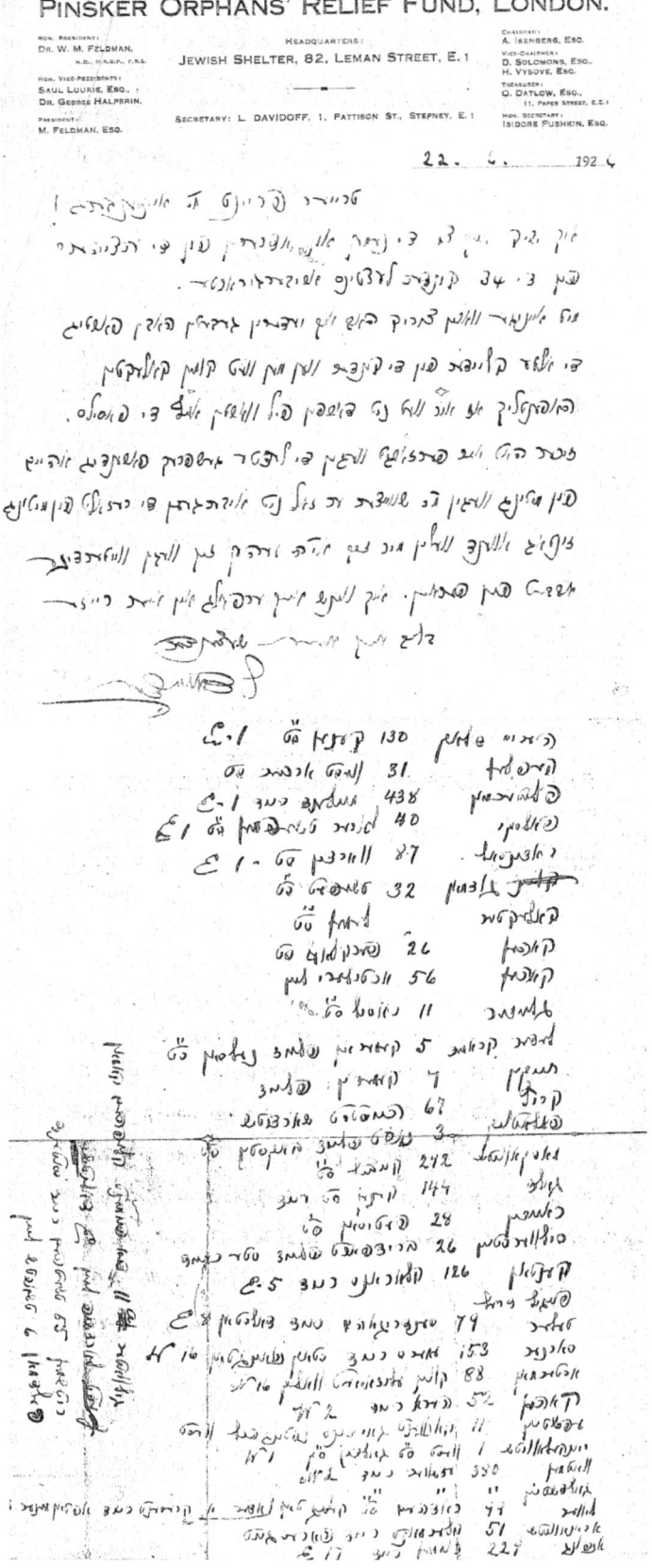

128

LIST OF1926 GROUP OF 34 CHILDREN
VACCINATED - 9 April 1926 Danzig

1.	Chaya	Gitelman Y
2.	Esther	Feldman/Ferdman Y
3.	Hejsu	Lev
4.	Leah	Dorfman
5.	Gitel/Gisla	Davidsky
6.	Masha/Miriam	Freilkoff
7.	Chaske	Isenberg
8.	Meyer	Dorfman
9.	Chaya/Sheine	Pinsker
10.	Meyer	Pinsker
11.	David	Robrowitz
12.	Chasre	Segalowitz
13.	Sholoma	Arenberg
14.	Pesse	Lev
15.	Chaya	Levin
16.	Chana	Gitelman
17.	Mulka	Wagman
18.	Sarah	Rubacka
19.	Sarah	Pragner
20.	Sime	Faksman
21.	Israel	Robrowitz
22.	Selio	Kagan
23.	Hillel	Rakalowik
24.	Fruma	Kovalski
25.	Furje	Higdalowicz
26.	Yizhok	Ziperstein/Ciperstein
27.	Chaya	Rubarka
28.	Rosa	Dorfman
29.	Shmuel	Pocrinka
30.	Chasre Gitel	Lichstein/Luhtewstein
31.	Feigel	Drel
32.	Sarah/Sisie	Bregman
33.	Shulem	Fialkow
34.	Pro	Hescel

3 DANZIG 3

Poland U.S.A. England

Staatliche Desinfektionsanstalt Danzig

S. S. Company Physician

Name. Chasre Gitel Luhtenstein

Vaccinated

Date - 9. April 1926

Upper space is for the stamp of the Disinfection Camp, or signature of surgeon certifying vaccination and disinfestation (one or both, or inspection alone as indicated on other side of card). The other space above is for stamp of local S. S. Company physician, passing the results as satisfactory, and as obtained by methods complying with U. S. P. H. S. regulations.

Name, origin and destination (Poland and U. S. A. respectively, unless otherwise indicated), date of commencement of 14 day period, also vaccination and disinfestation (except where V or D respectively is crossed out), as indicated above, are all certified by the stamp or signature in the upper space on the other side.

As a transmigrant certificate for the U. S. P. H. S. this card is valid only when bearing the U. S. P. H. S. stamp in space above. This stamp certifies compliance with all prescribed sanitary regulations according to class, origin etc., but does not certify absence of physical or mental defect nor admissability to the U. S. A.

For the information of ship surgeons physical examinations by local SS Co. physicians may be certified at bottom of card, other side.

United Baltic Corporation, ~~WHITE STAR LINE.~~

Steamship Company

DRUKARNIA GDANSKA A. G. 2076/25

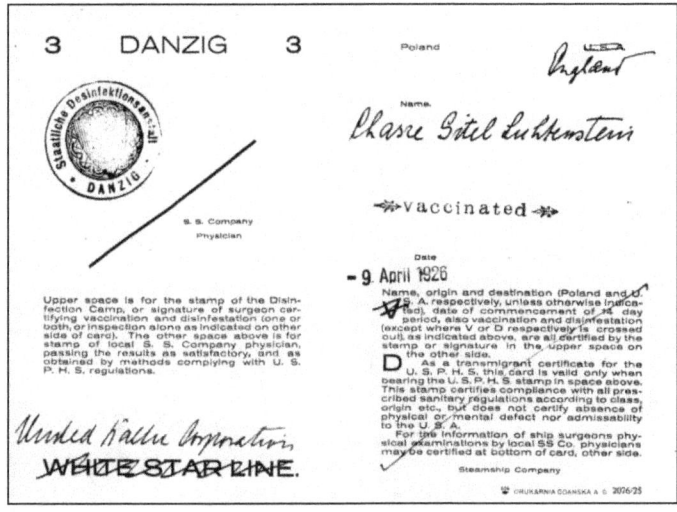

Vaccination Certificate of Chasre Gitel Luhtewstein
Danzig 9 April 1926 -

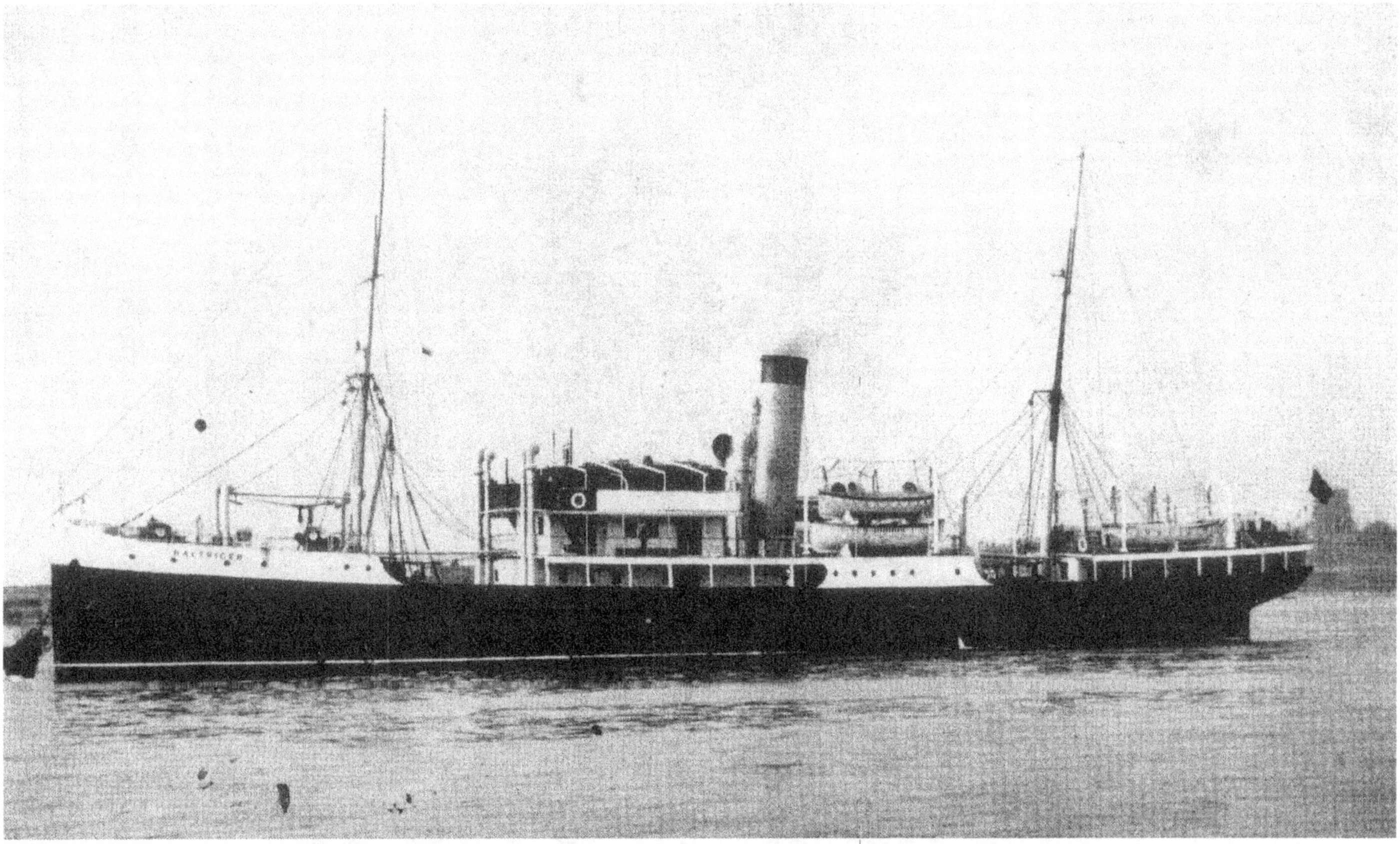

SS Baltabor, the ship that transported the 1924 group from Danzig to London

Chapter 23 - Group Photos

The 19 Pinsker Orphans that arrived in London in December 1924 - photo courtesy Ann Fine

The 34 Pinsker Orphans that arrived in London on board the Baltricer, in April 1926 photo courtesy John Segal Esther Waxman in front of funnel, Chana/Anne Gitelman is standing to the right of the boy holding up a picture, Eva/Chaya is more or less at the right end of that same row, holding a suitcase in front of her and Malka Woqman is seated in the third row on the left and two to the left of the boy

Pinsker Orphan Reunion - 1930s   photo courtesy John Segal

Tsirel Needleman (Sapoznik) the eldest of four sisters is holding her baby Sam, seated to her right (we think) are Eliyohu Holtzman, founder of the first orphanage in Pinsk and Ze'ev Lev (the secretary). Behind and between them is third sister Debbie Sapoznik. The youngest sister Claire(Chaia) Sapoznik is not in the picture. Fagel is seated to the right of Ze'ev Lev and Esther (Waxman) is in front of her (bottom right) Standing behind Tsirel and son is Silvia and her sister is the young lady with glasses on the left second from the top."   Sam Needleman

Yocheved Kniplech (Hetty Brand) is at the very end of the second row from the top (right side). Her fur collar and necklace are clearly visible. Chana Gitelman is back row, right side on the left standing behind Chaya Gitelman who is wearing the white fur collar.

Eliyohu Holtzman and Ze'ev Lev with the people who adopted (took in) the children - 1930s photo courtesy John Segal
Eliyohu Holtzman is in the centre of the back row and Ze'ev Lev on the far right of the back row. They are also in the centre of the photo above.
"Yetta Franks, who took in her four Sapoznik nieces is sitting front row 4th from the left." Sam Needleman
"Possibly the man - third from right in the second row may be the father that adopted their grandmother / mother Sora Basha Bregman."
Marilyne and Adam Rose

"The lady in the middle of the second row from the front (wearing a V-neck outfit with stripes), is possibly Yocheved Kniplech (Hetty Brand)." Josephine

A New Year's greeting card for Rosh Hashana 5687 (September 1926) from the youngsters of the Jewish orphanage of Pinsk

Youngsters in the Jewish orphanage in Pinsk, following the First World War - photo from Pinsk website

SECTION 5

THE LIFE STORIES OF THE OCHBERG ORPHANS

This section contains the histories of the Ochberg Orphans as related by their children and grandchildren that were not included in the first volume.

These histories are in two parts: the children placed in the care of the Cape Jewish Orphanage (Oranjia) and those who were placed in the South African Jewish Orphanage (Arcadia).

Included are the histories from newly discovered descendants and also, in some cases, additional information on orphans previously reported upon.

We also include histories that were included in More Arc Memories published in 2008.

When the Ochberg Orphans arrived in Cape Town half of the children went to live in the care of the Cape Jewish Orphanage later to be called Oranjia. The other half were taken by train to Johannesburg and initially placed in the care of the The Jewish Relief, Reconstruction and Orphans Fund and then later in the care of the South African Jewish Orphanage, later to be called Arcadia.

Oranjia, built by the Cape Jewish Community and completed in 1916 to house the children of the Cape Jewish Orphange. (This cover of Memories of Oranjia - The Cape Jewish Orphanage was designed by Benni Hotz).

Following are the histories of some of the children that were placed in the care of the Cape Jewish Orphanage later to be called Oranjia.

Chapter 24 – NAOMI (STEIN) MILLER (NECHAMA LERMAN) (1917-1970)

NAOMI (STEIN) MILLER (NECHAMA LERMAN)
an Ochberg Orphan who lived in Cape Town
Written by Jules Miller

Group Passport Photo of Ochberg Orphans - 1921
"I'm 90% sure that my mom is in the front row 2nd from the right, and her sister is in the 2nd row, 3rd from the right. Her older sister has features which I recognise. I have a later photo of my mom when she was probably 5 or so years and I think I can see a resemblance to the passport photo."

My Mom, Naomi, (or Nechama as she was then known) was born in Domachevo, Russia later Poland and now Belarus, in 1917 and it was there where my Mom first came into contact with Isaac Ochberg. She must have been four at the time when she and her older sister, Devorah (Dora), arrived in Cape Town with the Ochberg Orphans in 1921.

My late Dad, Harry, told me that he remembered being taken to the Cape Town docks by his own father to meet the "Ochberg children" along with many members of the local community. He was then 11 years old and married my mom in 1940, 19 years later!

My Mom and sister spent a short time at the Oranjia Cape Jewish Orphanage. My Mom was then adopted by a lovely couple, Louis and Bluma Stein. Her sister Dora was adopted by the Kagan family, also in Cape Town.

My Mom married, Harry Miller, in 1940. My Dad's parents, Isaac Miller and Annie Briss had emigrated from Lithuania after Annie's father, Menasha Bris had arrived in South Africa from Lithuania in about 1897. Both of my paternal grandparents (Isaac and Annie) had died before I was born in 1949 so, the only grandparents I knew were my Mom's "adopted" parents (Louis Stein and by then his second wife Leah, as Bluma had died earlier). My Mom spoke very fondly of Bluma and in fact my late sister Blume was named after her. My Mom always said she was very well cared for by the Stein family.

My Mom, whom I and my sisters adored, did not speak about the Ochberg episode, and it was always assumed that the memory was either too unpleasant or that she had been too young to remember the details. She did, however, suffer from recurring nightmares but would never discuss them with us. How I now wish that she could have talked to us about this.

I remember her as a loving, caring and devoted mother. She had many friends and was very active in the Bnoth Zion.

She died aged 53 in 1970 in Cape Town but had previously been in good health. My Dad passed away in Cape Town in 2002. He never remarried.

My mom and her older sister a few years after arriving in Cape Town

My parents' wedding photo in 1940

My Mom and Dad, my sister Bluma (in the middle), my sister Mary-Anne and myself in the mid 1950s. Blume unfortunately died in 1986.

Chapter 25 – HYMIE ROSIER (CHAIM RAZU)

YETTA CHAIM AND ITZIK ROSIER (RAZU)
Written by Tania (Bornstein) Jacobson, both whose parents, Yetta Razu and Isaac Bornstein, were born in Brest Litovsk and came out with the Ochberg Orphans to South Africa in 1921.

My mother spoke to me throughout my childhood of her experiences and the circumstances of her coming to Cape Town which I will try to relate to you.

The family was very poor and my grandfather was a teacher. They lived through a time when the Cossacks would come riding into the village and they would have to flee for their lives. My grandmother gave birth to her youngest child on the road out of town. There were five children and an adopted daughter. At the end of the 1914-1918 war conditions were very bad and a flu epidemic broke out. My mother told me how both parents landed in hospital and she would visit them every day. One day she came there to find both their beds were empty. They had died during the night.

The family could not do much for the children and suggested that the baby, Yossele, aged three, go into an orphanage. They promised to take care of him, but he unfortunately died. The oldest daughter, Elka, was taken to a nearby village to live with an aunt with a view to finding a shiddach for her. She met someone and later went to settle in Palestine and finally got to America where she prospered.

Meanwhile the rest of the children, Yetta, Chaim and Itzik, were left to their own devices. Hearing about a man who wanted to take some children to Africa, my mother discussed this with her brothers. She at the time was ten and the others eight and six. They met with Isaac Ochberg who agreed to take them and so their journey began.

As we know, they travelled from Warsaw to Danzig and then to London where they were cared for before leaving for Cape Town. The children were all medically examined

Itzik, Yetta, and Chaim Rosia (Isaac, Yenta and Chaim Razu).
Itzik was killed by gun fire from Rommel's army while fighting with the South African Military in North Africa. Chaim was up North, there, as was Celia's brother Wolfie who was with Itzik when he was killed.

and my Uncle Chaim was found to have a strange black patch on the back of his head. He was kept behind for further investigation till it was found to be a mark from his pen which he wiped on the back of his head. I hate to think of the trauma it must have caused the children to be parted from him.

ELKA RAZU – AN OLDER SISTER LEFT BEHIND
Dawn Goodman writes:

In the 1960s my Dad Chaim Rosier, got a phone call out of the blue, from the International Red Cross to ask whether he was related to a certain Elka Rozu who was living in Los Angeles and had been searching for her two brothers and a sister. The little ones had been separated from her when their parents had died of the flu epidemic raging through Eastern Europe around 1917, extreme poverty and starvation. That is what it says on my father's passport about his parents' death.

Elka was too old to be part of the Orphan group, and had a boyfriend anyway with whom she had decided to attempt to reach Palestine, which she and her future husband successfully did, going on to New York then LA as they became more affluent over the years.

The Rosier family details as recorded on pages 17, 19 and 21 of the register at the Cape Jewish Orphanage (Oranjia).
1 Names and surname: Yetta, Hymie and Isaac Rosier
2 Father: Aaron   3 Mother: Tilly
4 Ages: 10, 9 and 8 years 5 From where: Wlodawa
6 How orphaned: Both parents
7 Both parents suffered a lot during the War. They have both died within a week of hunger and typhoid fever.

Anyway, my father was quite shocked to learn that their elder sister was alive and trying to contact him and his sister and their younger brother Itzak, who came from Poland with them and sadly died in a battle in North Africa with the Germans as part of the South African Army Corp during World War Two.

In those days it took Elka two months to get to South Africa. She spent a few months here, and all I can remember of her visit was that every evening after work my father would go to Auntie Yetta's flat and the three of them would just weep and chat for hours- the weeping never stopped! Quite extraordinary!

Wedding of Chaim (Hymie) Rosier to Cecelia Kodesh

The long lost sister Ella (Elka Razu) with her children Alan and Ellen Rosen.~ 1952

HYMIE ROSIER a white Jewish member of the Congress of Democrats by *Dawn Goodman*

My father fought with SADF against Rommels army in North Africa-where Itzik, his brother, also an Orphan, was killed by enemy fire.

He also turned to be a white Jewish member of the Congress of Democrats, which was the white wing of the ANC in the very early years when whites and blacks could not be part of the same party, of his being the influence on twins, my mother and her twin brother Wolfie Kodesh who was, Umkhonto We Sizwe head of logistics, (the fledgling ANC's money collector man). When Nelson Mandela was on the run Wolfie hid him in his flat, then was the connection with the Leaders of the underground ANC while Madiba was in hiding at Lilies Leaf farm, Rivonia, now a truly superb Museum of the history of the ANC. He was one of the few white Jewish Commanders of Umkhonto We Sizwe, the underground of the ANC in exile.

My father elected to remain in SA during apartheid years under really difficult circumstances, being under house arrest, watched by the special branch of the SA Police, a vicious organisation I can tell you, while their comrades and friends had left this country. I could never. I figured this all out with the help of professionals- it makes for an interesting story…much to do with where Chaim came from actually…..understand the reasons why but years and years later I met Madiba….at the funeral of Wolfie Kodesh my uncle, specially flying down for the occasion- nothing to do with my dad but interesting to tell you nevertheless, because it is not usual to know about a white Jewish family being on that side of the political spectrum, standing up for the black man to the extent that they will sacrifice their lives in a way of speaking, which is what Chaim was prepared to do, and passed this on to his wife and her twin, all of them taking the ball so to speak and running with it for the rest of their lives, despite being ostracised for many many years by the society within which they lived. Well look how it turned out now! Who was right and who was wrong….who was brave and who was cowardly?

TRYING TO FIND INFORMATION IN POLAND ABOUT MY LOST FAMILY By *Dawn Goodman, the daughter of Hymie Rosier(Chaim Razu)*

While I was growing up, the subject of my father's life before South Africa, was never part of our discourse. As with many deep trauma sufferers, the past remained locked in a portion of his brain, never to be opened, like a safe… the past I now realise, was simply too painful to think about and remember. Looking back at my childhood,my parents were totally wrapped up in the Anti Apartheid movement, the future was all that mattered and Chaim's past was neither thought about, nor discussed.

I hardly questioned my father about family left behind in Poland. I do know for sure that Chaim had two older sisters, both almost teenagers when their parents died of the flu, an epidemic raging through the Pale of

Settlement at that time. They, and an infant brother remained behind in Poland. That little one I was told, remained with an aunt, possibly dying very young, the one sister had a non Jewish Polish boyfriend, we have no knowledge of what became of her and the other joined a group offering passage to Palestine, with her childhood sweetheart whom she married, ending up in the USA.

About six years ago I came across a novel, *The Puppet Boy of Warsaw*, the fictional story of a young boy living in the Warsaw Ghetto and a young German soldier who was conscripted into the German Army. This story was fascinating to me, two parallel tales, about before, during and after WW11, about the connection between these two disparate characters, putting into perspective what such lives must have been like and how it affected them on opposite sides of a most ghastly situation. It caused me to start thinking of my lost family.

The unexplained, started haunting me. I started wondering about my family. Both my grandparents had had at least eight siblings and that makes for quite a large family.

Reading this book had opened my blinkered eyes and got my brain churning over, to a situation I had never thought of before. Surely I thought, there must have been some family who survived the the early 1900's, the pogroms, the blood thirsty Red, White and Cossack armies decimating Jewish villages and homes, the famine, the flu epidemic which took the lives of my still young grandparents.

I contacted a relative in the USA, a reclusive man, difficult to keep contact with, asking him whether his mother had had knowledge of any family left behind in Poland. He told me that indeed there had been, close family, all sent to the Warsaw Ghetto but believed through some sort of extended family or friends network, all had died at Auschwitz.

This led me to research the possibility that there might be some information about my family in archives. A friend works for an Anti- Semitic Institute in Hamburg. She started me off in the right direction, enabling me to go ahead with my amateur investigation.

First I contacted the Emanuel Ringleblum Jewish Historical Institute of Jewish Geneology, and family Heritage Centre, in Warsaw.

A researcher immediately made contact with me and we had many interesting conversations by email. Very little fruitful information came out of my search however, but nevertheless I decided to visit Poland and see for myself, first hand. Walk the streets my ancestors might have walked once upon a time....pay homage to my lost family at their end destination. Very emotional stuff.

Alas my quest came to nothing, no information was available, all that could be found was that the surname on my father's passport was Romanian. The researchers suggested that perhaps I had made a mistake and that the family were from Romania...not Poland.

They had even checked with archivists at Yad Vashem. My thoughts from that piece of information were thatmany centuries ago the Rozu family had migrated to what is now Poland. My father's place of birth was definitely Poland. That I knew for sure.

Towards the end of 2015 I set off, intrigued at what I might find, how I would feel. Firstly checking out enormous vibrant Warsaw then checking in wiith the researcher I had been communicating with, who confirmed again face to face with me, that no records were to be found in or around the town where my father was born. The researcher told me that vast quantities of personal files belonging to the Civil Service were destroyed during and just after the war.

The Institute of Jewish Geneology is really most imprlessive. They have a bank of researchers, all highly qualified, who attend to anyone who has any questions about Jewish Polish ancestry. One can simply walk in off the street and they attend to you, with sympathy, patience and grace. A truly marvellous facility. I dropped off a copy of the Ochburg Orphan documentary with them. By the way, the Institute has a good museum display of the history of Polish Jews on their second floor.

The truly magnificent modern Warsaw Polin Museum of Polish Jews is in every way a superb world class museum designed by a great Finnish architect situated exactly where the Warsaw Ghetto had been. There too I dropped a copy of the film of the Ochberg Orphan story. The museum researcher I spoke with had no knowledge of the amazing Ochberg Orphan story and was fascinated with the little I told her. They were keen to see the books as well.

Next stop Krakow, to pay homage to my family at Auschwitz. However upon arrival at the camp I was told by an authoritative guide, that my family would have been taken to Treblinka, not Aushcwitz. I was disappointed and saddened but nevertheless of course found the experience extraordinarily moving.

Quite a few synagogues in the city of Krakow are now Jewish Remembrance Museums. One extensive display particularly impressed me. It was a large series of blown up photographs of Jewish citizens of Krakow with explainations of why they, and their families had remained in Poland after the war right up till today, and why they had not considered moving to Israel.

Wandering around Krakow one can feel the spirit of the Jews in and around the old Jewish quarter. Cafes, Bagel shops and restaurants are filled with people day and night, music from Klezmer bands fill the air, the beginnings of restoring what were Jewish houses, outdoor art displays and huge graffiti with Jewish symbols, all add to the atmosphere of a charming section of that city.

I feel satisfied that I had gone on a quest and although the result was not what I would have preferred, it still gave me a sense of satisfaction that I had done my best in my search regardless of the outcome.

My ancestors knew I was there!

Chapter 26 – MOLLY COHEN (MALKA SCHAPIRA) (1913-2013)

The records show that Malka was born in 1913 in Sarny and was placed in the care of Oranjia.

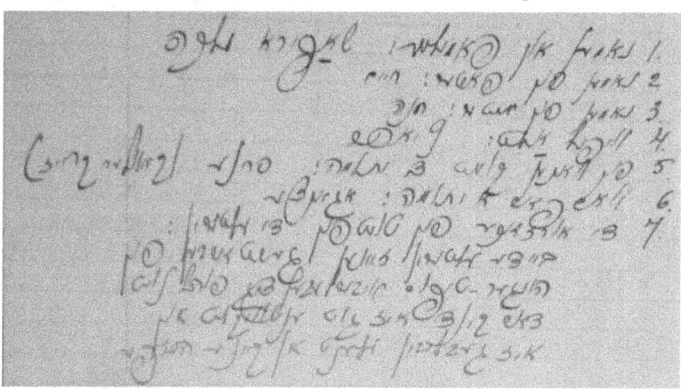

Family details of Malka Shapira as recorded on page 117 of the register kept by the Cape Jewish Orphanage (Oranjia).

1 Name and surname: Malka Shapira
2 Father: Hayim
3 Mother: Hannah 4 Age: 9 years
5 Place of origin: Sarny
6 How orphaned: Both parents
7 Cause of death: Both parents died of hunger and Typhus experiencing much hardship. The child was well developed and was left alone without any help.

Malka Schapira

*Malka Schapira, is the little girl front row, 5th from the right
Group passport number 8*

Wedding of Isaac Cohen and Molley Schapiro - 1934

LASTING LEGACY - MEMORIES OF MOLLY
by Charlotte Cohen, Molly's daughter-in-law
October 2014

Sometimes relationships exceed their delineation. Sometimes they extend past the term 'friendship' – leaving one inspired, uplifted - and with more insight and understanding.

Molly Cohen passed away in November 2013 – just 9 days short of her 100th birthday which would have been on 18th November. Prior to her death, she was the last surviving Ochberg orphan in Cape Town.

In an article 'Connections and Recollections' first published in the 2006 (later in David Solly Sandler's book, 'The Ochberg Orphans'), I wrote about Molly's early life in war-torn Eastern Europe, being rescued by Isaac Ochberg and growing up in Cape Town at Oranjia. Molly married before she was twenty and had two sons. With the untimely and sudden death of her husband at the age of 33), she was left a very young widow. Although she always worked hard and nothing was handed to her on a plate, Molly was 'a lady to her fingertips'. Without airs and graces, she was beautiful in appearance; her manner restrained and gentle.

Molly became my mother-in-law in 1959. Our relationship was respectful and cordial. After my divorce in 1987, our paths separated. However, after my younger son, Steven, married in 2003, my association with Molly was renewed. So much had happened in our lives in the interim, that the formal roles of mother-and-daughter-in-law became more undefined.

With shared concerns and convictions, we became friends.

One never knows how life will deal the cards or anticipate how lives will intertwine.

Both of us had experienced great trauma: For the first years of her life, she was an orphan. Her two young sons were also orphaned at a very early age.

Tragedy had also overtaken my life in that my sons – (and Molly's grandsons) aged 45 and 42 respectively, died within 4 years of each other. Both of us (despite enjoying a laugh, a joke and good company) had met head-on with the 'slings and arrows of outrageous fortune.'

One of the greatest acts of compassion and kindness - and one which I will never forget - was when Molly attended the funeral of my younger son, Steven, in May 2010. Although a chair for her was at the graveside, Molly, aged 97, refused to sit. She stood before the grave with her arm around me – never removing it and never leaving my side. After the burial, both of us sat on a bench erected at the cemetery in memory of Rodney and Steven - my sons and her grandsons. Molly and I were blessed by Rabbi Richard Newman. It will remain ingrained in my memory for as long as I live.

As well as many others on whom she had a profound effect, Molly became an integral part of my life in the years before her death. I often think of the times she would phone me to chat - or the talks we had when I popped in to see her. Even at age 99, she would still insist on making tea, which was brought to a small table by the window where would sit and discuss things and exchange ideas. What Molly said was clear, simple and meaningful.

Despite her gentle approach, Molly was not hesitant to speak her mind; and even though she was in her late nineties, when she felt I needed to hear some sense, I would receive a firm lecture from her.

In fact, being there was like a haven. It was therapeutic.

On one occasion she remarked: "People are mean to you because of three things: They are either jealous, they feel inadequate or they want to be 'top dog'. How true, those words! The three factors she cited are food for thought: Think of anyone who falls into one of these categories - whether they feel inadequate, or jealous or that you are invading their space, it doesn't matter what you try to do try and win them over. It is not going to happen. No matter how you knock yourself out trying to please them, they are never going to 'like' you ... because the fault lies with them - not with you.

So you are wasting your time. Best thing is to 'move out and move on.'

It changed my thinking and attitude

It was going to be Molly's 100th birthday on November 2013. A party was planned for her centenary celebration by Arthur and Nesta - her son and daughter-in-law. I planned to ask her about some of the influences that had shaped her life and write them down. Unfortunately, she became ill a few weeks prior to turning 100, and died just 9 days short reaching her century.

However, the exchange I had with Molly only a few weeks before, was one of the most meaningful I have ever had. It has also impacted on many others to whom I have posed the same question and related what she said.

I asked her "What about yourself has made you most proud?" (What would that response be if that question were asked of you?...)

Without hesitation, she answered "When I said I would do something, I did it!"

"So you could be trusted?" I said.

"Yes,' she replied simply.

What an incredible thing to be able to say about oneself: "I could be trusted."

Of course, the statement goes even further than that in that it also shows commitment and determination.

There are two things that cannot be bought. They have to be earned. They offer rewards greater than any money can buy – not only for you - but on those who have been in contact with you. (If you lose them, no amount of money can buy them back). They are trust and respect.

Molly epitomised those qualities. And what a remarkable lady she was!

With a life that typified trustworthiness, determination, courage and kindness, she personified the same characteristics of those that exemplified Isaac Ochberg:

Molly is missed by all who knew her. (I still have an overwhelming impulse to phone her whenever there is 'news' - or visit her at Sea point Place when I drive past.)

But her legacy of wisdom, friendship, understanding and good advice remains with all who were privileged to have known her.

The full life story of Molly is told in chapters 37 and 48 of the first volume of The Ochberg Orphans

REMEMBERING MY MOM MALKA [MOLLY] COHEN
by her son Arthur Cohen

My Mom. Malka [Molly] Cohen was born in Eastern Europe in what today is the country of Belarus and almost exactly 100 years later passed away in Cape Town. In those years she saw not only geographical upheavals but also vast changes in people's attitudes to what is or is not acceptable norms. At age seven she was rescued by Isaac Ochberg from the horrors that the Jews of the Pale of Settlement were suffering, and arrived in Cape Town in 1921 with the group fondly known as the Ochberg Orphans. She was placed in the care of Oranjia (The Cape Jewish Orphanage), and there it was that she made lifelong friends with other members of the group.

When Molly married my Dad in 1934, the members of the committee of Oranjia were honoured guests. Molly and her husband (my Dad) started a small shop in the front of a rented house near Mowbray. My brother was born in1935, and I followed in 1938. When my parents had saved enough to buy their own house, they moved the shop to Athlone.

In 1944 Molly was widowed. Finding herself again alone, and with two small children, to whom she needed to be comforter, confidant, behavioural example, and also provider, instilled a strongly independent streak in her. She determined it better to keep the shop going rather than seek employment, but the long hours it entailed soon made her realise that my brother and I were too young to be left alone. She therefore was forced to sell the house and turned to the people she trusted (the Oranjia committee) and placed us in their care for a few years till we were able to manage on our own. We were then transferred to Boarding School for a short while, before Molly decided we were ready and so again set up a permanent home for the three of us.

When Molly was still at Oranjia, a surviving brother was traced and had reached Israel, were he was married and had three children. Molly went to Israel in the early 1950s to meet them, and I and my wife also did so in the late 1960s. In later years the one son Moshe, her nephew,

Molly Cohen (1913-2013)

my first cousin, made numerous visits to Cape Town and grew very close to Molly.It was from Moshe that a second surviving brother of Molly and living in Israel, also then became known . On a subsequent solo trip by Nesta,my wife, to Israel, Moshe took her to meet the second surviving brother and his family and she reported back to Molly thereon, but they never physically met again.

When Molly returned from her visit to Israel, she found the shop was completely run down. She therefore elected to pay its debts and closed it. She then worked for a while in the hotel industry, and as a commercial traveller, and eventually ended up importing and selling to offices, and staff copies of old master pictures which she hauled all over Cape Town, travelling on buses in all weather and enjoying it. She said it was her way of getting out and about, and paid her way so as not to be a burden to anyone.

Molly lived for her children, and never remarried because she felt that no one was going to treat us in the same way that they treat their existing biological children. It is therefore incumbent on her descendants to see that her sacrifice is for a worthwhile purpose and teach others that adversity is a spur to dig deep within ourselves to tackle and solve whatever problem comes our way.

Inspite of suffering loss of both parents and many of her siblings as a child, of her husband whilst still a young women, of a son, and of two grandsons, and continuing to work until over 80 years old, Molly was uncomplaining, refined, gracious, gentle, and modest right till the end of her days. To her eternal glory she never let her circumstances compromise her principles, or her concern and commitment to ensure as best she could for the well-being of family and friends.

With love

Arthur (son)

Mollie's sons - Hymie and Arthur

Chapter 27 – SZLEMA (SOLOMON) SHTERN
LATER CALLED SOLLY CHIDECKEL

SZLEMA (SOLOMON) SHTERN
Later called Solly Chidekel

The records show that Solomon was born in 1912 in Wlodawa and was placed in the care of Oranjia.

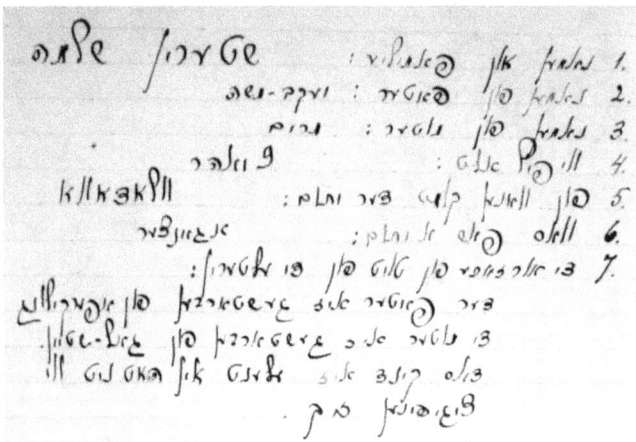

Family details of Szlema (Solomon) Shtern as recorded on page 15 of the register kept by the Cape Jewish Orphanage (Oranjia).

1 Name and surname: Shlomo Stern
2 Father: Jacob Moshe
3 Mother: Miriam
4 Age: 9 years
5 Place of origin: Wladawa
6 How orphaned: Both parents
7 General Comments: Father died of the flu. Mother died of gallstone
   The child had nowhere to go to.

SOLOMON SHTERN LATER CALLED SOLLY CHIDECKEL *by Stanley Loon.*

Here is the story of Solly Chideckel as told by my mother: In the 1930's, her uncle and mentor, Baruch Chideckel, vice chairman of the Jewish Board of Education in Cape Town, and his wife Ziporah were childless and they decided to adopt an Ochberg orphan by the name of Solomon, now well into his teens. Solly was soon treated as a brother by my mother and her sisters.

In 1939, Baruch died and when war broke out, Solly joined the South African army. He was sent up north as a tank driver with the 6th Armoured Division. He wrote home regularly and my mother or one of her sisters would read the letter to Ziporah who was in poor health and nearly blind.

On the 12th of June, 1942, Solly was killed in action in Tobruk and is buried in El Alemein. The family did not know how to break the news to Ziporah as it would certainly have killed her. They decided not to tell her and so for months afterwards until she succomed to dementia, they read old or fictitious letters to her. She died in 1946.

Another Ochberg orphan in our family, is Gawa Piatkin (Chawa Pianka) who changed her name to Eva. She married Baruch Chideckel's half brother, David Smulowitz. David Smulowitz and my grandmother were full brother and sister. Eva had the distinction of being the first Ochberg orphan to marry.

I remember going to her funeral in Pinelands in 1983 and I never knew that she was part of this historical event.

In the book "Jewish Responses to Persecution 1944-1946" by Leah Wolfson, 2015, there is a discussion concerning the estate of South African corporal Solomon Chideckel, who was killed in action in WW2. In the article, it is mentioned that he had left an estate of unknown value to the Schtern family. Also in the article is a letter to Poland trying to trace the Schtern family.

MEMORIAL PLAQUE AT ORANJIA

A Memory Plaque to commemorate those who made the supreme sacrifice in WWII and the Israeli War of Independence was erected in the children's playground. It bears the following names

In WWII
   Trouper Solomon Chideckel, Service details below
   Sergeant Abe Isadore Gottlieb,
   Lieutenant Ernest Louise Jacob Hazeldine,
   Private Harry Miller,
   Lance Corporal Isaac Rosier,
   Private E Stone

In the Israeli War of Independence
   Pilot Officer Nathan Friedman

SERVICE RECORDS OF SOLOMON CHIDECKEL

Name	Given Name	Initials	Regiment	Unit	Cemetery	Country	Locality	Date of Death
CHIDECKEL	SOLOMON	S	South African Tank Corps	6th Armoured Car Regt.	ALAMEIN MEMORIAL	Egypt		1942-06-12

Service Details

Name:	CHIDECKEL
Given Name:	SOLOMON
Initials:	S
Service No:	15479
Rank:	Trooper — Other Casualties of this Rank
Regiment:	South African Tank Corps — Other Casualties from this Regiment
Unit:	6th Armoured Car Regt. — Other Casualties from this Unit
Date of Death:	1942-06-12 — Other Casualties on this Date
Cause of Death:	Missing, Death Presumed
Additional Information:	No additional information known at this time

Commemoration

Country:	Egypt — Other Casualties commemorated in Egypt
Cemetery:	ALAMEIN MEMORIAL — Other Casualties commemorated in this Cemetery

OTHER ON THE MEMORIAL PLAQUE AT ORANJIA THAT MADE THE SUPREME SACRIFICE

GOTTLIEB	ABE ISADORE	A I	Royal Air Force Volunteer Reserve	44 Sqdn.	RUNNYMEDE MEMORIAL	United Kingdom	Surrey	1942-06-06
HAZELDINE	ERNEST LOUISE JACOB	E L J	South African Air Force	4 Sqdn.	EL ALAMEIN WAR CEMETERY	Egypt		1943-01-05
ROSIER	ISAAC	I	Duke of Edinburgh's Own Rifles, S.A. Forces	1st	HALFAYA SOLLUM WAR CEMETERY	Egypt		1941-12-03

Chapter 28 – FEYGA SHTRASNER LATER CALLED FANNY GOLDBERG

FEYGA SHTRASNER
Fanny Florence (Goldberg) Wise

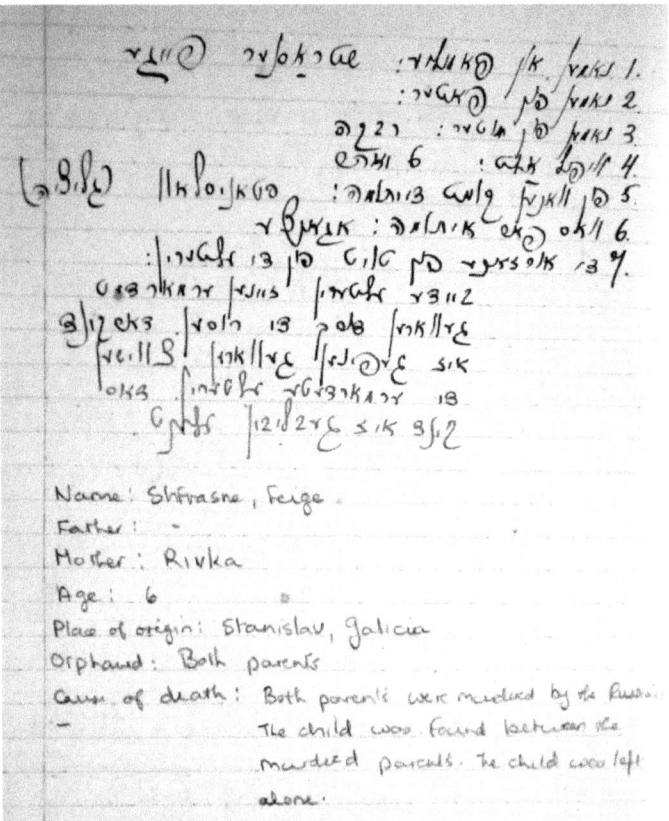

The entry in the register of Oranjia for Feyga Shtrasner (later Fanny Florence (Goldberg) Wise)

FEYGA SHTRASNER
FANNY FLORENCE (GOLDBERG) WISE

Establishing that Fanny Florence (Goldberg) Wise was in fact Feyga Shtrasner took many many months of correspondence with Channelle and Olga Rubie

Channelle and Olga Rubie initially wrote
"We are descendents of Fanny Florence Goldberg. She was an Ochberg orphan. She was born in Poland in 1915. She was 11 years old when she came out to South Africa. She stayed in the Cape Jewish Orphanage. She was my (Channelle) great grandmother and my mom's (Olga) maternal grandmother. She didn't speak about her life as an orphan so we didn't know much about her apart from the basics. She married a South African man and had six children, Gerald, Linda, Edna, Mercia, Maureen and my mom Olive. Two of them are still alive. She died at the age of 59 when my mom, Olive, was 16 years old."

As the given names were not on record, I suggested she may have been adopted and Olga replied. "These are the only names I know she had being Fanny Florence Goldberg. She married and became Fanny Wise. I never heard any mention of her being adopted. She had no siblings and growing up she never mentioned being adopted. I was only 16 years old when she died.

Fanny as a young lady.
Olga writes "this picture of my gran is one she sent to my grandfather it says "To Lesley fondest love Fanny" probably when they were dating."

If she had lived longer I would have had the opportunity to ask her questions but at 16 one doesn't think like that.

A couple of years ago we went to the Jewish Museum to see if we could find anything but unfortunately not. They said they would check the archives but never got back to me. My aunt and uncle are still alive. I have occasional contact with my aunt and I'm going to try get more information from her. Its not that easy as she is ill with cancer. We live in Cape Town."

I replied "I can help you but there is a missing link with the name. Please ask the older generation in your family for more information. Did you know the names of Fanny's parents? Do you have photos of Fanny as a young girl? Can you give me any more information that can help me identify your grandmother?

Later Olga Rubie wrote
"I got some news which I find exciting. My family had a little reunion last weekend and my mother's brother and daughter Colleen were there and I have not seen them for many years (I knew they were going to be there).

Colleen had pictures and documents of my gran which her father gave to her to keep. Well she phoned me today and there is a picture and the name behind it is Fanny Strasone. I am so excited does that help us now. We all went to my mothers sister who I told you was ill. She then passed away on Thursday. Colleen is going to make copies for me of everything she has and I am going to get the pictures and make copies. I am so excited by all this

I responded "I've been looking for the name Fanny Strasone on pages 216 and 217 and on pages 636 to 640. There is no surname Strasone.. There is also no Fanny but this may well have been an Anglicised version of Feiga. I have found it. There is a **Feiga Shtrasner on page 639** and she remained in the Cape in Oranjia and we have not made contact with her or her family and so I would say **Feiga Shtrasner is** your Gran. From page 639 you can see she was born in Stanislav in 1915 and was placed in the care of Oranjia. On page 217 she is number 62 on one list and 27 on the other list. On page 98 she is number 20 on the group passport and would be one of the girls in the photo!! Can you recognize her??

Look at the little girl with short hair in the middle at the back with a 20 written above her. This may well be her!!! What do you think?

Extract from group Passport One

Olga Rubie wrote
Well that looks like her she had straight dark hair and she was a short woman. I am almost positive that is her. Judging by the other girls I can tell a mile off none of them look remotely like my gran. That is her face. David I am so excited it seems like everything is falling into place. This book is truly amazing you have done extraordinary work !! Thank you !!

Later Olga Rubie wrote
Thank you so much for your response David!! I am not aware of this memorial site *in Israel.* Would you please send info on it. This is getting so interesting for me after all these years. Years ago when I could not find anything on my gran I reluctantly just gave up and all these new doors have opened thanks to you. I am very grateful to you !!

The pic of my gran you have is one she sent to my grandfather it says "To Lesley fondest love Fanny" probably when they were dating. Looking forward to putting this all together!!

I am so happy (that's an understatement) to have pics and post cards of my gran which my daughter Channelle mailed to you on my behalf. (see below) I am going to make copies of everything and then give it back to my cousin. I have a couple of other photos of her too also her green I D card. On the one card I sent to you there is the name Goldberg!!

Anyway I am doing some more research just waiting for the Oranjia to get back to me. Still trying to contact the UCT there is always an answering machine on. I read the pages you quoted to me of the *entries in the register of Oranjia* and I understand what you mean. Hoping to get to the grave tomorrow

I was paging through The *Ochberg Orphans* book and what a small world !! The Kapelus family is in there and I used to date Arthur Kapelus. My parents bought furniture and goods from him many times and he became part of our family in a sense. He had lunch with us almost every Saturday and visited quite often. And when I got older we dated. He was 14 years older than me. I just cannot believe reading this and seeing the pic. Pages 344, 345 and 346. There is Arthur in the picture in the back row with specs on. Just can't believe it.

THE THREE POSTCARDS OF FEYGA SHTRASNER (FANNY GOLDBERG), AN OCHBERG ORPHAN

These postcards sent in by Feyga's grand daughter, Olga Rubie, establish that Fanny (Florence) Goldberg was in fact originally named Feyga Shtrasner.

The photo on the first postcard. Sybil Keats the daughter of Polly Stanger (an Ochberg Orphan) writes. "As for the two beautiful girls, one is my mother and the other girl could be one of the Gonifas sisters."

Photos of my gran, Feyga Strasner later called Fanny Florence (Goldberg) Wise

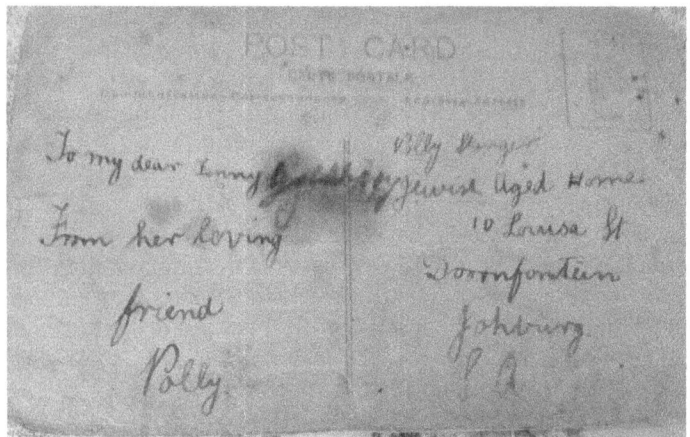

The first card is from Polly Stanger (an Ochberg Orphan then living in The Old Aged Home in Doornfontein) and her daughter Sybil Keats writes, "I have never seen that picture of my mother, (on the right), the other woman and the good looking man."

Fanny as a young lady

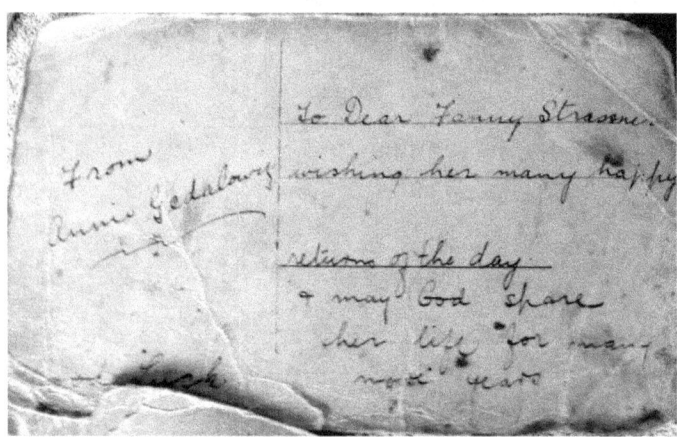

The second postcard is a happy birthday greeting addressed to Fanny Strasner and is from Annie Gedalowitz. Olga writes " There is no one in South Africa. with the surname of Gedalowitz. I phoned our telkom and they searched nationally for me. "
Sybil Keats writes about the photo, "I think the photo of a woman on the couch could just be a postcard."

Fanny and her husband, Lesley Wise

The photo above is on the front of the third postcard and the message on the back of the card reads.
"To Fanny - with love from Phoebe"
Olga says Fanny is on the right

My gran

Meeting up with Sybil Keats, Polly Stanger's daughter.

When Sybil came to South Africa last year (2016) we met. It was wonderful to meet Sybil, Polly Stanger's daughter. I felt a connection with her as her mother and my grandmother were friends as we can see from the post card.

Olga Rubie and Sybil Keats meeting up in South Africa in 2016

Family Photos

My mum, Olive Wright

My husband (Keith) and I

My son Garth and daughter Channelle

Garth, his wife Megan, their son Jesse and their daughter Hannah.

Chapter 29 – YAKOV YAGALKOVSKY

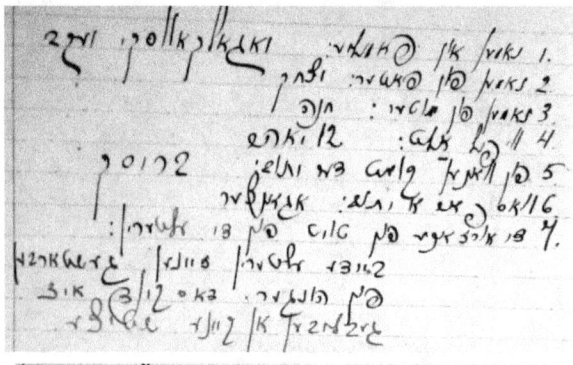

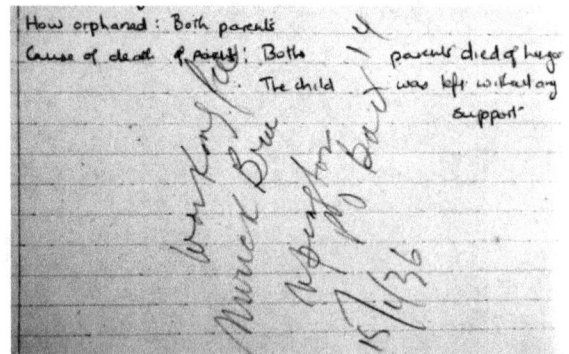

Family details of Yakov Yagalkovsky as recorded on page 135 of the register kept by the Cape Jewish Orphanage (Oranjia).
1 Name and surname: Yakov Yagalkovsky
2 Father: Yitzhak
3 Mother: Hana   4 Age: 12 years   5 Place of origin: Brest
6 How orphaned: Both parents
7 General Comments: Both parents died of hunger.
The child was left without any support.
Note dated 15/1/36: Working for Nurick Bros. PO Box 14 Upington.

JACK YALKOVSKY (YAKOV YAGALKOVSKY)
Written by Sally Sher from Israel.

I wonder whether Jack Yalkovsky's name has been recorded as an Ochberg Orphan. I dont know anything about his early life besides that he did live in the *Oranjia* Orphanage and had been brought to Upington by a childless couple Mr and Mrs Gotschalk.

From a young age he worked for my grandfather Abraham and his brother Morris Nurick in the shop on their farm Exteenskuil. He never married. He did not come into town and associate himself with anyone and to use my father's expression "he threw himself away." He was a real recluse. However he was loyal and worked well.

Morris was the elder. The firm was Nurick Bros. (Pty) Ltd. The address was P O Box 14 Upington. Jack probably worked in the farm shop for about 20 years. It would be interesting to know how he came to work for The Nuricks.

The farm Exteenskuil was about an hour by car from Upington. My family lived in Upington and went daily to the farm whereas Jack lived on the farm. He occasionally went to Upington to get stock for the shop that he ran on the farm. I found amongst our family tree Jack's surname spelt Yalkovsky.

My uncle Abe Rosman, now aged 90, who lives in Sea Point. together with my father ran the farm and produce section of the business. Abe said that Jack bought a piece of farming ground adjacent to Exteenskuil which he farmed until he was murdered. My grandfather bought the ground. Abe does not know what happened to the money and Jack's estate. While I have such a clear recollection that Mr and Mrs Gottschalk were instrumental in bringing Jack to Upington, Abe has no recollection of this.

Neither Abe nor I had ever seen a photograph of Jack. As far as descendants go Abe said that Jack had a coloured daughter. The girl's mother was a coloured woman living on the farm. I can't recall ever seeing the mother or daughter. I always heard about the relationship. Abe does not know what happened to her after he died. As I said previously he was a recluse.

Sadly one night in December 1956 two coloured men, an older one and a younger one, knocked on his door with the pretext that they needed petrol. The petrol pump was outside his house. They murdered him for the money in the safe.

> A very sad story relating to one of our employees is that of Jack Yalkowsky, who was murdered when working at Eksteenskuil. He was called out one night by two natives saying that they needed petrol. When he came out of the house they demanded money and when he refused, hit him on the head with an iron bar, killing him. When arrested one of the men turned king's evidence and the other was sentenced to death. As Jack was one of the "Ochberg Orphans" brought to South Africa after the horrific pogroms in Poland in 1921 and was unmarried, this seemed more than tragic as there was nobody to really mourn for him. He left all his worldly possessions to the Upington Hebrew Congregation.

Extract from a book on the Nurick Family

Rhoda, Sally's sister writes

Although Jack was like a ghost in the background I was always intrigued by him and felt so sorry for him. I would have liked to hold his hand or kiss him. I definitely knew that originally he came to stay with the Gottschalks but they could not communicate with him, hence him going to live on the farm.

I remember going with my father to the farm and Jack had lunch with my father and Abe. He was clean and nicely dressed.

He used to come to Upington for Yom Kippur and I remember him sleeping over on the stoep. When my mother asked him if he slept well, he said he couldn't sleep there was too much traffic! My parents thought that was so funny. On the corner of our house was a stop street sign and maybe three cars at the most might have stopped there in the early evening!

I remember when he was murdered and the three murderers were apprehended near Kenhardt. They had used an axe to slice open his head and they were later hung! I remember hearing my father speak and arrange a tombstone to be put on his grave.

What I never ever heard was that he had a daughter and we suppose her mother was a coloured lady. I'm pleased he had some sort of normal life.

The above page, chapter 85 of The Ochberg Orphans, has been repeated for completeness and now the photos following are included.

PHOTOS OF JACK YALKOVSKY

Jack is on the extreme right.

Jack is on the pillion of the bike
The photos were kindly sent in by Pearl Chazan (Nee Nurick) from Israel and as stated on Jack's page in the Oranjia Register her brothers employed Jack

Chapter 30 – GROUP PHOTOS OF THE ARCADIA CHILDREN

When the Ochberg Orphans arrived in Cape Town half of the children went to live in the care of the Cape Jewish Orphanage later to be called Oranjia. The other half were taken by train to Johannesburg and initially placed in the care of the The Jewish Relief, Reconstruction and Orphans Fund and then later in the care of the South African Jewish Orphanage, later to be called Arcadia.

Some of the Ukrainian Pogrom and War Orphans(Ochberg Orphans) in Johannesburg, brought to South Africa by Isaac Ochberg~ 1922. Isaac Ochberg is in the middle, Clara Tannenbaum is left of him (in the striped dress) and Sally Tannenbaum is standing behind him on the right. On his right is Leah Zaika. The two little children held by Isaac Ochberg are Hymie and Phyllis Wolchuk.

COMMENTS

Top row second from right is my aunt, Cywje Joffe. **Peter Larson**

The first boy on the left in the middle row (third) is definitely my uncle Isaac Helman and I think the first little chap in the front row on the left is his younger brother Benjamin Helman. **Julie Ross**

Chaim Altuska is the last boy on the right in the bottom row. **Ursula Rembach**

Fourth row, fifth from the left is Annie Borowik. **Barry Berelowitz**

In the middle of the back row is my mother, Blume Faifer and her sister Lily is to her right. **Louise Bird**

Second row on the extreme right hand side are Annie (Chaya) and Charlotte (Cherna) Guber, with hand on hip.

Third row third from left is Tasha Altuska, one of the 'Nurses" without her glasses.

Ochberg Orphans placed in the care of the South African Jewish Orphanage (Arcadia) in 1921

COMMENTS

I think my uncle David Rubin is the boy with his hands on his hips in the top left hand corner of this photograph and my mother Chana Rubin is the little girl third from the left in the front row. **Rhoda Fowler**

My mother Helen Penzik /Meyerovitz /Green is standing behind the bottom row of seated children and is 5th from the right wearing a hat. In the photo is also her brother David Penzik - top row standing on the right with a striped belt without a hat. Her sister Mindel Penzik/Davidow is also in the photo standing in front of David in the white dress. I unfortunately can't find her other sister Hannah Penzik/Sandler/Kahn in this picture, but am pretty sure she's somewhere there. **Yvonne Chenik**

In the 3rd row, there is a tall woman wearing a dark dress. To the right of her is a little boy. Behind him is my Aunt Clare Tannenbaum. My Mom, Sally Tannenbaum, is on the little boy's right. Sally has her arms around the child in front of her. **Helen Kuttner**

I think but I'm not 100% sure that Zeidel Feinschmidt (Jack Fine) is in the back row, 5th from right. **Brian Fine**

2nd row extreme left is Cywje Joffe and 3rd row on left side of lady in dark dress is Freidel Joffe. **Peter Larson**

Third row from top, second from right could be Gittel Gonifas and third from right could be Leah Gonifas. **Dorothy Pantanowitz**

My dad Osher (Oscar) Echstein is third from the right in the bottom row standing, behind the row seated. There is a very strong Echstein family resemblance. **Harold Echstein**

The girl with her arm around the woman in the patterned dress could be my mom or aunt, blume or Liba Faifer. **Louise Bird**

Mavis, the Matron and Morris Isaacson, the Chairman, with the Ochberg Orphans ~ 1924

COMMENTS

Ursula Rembach, daughter of Leah Altuska, who sent in this photo identifies the three Altuska sisters. "Leah is on the right end of the first row of seated girls, Tasha is behind her with glasses and dark dress and Sarah is top row third from the right."

Jeff Isaacson living in Israel writes about the two adults in the second row
"Those are my parents, Mavis and Morris Isaacson, all right, but that's not the picture I had at home. There were many more children in my picture. In the picture my parents looked so young. What an extraordinary find! They must have been 24 and 46 respectively at the time."

Front row extreme left sitting on the grass is Cywje Joffe and back row 2nd from the right may be my mother, Freidel Joffe. **Peter Larson**

The little boy, in the front on the grass is probably Hymie Wolchuk. **Francine Blum**

The first girl on the left in the second row from the back is my mother Chassa Helman (Essie Zagey). **Julie Ross**

Second row, third from right Leah or Molly Gonifas, and third row, second from right is Gittel Gonifas. **Dorothy Pantanowitz**

I am sure my mother, Salsa Blind or Sadie is in the middle row third from left, just behind Morris Isaacson. Her arm is around another girl. **Edna Rudnick**

Back row fifth from the left is Annie Borowik. I think that her sister Rachel is to her right. **Barry Berelowitz**

Following are the histories of some of the children that landed up in the care of the South African Jewish Orphanage, later to be called Arcadia.

Chapter 31 - SARAH (ALTUSKA) SLIER (1910-2001)

Sarah was born in 1910 and was in the care of the South African Jewish Orphanage from age 11 to 17.

She had two older sisters, Natasha and Faiga, and a younger sister and a brother, Leah and Chaim. All bar Faiga were brought out to South Africa in 1921 by Isaac Ochberg.

Faiga, the second oldest sister, was in hospital at the time the children were selected, and was sadly left behind.

MY MOTHER, AN OCHBERG ORPHAN
Written by Yvonne (Slier) Phillips, Sarah's daughter.

What was it like growing up with a mother who lived from the age of 11 to 17 at Arcadia Jewish Orphanage?

This is her story as I remember it.

My mother's name was Sarah (Altuska) Slier. She was born in Brest-Litovsk. Belarus on the 23 May 1910. Her parents had five children, four girls and a boy who was the youngest. She was the third child. She was four years old when the First World War broke out. The family was caught in the middle of the battles between the German and Russian armies and somewhere along the line, the parents disappeared and the children were left in the care of the oldest sister, Natasha. They survived as street children, in rags, broken shoes and very little food. They often took shelter in the Shul.

Sarah at the back, Chaim in the middle and Jack Feinschmidt is the other boy. The others are not known. Jack has a son, an optician, living in Sydney Australia.

When the German troops arrived, they were friendly, gave the children chocolate and they were able to communicate; the children speaking Yiddish to the soldiers. The children were taken to work on the farms picking potatoes. One day they would eat potatoes and the next day the skins. As the battles waged backwards and forwards the children sought shelter in the Shul again. The war ended in 1918.

One day in 1920 a man called "Daddy Ochberg" arrived and picked out children that he wanted to take to Africa. The children had no idea what Africa was. Ochberg's brief was that he could only take genuinely orphaned children; if one parent was alive they were disqualified. He could not take sick or disabled or retarded children or any over the age of 16 years.

The second sister was in hospital when Ochberg arrived, but he still took my mother, a younger sister, Leah and the brother, Chaim, with him. The oldest sister, Natasha, was 20 years old, so Ochberg pleaded that he needed at least five nurses to help look after the girls. She became one of the nurses. He also took five older boys to look after the youngsters. In all Ochberg took 200 children, the number he was allowed to bring into South Africa according to a prior

Sarah and Leah sitting in front of two unknown girls

agreement with Prime Minister Smuts. He ignored certain other conditions.

Eighty seven children eventually arrived in Johannesburg, the others remained in Cape Town and some were housed in the Jewish Children's Orphanage which was in Benbow Street in Kensington at that time. The others, including my mother, were put up in the Jewish Old Age Home in Louisa Street, Doornfontein.

My mother so hated it there that she often made me promise that I would never ever put her in an Old Age Home when she was old. (She lived with me in her old age and passed away in March 2001).

In 1921 the Jewish community purchased Arcadia in Parktown, the home of Sir Lionel Phillips and his wife, Florrie. He was one of the richest Randlords – a mining millionaire.

Chaim stands next to Tasha and Leah wears a white ribbon. Sarah is behind Tasha. Other girls unknown.

Growing up in Arcadia was not easy. They had very strict rules about almost everything. The Committee who ran the Home were mostly of English descent and they kept a very strict Jewish religion. People used to come and visit the children on Sundays and bring fruit and sweets, but my mother said that the staff kept most of these for themselves. Of course there were many local children at Arcadia and they all mixed happily together. The newcomers were known simply as "The Russians". My mother spoke about Pesach and how the children were not given anything to eat until the Seder when food only arrived at about ten o'clock at night. This always stuck in her memory.

Yet the children grew up reasonably happy and healthy. My mother was sent to Hebrew High School in Wolmarans Street, opposite the Shul; the younger children went to Jewish Government School in Doornfontein and of the older boys many went to Parktown Boys' High. When my mother was 16 she was sent, together with other girls of her age, to work as a counter-hand at the CTC Bazaars in Johannesburg. The boys were put into trades.

At the age of 18 my mother met a Hollander Jew and before he could marry her, he had to appear in front of the Committee who grilled him about his ability to support her. He, of course, was my father.

Girls in gyms (Sarah standing next to teacher) Polly Stange second from right.

Now a wonderful life began for her. She had a nice home and family but what lingered was the fear of running out of food and she and her siblings had this in common – they always stored a lot of food in their homes. She also insisted that her children learnt music and the girls had to do dancing. She said, "I want them to have what I did not have as a child." She had a passion for shoes and when she died she had over 50 pairs of shoes.

My mother was always embarrassed about the fact that she came from an orphanage, although most of her adult friends were 'orphanage girls.' Her brother absolutely denied that he was ever at Arcadia.

Of course, conditions improved for the children in the thirties and later with the Committee and staff having some psychology knowledge in their background and understanding of the children's situation. So much so, that today ex-Arc children will tell you about the wonderful times that they had at Arcadia.

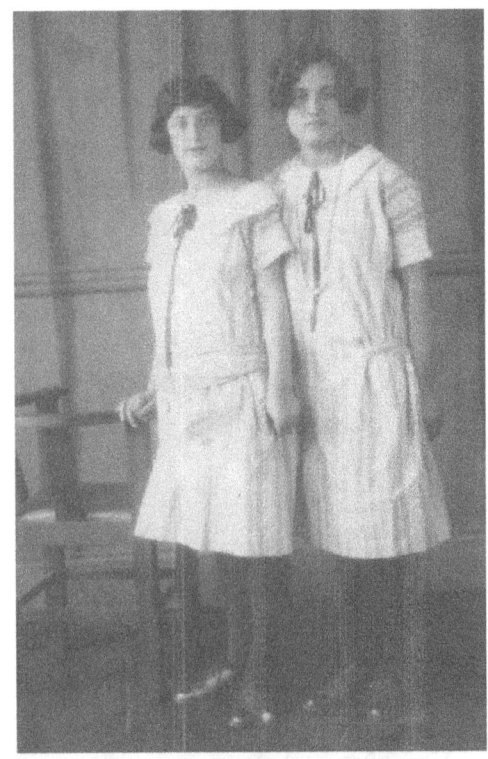

Unknown girl and Sarah

A group from South African Jewish Orphanage – ~1921

1922 class at Hebrew High - Sarah is the 2nd in the middle row and Miss Diamond on right is the teacher

Sarah and Polly Stange

Sarah next to a Girl Guide.

Goup picture (Sarah 2nd from right)

Sarah and girls

Sarah holding hands with young girl

Lionel Slier (Sarah's son) continues

It is remarkable that my mother kept all these photos because when asked about life in Russia and even in Arcadia, her standard reply would be along these lines – "There is nothing to talk about. I have only unpleasant memories. Arcadia in those days was very strict and very hard for all the children."

There was this belief that somehow it was the fault of the children themselves that they were there. Later some ex-Arcs became committee members themselves, and this together with a greater understanding of the children, meant much better understanding and conditions.

I remember Mannie Lipshitz telling me how much he loved being there. "I had so many brothers and sisters and friends," he would say. Jules Gordon also said he loved it.

My mother was shot in the leg at some stage during the war, or even perhaps later when the revolution took place. She either did not remember or else blotted the circumstances out of her mind, but we never found out what had happened. She would never wear shorts as she was conscious of the scar in her calf.

My mother lived from May 1910 to March 2001.

Isaac Ochberg had accepted as one of the conditions that he was not to break up families.

The second sister, Faiga (or Feigel), was in hospital at the time when Ochberg arrived in Brest Litovsk when the children were living in the Shul.

Ochberg took Tasha as a nurse and my mother, Leah and Chaim and left Faiga, the other sister behind. Either he did not know of her, or else he believed that he would come again and get her.

Ochberg really had planned to make more than one trip but the Communists took over and they said that none of their children would be allowed to go to a capitalist country. Ochberg could not get permission to go there again.

We know that Faiga married a man called Milztein in 1925 and they went to live in Argentine. My mother and Leah met her in 1971, but language difficulties meant that there was no real contact.

However my younger daughter, Hayley, is a flight attendant on British Airways and she went to the Argentine where she made contact with a grandson of Faiga, who passed away many years ago. His name is Gustavo and through a girl friend of his who spoke good English, we heard the following:

When Faiga came out of hospital she was shocked and horrified to find that her sisters and brother had gone with a man to Africa. According to Gustavo she never got over the shock and spent her life in morbid depression; she simply never recovered from it. Imagine a girl of 13 finding herself alone and abandoned in a country recovering from a war and a revolution. She really was affected her entire life.

The photos were in the collection of my eldest sister, Yvonne, who has always kept them. They were sent to you by Phil Levinsohn, who married Phyllis the youngest of my three sisters.

In Isaac Ochberg's will, he left a sum of money with his daughter for a 50 year reunion of the children to be held in Cape Town. There was money to pay for all 'children' who could not afford the fare to get to Cape Town and for their accommodation to be met. My mother, Sarah and her sister, Leah, went to the reunion in 1971.

He truly was a wonderful man and a remarkable human being.

SARAH'S FAMILY

Sarah married Jack Slier in 1928 and they had four children; Yvonne (now Phillips), They have 14 grandchildren and seven great-grandchildren.

Deborah, Lionel, Sarah, Jack and Yvonne with Phyllis in front Durban 1948

Yvonne, and Lionel behind and Sarah and Phyllis in front

Jack Slier

Chapter 32 – LEAH (ALTUSKA) ROSENBLATT (1912-1993)

LEAH'S STORY *Written by Ursula (Rosenblatt) Rembach, Leah's daughter.*

My mother, Leah Altuska was the fourth of six children born to my grandparents Labe and Yetta Altuska. The family lived in a village (Shtetl) on the outskirts of the city of Brest Liktov. Brestliktov was quite a famous place, being the border between Russia and Poland. It was here that in 1918 The Treaty of Brest Liktov was signed which exited Russia from WWI.

Being a border town it was continuously the site for civil wars which raged between the Bolsheviks, Finland, Latvia, Lithuania, Ukraine and Poland. The area was part of what was known as the Pale of Settlement established in the late 1700s. Besides the great cities of Poland this was the only area where Jews were permitted to live, and their communities were large and vibrant.

My mother remembered little of her life there prior to the events in 1920, when she was eight years old, and the family would be decimated by the events of Pogrom, wars, famine and disease.

She remembered the many happy times spent visiting her maternal grandparents, Sheine and Shepsel Pavin, who lived in the nearby city which may have been Brest Liktov. The house was unusual in that it was a large double storey with a bannister where the children could have fun sliding down.

In another Shtetl nearby, she recalled visiting her aunt and uncle and two boy cousins. She couldn't remember their names, but knew that the uncle was her father's brother. Of her own home she recalled a large oven above which she and her siblings slept covered in warm eiderdowns. Of her parents she remembered little, except that they had blue eyes and that her father spent time drawing pictures of houses. He may have been an artist, a builder or even an architect but we will never know for sure.

Sometime during the year of 1920 Labe died. Whether his death resulted from one of the very many pogroms inflicted on the Jews or from disease, or other misfortune, it was not unlike the fate of very many Jewish families at that time and place, and was to change the history of the Jewish People of the Pale.

Sometime after this event, whether it was weeks or months, no one could remember, their mother Yetta also died. She left behind the six children. Tasha (Natasha) aged 16, Fagele, (Fanya) aged 12, Sarah aged ten, Leah aged eight, Chaim aged five and an infant daughter called Rochele. My mother thought that her mother may have died of Typhoid. She recalled being taken to a hall, which may have been a hospital or a morgue where her mother was laid out. Her body was swollen and when the infant Rochelle saw her mother she cried out trying to reach her dead body to feed. Leah recalled her mother being buried in a cemetery. Both her parents, Labe and Yetta were not yet 40 years of age.

Leah before her departure from Russia.

The children were left with precious little to survive on. Chaim, the only boy of the family was able to show his sisters a secret place in the leg of the dining table where their father had hidden coins.

It was a near impossibility for the children to care for their baby sister who was still so young she had been breastfed. There was neither feeding bottle nor formula available and they tried to feed her using watered down potatoes, dug from the frozen earth at the back of their small wooden house, sieved through a linen sack which the baby tried to suck. In desperation Leah and Chaim walked to the next village to try and find their aunt and uncle who would surely be able to help them. The two children walked, for what my mother thought was a day and a night, only to find the village had been burned to the ground and no one was left. When they got back home the baby had died. They buried her wrapped in their father's Tallit.

The remaining five children survived alone. For how long we don't know. It may have been days, weeks or even months. My mother could never understand why her grandparents, Sheine and Shepsel Pavin didn't rescue them. This too, we will never know. Perhaps they too were dead or had fled and were not aware of the plight of their grandchildren. What had become of her aunt and uncle and her two boy cousins was a mystery. Except for the fact that the name Shepsel Pavin appears on the 1912 Voters roll of the district, they may have simply been a hopeful figment of my mother's childish imagination. Of other family, which their surely must have been, we have no knowledge or recollection, but right up until 1942 when the holocaust overtook the few remaining Jews in the area, there were people living there with the family name of Altuska.

The children on the day they had their passport picture taken. Small boy third from left with the white top is Chaim, The little girl on the extreme right with the white clip in her hair is Leah. She is holding a small porcelain doll which she told me she placed on her mother's grave

During this time the children must have faced extreme danger and suffered unspeakable terror. My mother recalled being chased by Cossacks through the forest towards the river. She was aware of the horses' hooves as they rushed towards her, she could recall her blind terror as she felt something strike her head and she fell down, her eyes tightly shut, thinking that she had died. She was afraid to open her eyes. It may have been at this time that Sarah suffered a gunshot to her leg. She also remembered hiding in a wooden barn while fires and fierce fighting raged around them. She recalled the terror as the wooden sides of the barn splintered and smashed under the horses' hooves as they were cowering inside. My mother said that the Germans were not so bad, they never harmed them; unlike the Russians who made a sport of killing Jews.

After my mother's death, I found several notebooks where she had written some of these terrible incidents that had remained with her all her life and which she was not able to speak about. She wrote that from a hiding place she was witness to the Cossacks chopping off the beards of religious men, often slicing through their chins, blood splashing to the ground. Of the times when they had no food and she went from yard to yard searching for food in the rubbish. Of being cold and having no boots or being sick with fever and having no help except the Rabbi's prayers.

At some time, a man, known to the children, (could have been a relative) came to the cottage and took them to a large school house that had become an orphanage for the many Jewish children in the area. Conditions at the orphanage must have been extremely bad. Many children were sick and they were often hungry and cold. My mother recalled that adults would frequently come to the orphanage and look at the children. She never knew why, but it may have been the result of many families being separated at the time and people were looking for their relatives.

When Isaac Ochberg arrived in 1921 the children were told that he would be selecting the best and brightest to take with him to Africa. The children were excited and keen to be part of the group he would choose to take with him on this adventure. My mother clearly remembers the day when they were washed and their hair cut and pictures were taken to prepare them for the journey. The picture of the children grouped around their carer shows my mother standing on the right with a bow in her hair. She is holding a small porcelain doll. On that day she was taken to her mother's grave and placed this small doll on it. It was not long after that the children left for the first leg of their long journey.

It had been Ochberg's intention to keep children within their family groups and not separate them. It is a mystery then that Fagele the 12 year old sister was not included. It would be more than 50 years later that Sarah and Leah would trace her whereabouts.

In the meantime, Jewish communities in South Africa were busy arranging functions, raising money for the arrival of the 200 orphans. When the *Edinburgh Castle* arrived from London in September 1921 it docked in Cape Town the children were welcomed by many of the Jewish community. Some children were to remain in Cape Town, but others, my mother and her siblings included, were to travel by train to Johannesburg. In Kimberly the train was met by the local Jewish Community. The children were given gifts of sweets and toys. Amongst them was a young man by the name of David Rembach, a new arrival just escaped from the clutches of the Ottoman army in Palestine.

While Leah and Sarah settled down to their new life at Arcadia, the brother Chaim, was adopted and his name was changed to Harry Gordon. Chaim was not happy and after running away several times he was returned to Arcadia.

Tasha then aged 17 who was too old to be termed an orphan left to work as a seamstress in a clothing factory and took up lodgings in a boarding house in Doornfontein. At her place of work she met a young woman called Bella Krauthamer, newly emigrated from Palestine. The two became firm friends and shared their lodgings.

Together the two friends would visit the children at Arcadia on the weekends, taking them for day trips and treats. Tasha met a man called Harry Rachman and began dating him. Harry Rachman was a chemist and worked in a pharmacy in Judith's Paarl. At the pharmacy, an optician David Rembach had recently been employed. Since David was an immigrant from Palestine, Harry thought it was a good idea to introduce him to Tasha's friend Bella, also recently arrived. The two couples later married and were "Unterferers" at each other's weddings, their friendship enduring all their lives and also involving in the coming years the families of Sarah and Leah. In fact I, the youngest child of Leah was to marry the youngest child of Bella and David Rembach. We have known each other since we were infants. I am a strong believer of Besheit... fate.

1922 Girls at the South African Jewish Orphanage – Judith in front on left

Ever since I could remember my mother spoke about her life in Arcadia with fondness and gratitude. She spoke of wonderful friendships that lasted a lifetime and of a kind patron that cared about them. There was the real thrill of living in a real mansion.

She had survived war and pogrom, hunger and cold and was privileged to be amongst the chosen to leave all of that behind and be given the gift of a new life in a wonderful country.

She spoke of the beautiful gardens, spacious rooms and plenty of good food. She said they always had lovely clothes to wear, attended good schools and those who wanted it - the opportunity to recover, grow and make a good life. There were music and dancing classes and on weekends there were outings. On some Saturday nights there was entertainment for the children.

At Arcadia entertainment was often organised for the children. Two step brothers, Harry Gers and Maurice Rosenblatt, who were violinists, playing in a band, would visit Arcadia and play for the children. There Maurice found the teenager Leah and fell helplessly in love at first sight, as my mother told me. In fact he would write endless love letters to her, pleading with her to marry him or he would kill himself. When my mother passed away in 1993 I found such a letter and still have it today. My mother told me that for her to get married she would have to have finished school. I have the minutes from a board of trustees meeting at Arcadia where she seeks permission to do so. Before her 18th birthday on June 8 1930, Leah married Maurice.

Leah and Morris when they got engaged – 1930

The Chupah took place on the lawns of Arcadia. The reception was a grand affair with 300 guests entertained at Arcadia, complete with a jazz band and children's choir from Arcadia. It was reported in *The Zionist Record* of June 13, 1930, a copy of which is one of my most treasured possessions.

A WEDDING AT THE ORPHANAGE
THE ZIONIST RECORD – June 12, 1930

Arcadia, once again was the scene of a wedding last Sunday, when Miss Leah Altuska married Mr Rosenblatt of Benoni. She was the fifth bride of *The Pogrom* orphans to be married at Arcadia, while two others had married elsewhere.

These girls leave the Home, and live out, boarding at private houses or as in the case of the latest bride, with relatives. But they all like to come back to Arcadia, with its spacious lawns and beautiful rooms, to be married.

The *Chupah* was on the lawn, and the happy and excited children were sitting around a square enclosure, waiting eagerly for the little bride they had known as one of

Leah standing with some offical guests

themselves a very short time ago. She was indeed young and small – but 19 – and she looked a sweet and shy little thing as she stood beside her tall, also young husband, under the *Chupah*. She was the regulation bride as to dress, quite the latest in dainty pale pink, long and flouncy, with a lovely veil and head dress.

One of the old girls was her attendant – dressed in yellow. The Unterfuhrers were Mr and Mrs Nathan (the latter a great advocate of matrimony among girls, and a real kindly 'mother' to them), and Mr and Mrs Slier (sister of bride). The Canopy Holders were four old boys of the Orphanage.

As the bride and party at last came down the stately terraces to the lawn, the children's choir burst into *Borouch Habo*.

The ceremony was performed by Dr J L Landau (Chief Rabbi) assisted by Cantor Rabec, and was most impressive.

After the ceremony the bridal party and friends, committee and a crowd of probably 300 people adjourned to the house where tables were beautifully laid in the two large reception rooms and verandah. A crowd of children immediately commenced to wait upon the guests. Afterwards there was a little dancing to the strains of a jazz band, and the bride and bridegroom left early. The bride was the recipient of some nice presents in cheques, presented to her by the Chairman – Mr Hillman, who made a fine speech at the table, welcoming visitors and congratulating the young couple. The health of the bridegroom was proposed by Mr Kaumheimer, to which, on behalf of the bride, the bridegroom suitably replied.

And so Sunday, 8 June 1930, another great day is written in the annals of Arcadia.

In those days the main objective was for girls to be married off at an early age and when my mother and father married at Arcadia they were given a real "society" wedding, seemingly with no expense spared.

The Ladies Committee set up a trousseau fund for the Ochberg orphan girls so that they would go into marriage like any other girl, with new wedding dresses and a trousseau. This fund was continued for many years and when I married in 1969, I was considered a part orphan because my father had died when I was still a young girl, I too received a trousseau. I think that my mother considered Arcadia to be her home, the place where she grew up and was cared for. I don't think she ever thought of herself as an underprivileged orphan but rather someone special who had been given the gift of opportunity.

Isaac Ochberg, Leah Zaicka, Clara Tenanbaum, and Tasha Altuska

Of the 14 children born to Tasha, Sarah, Leah and Chaim, the children that Isaac Ochberg saved in 1921, there are today more than 70 offspring around the world living in South Africa, Israel, England, Canada, USA and Australia. We have produced doctors, lawyers, medical scientists, journalists, artists, business people, kibbutzniks, IT specialists, teachers, veterinarians, jewellers, university professors, and others I haven't yet met.

Thank you Daddy Ochberg, without you we would not be here to tell the tale.

The three sisters Sarah, Leah and Tasha.   Leah below

Leah's Family in 1954 on holiday in Durban Sylvia, Leah, Leonard, Maurice. Ursula in front (Eldest daughter Yulanda was already married)

FINDING FEYGELE

During the late 1950s my mother, through the Red Cross located their sister Feygele. She was living in Argentina. She had married a wood chopper and had seven children. The family was desperately poor. We tried, with the help of the politician Helen Suzman, to gain them entry into South Africa but were unsuccessful.

Finally in 1973 my mother and Sarah travelled to Argentina and met Feygele and her family. Today we have minimal contact with our cousins in South America, language being a great barrier.

Leah's lost sister Faygele with her husband and three of their seven children in front of their home - mid 1950s.

Also during the 1950s through the Red Cross it was discovered that one of the cousins that my mother remembered had eventually made his way to Cuba. My mother made contact with him and although he acknowledged that he was in fact the missing cousin, he asked not to be contacted as he did not want to be known as a Jew.

In 1981 after my family had migrated to Australia my husband Don was walking in the Melbourne Jewish Cemetery when he happened to notice a tombstone with the name *Altuski* on it. On his return home we immediately looked in the telephone book and located a George Altuski. He was in fact the son of my mother's other missing cousin. There is an uncanny resemblance to my late uncle Harry Gordon. George told me that his father always spoke about the family of cousins that had simply disappeared out of their lives in 1920. They had been in hiding in Russia until after the holocaust when they made their way to Australia. In 2007 George made contact with the family of his uncle in Cuba and travelled there to meet them.

Post script.

I have tried for many years to find out more about my grandparents and the events that took place in the fateful years of 1920/21. There is precious little to find. I will always want to know who my grandparents were; what did they look like? When I look into the blue eyes of my beautiful granddaughters I wonder if they have the same blue eyes. When I see my son producing magnificent drawings I wonder, did he inherit his talent from my grandfather who, so long ago drew pictures of houses? It is forever a void in my heart.

Although I knew there was nothing there and I had been told that the old Jewish cemetery had been desecrated, the tombstones used to pave the sidewalk and the actual site was now a football field, in July 2007 I travelled across Eastern Europe. I stopped off for a short time in Brest (Liktov, now a sad town in Belarus not far from Chernobyl). I wanted to step into a space where perhaps my Zaide once stepped, I stood awhile in a spot where perhaps my Bobba stopped to chat with a neighbour or stopped to buy a Shabbos chicken...... I saw the same small wooden cottages where the Jews once lived. They are old and poor, some leaning dangerously in decay, others lovingly restored and brightly painted and I wondered was it in one of these that my mother and her siblings had lived, loved and played for a short tragic childhood some time in history, once upon a time.

THE CHILDREN OF LABE AND YETTA (PAVIN) ALTUSKA

- Natasha born 1904 died 1971 Johannesburg. Married Harry Rachman, three sons Bernard, Lionel & Stanley (Jackie)
- Fanya born 1908 died Argentina 1975. Married Millsztein, seven children
- Sarah born 1910 died Durban 2001 Married Jack Slier four children Yvonne (Phillips), Deborah (Shine) Lionel and Phyllis (Levenson)
- Leah born 1912 died Melbourne 1993 married Maurice Rosenblatt four children Yulanda (Janet) Leonard, Sylvia (Tobiansky) Ursula (Rembach)
- Chaim born 1915 died Johannesburg 1990 married Corrie three children Cheryl, Ian and Keith

Ursula, Maurice and Leah **Leah and Sarah 1960s**

Leah and Maurice 1957

Leah and all her children at Ursula's wedding
Leonard, Ursula, Leah, Sylvia and Yulanda

Leah and Albert Burts   **Don and Ursula 1966**

My mother had a second husband that in itself is another story. My mother had been a widow since 1960. Being an attractive woman she had many suitors, but was never interested in any permanent arrangement. In 1988 at the tender age of 76 she met a man called Alfred Burts in Durban. She told me that she fell madly in love with his blue eyes. My brother and I were already living in Australia but my sisters were still in South Africa. While I knew about Alfred, I really didn't think anything would come of it except perhaps a friendship between two older people. Well, not so....they eloped. I did not hear about it for about six months. Apparently my mother had sent me a letter after the event, but, I never got the letter. They were truly in love and I got to meet Alfred when they visited in 1991. Their marriage was short, but they truly loved each other and enjoyed those years together. My mother was really a very special person. Quite feisty and a true survivor.

Chapter 33 - SARAH, EVA AND HARRY GAYER (OCHBERG ORPHANS)

This history of the three Ochberg Orphans, Sarah (nee Gayer) Gilinsky, Eva (Chava) (nee Gayer) Queit, and Harry (Maisha) Gayer (aka Friedman) was kindly researched and written by Anne Lapedus Brest

SARAH (GAYER) GILINSKY (OCHBERG ORPHAN)

Sarah Gayer was born in Opalin, Poland in June 1909 to Eliahu and Rachel Golda (Lederer) Gayer. Opalin is near Chelm, on the border of the Ukraine and Sarah grew up there as a little girl together with her sister Chava (Eva) and brother Maisha (Harry).

Her father went off to Detroit, MI, USA, probably around 1915, leaving the children with their Mother. When the mother died in Poland, the children were orphaned but were lucky enough to be brought over to South Africa in 1921, by Isaac (Daddy) Ochberg.

They arrived in Cape Town and then came up to Johannesburg where Sarah went into Arcadia, with Eva and Harry. Eva and Harry were later adopted by the Friedman family of Fordsburg, Johannesburg.

In June of 1928 Sarah married Solly (Israel) Gilinsky in Arcadia.

WEDDING OF SOLLY GILINSKY AND SARAH GAYER
The wedding article and the photo which appeared in June 1928 in the "Star".

Miss Sarah GAYER eldest daughter of the late Mr and Mrs E Gayer, was married last Sunday at the South African Jewish Orphanage, Arcadia, in the presence of a large gathering, to Mr Solomon Gilinsky, son of Mr and Mrs S Gilinsky.

The Chief Rabbi, Dr J L Landau officiated, assisted by Rev N Lopati, and the Unteferers were Mr and Mrs M Lang, Mr and Mrs S Gilinsky, and Mrs M Alexander and Mrs Bernard Alexander.

The canopy bearers were Messrs M Lang, A Erms, H Kaplan and S Isakowitz.

The pretty bride wore a Victorian frock of ivory taffeta and silver lace and her train of pale pink georgette was carried by Tilly Kaplan and Eva Friedman. Her veil of embroidered silk net was arranged in a Spanish fashion, and she carried a bouquet of white roses and pink carnations.

Her bridesmaids, the Misses A Gilinsky, P Potash, T Kaplan, E Friedman, E Shamao and C Knubowitz wore

Sarah married Solly (Israel) Gilinsky in Arcadia.

dainty frocks in varying pastel shades of crepe de chine and Victorian headdresses of folded tulle.

Ettie Lazarus the little flower girl was in pink tinsel with a headdress to match, and carried a basket of flowers.

The Bridegroom's Mother wore a smart dress of black and silver, and a black hat. A very large number of guests attended the reception, which was held on the lawns at Arcadia.

The honeymoon is being spent at the Natal Coast, and the bride travelled in a tailored three-piece suit of navy blue face cloth, and a grey felt hat, worn with a stone marten choker tie.

Note *The article described her father as the "late Mr E Gayer" but he was alive and well, having gone off to America from Poland, before 1921 leaving his wife and three children behind in Poland.*

SARAH (GAYER) GILINSKY
Seen through the eyes of her son, Lionel Gilinsky

I believe after my parents married, they worked for my aunt and uncle Morris and Eddie (Edith) Lang in a Native Trading Store in Crown Mines, which is near Mayfair. They lived in a small room at the back of the store. My Dad used to sell empty bottles and bags, while mother worked behind the counter, attending to customers.

Years later, don't know how long, Mom and Dad started a grocery store (Model Grocery) in Mayfair, over the road from the railway station. It was there that I became involved with the family business, helping my parents in the store, packing and marking the stock and sometimes delivering the orders to customers and running errands like banking and Post Office.

At this time we were living in a house in 9th Avenue, Mayfair, which is where I was born.

As life for my parents improved, Mom had decided to start a Ladies Dress Shop, also in Mayfair, at the Mayfair Tram Terminus, opposite the Grosvenor Railway station and at that stage we had now moved across the railway line to a house No. 27, 7th Avenue, Mayfair.

In 1947, I (Lionel) contracted Polio and so my mom, Sarah, decided to sell the Dress Shop in order to raise sufficient funds to take me to the USA for treatment for the Polio.

I was in the Sister Kenny Hospital and also the Oakland County Hospital in Pontiac, Michigan. where I was undergoing treatment. I think I was there for six months and by the time we returned to South Africa, I could walk unaided.

Sometime in the middle of the 1950s Morris and Eddie Lang had bought a building in Welkom in the Goldfields of the Orange Free State and persuaded my parents to start a General Dealers Store in one of their shops in the building, which they did, and that is where they spent most of their life living and working together. They built their own building alongside the Lang's building and that's where they lived until they retired and moved to an apartment in Berea, not far from the Berea Shul, where they became members.

It was in this apartment that Mom started a little catering business (Sarah's Kitchen) as a side line and built it up to be a huge success so much so that she began retailing her products from Esther's Food Shop in the Linksfield Shopping Center. Esther eventually gave up the store and Mom continued to work out of her apartment.

Dad passed away in December 1979, just six months after celebrating their Golden Wedding anniversary and Mom continued living and working in the apartment.

She earned a reputation for baking and cooking. Her cheese cakes were the order of the day and her taiglach became world renowned, shipping them to London, Los Angeles, Tel Aviv and many other places.

Come the Yomtavim, there was no place in the flat to sit down and enjoy a cup of tea and a piece of cake or taigel. Apart from the baking of all types of cakes, she was making on a daily basis for orders, kichel and chopped herring, Danish herring, curried fish, fish cakes and many other dishes, too numerous to mention.

She loved doing what she was doing and we, her four children, loved visiting her, as we always left with something in our hands for our own kitchen.

It was during her latter years that her hips needed replacement and it was after Dr Weeber performed the second hip replacement that Mom passed away at the Sandton Clinic from shooting an aneurism.

Sarah and Eva

SARAH AND SOLLY'S FAMILY

Sarah and Solly had four children; Rochke (Rochel) Gilinsky (later Hesslberg), Esther Clara Gilinsky (later Shuster), Lionel Gilinsky and Raymond Gilinsky.

Rochel (Rochke) Gilinsky Hesselberg was married to Sammy Hesselberg, who was also in Arcadia together with his two sisters Leah and Becky.

Esther, Alana and Rochke

Rochel (Rochke) Gilinsky Hesselberg was married to Sammy Hesselberg, who was also in Arcadia together with his two sisters, Leah and Becky.

Rochke and Sammy (both now deceased) had four children
–Mervyn who married Marcelle and had three children: Shawn, Gary, and Lara with three grandchildren
-Merle who married Eric Roy Alexander and had one son Jonathan Craig with one grandchild
-Sharon married Darryl Myers and they had two children and three grand children and
-Edith who married Simon Efune and had two daughters Tony Jade and Jodi.

Esther Clara Gilinsky married Hymie Shuster and they had a daughter Alana, who married Mark Fishel, and they had two sons Yaniv and Edan.

Lionel married Ros Sonic and they had three children and one grandchild.

Lionel Gilinsky and Selwyn Queit (Eva's son) 2008

Laureen Gilinsky, daughter of Lionel (and grand daughter of Sarah) passed away 8 July 1988.

Raymond married Irit Gertzman and had two children and two grandchildren.

So in total Sarah and Solly had four children, 10 grand children and 14 great grandchildren.

EVA (CHAVA) (GAYER) QUEIT (OCHBERG ORPHAN)

Eva was born in Opalin Poland on 3 November 1914, and lived there until she was eight years old when she came to South Africa as part of the Ochberg Orphans.

She was adopted by the Friedman family, in Johannesburg, Mayfair. Mr. Friedman owned property in Mayfair in those days. Eva was never happy with the Friedmans and she kept running away and back to her sister Sarah.

THE WEDDING OF EVA AND ISAAC QUEIT

Eva married Isaac Queit (born 3 March 1890 in Taurogen, Lithuania) on 1 January 1941 in the Berea Shul, Johannesburg,

Eva on her wedding day – above and below

In the wedding photo on the previous page Sarah (Gayer) Gilinsky is to the right of the Groom but behind him and a fellow's hat is cutting out part of her face. Lionel Gilinsky is the little boy on the right of the photo (he's half out of the picture and was so short then) and the little girl next to him is his sister Esther Gilinsky (later Shuster).

Lionel Gilinsky is the kid on the right with hat on and the girl next to him is his sister Esther Gilinsky Shuster, the children of Sarah Gayer Gilinsky (Ochberg Orphan). Behind Esther is Rochke Gilinsky (later Hesselberg)

Eva and Isaac had two children, Selwyn Queit born 29 November 1941 in Florida, Roodepoort and Jack Queit born 7 October 1944 in Johannesburg.

Selwyn is married to Hazel Abraham and they had three children Alan, Kevin and Brett.

Jack is married to Joan Serebro and they had three sons, Gavin, Rael and Joel Queit and live in Melbourne Australia. Gavin is married to Michelle Stein and they had two children Danielle and Erin.

EVA (CHAVA) (GAYER) QUEIT
As seen through the eyes of her sons, Selwyn and Jack, and daughter in law Joan Queit

Eva was one of the most generous people, always looking out for the family. Any problems that anyone had, they would run to see her. She kept an open house. Everyone was always welcome. She always had friends over, and she idolized her husband, Isaac.

After Eva got married, she didn't work in the first few years. When she and her husband, Isaac, moved to Thabazimbi, they owned a business called "Vliegpoort Trading", which was a general dealer shop in Thabazimbi, North West Province. She served at the counter, and did the accounts.

They were one of two Jewish families in Thabazimbi, the other being the Milner Family. Eva and Isaac had an open home, often filled with family visitors, in particular Sarah's children as well as many Jewish travellers who would spend a Shabbos meal and even a Yom Tov dinner with them.

Eva was an excellent cook. Her Jewish cooking skills were amazing and still today, Jack is my chopped herring taster to make sure it is as close to Eva's as I can make it.

From Thabazimbi they went to Welkom so that Eva could be close to her sister, Sarah (Gayer) and Solly Gilinsky. She worked in her husband's business "IQ outfitters", until they sold it. In 1981 they moved to Johannesburg permanently and at that time Selwyn was living in Cape Town and Jack was living in Johannesburg.

They lived in New Carlington Heights, Corner Claim and Goldreich Street, Hillbrow, Johannesburg.

Eva lived there until her husband died in February 1978, then she moved into a residential Hotel called the "Courtleigh Hotel" in Berea, and she died there.

HARRY (MAISHA) GAYER (OCHBERG ORPHAN)

Harry Gayer, was six years of age when he left Opalin Poland, to come to South Africa, with his sisters Sarah and Eva, as one of the Isaac Ocberg Orphans

Harry never married, and died at the age of 29 in Beaufort West, from TB.

He is buried in Brixton Cemetery in Johannesburg.

He was known as Harry Friedman, the surname of the people who adopted him.

Sarah, Eva and Harry Gayer (three Ochberg orphans).

Chapter 34 – HERSCHEL LIDVENITZKY (HARRY LIDVEN) (1908-1957)

OUR FATHER HERSCHEL LIDVENITSKY (HARRY LIDVEN)
Written by Laurane (Lidven) Klingman and Anita Lidven

Our father Herschel Lidvenitsky was born on 23 May 1908 in Pinsk. His parents were Gershon Lidvenitsky and Leah Foeterman, who was born in Russia.

We don't know if there were any other siblings or what happened to his parents.

Our father never spoke and would not speak about his life in Eastern Europe. The only thing we remember is that he told us about the Soup Kitchens. He said he stood for hours in the lines, in order to receive some food.

At that time we, as kids, did not realise that we would in later life, want to find out or know more about his life in those early days. He died so young at 49 years old when we were only 17 and 12 years old.

All we know is that he landed up in an Orphanage in Pinsk and was part of the group of children selected by Isaac Ochberg that was brought out to South Africa in 1921 and his gratitude to Isaac Ochberg was indescribable.

Herschel Lidvenitsky (Harry Lidven)

Isaac Ochberg in the middle of a group of children in school uniform – Johannesburg ~1922

Harry and friends unknown 1926, 1929, 1930 and undated

Harry and friends unknown 1930, 1934 and undated

Harry and Dora on their wedding day 20 February 1938

Our father was part of the group that was sent from Cape Town to Johannesburg and placed in the care of the Orphanage in Johannesburg (Arcadia) at the same time as all the other orphans in 1921. He was grateful for the opportunity and security the orphanage offered him and it protected him and gave him the opportunity of further learning. He left Arcadia around 1932. He was friendly with Molly Gafinowsky (Blumberg) another child from Arcadia.

After he left Arcadia he studied to become a Reverend and his first assignment was in Bothaville in the Orange

Free State (OFS) and then to Bethlehem also in the OFS and to other towns in the OFS.

It was while he was working in the OFS that he met our Mom. She lived in Parys OFS which was near to Bothaville. We assume they met at a function or were introduced. Our father changed his name to Harry Lidven and on 20 February 1938 he married our mother Dora Bloom. Dora, born in South Africa on 14 March 1914 was the daughter of Joseph and Sophie Bloom.

Soon after marrying they moved to Leshoane (just outside Pietersburg) to join his brother and sister in law, in starting and running a store. He was a storekeeper as well as the Chazan at the Pietersburg Shul and was also a member of the Chevra Kadisha.

Harry and Dora had us two daughters; Laurane born 21 May 1940 and Anita born 11 February 1945. We both grew up in Pietersburg and completed all our schooling there

Herschel Lidvenitsky (Harry Lidven)

We remember out father as a kind, caring and devoted Father and husband. His first concern was for his family. He taught us the value of family and the appreciation of our Jewish Heritage and roots. He was always there for us and gave us all the love and guidance that he had been denied in his own youth. He was always willing to assist his neighbours and friends in times of joy and sorrow. He extended his time and knowledge to the Jewish community by conducting the Friday night services and Yom Tov services when called upon to do so. Testimony to his fine singing voice and his renditions are still remarked upon today by the then youth (as adults today) and the few remaining adults of that time. A proud moment for our Family is when we are reminded of his fine qualities.

He was a devout Jew, a Hebrew teacher as well as the Chazan at the Pietersburg Shul. He also assisted with shechita.

In Pietersberg there was a large Jewish population for a rural area, with about 120 Jewish Families. Other Jewish families in the surrounding areas utilized this Shul as well. To this day our Father is remembered for his renditions and his beautiful singing voice.

Harry died on 9 May 1957 and Dora in August 1990. They have been blessed with two grandchildren and nine great grandchildren.

THE HISTORY of the PIETERSBURG JEWISH COMMUNITY Extract from book written by Charlotte Wiener

When Rev Levine *(the reverend of the Pietersburg Synagogue)* was unable to perform *shechita*, Mr Harry Lidven, a trader in the Pietersburg area, used to assist him in the 1940s or the Rabbi from Warmbaths would travel to Pietersburg for this purpose.

Mr Harry Lidven was born in Pinsk on 23 May 1908. He was an 'Ochberg Orphan' who was brought out to South Africa in 1921 by Isaac Ochberg, a leader of the Cape Town community and the president of the Cape Jewish orphanage. Mr Ochberg had gone to Russia and had brought back 167 orphans to South Africa. These Children had witnessed the terrible atrocities that had occurred in the pogroms in Eastern Europe.

Mr Lidven lived in the Arcadia Orphanage in Johannesburg, where he studied to be a Reverend. He was the minister in Bethlehem and Bothaville before coming to Pietersburg around 1938. He settled at Leshoane, 45 kilometres outside Pietersburg as his wife, Dora's sister, Sarah Jedwood, already ran a general dealer's store there on a trust farm with her husband Joseph. He also assisted in conducting the services in the synagogue, singing in a beautiful voice. He died in 1957 in Pietersburg.

Herschel Lidvenitsky (Harry Lidven)

Chapter 35 – ROSA LILA (LATER CALLED ROSA BRAUDE)

LIST OF CHILDREN GOING TO THE SOUTH AFRICAN JEWISH ORPHANAGE IN JOHANNESBURG

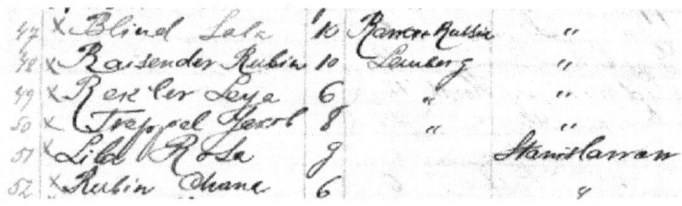

Children sent to Johannesburg showing name, age, where born and where taken from

FROM THE SOUTH AFRICAN JEWISH ORPHANAGE REGISTER

Name of child	Child placed in the care of
51 Lila Rosa girl 9	Standerton Young Israel Society

This is the plaque on Ramat Menashe in Israel there is a bit of limestone on the stone that can easily be washed off.

MY MOTHER, ROSE LILLE
by Joyce Wingrin

"My late mother, Rose Lille was born in Poland in a village called Lile (as far as I know). At a young age her brothers sent her with the Ochberg children on the boat as organised by Mr. Isaac Ochberg. Her parents (my Grandparents) were killed by the Cossacks.

She was sent to the Arcadia Orphanage in Johannesburg. She did a shorthand typing course. She did very well. She was very efficient and got a job at a law firm in Johannesburg.

While she was in the orphanage she was adopted by a Mr and Mrs Glass. They lived in Homedean in Standerton. She spent many a holiday with them. My Mother was the only child that they adopted and I'm most grateful to them for all the care they gave her. They had no children of their own. Should anyone know about the Glass family I would welcome them getting in touch with me.

She met her husband, Morris Braude, while on holiday in Durban. Once they were married they went to live in a small village called Bronkhorstspruit, which was then an hour and a half drive from Johannesburg.

They had two daughters, Frume and myself. Fruma married Max Lubinsky and had two children, Rose and David. Sadly Frume passed away in 1974 and Rose passed away in 2004 while living in Canada with her husband, Stephen Katz and their daughter, Franki.

David is living in Johannesburg with his wife Debbie and they have four children, Baruch, Talya, Tova and Naomi

I married Barry Wingrin and live in Pretoria. My husband passed away in 1991. I have five children B'H, Shaun, Rochelle, Rael, Miriam and Moshe Michael, who live in Johannesburg and surrounds.

My Mother passed away in 1956 at the young age of 43 when I was 12 years of age. She was a very kind, pleasant, capable lady and helped her husband in their general dealer business in Bronkhorstspruit.

Before she got married she insisted that her husband had his own business as she felt she needed some security. She was 25 and he 35 years old when they married. They lived in a tiny house at first in Bronkhorstspruit.

They spent many happy years in this country town. They always hosted the country Rabbi when he came for Yom Tov to Daven at the Bronkhorstspruit Shul.

In those days there were about 40 Jewish families living in Bronkhorstspruit.

My parents were well liked by the community.

I have very special memories about my dear Mother a"h. May she rest in peace "

Chapter 36 – BEILA NEMET LATER CALLED JUDITH SMITH

The records show that Beila was born in 1915 in Kyntchyn and was placed in the care of Arcadia.

JUDITH SMITH (BEILA NEMET)
Written by her daughter Joy Chazen

My mom, Judith Smith, Beila Nemet passed away yesterday (23 May 2012) at the age of 96 in the retirement village where she has been living for some time.

My mom came to South Africa when she was about five and was adopted by Bertha Friedland who changed her name to Judith. My mother never spoke about her past. She told me once a long time ago that she was brought out from Lithuania by a Dr Hochstader with a group of children but never spoke about it again saying that it was too sad. She told me that she thought that her parents had died of flu. A friend of mine went to the Kaplan Institute in Cape Town and she brought me a cutting from a newspaper about Dr Hochstader and we found out that he was connected to the orphanage. We then saw an article in the Jewish Report and only then did we find out that my mom was an Ochberg orphan.

When my mom was young, her sister Hilda (who ended up in America) managed to contact her and her adopted mother refused to let her have any contact with my mom. She said that she mustn't contact her again because she didn't want to dredge up her traumatic past.

In 1961, Hilda advertised in a Jewish newspaper because a cousin was coming on a cruise to South Africa and was hoping to find my mom which she did. A year later, Hilda came to visit us in South Africa and in 1969 I went to Europe, London and Israel with my mom and Hilda came to join us in London and Israel. Hilda's one daughter, Lorraine, came to South Africa to meet us all in 1989. My brother Michael and his family have met the entire American family.

My mom was a devoted wife to Reuben for almost 75 years (he passed away at the age of 99 in October 2009), mother to Bennett, Michael and Joy and granny to eight grandchildren and six great grandchildren.

I don't think that my mom was at Arcadia for long. She was adopted by Bertha Friedland and went to live in Braamfontein. She went to Spes Bona school. My father, Reuben, was a Chartered Accountant and was the Honourary Secretary of Beaconsfield Club for many years. My parents lived in a flat until Bennett was born and then moved to a house in Greenside.

My mom never worked. She spent her days caring for her family and her beautiful garden, where she gave new meaning to the term 'green-fingers'. Her skills could not be limited to the garden. Her beautiful hand-knitted jerseys kept all of us warm in winter. She was an amazing cook and we will not forget about the wonderful smells that used to come from her kitchen, and her unforgettable roast chicken and freshly-baked biscuits and cookies which we used to receive on a regular basis.

When she found the big garden and house too much for her to handle, they moved into a flat in Killarney where she used to do all her own cooking and housework. After living there for about 10 years my father's health began to deteriorate and she couldn't manage to help him anymore and they were forced to move into a retirement home.

When her grandchildren were born, my mom's name changed again...this time to 'Gran'. She was extremely proud of her children, grandchildren and great grandchildren and loved to hear of all their successes and adventures both here and abroad. In the last few years of her life, she lived for the daily and weekly visits from her family. She really was a GRAND-mother in the truest sense, and was always there, showing her love and support to her family.

My mom really was proof that dynamite comes in small packages. Her feisty nature and witty sense of humour always kept her family on their toes! She will always be fondly remembered and sorely missed

Judith Smith
4th row from top - second from right with clip in hair

Chapter 37 – DAVID PENZIK (1908-1992) AND CLARA GABBE (1907-1987)

MY PARENTS, DAVID PENZIK AND CLARA GABBE.
Written by Bennie Penzik

The orphans who made the epic 1921 journey from strife-torn Eastern Europe to South Africa under the divine guidance of their saviour, Isaac Ochberg included four members of the Penzik family from Kupichow and three Gabbe sisters from Trysk.

Five Penzik siblings: David and Mindel at the back with Chana (Hannah), Chaia (Helen) and Isaac, the oldest brother, in front
Taken around early 1921 in the Ukraine

It has never been established with any certainty why the eldest Penzik, Isaac, did not make the trip, although we always understood that Mr Ochberg did not wish to separate siblings. We have accepted the reason as a 'cut-off' age as Isaac would have been over 16. The last word we had from him was in 1941. Isaac, his wife and two daughters are presumed to have perished in the Holocaust.

My Dad is indeed on the passport – he is on the extreme left at the top row

Two years after arriving at the Arc, my Dad, then aged 15, joined the firm, L K Hurwitz and Son, and spent the next 55 years in the cycle industry, most of those years as an independent wholesaler in Pretoria.

My late Dad made a point of checking with the Arc when a vacancy came up and I have a clear recollection of Bobby Gordon as a young blond guy who worked for a time at Reliable Cycle Co - the Penzik family business in Pretoria.

He remained active as a staunch supporter of Arcadia well into his twilight years and I have fond childhood recollections of doing the Sunday morning rounds of the Pretoria Jewish community with him and his receipt book collecting 'half guinea' subscriptions.

The 1920s saw him at Twist Street School in Johannesburg, playing club-level rugby (a speedy winger) and a motorbike enthusiast and rider on his Montgomery, a frequent traveller between Johannesburg and Pretoria on social visits!

David Penzik (born 1908) married Clara Gabbe (born 1907) on 15 February 1931 at a ceremony held in the grounds of Arcadia and my sister, Rita, and I are the offspring of that union.

Neither of my parents were able, or perhaps willing, to share memories of their early childhood and from the sparse details, I recall only bitter and tragic recollections of their parents who died from typhus, harsh winters, desperate living conditions and a harsh physical working environment, despite their very young age.

Dad had a close relationship with his three sisters, the youngest of whom, Helen (Green), spent the last years of her life as his neighbour at Jaffa, the Pretoria Jewish Parents Home. Mindel (Davidow) passed away in the fifties and Hannah (Sandler) is today a resident of Sandringham aged 95!

Mom was the 'giant' of her siblings at four feet ten-and-half. Sisters Peggy (Greenberg) and Gittel (Shnaps) continued to live in Cape Town after their spell at Oranjia.

In the attached letter from Mr Ochberg to my Dad on the occasion of their engagement in 1930, he writes – "…and congratulate you on securing Clara as your partner in life. I am sure that you have by now found out that she has a golden character and is really a sweet little woman and I am sure she will make you very happy. I am glad to have your assurance that you will do everything in your power to make her happy – she fully deserves it."

My Mom and Dad - approx 1932

I believe that this was the first marriage of Ochberg orphans.

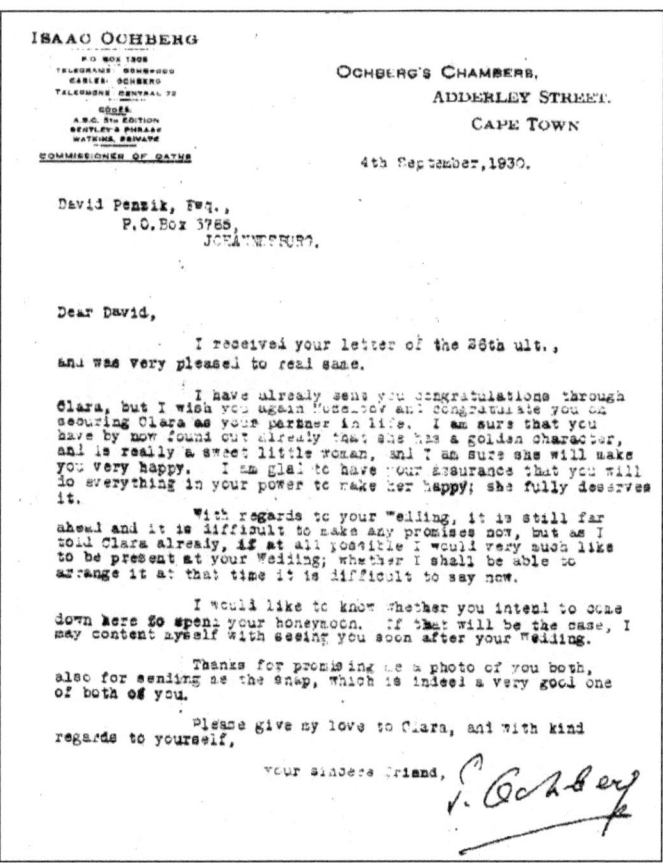

I can attest to the indisputable fact that they both honoured their commitments to Mr Ochberg and to each other. The harmonious life they led was truly blessed and has been an inspiration.

Mom passed away in 1987 and Dad in 1992

THE PRETORIA CONNECTION TO THE OCHBERG ORPHANS
Written by Bennie Penzik

Reference is made, in an extract from a book titled THE STORY OF THE PRETORIA JEWISH COMMUNITY UP TO 1930, of a meeting held in Johannesburg in 1920 to discuss a fund-raising effort designed to send Eastern Europeans orphans to Palestine. The Pretoria delegate proposed that the children be brought to South Africa. The proposal was defeated but the delegates were later informed that Mr Isaac Ochberg of Cape Town was being sent to Europe with the aim of bringing orphans to the Cape Province.

Pretoria generously offered their assistance in all matters relating to the orphans including a suggestion that adoptive parents be sought there. After much discussion, a meeting in 1921 decided that 250 orphans be brought to the Rand, of whom 20 would be settled in Pretoria. A mass meeting was called with appeals printed in English and Yiddish and distribution was made to the community together with application forms for the ladies sub-committee which was to investigate adoption options. Mention is made of Mr B Alexander, Chairman of the South African Jewish Relief Reconstruction and Orphans Fund, based in Johannesburg. The Chevra Kadisha of Pretoria contributed 150 pounds and agreed to set aside a further 1000 pounds towards bringing the children from Europe to South Africa. Mr Semach Jaffe became chairman of the Fund and Mrs Lena Janover, the secretary.

Many meetings followed and suggestions were considered including one to build an orphanage in Sunnyside. At one stage it was recommended that 20 children would come to Pretoria for Yom Tov but continuously, as funds were raised, the committee haggled over the future of the orphans. Finally, when 177 'Ochberg Orphans' arrived in Cape Town in September 1921 and half were relocated to Johannesburg, none were allocated to Pretoria. Eventually it was proposed that a new orphanage be built in Johannesburg and the Pretoria community would be called upon to support the project.

It then transpired that twelve of the orphan group were brought to Pretoria for a 10-day holiday and were lodged with a number of residents whose names will be familiar to many readers of Vignettes - Galgut, Roseman, Rudolph, Neifeld, Orkin, Etin and Shapiro among them.

The section concludes with the statement that only years later did three Ochberg Orphans eventually settle in Pretoria - David and Clara Penzik and Janey Oddes. I believe that Abie Kruger was a fourth.

I am indebted to David Solly Sandler of Perth for alerting me to this information.

REMEMBERING MY DAD AND PAYING HOMAGE
If I am to be permitted to end on a personal note....

My earliest recollections of my late Dad's commitment to the Arcadia orphanage in Parktown, Johannesburg, were how much he had enjoyed his sojourn, which period included both his Bar-Mitzvah and wedding.

He was intimately involved in the support of Arcadia for 50 years. I recall the Sunday drives in the '34 Vauxhall with Dad and his little receipt book with its crumpled piece of carbon paper canvassing half-guinea donations from each Pretoria Jewish family.

To my everlasting chagrin, his requests of me as a teenager to accompany him on trips to the Parktown orphanage often fell on indifferent ears - after all, I had to play soccer or attend a Betar meeting so I was pressed for time.

I have ultimately joined the ranks of those who now want to ask questions and no-one is left to respond.

However, and this is the message I wish to convey to all descendants - it is never too late to pay homage.

Now that I have been so intimately involved in the organisation of events in honour of his 'Daddy Ochberg', I pray that, *in absentia,* my Dad may be aware that I have endeavoured to live up to his expectations of me.

It is exactly 40 years ago that he played an active role in organising the Golden Jubilee gathering of the original orphans and their families in Cape Town in 1971.

I urge you all to step up to the plate and remember and honour Isaac Ochberg as befits his memory.

Without him, we would not have been!

Bennie Penzik February 2011

Benny Penzik addressing the audience at Ramat Menashe

Benny Penzik and the monument to Isaac Ochberg.
Photos July 2011 courtesy Anne Breat

Chapter 38 – MINNIE DAVIDOW (MINA PENZIK) (1905-1956)

MY MOTHER MINNIE DAVIDOW (MINA PENZIK)
Written by Rita Chimes (Davidow)

My Mom Mina didn't talk much her life before coming to South Africa. She told me that they nearly did not let her come because she was already 15 years old. They let her come so that she could look after Helen (Chaia) who was a baby. Also they let her younger siblings David and Hannah (Chana) come but, not her older brother Isaac who was then 16.

The wedding of Mina Penzik and David Lazarus Davidow

A WEDDING AT ARCADIA – 26 March 1926
From a news cutting

Arcadia was en fete last Sunday, when the wedding of one of the Ukrainian orphans was celebrated. The beautiful garden, with grassy lawns, its terraces, shady trees and purple bougainvillea made a delightful setting for a simple, dignified and impressive ceremony. There must have been between three and four hundred visitors besides the one hundred and sixty children gathered round a square in the middle of which the 'Chupoch' was held in place by the brothers of the bride and bridegroom and two orphanage boys.

Judging by the eagerness and intense, if restrained excitement on the faces of the children, one could well imagine that this wedding day was the culminating point of days of interesting speculation, and that with the receipt of each fresh present and at each ring of the telephone bell, this excitement had been growing and growing. It is a wonderful thing for any girl to be married even in her own home, but when it is the oldest of about 80 orphan girls, with the most of the older ones speculation on whose turn it will be next, one can imagine what an extraordinary event it must be.

The bride, Miss Mina Penzik, was dressed in a simple white crepe-de-chine dress, and wore a lovely veil attached to a pearl-ornamented headdress. Her demure

Four Penziks in 1922 at Arcadia - Mindel (Mina), Chana (Hannah) and David standing with Chaia (Helen) seated.

She was very happy at the orphanage Arcadia, and also worked there, and stayed there until she got married. She also told me that a family wanted to adopt her, but she would not go without her brother and sister. When Helen and Hannah were adopted she worked at Arcadia.

I don't think that my Dad had any connection to Arcadia and I remember him telling us that a friend, whose name I don't remember, brought him with to play tennis at Arcadia. That's where my Mom was introduced to him.

They were married on the 26 March 1926 when she was 21 years old.

bearing and rich natural colouring, caused the whisper of 'What a pretty bride' to run round the large concourse of people. The bridegroom, Mr Davidow, awaited her at the 'Chupoch' and as she crossed the grassy lawn, the orphanage choir greeted her with a lusty Boruch Habo. She was accompanied by the bridegroom's mother and sister, the Unterfuhrers; Mr and Mrs Nathan, her two young sisters, both adopted children, and her one bridesmaid, Miss Sarah Cater, of the grown-up orphanage girls.

The ceremony was performed by the Chief Rabbi, Dr J L Landau and the Rev S Pinkasovich. The latter rendered the Hebrew portion of the service in his usual beautiful manner, while Dr Landau delivered an eloquent address, during which there was scarcely a dry eye. He spoke of the bride's loneliness in a strange land, but noticed that she had many friends. He begged for her to be true to her Jewish ideals, not to be lead away by others to disregard her holy religion, and to keep her home as a true Jewish woman.

The signing of the register, and congratulations followed, and when the young couple reached the house, the orchestra played the wedding march – after which Kiddush, and more speeches – difficult to follow owing to the coming and going of the huge crowd. Refreshments kindly provided by the friends of the committee, were handed round by the children, and dancing was participated in until 7 o'clock. The bride and groom then departed, to celebrate further in the bridegroom's home, and so a day never to be forgotten in the annals of Arcadia, a day to be talked of for months to come, came to an end.

We understand that the individual members of the committee subscribed sufficient funds to enable the bride and bridegroom to establish themselves in a nice comfortable home, as well as providing the wedding dress and a trousseau.

Ekkie Litvin (Levine) remembers

I remember the weddings held under the big eucalyptus tree (fat tree) and the great excitement of the children who practiced singing for the wedding and who were part of a great crowd of three or four hundred people who attended the weddings and the hush of the crowd as the bride made her way from the main building down the steps and through the crowd to the open air chupah. There was a Miss Judith Ratzer, an Ochberg Orphan who later stayed on to work as a housekeeper in the Arc. They were called the Russian Orphans or the Pogrom Orphans or the Ukraine Orphans, but never called Ochberg Orphans.

Rita continues

I have the cutting from the newspaper about their wedding, which I had laminated for me and my sister Bessie. Another thing I remember my Mom saying was that somebody by the name of Sarah Gayer was her bridesmaid.

OUR FAMILY

My Dad, David Lazarus Davidow was born in 1893 and my mother in 1905, and they had six children.

> Sidney born in 1928 and died in 1992 of a heart attack
> Reuben born in 1929. He was the first to die, of heart problems.
> Joey was born in 1930 and died in 1995 from brain tumour.
> Rita born 10 April 1931 and thank G-D am well and happy.
> Morris born ~ 1932 and died 17 December 2000 of heart attack.
> Bessie born 26 Jan 1934 and living in Johannesburg.

Back: Morris, Reuben, Joe and Rita
Front: Bessie, David, Mina and Sidney.
The photo was taken two months before dad passed away

Dad was a very quiet person and during WW1 he was stationed in Pretoria in the army. He acquired airplane propellers and fashioned beautiful clocks from them for the family and also for the Red Cross, for a raffle. He was a very skilled French Polisher, and did work for Lincoln Brothers who had a furniture factory and made pianos that he polished.

Dad had many small heart attacks and when he was in Pretoria staying at uncle David Penzik he had a massive heart attack and passed away on 23 August 1947. My brother Sidney had to go to Pretoria to come back with the vagter as he had died on a Saturday.

Mom was well liked by everybody. She kept a strict kosher home, and on Friday morning always made her own challah and bagels, and also would give some to our neighbours. We lived in Doornfontein for some years and then moved to Yeoville. Mom was a very friendly and lively person and passed away on the 27 January 1956.

I was married on 12 April 1953 to Solly Jack Chimes who was born on 19 March 1924 and we had four wonderful children. Solly passed away on 18 October 1991 from cancer of the liver.

Chapter 39 – HELEN GREEN (MEYEROVITZ) (CHAIA PENZIK) (1916-1990)

OUR MOTHER HELEN (CHAIA) PENZIK
Written by Renée Aron and Yvonne Chenik

Our Mom, Helen (Chaia) Penzik was born 5 November 1916 and was five years old when she came to South Africa. She wasn't in Arcadia for very long before she was adopted by Morris and Eva Meyerovitz. They were very special people who loved Helen and kept her in touch with her biological siblings (Mindel, David and Hannah) by inviting them over every weekend.

Despite many hardships in her life, Helen had the most wonderful disposition, and never complained. She was an angel and was a loving, caring, compassionate and wise woman.

Helen married our Dad, Harry Green during WW2. They had three children, Renee, Yvonne and Errol. Sadly Errol died of cancer at the age of 15 years after terrible suffering.

Harry and Helen started their married life in Amersfoort, Transvaal where they lived happily and Renée and Yvonne were born there. They then moved to Johannesburg where Errol was born and lived there for 12 years. They then moved to Klerksdorp where very happy years were spent.

Helen had a terrible motor car accident and spent two years in hospital. During that time, she always had a smile, encouragement and good advice, despite her discomfort and pain.

Helen, Mindel and David - ~1924

The doctors said that she would never walk again, but against all odds with determination and courage, she did. She also became a bowls player and drove a car again.

1921 - Ochberg Orphans placed in the care of the South African Jewish Orphanage Arcadia

Helen (Chaia) Penzik age 5

Wedding of Harry and Helen Green "The most beautiful couple inside and out"- 21 July 1940

Helen as an adult with her adoptive parents Morris and Eva Meyerovitz

Both our parents (Harry and Helen) were very popular and were "loved by all who knew them."

Renée married Albert Aron from Bulawayo, Rhodesia. They have two daughters and five grandchildren and all reside in Australia.

Yvonne married Alan Chenik from Greenside, Johannesburg. They have a son, a daughter and one grandson.

Errol sadly died at the young age of 15 years after suffering with a brain tumour.

Helen passed away 13 August 1990

Helen, Harry, Errol, Yvonne and Renée – January 1949

Helen with daughters Renée and Yvonne

HANNAN (CHANNA) PENZIK
Written by Yvonne Chenik in 2008

Helen and her sister Hannah

Purim 1952 - Renée, Errol and Yvonne

Hannah married Joe Sandler (who died aged 51 in 1951) and re-married Max Kahn who subsequently passed away.

Hannah is now 97 years and is in the hospital section of Sandringham Gardens. Sadly doesn't remember much. She knows me and I often show her old photos which she identifies and when she sees a photo of my Mom, she'll look at it and say "my sister Helen" etc.

Her daughter Rhoda Gien lives in Israel. Another daughter Berry Lazarow lives in Melbourne and her son Stanley lives in Johannesburg and visits her every day

Chapter 40 – JUDITH, NATIE AND PHYLLIS RATZER (OCHBERG ORPHANS)

Leib (Abraham Marcus Ratzer) and Beile Bokser (nee Kodisch) lived in Stanislaw in the Ukraine and had many children. There were some older siblings, including a brother Fischel and a sister Chancie, and three younger siblings; Phyllis, born 1908, Judith born 25 June 1910 and Natie born 1914.

Leib and Beila died in ~1921 during the influenza epidemic and the older children put their younger siblings into an orphanage. The three younger siblings were very bitter that their older siblings had placed them into the orphanage.

In 1921 the three younger siblings, Phyllis, Judith and Nathan were brought out to South Africa with the rest of the Ochberg Orphans by Isaac Ochberg.

Fichel an older brother remade contact from Stanislaw in 1937 and an older sister, Chancie Ruchel in 1939.

The family made contact with the older brothers and sisters who ended up in New York and had the name Racer.

Group Passport Photo number one 1921
We can positively identify our uncle Natie. He is in the front row, second from the left (next to 15). We think that our mother Judith, is the first girl behind him (third left back row). It stands to reason that she would be close to her little brother. Her features and hair style are the closest to hers as we remember her and from past photos also she must have been nine years old at the time. Perhaps then, Phyllis is on Judith's right, we cannot recognize her, though. She would have been 11 years old.

Our Grandmother Beile Bokser (nee Kodisch)
"Our mother always had this photograph next to her bed"

OUR MOTHER, JUDITH.
Written by Rachelle and Rosalie

Our Mother Judith, had a deep elongated dimple-like indentation at the back of her left calf. She told us that a rat had bitten her on the boat coming here. Perhaps it had become infected and some flesh had to be removed, resulting in this crevice. We thought it might be a bullet hole wound but this does not seem likely now. She never related any fond or other memories of her childhood and time at the orphanage.

Rosalie does vaguely remember her mentioning a Matron that was very strict and not particularly kind or sympathetic towards the children.

We know that she worked in the laundry and was a good organizer which was evident throughout her life. She did tell us that Phyllis was adopted and lived away from the orphanage. She never mentioned that she was fostered but from the records received by us she was. So was her little brother Nathan.

She told us that she remained at the orphanage and that Natie was adopted or fostered but was unhappy and missed her so he ran away back to Arcadia. She did help to look after younger children and became a nurse working in Arcadia. We have photos to support this.

She remained in touch with her siblings and was very close to Natie who incidentally, married Tilly Goldstein from Arcadia.

When she left Arcadia she went to work for the OK Bazaars and worked herself up from a sales girl to running the millinery department. It appears that she was very capable and highly thought of. She seems to have made many friends there and we have quite a number of photos from this period in her life, although we do not know any of the people in the photos.

Natie and Judith at the seaside   *Natie and Judith at Arcadia*   *Judith 1929.*

Judith in front centre and Mr Shaer on right   Judith is on the end in both these photos of 1924 Arcadia'nurses'
Judith apparently helped look after the children and must have stayed on and worked at Arcadia.

Two unknown Arc nurses   Judith in tennis outfit   Natie looking very smart   Judith with unknown friend

MEMORIES OF THE ORPHANAGE AND ARCADIA

Rosalie Fisher (Judith Ratzer's daughter) writes

My mother and her siblings were so ashamed that they were in an orphanage and they never spoke about it

Gerard, Natie's son, said his Father never spoke about Arcadia. Rene Rabinsky, an ex Arc Girl, I met in the USA, did not want to talk about that part of her life and another fellow Walchick, whose father was there, said the same. They didn't like to talk about their time in the orphanage.

My Mom mentioned that there was a matron in charge in the Orphanage who she did not like. She would give to charity for everyone but not to the Arc. If our clothes were not straight she would go crazy. She must have got that from the Arc.

Natie was fostered out, but returned to the home, so he had the same name.

Beryl Ratzer (Natie Ratzer's daughter in law) writes

My husband's parents were at Arcadia in the 1920s

As far as Maurice can recall his late father never spoke of the time before he got to the orphanage or even of the orphanage itself.

Maurice's late mother, Tillie (nee Goldstein) was born in South Africa but her parents couldn't care for her and her many brothers and sisters and they were placed in Arcadia. She often told stories of the difficult times they had in the orphanage. They would have been there until about 1932.

According to Tillie, they were not very well treated. Actually she had a number of real horror stories!

Natie was an Ochberg orphan, something he never mentioned and which I only recently found out. Natie was a wonderful person and was chief projectionist at His Majesty's theatre.

Rene Simpson (Phyllis Ratzer's daughter) writes

My late mother Phyllis Ratzer, born 31 May 1908 (may her soul rest in peace) was one of the children rescued by Papa Ochberg as he was to her, her brother Natie and her sister Judith.

Initially she was there at Arcadia together with Natie and Judith.

She was very lucky to have been adopted by a wonderful family by the name of Woolf and she subsequently took their name.

She did tell me that she did visit her siblings regularly at Arcadia and they were always close to each other.

My late mother survived both her siblings and passed away at the age of 94 in 2002.

Essie Ratzer, (Natie Ratzer's daughter in law) whose sister Mary (Aronovsky) Flax was in the Arc, writes;

I do not know if you are aware that Gerard's Mother Tillie Ratzer (nee Goldstein) also had her two sisters Rosie Zeff and Janie Kruger in the Arc with her. Three of her brothers were also there Jack, Leslie and Mendy Goldstein. Gerard is not sure if the other two brothers, Michael and Alec Goldstein, were also there.

I think that every Jew in South Africa had some relation in the Arc at some time.

OUR FAMILY
Written by Rachelle and Rosalie

Our father, Nathan Sherksne, arrived in Cape Town 1919 and was a butcher. Judith married Nathan Sherksne around 1943.

Wedding picture of Judith and Nathan

After they got married the family first lived in Doornfontein. The father's butcher shop was at the corner of 46 Derby and Queen Street in Doornfontein. Our mother helped our father in the butcher shop and played bowls well and was the Treasurer of Ellis Park Bowling Club.

Nathan and Judith had three daughters Rachelle born 15 February 1945, now Meskin, Marion born 18 January 1947 now Katzel and Rosalie born 28 October 1949 now Fisher. In about 1949 just before Rosalie was born, they moved to Cyrildene.

Judith and Marion

Rachelle, Rosalie and Marion

Marion, Rosalie and Rachelle

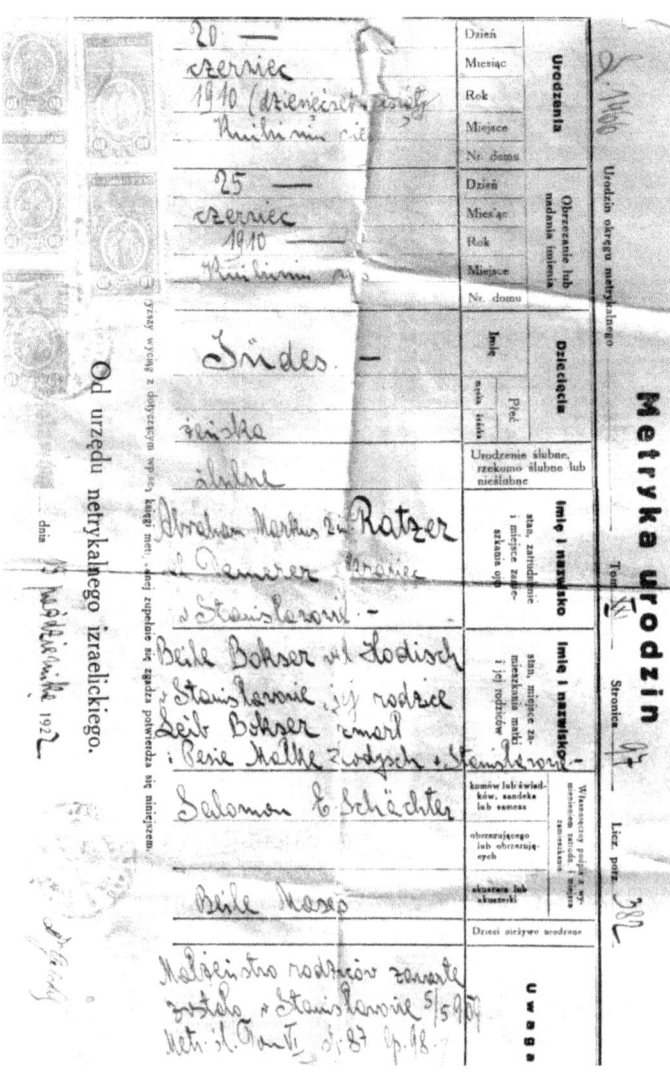

The birth certificate belonging to our mother Judith Ratzer

We have ascertained that she was born on 25 June 1910.

Judith passed away on the 14 August 1965.

REMEMBERING THE RATZERS

Alec Saul from Israel writes

The Ratzers where well known to me. Natie was at one time a business partner of mine and he married a Tilly Goldstein who was also in Arcadia. They had two sons Morris and Gerard who married Beryl and Essie. While Morris and Beryl and their children live in Israel, Gerard and Essie live with their children in South Africa.

Judith Ratzer married Nathan Ratzer (Shirksner) and I remember they had two daughters. My memory of the second sister, Phyllis, is vague. She had a farm in Eikenhof, in the then Transvaal.

Natie and Tilly

Michael Perry Kotzen from Sydney writes

I remember Natie Ratzer very well. Natie had already left Arcadia when I was brought there in 1933. When I left Arcadia at age 18 in 1941, my first job was as an assistant cinema operator for ACT, (African Consolidated Theatres) I was assigned to the Plaza Cinema in Rissick Street. Natie Ratzer was the chief operator (Projectionist) at the Plaza bioscope. I was one of Natie's three assistants. I worked under Natie in the projection booth for over a year. Then Natie was promoted to chief operator of the new His Majesty's theatre in Commissioner Street and I joined the army and was sent up to North Africa.

After my discharge in 1946 I worked backstage for a number of theatrical producers. By the 1960s I had attained the exalted position of manager of the Empire Theatre in Commissioner Street. Natie was then chief projectionist at his Majesty's, the "flagship" of A C T.

I knew Natie well, though I never did meet his family. He told me he had come out of Arcadia. He may also have told me that he was "An Ochberg child". I do not recall. Through Natie I met Polly Joffe, a widow living in Kensington with her two beautiful daughters Sybil and Myra. Polly had spent her childhood in Arcadia. Today, Sybil, Polly's daughter is Mrs Michael Keats. Both Polly and Myra have passed away.

I remember Natie as a kind and decent man who taught me cinematography and encouraged me in my chosen career.

FISCHEL RATZER, JUDITH'S OLDER BROTHER

In 1937 Judith did hear from a brother that remained in Stanislaw. Here is a wedding photograph of him and his bride that was sent to her.

To my dear sister - a keepsake (to remember me) from your brother Fischel Ratzer   24 May 1937

Two years later this same brother sent her a photo of their late mother with an inscription on the back. My mother always had this photograph next to her bed.

CHANCIE RUCHEL (RATZER) JUDITH'S OLDER SISTER

A postcard dated 27 January 1939 sent to Judith.

A keepsake (to remember me) from me your sister Chancie Ruchel

Chapter 41 – CHAIM AND ABRAM REICHMAN

MY FATHER WAS AN OCHBERG ORPHAN
Written by Karon Reeve Richman (Israelsohn)

I discovered in 2011 that Chaim (Hymie) Reichman, my father, and his brother Abram (Abie) belonged to the group of children known as the Ochberg Orphans. I found this out because one of the producers of the documentary on Isaac Ochberg contacted my brother in South Africa to inform him and request information.

The only information I ever got direct from my father was that he was from Pinsk in Belarus. He didn't speak to me about his childhood and his roots.

Other information over the years that I gleaned from various sources is that my grandparents owned a forest and flour mill and also raised horses for the Tzar.

I learned that my grandfather Pincus Reichman was taken for ransom by the Cossacks, and even though they received the ransom money from my grandmother they murdered my grandfather. I am told by my brother, who got the information from my uncle Abie, that it was done in front of my grandmother. I have been told that my father witnessed this atrocity. He was hiding in the forest and watching from there.

I was originally told that my grandmother sent her two youngest children, my father five years old and my uncle eight years old, with a servant to the Polish border where they were met by a priest and put on a boat to South Africa. When they arrived in South Africa they were adopted by different families.

However in 2011 I received information from David Solly Sandler, who has done much research on the Ochberg Orphans and has written books on them.

David told me that the 1921 records show the boys were then aged 9 and 11 and were born in Turow. They were selected from the Pinsk Orphanages by Isaac Ochberg and would have been accompanied and looked after by Alter Bobrow on their journey via London to South Africa.

After arriving in Cape Town South Africa they were sent by train to Johannesburg and placed in the care of The South African Jewish Orphanage, later called Arcadia."

From there Chaim, my father, was placed in the care of the Israelsohn Family of Pietersburg (Max Israelsohn) and Abram, my uncle, was placed in the care of the Kruger Family also of Pietersburg so at least the brothers were close by to each other and would have stayed in touch.

Extracts from the Address book of Isaac OCHBERG.

NAME OF CHILD	NAME OF ADOPTIVE PARENT
No.30 RAICHMAN Chaim 9	To Max Israelsohn, Pietersburg
No.29 RAICHMAN Abram	To Kruger, Pietersburg.

ADOPTIVE PARENTS	NAME OF ORPHANS
38. ISRAELSOHN 134	REICHMAN CHAIM 30
19 KRUGER 23	ABRAM REICHMAN 29

PINCUS (PINYA) REICHMAN, MY GRANDFATHER

Pincus was one of six siblings -
1. Grunia (married Max Gittleman) came to USA,
2. Pincus (married Rivka),
3. Max,
4. Nichoma,
5. Saul (Sol - married Bella) lived in LA USA
6. Fannie (Fanya - no children)

Pincus (Pinya) Reichman

Pincus married Rivka and they had five children. The older three children are unknown, Abi was next and Hymie the youngest.

I don't know anything about the older three. I think they all remained in Russia. My uncle Abie did communicate with his brother, who stopped communicating when uncle Abie offered to bring him to South Africa. I think that two were male and one female. I believe the female was raped.

RIVKA REICHMAN, MY GRANDMOTHER

Rivka's maiden name is unknown. She married Pincus Reichman and is the mother of Abram and Chaim Reichman.

Rivka Reichman

This photograph which is life size somehow came to South Africa with the children. How they transported the life-size photographs of their parents is hard to imagine. They must have been laid on the bottom of the suitcase, or rolled and placed in the suitcase. However, did the children have suitcases?

My mother Ettie Penkin was born in Cape Town. Her parents came from Rakishker, Lithuania. She was a descendant of the Penkin, Ruch family tree, and was an orphan by the time she was eight years old. However my mom had a large, caring, supportive, and close extended family in South Africa

PHOTOS OF CHAIM AND AVRAM REICHMAN FROM THE TRAVEL DOCUMENTS ISSUED BY THE PINSK MAGISTRATE

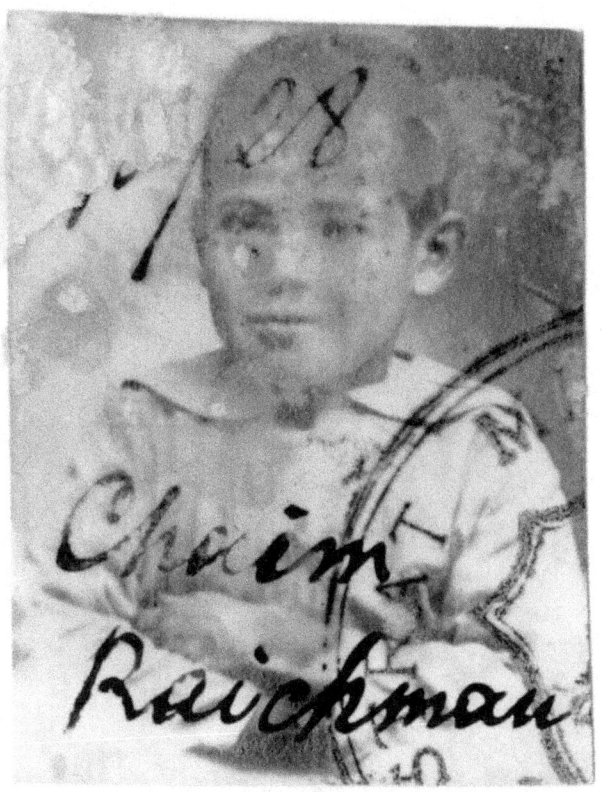

Chaim Reichman - aged five - photo on Pinsk Travel Document

Abram Reichman - aged eight - photo on Pinsk Travel Document

GROUP PASSPORT TWO AND LIST OF NAMES ACCOMPANYING GROUP PASSPORT TWO

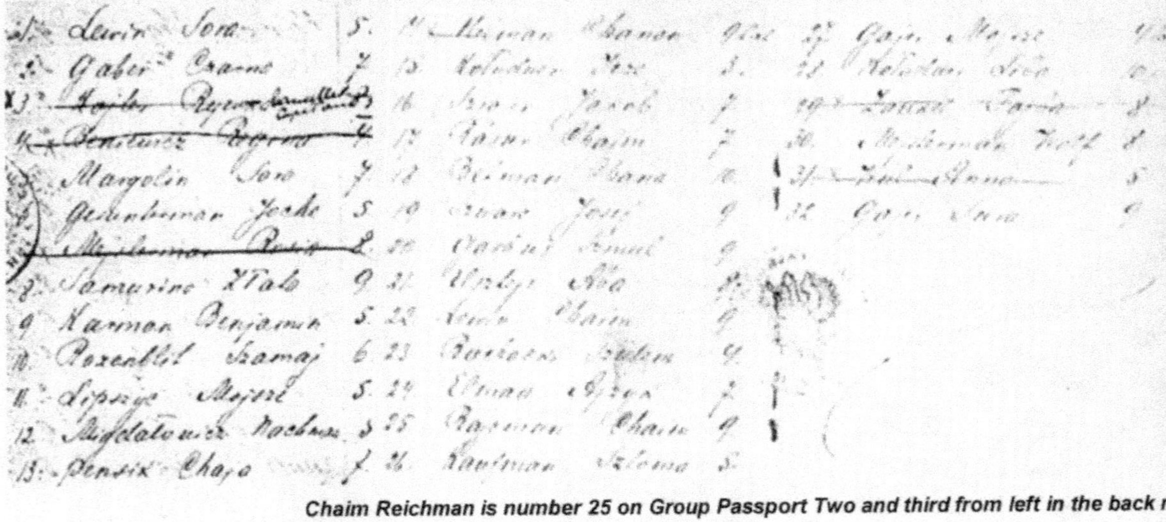

Chaim Reichman is number 25 on Group Passport Two and third from left in the back row and enlarged above

GROUP PASSPORT FOUR AND LIST OF NAMES ACCOMPANYING GROUP PASSPORT FOUR

Abram Reichman is number two on the Group Passport Four list and in the middle row last on right and enlarged above.

CHAIM REICHMAN, OUR FATHER
Karon Reeve-Richman (Israelsohn) writes

Chaim (Hymie) was the youngest child of Pincus and Rivka.

He was adopted by the Israelsohn family and lived with them in Pietersberg, until he was 16 years or younger. He was known as Hymie Israelsohn. I believe that he did not get along well with his adopted family. I think the only one who liked him and was good to him was the father. When the father died, it became difficult for him and so he left and went to Rhodesia and I believe he did well for himself in the textile business.

He met my mother Ettie Penkin, also an orphan, when he gatecrashed a wedding of one of my mother's cousins. He proposed to her after that. Very romantic, but it was not a happy marriage.

Hymie top left and Ettie bottom right
15 February 1950 at the Barmitzvah of Charlie Bacher

They had three children and lived in Johannesburg
1. Preston Michael Richman Israelsohn (Hebrew name Pincus)
2. Raymond Richman Israelsohn
3. Karon Reeve-Richman Israelsohn (Hebrew names Kazriela Rivka)

My Dad didn't even know his real birthday. His given birthday was 8 December.

Unfortunately my dad's story and our family life wasn't a big happy family event. My parents eventually divorced when I was in high school and this was after a number of separations and coming together again - mostly separated.

My father unfortunately served time in prison for tax avoidance and the horrible thing about it is that the people whom he took into his business, my mother's cousins, turned Queen's council against him. They got off and he took the punishment. When he came out he was very bitter. He had been a wealthy man and lost everything. He never quite made it again.

My mom, brothers and I lived in Cape Town for a few years. My brothers were boarders at SACS, and I started my schooling at Good Hope Seminary.

My father didn't have a close relationship with any of his children. I think I was the closest when I was older although I am the one who provoked him and fought with him the most as a child and while growing up until the divorce. After that I kept sporadic contact with him.

In his senior years he met and married a Greek woman by the name of Veronica.

Ettie, Hymie and Karon

Ettie

Hymie

Hymie's passport photo

Raymond Richman Israelsohn writes

Perhaps apocryphally, Abram (my uncle) and Chaim (my father) Reichman (sometimes Raichman) witnessed the slaughter (decapitation) of their family in Ukraine at the hands of the Bolsheviks at the ages of seven and five. They hid in the bushes and later stole away.

The family was, I understand, well established and relatively prosperous in the area in which they lived, owning an estate on which they conducted the businesses described by my sister, Karon. They also, I understand, bred, reared and trained horses for the Czar's cavalry, and may even, if I understand correctly, have served in the Czar's cavalry. I heard accounts of the Reichman men riding together on their horses into the neighbouring village (which somehow bore the name *Reichman* or some derivative thereof) from time to time to rout pogroming Bolsheviks.

After stealing away after the slaughter, the boys wandered away in the snow, which they sucked – with stones my uncle said – for water but had no food. They eventually found their way to a Jewish Orphanage – such as may have existed then and there (or were found and taken to the orphanage). The rest is general and well documented. Growing up in South Africa, my father was reportedly unhappy and unliked. He ran away from his adoptive family (Israelsohn) during his teenage years and made his own way …to Rhodesia, I understand.

Only my uncle would talk of the experiences, albeit inarticulately and when pressed. My father, who was traumatized by the experiences, never uttered a word. The effect on my father was damaging; and from about my seventh year he got involved in fraudulent activity for which he was convicted.

The traumatic experiences of his young years rendered him chronically insecure, and to this I attribute his vulnerability and vicissitudes.

My father was adopted from the South African orphanage by the Israelsohn Family, and he assumed that family name. Similarly, my uncle, Abie, was adopted by the Kruger Family, and he assumed that name. When they both had children in due course, it would seem that their memorial gesture was to give each child a middle name *Richman* – an anglicised *Reichman* (not double-barrelled). So I was *Raymond Richman Israelsohn*, my brother *Preston Michael Richman Israelsohn*, and my sister *Karon Reeve Richman Israelsohn*. Similarly as far as I'm aware, my cousins, uncle Abe's children eg *Mervyn Richman Kruger*.

When I became aware of the richly tapestried history of my paternal family-line, I alone, not in association with any of my siblings or cousins, sought to embed the paternal family name *Reichman* more securely by a formal registered change of name by substituting the *Richman Israelsohn* with *Reichman-Israelsohn*. This I did in 1979 since when I and my family have carried the double-barrelled name on our Identity Documents, Passports, and generally.

Relative to my firm's name *Reichmann and Israelsohn*, which has the two n's in Reichmann and the word *and* instead of the hyphen, this is a product of *gammatria* (numerology). It is a play on the two names in order to produce the richest emergence of harmonic resonance from them according to principles of *gammatria*.

Preston Israelsohn writes

I remember my father as a quicksilver type of personality whose every emotion was graphically expressed on his face as he felt it. I knew how he felt merely by glancing at his face.

He was highly volatile and I remember most of all his fearsome temper. He was an angry man most of the time.

He had a silver tongue and could sell snow to an Eskimo. I think his success in selling had something to do with his passion/intensity or belief in what he was doing albeit delusionary. I think this probably lead to the fraudulent aspects of some of his business dealings.

He was a larger than life personality and held his audience caprice with his stories of his past experiences.

He seemed to have associated with some of the early colorful entrepreneurial characters of his time, mining magnates etc about whom he used to tell stories.

He was a very successful business man and had some amazing brands of products such as Horrickses Fabrics for which he had the South African agency.

He owned extensive land which at one time in his hey day extended large distances from Johannesburg to Pretoria, which today had an incredible value.

I remember going with him to a farm he owned in the Orange Free State which he had named Presthyme.

We, early in my life, lived in a mansion on large grounds on the top of a ridge called Mountain View which had a brilliant view of the suburbs below it.

The house was on large grounds with tennis court, rockery, children's play equipment and had a multi car parking garage which had pits under the cars with steps leading down so one could inspect the cars from underneath.

The garage housed large luxury cars such as the Lincoln Continental V12 and other luxuriously American cars of the time.

His fiery temper I believe lead to the beginning of the end of his empire by antagonizing internal revenue authorities who visited his business premises and promptly got thrown out by him. I assume super confidence and indiscretion lead to his downfall.

Preston (my oldest brother), Karon (me the youngest), Ettie (my mom), and Raymond (my middle brother).

This photo taken outside my uncle Jack Penkin's apartment on Kloof Nek Road, Tamboerskloof. Jack was my mother's brother.

I remember him as subsequently becoming locked into the past and what was, and only looking back not forward. Consequently, he was unable to recover and rehabilitate and rebuild.

He was obsessed with recovering his lost past and clearing his name which left little energy for going forward. He carried grudges from the past and could not let go of them.

I remember he used to dominate my mother who was a rather meek and mild lady who was suppressed and oppressed by him. I believe her stress engendered by her relationship with him lead to her serious illness of breast cancer resulting in a radical mastectomy at very young age. This is purely my opinion and obviously not a medical one.

My experience with my father was from birth to around eight years old when he went to prison and I and my brother went to boarding school in Cape Town for three years. On our return to Johannesburg I was 12 and my brother nine. I don't remember much about my father for the next few years. He was never prominent in my life, never came to my school affairs, such as athletic meets, rugby matches etc in which I participated.

He then disappeared for another three years for fraud. I didn't see much of him. However, he and my mother divorced and I remember he had a girlfriend who was eventually followed by another woman whom he married and he eventually died of a heart attack. I attended his funeral and that was the end of the chapter in my life of Chaim my father.

My mother Ethel I remember as a quiet unobtrusive person, more introverted than extroverted. Always very well groomed and immaculately presented. She also had very good taste in clothing, home interiors etc.

However, she somehow survived through all this successfully.

Hymie holding Karon's son David and daughter Tanya - ~1971

Kenny Penkin, a nephew of Hymie, writes about Hymie

He was always warm towards me and most generous in providing me with a home in our July school holidays – especially in Mountain View. I also remember 10 Hettie Street, Cyrildene as a lovely much smaller home. He was also a very handsome man. His oft quoted tax case was an interesting one and I always felt good as a Chartered Accoutant that here was an important tax case and it was my uncle.

He set a legal precedent when he took on the South African tax authorities in the well known and oft cited case of **Israelsohn v CIR** (1952) (3) SA 529 (A), 18 SATC 247).

ABRAM REICHMAN, OUR UNCLE
Karon Reeve Richman (Israelsohn) writes

Abram was the second youngest child of Pincus and Rivka and was adopted by the Kruger family and lived with them in Pretoria. He was known as Abie Kruger.

Abie married Bella and they had three sons and lived in Pretoria

1. Pierre Richman Kruger
2. Mervyn Richman Kruger
3. Billie Richman Kruger

Uncle Abie was my favourite uncle and I loved him very much. I used to wish he was my father. My mother and I used to travel to Pretoria regularly while my brothers were in boarding school. We visited my uncle Abie almost every weekend and we often stayed over for the weekend.

I loved being with my boy cousins Pierre, Mervyn and Billie. They were always so kind to me and allowed me to "schlepp along". They taught me how to ride a horse and I will never forget that. It was so scary and exciting at the same time. I felt like a princess every time we went horse riding.

Being the youngest and the only girl amongst the five Richman boys was a privilege I grew up with. I think my Richman Kruger cousins were especially nice to me because I was the youngest and the only girl.

I used to love it when I was taken to uncle Abie's shop. It was so exciting because I never left without something new and useful to wear. I also loved my auntie Bella. She was fun to be with and we used to tease each other. She often reminded me of when she visited my mom and I in Muizenberg and I used to lie with my head on her tummy on the beach and complain about the noises I could hear in her tummy.

She loved telling the story of how she came to fetch me from school one day and found me kicking my suitcase along instead of carrying it, because it was too heavy and I didn't want to carry it. She was very cross with me so I ran ahead of her and then she was worried I was going to let her get lost. Those were the days...

Something I remember about my uncle Abie is that he used to swim every single day, summer and winter throughout the year - he did not skip a day.

My uncle Abie Kruger holding my son David ~ 1969

My uncle Abie was a down-to-earth, reliable, solid citizen who owned his own general dealership business in Pretoria, and was well regarded by the local Jewish Community. His business comprised a large shop extending from the front of the building right to the back, and containing virtually everything but the kitchen sink.

I believe he owned the building as well and other properties. I know that he had the same business during my entire relationship with him from when I was a small child to when he passed away. He must have had the shop for 50 plus years.

Comparing my father with uncle Abie is difficult due to the circumstances in which each of the brothers conducted their lives. My father was the very opposite to Abie in that he displayed none of the solid, reliable and consistent attributes of his brother. My father was obviously very smart, good looking and charming and had made a tremendous success of his life by amassing considerable wealth at a very early age. He was a founding member and contributed substantially to the establishment of the Cyrildene Hebrew Congregation in Johannesburg. However, unfortunately he lost everything. I estimate that it was probably before he turned 40 years old, and shortly before I turned five. This hit him very hard and he did not manage to regain his confidence and his success in business. Perhaps if he was less reckless and more like his brother he would have managed to sustain his success.

Maybe my father, being younger than Abie was more affected by the horrific experiences of their early childhood. Maybe my uncle had a more secure upbringing with his adoptive family. I wish I knew if the brothers spent any reasonable amount of quality time together as young children. They must have missed each other desperately after having shared such a traumatic experience during their formative years and then been pulled apart and adopted by different families. This is something that will always bother me. Why separate two brothers who had no one left but each other? I think that was a big mistake – if they could not have gone to the same family at that time, it may well have been better to have kept these young children together to have the benefit of each other's company until a family was prepared to take both of them. I think this was a most insensitive action on the part of the authorities at that time, and may well have contributed to the insecurity of my father. Whatever it was - the brothers were very different in the way they conducted their lives. This difference also extended to their family relationships. Uncle Abie was more of a family man than my father who did not manage to acquire parenting skills.

I wonder what part heredity played versus environment in the enacting out of their lives. It will remain unsolved. The poignant fact is that it is due to Isaac Ochberg that I am here to tell this story, and through his beneficent actions that I have brothers, nieces, nephews, children, grandchildren, and cousins all doing well in our different ways.

Preston Israelsohn writes

Abie (Avraham) as opposed to my father was a stable family man who ran his outfitting/dry goods store in Pretoria for years (most of his life) and owned the building in which he ran his shop.

We used to visit my cousins in Pretoria from Johannesburg occasionally and I remember a normal family experience.

In fact shortly after my marriage uncle Abie was closer to me than my father and even helped me in a small way to get started.

Uncle Abie and I attended my father's funeral.

PLAQUES AT RAMAT MENASHE
Karon Reeve Richman (Israelsohn) writes

I would like to thank both Bennie Penzik and his committee, for persuading the JNF to erect the monument to Isaac Ochberg with all the plaques to the Ochberg Orphans at Ramat Manashe, and David Solly Sandler, for documenting for perpetuity, the lives of these special orphans.

The story and the monuments together have something positive to show for the life of my father and uncle. I am looking forward to visiting the monument site at Ramat Manashe G-d willing next year 2014.

Above and below are the plaques to Hymie and Abie Reichman at Ramat Manashe

GRUNIA REICHMAN
Karon Reeve Richman (Israelsohn) writes

Grunia, the sister of my grandfather Pincus, married Max Gittelman and settled in the USA. They had three children Sonja, Rose and Max.

The Reichman Gittelman Family

Sonja married Sam Gold and they had a son Fred who in turn had two children. Rose married Sam Schwartz and had two children, Martin and Leonard.

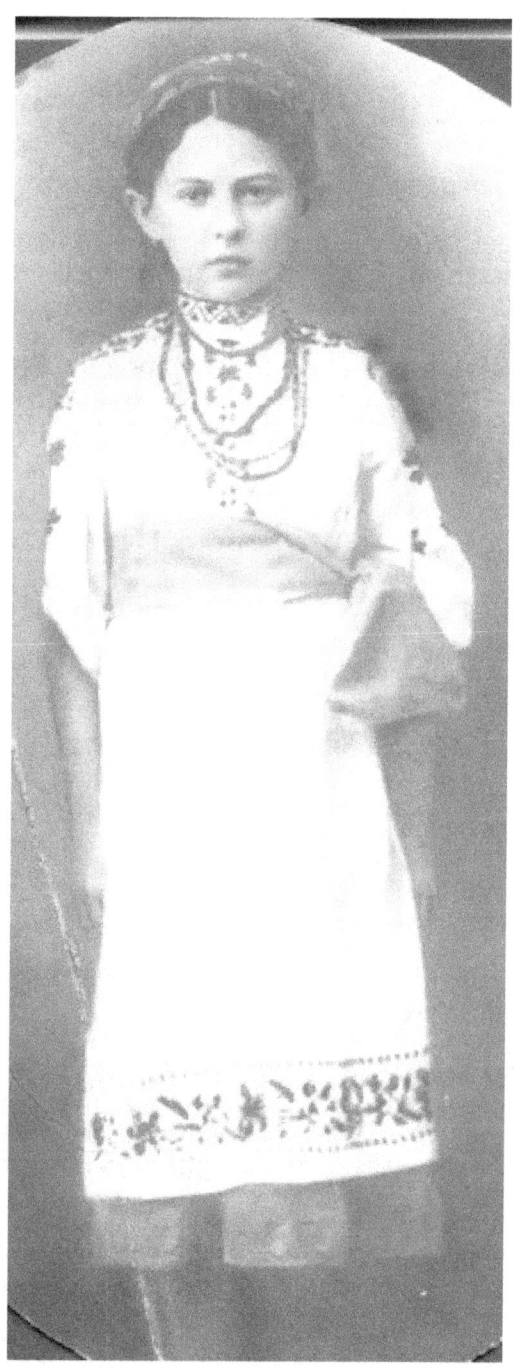

Sonia as a young girl

When I eventually met my aunt Sonja she spoke about Hymie with such love and concern, as did my aunt Bella Richman in LA. They remembered the boys and the heartbreak of losing them when they left Russia.

It was through Sonja that I learned about the ransom and about the flour mills and forests that my grandfather owned.

Chapter 42 – RUBIN REISENDER
AN OCHBERG ORPHAN SENT TO THE USA

RUBIN REISENDER
AN OCHBERG ORPHAN SENT TO THE USA

Jenny Segall (1) sent in the photo below and wrote

I want to let you know that the photo of the 'Ochberg Orphan sent to the USA', the man with the hands behind his back, and the young lady is definitely a Rubin. We cannot remember his last name, and it seems he left to go to America when he was about 18 or 19 (not earlier age as we thought). He did not have a sister, so the photo might be a cousin, as we know he never married. Hope that helps somewhat.

David Solly Sandler wrote

The man in this picture was an Ochberg Orphan who was sent to the USA as he had an aunt there.

The only Ochberg on the list named Rubin is Rubin Reisender. Does this ring a bell?

Jenny Segall emailed from Houston

Yes, it is Reisender!!!! The minute I asked my hubby Chaim if that is the name he said definitely.

So after going round the bush for quite a long time we have his full name.

He definitely did not leave the Men's Residence in Cape Town until he was 19 or 20, because the Aunt in America asked him to come to them, which he did, but he asked my mother Ruza Hans to marry him and go with him and she said "No" and so he went.

Chaim, my husband, was on a scholarship from the South African Board of Deputies and the South African Government at the Yeshiva and New York Universities for 18 months, and in spare time he was lecturing all over America on South Africa. In those years he had to be very careful what he said. At one of the lectures he spoke about South Africa and Cape Town, and after the lecture this man came to Chaim and asked him "Is Cape Town still so beautiful?" and a conversation started. He then told Chaim that he was an Ochberg Orphan and had been brought up at the orphanage. Chaim then told him his mother-in-law was also there- name Ruza.

They spoke for several hours, and straight afterwards Chaim wrote us a letter and told us about the meeting. It was that letter we were looking for to let you know the name. So there you have the little story attached to him. This was in 1958/59 approx.

Rubin Reisender
the 'Ochberg Orphan sent to the USA',

I am so happy you have finished the book, and I am sure as time goes on, more descendants will now have heard about it and want to write to you. Your work on this book and the Arc books is something no words can express. I want to thank you from all the decendants and their families for having had the 'kaychas' as they say in yiddish to do this remarkable job of work and with such love and no payment.

Note 1

Jenny (Flink) Segall, the daughter of an Ochberg Orphan, not only wrote about her Mom and Aunt, Ruza and Neta Hans, who were Ochberg Orphans (in The Ochberg Orphan's book) but also sent the wonderful photos of "The young ladies in the "Ladies Section".

Jenny also wrote about Chava Berkowitz another Ochberg Orphan who was an Actress in the Yiddish Theatre

Chapter 43 – GDALIA ROSENBLIT (ROSENBLATT) (LATER CALLED GERALD NADELMAN)

Gdalia Rosenblit, born 1913 in Rovno and his brother Shamay Rosenblit, born in Rovno in 1912 were part of the half of the Ochberg Orphans who were placed in the care of the South African Jewish Orphanage later called Arcadia.

While Shamay Rozenblat is in Group Passport Two Gdalia is in Group Passport Nine

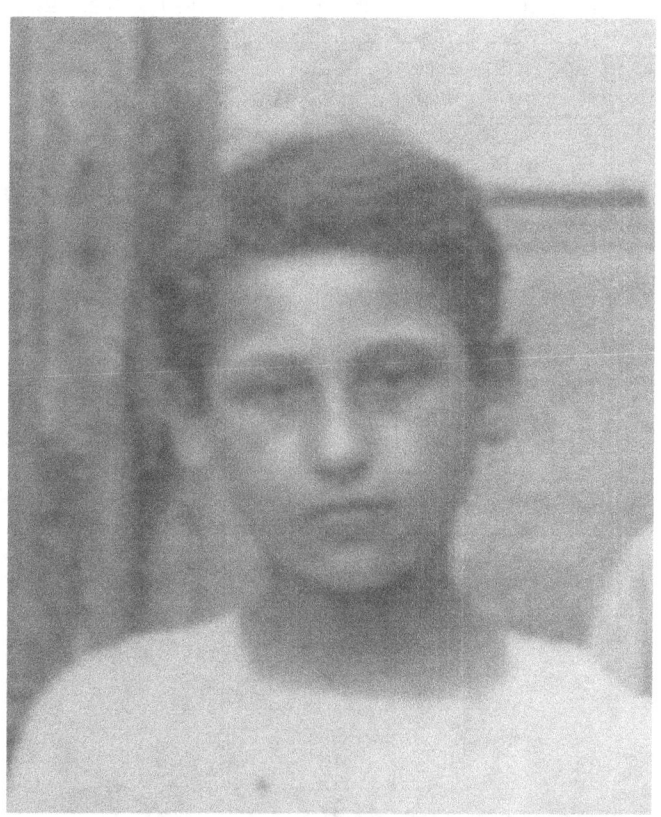

Gdalia identified by Gerald in Group Passport Nine

LEARNNG MY FATHER WAS AN OCHBERG ORPHAN
by Arnold Nadelman, Gerald's son

I read in the Melbourne Jewish News (July 2011) about the Ochberg Orphans. My late Father Gerald Nadelman came as an ophan from Russia with his Brother Sam Rosen and that is all I know to date. I am now 68 and know nothing about my Late Father other than he was an orphan from Russia.

My Late Father Gerald (Gdalia) was adopted by Avraham Nadelman and it appears that his brother Sam(Szamay) was never adopted - so that is why his name remained Rosen.

I went on line and found this article "seeking Ochberg Ophan Descendants from South Africa" and was blown away when I found my Late Father's name and his brother under Rosenblit. My Father never ever spoke about his childhood. All I ever knew was that he and his brother came on a boat as orphans to South Africa after the pograms in Russia. We think there were three brothers in total, one being a baby who supposedly went to Israel. Unfortunately we were never able to find him as we didnt have a name. Maybe now you have a list of a boy Rosenblit or his descendants who we could contact in Israel.

I am quite overwhelmed by finally after 68 years discovering something about my Late Father Gdalia Nadelman (Rosenblitt). Please be in contact with me as I am seeking anything on my Late Father Gdalia.

Gdalia as a young man

GERALD (GDALIA) NADELMAN BORN ROSENBLIT
As remembered by Arnold Nadelman

I knew my Dad was adopted, born in Russia and that was all I knew. It was never discussed. He died at the early age of 44 soon after my Barmitzvah.

My Dad married Dora (Doris) Simson in 1933 and had three children; Fay born 1934, Ruth born 1937 died 1963 and Arnold 1943.

We lived in a semi-detached house in Francis Street, Yeoville when I was very young and then moved to a house in Becker Street, Yeoville. When I was nine we moved to a lovely home in Sydenham until Gerald (Gdalia) died in 1956.

I was the apple of my parents eyes as I was the youngest and the only boy. My Dad spoilt me rotten. He was a hard working man and had a scrap metal business.

My Dad, Gerald and Arnold (My Dad and I)

I have wonderful memories of my Dad. He loved sport and was very involved in swimming and water polo at Yeoville Baths. He was also very involved at Balfour Park with the soccer. I am constantly reminded by people who knew him that he would fill the Jeep with as many kids as possible to take them to their matches. My life as a little boy was spent between Yeoville baths and Balfour Park. What wonderful memories I have of those young days.

I believe that there were two brothers and only my Dad and Samay (Sam) were saved by Isaac Ochberg. Samay (Sam) Rosen (Rosenblit) the older brother of my Dad Gerald (Gdalia) lived in Greenside with his wife Lily and had two sons, Jossie and Ralph. When I was about seven Sam seperated from his wife. He too died at a young age from a heart attack. Even though they had different surnames they grew up knowing they were brothers.

My Grandfather Avraham Nadelman who adopted my Father was very much part of our lives. When he lost my grandmother he lived with us in Sydenham until he died in 1950.

I am so grateful to finally find out a little about my Father, when he was born and where. I feel so heartsore knowing that his young years were so difficult, having his parents slaughtered in the pogroms.

I am extremely and eternally grateful to the wonderul Isaac Ochberg and all the people involved in saving my Father's life as well as the other orphans.

Ruth Nadelman (my late sister) and I

Gerald(Gdalia), Arnold and cousin Ralph Rosen son of Samay Rosen (Rosenblit)

Gerald(Gdalia) with the eldest grandson Geoff Ginsberg (Son of eldest daughter Fay Ginsberg)

FAY AND RUTH NADELMAN
By Gail Nadelman

Arnold's eldest sister is Fay Ginsberg married to Henry Ginsberg with three children, Jeff, Alan and Glenda. Fay Ginsberg was a well recognised Table Tennis Player in South Africa.

Arnold's second sister Ruth was married to Solly Rabinowitz and died shortly after having a baby whose survived and is named Gary Rabinowitz. All Arnold's family have remained in South Africa.

GERALD NADELMAN AND FAMILY

I married Gail Katz on 27 June 1965 and we had three children: Grant born 1966, Jeff born 1968 and Dana born 1972. Gail and I emigrated to Melbourne Australia in December 1978 with our three children Grant, Jeff and Dana. We now have seven grandchildren.

Within six months of being here we opened the first of the *Baby Bunting* chain. Our children after being educated at University joined the business.

We both play bowls and I play golf too. Gail was inducted into the Maccabi Hall of Fame for bowls in 2016.

Fay and Henry Ginsberg, their two sons Jeff and Alan Ginsberg, daughter Glenda Ginsberg as well as their grandchildren from the two boys,

Gary Rabinowitz son on the late Ruth Rabinowitz (nee Nadelman) together with Gary's Aunt and Uncle, Fay and Henry Ginsberg.

Our children and their spouses - Hadasa and Grant (eldest) Nadelman, Dana and David Felbel (our youngest) and Tammy and Jeff Nadelman (middle child)

Arnold and Gail together with their seven grandchildren. "Our seven blessings - Gabi and Jared Nadelman (Grant's family), two little boys and the girl with black dress next to Arnold are Dana's family: Coby, Jesse and Kami (Kamryn) Felbel. The tallest of the kids and the girl on the furtherest right in white are Jasmine and Dylan Nadelman (Jeff's family)"

Chapter 44 – SZAMAY ROSENBLATT LATER CALLED SAM ROSEN

INFORMATION FROM ORPHANAGE APPLICATION FORM IN POLAND COMPLETED IN YIDDISH

Names: Rozenblit, Gedalyahu and Shamai
Father: Yosef: Mother: Chana
Surviving relatives: An aunt Zvia Rozenblit in Rowne and a brother in a Rowner Orphanage.
School attended: Talmud Torah
Languages: Hebrew, Yiddish, Russian
Born into an intelligent family. Father was a photographer
Both parents were deceased. Father was killed, murdered by Petlurists in Gomel, the mother died of typhus.
Certificate of good health for the boys

LISTS OF CHILDREN GOING TO THE SOUTH AFRICAN JEWISH ORPHANAGE IN JOHANNESBURG

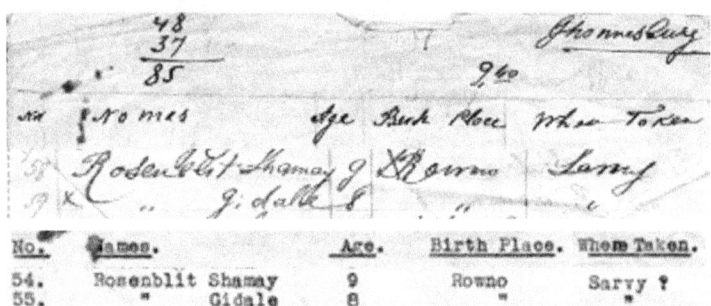

Children sent to Johannesburg showing age, where born and where taken

FROM THE SOUTH AFRICAN JEWISH ORPHANAGE REGISTER

Child placed in the care of		Name of child	
20	NADELMAN	102	GIDELE ROSENBLATT

Name of child	Child placed in the care of
No.59 ROSENBLATT Gidele boy 8	A. Nadelman Jeppe
No.58 ROSENBLATT Shamaya 9	CT

SAM ROSEN (SZAMAY ROSENBLATT) AND HIS DESCENDANTS *Written by Sheryl Daija (Rosen) James, Sam's grand daughter.*

Based on certain documents, it appears Sam was born in 1912 and was around nine years old when he came to South Africa as one of the Ochberg Orphans. Not much is known of Sam's childhood or his teenage years. As he moved into adulthood, Sam was a cabinet maker and lived at 28 Rocky Street in Bellevue. The address has significance because later it was the very same address of his son Joe's father-in-law's dairy (Bellevue and Willow Dairies) where Joe worked when he was first married.

On 7 October 1934 Sam married Lily Jacobsen (born 4 August 1908). They lived together with Lily's bobba, grandfather and brothers, Benny and Taffy in Doornfontein.

Lily had five brothers Wolfie, Alec, Benny, Taffy and another brother who died young. Her parents were Hynan Jacobson and Rosie nee Klaas Jacobson. Lily worked in a butcher shop as a bookkeeper for over 35 years.

Sam Rosen as a young man

Sam and Lily had two sons: Joseph (born August 11, 1935) and Ralph (born October 21, 1939). Joseph (Joe) was named after his grandfather Joseph.

When his sons were still very young, in 1940, Sam joined the South African army and during World War II he went up to North Africa where he built bridges for the army. After the war in 1945, he returned to Johannesburg where he worked as a salesman in an outfitter shop, Jackson's Outfitters. Joe worked with his dad there on weekends to earn some pocket money. In around 1947, the family moved from Doornfontein to Greenside.

Sam was a kind, soft spoken and gentle man. He never yelled or raised a hand to his children. He played cricket and would often watch his son Joe in boxing matches at school.

Legend has it that Sam was the nephew of the famous Chazan, Yossele Rosenblatt. Like Yossele Sam was a tenor and a good singer. In fact, he used to sing when guests came to visit and for his family at home.

Sam's brother Gerald Nadelman, also one of the Ochberg Orphans, was adopted from the Arcadia orphanage. Arnold and Gail Nadelman (son of Gerald) reminded Joe that Sam would take his wife and sons to visit with Gerald for tea. Sam did not drive so Gerald would fetch them in his Jeep. Ralph and Joe used to also meet their dad at the train station for a good lunch, which was a common place in those times.

Sam's life was not an easy one, and the knowledge of him as one of the Ochberg Orphans in part helps explain his challenges and wandering spirit. Not able to stay in one place for very long, in around 1950 Sam left his family to work in Port Elizabeth. After a year, he returned home, but soon he left again to work in a concession store in Uppington in the Northern Cape.

In 1956, Joe received a call from Sam's boss to say that his dad was very ill with a heart condition. Joe travelled to

Uppington and brought his father back with him where he was admitted to the General Hospital in Johannesburg. Joe visited him there often until Sam died from his heart condition on 14 December 1957. He is buried at Westpark Cemetery in Johannesburg - tombstone G246. Lily continued to live with her mother in Yeoville and died 19 May 1990.

Joe married Cecil Susman on 8 March 1959. During the early years of their marriage Joe put himself through university and graduated as a Chartered Accountant. They have two children Alan (born 18 June 1961) and Sheryl (born 4 June 1965) and will soon B'H celebrate their 58th wedding anniversary. Sheryl was named after Sam. Alan and Sheryl moved to the US in 1986 and 1987 respectively and Joe and Cecil emigrated to San Diego in 1996.

Alan, an Orthopedic Hand Surgeon, married Linda Clumeck on 8 July 1990. They live in Houston, Texas and have two children, Lauren (born 21 November 1994) who is a senior at Duke University and Evan (born 27 October 1998), who is in his last year of high school. Lauren is a state champion gymnast, a high school actress, dancer, choreographer, cheerleader and an avid sports fan. Evan is a high school athlete, performing artist and ardent sports fan of both professional and college athletics and will soon follow in Lauren's footsteps by attending Duke.

Sheryl Daija, an executive in the technology industry, married Rafael James on 13 January 2009. In 2010, they adopted their son, Abelli who was born 9 August 2008 in Ethiopia. They recently moved from New York to be close to Joe and Cecil in San Diego, CA. Abelli is in 3rd grade at the Chabad Hebrew Academy and has an equal passion for davening as he does for playing and watching competitive soccer.

Szamay Rosenblatt (Sam Rosen) as a young man

Joe Rosen and his family -- Rafael James, Sheryl Daija James, Abelli Daija James (front), Cecil Rosen, Joe Rosen, Evan Rosen, Linda Rosen, Alan Rosen

Joe Rosen and more of his family - Lauren Rosen, Evan Rosen, Cecil Rosen, Abelli Daija James, Joe Rosen

Sam's younger son, Ralph, married Jennifer Segal in Johannesburg on 31 January 1965. They raised two sons and a daughter, Stanley (born 29 January 1966), Darrill (born 4 October 1969) and Helene (born 4 April 1974), and recently celebrated their 51st wedding anniversary. Ralph inherited Sam's salesmanship and was also a tenor who sang in the Shul Choir.

Sam's younger son, Ralph, married Jennifer Segal in Johannesburg on 31 January 1965. They raised two sons and a daughter, Stanley (born 29 January 1966), Darrill (born 4 October 1969) and Helene (born 4 April 1974), and recently celebrated their 51st wedding anniversary. Ralph inherited Sam's salesmanship and was also a tenor who sang in the Shul Choir.

Their eldest son Stanley trained as a chef and has a daughter, Gabriella (born 7 January 1999), who is about to graduate high school. Gabriella dabbles in drama and is an animal lover, volunteering at the local SPCA. They live close to Ralph and Jennifer in Johannesburg.

Darrill emigrated to the US in 1999 after winning the Green Card Lottery. He married Heddy Lahmann (born 27 August 1981) on 24 November 2011. They live in Brooklyn, New York and both are involved in the arts.

Helene, a radiotherapist, married Eitan Zilkha (born 3 June 1974) on 26 June, 2008. They live in London with their son Zachary (born 18 September 2011) who exhibits the Rosen spark.

The family, beyond Lily and their sons Joe and Ralph, never met Sam who has existed up until now as somewhat of an enigma. From his photo and the little they have known about him they have thought of him fondly as dapper, magnetic and musical.

Zachary Zilkha

Ralph Rosen and his family - Heddy Rosen, Darrill Rosen, Helene Zilkha, Eitan Zilkha, Jennifer Rosen, Ralph Rosen (seated), Stanley Rosen, Gabriella Rosen

Chapter 45 – HARRY (HERMAN) ROTH (1910-1952)

HERMAN (HARRY) ROTH
an Ochberg Orphan who lived in Arcadia
Written by Arnold Roth

My late father's name was Harry Herman Roth but according to the records in Cape Town it is shown as Herman Roht with two dots over the "o". He was born in Lemberg in 1910 and there are no relatives that we know of.

He was one of the "Ochberg" children who was at Arcadia and apart from gleaning scant information from the Kaplan Centre Library at the University of Cape Town I have not been able to find out much about him. He moved to Rhodesia in 1928.

In 1946 he purchased a general dealer's store in Beitbridge and unfortunately died as a result of an accident in the Messina Mine Club swimming pool in November 1952.

It was soon after my Barmitzvah and I never had the opportunity to find out about my paternal grandparents as from the age of eight I stayed with my mother's family in Bulawayo where I went to school. I have some vivid recollections of happy times in Beitbridge with my parents and siblings during school holidays.

I never had the opportunity to discuss his childhood with my father and I don't think he was very forthcoming in that respect. I have a recollection of hearing that after the

Harry Herman Roth

war ended in 1945 he tried through the Red Cross to establish if he had any surviving family in Europe but without success. He did tell me he was Polish but as his Passport states that he was born in Lemberg – later Lvov – I note that it is now part of the Ukraine.

My research to date started after a discussion I had with Alec Grevler in Cape Town a few years ago. He had been a friend of my father's in Bulawayo and he suggested I contact Fanny Lockhitch who was an Ochberg orphan. She was a wealth of information and had amassed volumes of information which was with the Kaplan Centre at the University of Cape Town. She informed me that she had kept records of the children who went to the Oranjia Orphanage but my father was on of those who went to Arcadia in Johannesburg. Efforts to get information from there were also not successful. What I did get from the Kaplan Centre was the list of names and a group photo similar to what you sent me but was not able to identify my father.

I have been in contact with Alex Dunai in Lvov whose name was given to me by Lauren Snitcher and have asked him to make enquiries about my father and his family but again no success to date. I suggested to him in July that I should visit Lvov to initiate this research but he dissuaded me from doing so. Although I am not a member of the Norrice Lea Shul (Hampstead Garden Suburb Synagogue) I have ascertained that they have twinned with Lvov and amongst other activities they have assisted with the restoration of The Synagogue on Brothers Mikhnovskych Street. They arrange communal visits to Lvov from time to time and I hope to accompany them on their next visit.

Harry married Rose Gordon.
Rose, born in 1910 in Gwelo, was one of the six children of Robert Zelig Gordon and Mary Gordon (born Liptz). Rose and Harry had four sons, Arnold, Raymond, Marshall and Joseph and passed away on 4 March 1977.

WHAT I REMEMBER ABOUT MY DAD

At some stage after coming to Rhodesia in 1928 my dad had a small grocery shop on the corner of 4th Avenue and Fort Street in Bulawayo and as he had no home, he slept on the counter in the shop. He then had a shop and adjoining house built diagonally across the road from the original shop and I remember life as a five year old in that house. I am told he had a car registration number B12, but all I remember is catching my left index finger in the door and I still have a small scar to show for this

He purchased a trading store in Beitbridge and when I was eight my mother moved to Beitbridge and I stayed with my Aunt Bertha Gordon and Uncle Sox Gordon who had never married. Bertha was in the BSAP and Sox a bookmaker who, had at the age of 14, matriculated and won a scholarship which he cashed in so as to be able to pay for the education of his siblings. At school he held the record for the 100 yards and was a larger than life character who kept the family together.

Beitbridge had no running water, no electricity and was a 200 mile drive on strip roads from Bulawayo that would take six to eight hours. We had a Ford 1 ton truck that was used to carry goods from Bulawayo to Beitbridge and it was the happiest time of my life to be fetched and taken to Beitbridge for the school holidays where I spent a lot of time working in the shop. The Witwatersand Native Labour Association who recruited Malawian and Rhodesian staff to work on the mines in Johannesburg, would repatriate them at the end of their contracts and would send them by train to Beitbridge where the rail line ended. They would have to get buses back to their homes, but on arrival in Beitbridge usually at 8 pm they knew that they could come to the store to buy gifts to take home (blankets, material, clothing) and we would often be there until midnight on a Tuesday and Thursday when the trains arrived. The lighting was done with Tilley lamps using Paraffin and I became quite proficient in replacing the mantles. My Dad always said he should have bought the Garage (owned by an Irishman Patrick Murphy) or the Hotel (owned by the Dushah family, who I think were non-practicing Jews) as storekeeping was a hard life. In the afternoons he would always have a snooze for a half hour or so and would then kick a football with me. I was convinced he could kick farther than anyone else. Bread used to come by Road Motor Service buses twice or three times a week from Lobels Bakery in Bulawayo and often arrived mouldy but it was great to get "fresh" bread on the days when it came.

A little socialising was done in Messina with the Michalow, Chasen, Klaff, Cooper and Flax families (all Jewish) but whenever possible the family would congregate in Bulawayo for Rosh Hashanah and Yom Kippur as the shop was always kept closed on those days and my father was always the last to leave the vicinity of the Shul as he wanted to catch up with all his friends.

Christmas holidays were spent in Louis Trichardt where we relaxed at the hotel and did some scenic drives one of which ended up in the car getting stuck in the mud as there were only gravel roads and we had to be pulled out by a tractor driven by a local farmer who I think did far better financially from pulling out the many cars that had suffered the same fate as us, than he did from his farming.

In 1949, when I was 10, my father took his first holiday since arriving in Rhodesia 21 years earlier, and he took me with him. I got chicken pox the day before we were due to leave, but a few days later we took the train from Messina to Johannesburg where we nearly had one of our cases stolen and then on to Durban where we stayed at the Louis Hotel. In Johannesburg I had my first taste of a long awaited Coca Cola as there was none in Rhodesia at that time and I got my first Captain Marvel and Western comics, of which I became an avid fan.

In the same year my brother Raymond also joined me in Bulawayo for his schooling having had his nursery schooling in Messina and it was quite an achievement to get him to wear shoes for school as no one did in Messina. When it was time for my brother Marshall to start school my mother moved to Bulawayo so that she could be with her four sons. It was quite a wrench for us to leave the loving care of Bertha and Sox, but what a pleasure to be with my Mom and have my dad visit whenever he could and to continue to spend all our school holidays as a family in Beitbridge.

In December 1951 my Dad bought a Chevrolet Coupe Imp so that all the family could drive down to Cape Town. He arranged for someone to take care of the shop and off we went, only for the car to break down at Naboomspruit where we stayed for three days whilst parts were brought from Johannesburg for the car to be fixed. We then had to drive at 25 miles per hour for the first 1000 miles (nearly all the way to Cape Town) and you can imagine with four children aged 12, 10, 8 and 6 that it was not the most pleasant of trips.

A booking had been made to stay in Kalk Bay as the local Police Inspector from Beitbridge and his family had recommended the Hotel and would also be staying there, but it was not what was expected and we ended up staying at the Penlu Hotel in Muizenberg run by the Leibowitz family. I made friends with kids my age who are still, I am very happy to say, amongst my closest friends to this day. On the way back the car again broke down in Naboomspruit and we had the same delay, but it was a very special holiday.

After returning to Bulawayo I then had to cram my Barmitzvah studies and it culminated with a grand affair at the Jewish Guild Hall on 5 April 1952 where Mrs Plezner catered (ably assisted by one Bull Acutt who ran a restaurant and was a pal of my uncle Sox) and there was a band, but I was not too inclined to dancing with girls at that stage.

Sadly my father passed away on 23 November 1952 as a result of an accident in the Messina Mine Club swimming pool where he had gone to get some relief from the heat at that time of the year.

Chapter 46 – LETTERS AND PHOTOS TO THE STEINER BROTHERS IN ARCADIA, FROM THEIR OLDER SISTER CHAYA, IN PINSK

The Steiner brothers, Hersh, Isaac and Chaskel are introduced on page 86 of this book and their life stories are more fully told in The Ocberg Orphan book.

This chapter focuses mainly on the letters and photos sent by their older sister Chaya who remained in Pinsk. She married and her family perished in the Holocaust.

THE STEINER FAMILY
Written by Gila Waichman (Heather Steiner)

My father, Charles, fondly called Charlie, was born Chaskel in Libshei, Poland. His parents, Baruch and Brocha (nee Barenboim) had four children: Chaya, Hersh, Isaac and Chaskel. After Baruch was murdered during one of the many pogroms, Brocha fled with her children to her sister in Belarus. Soon after their arrival, Brocha died from pneumonia. Chaya remained with her aunt's family. She later married and her married name was Friedman. Tragically, she, her husband and two children, and the rest of the family died in the Holocaust. Sadly, this is all I know about that side of my dad's family.

The mother and sister of the three Steiner siblings Brocha (nee Barenboim) Steiner and Chaya

The three Steiner brothers; Charlie, Harry and Isadore

Thanks to the humanitarian kindness and generosity of Isaac Ochberg, the three little boys, Chaskel aged five, Isaac six and Hersh nine were among the lucky ones who were selected and sent to South Africa. At age 14 my dad left the South African Jewish Orphanage in whose care the boys had been placed and he (and I think also his brothers) went to live with Solly Bassman and his family in Bertrams Doornfontein. As far as I know Charles did not stay in touch with any of the other orphaned children.

He never ever spoke about his parents and sister, or his life as a child, adolescent or young adult. All I really knew was that he grew up in an orphanage, and his only immediate family were his two older brothers, Harry (Hersh) and Isadore (Isaac). I did not know much about Israel until the Six Day War and until I immigrated to Israel in 1969. I had no inkling of pogroms, the holocaust or anti-Semitism. We were just an average South African family and I was too young to even think about asking about our "roots".

LETTERS FROM CHAYA STEINER IN PINSK TO HER THREE STEINER BROTHERS IN ARCADIA

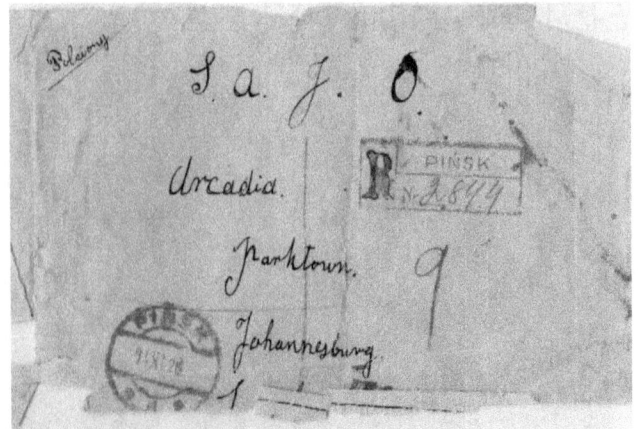

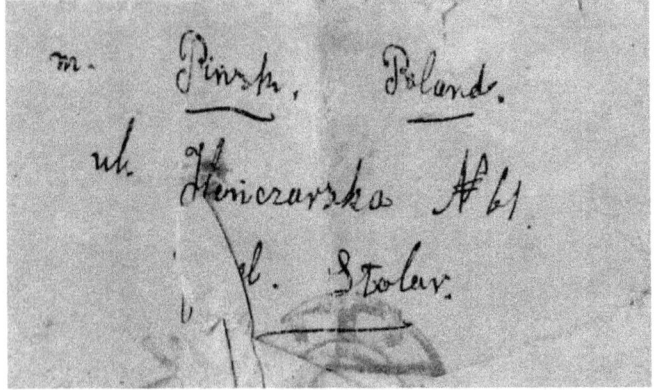

Front and back of envelope dated 12 8 1926 from Chaya in Pinsk to her three brothers in Arcadia

Letter 1
To my much loved and dear little brothers. May they live and be well. Firstly I want to write that I find myself well. Please G-d to hear the same from you. Dear little brothers, I have received your dear lovely letter and now I send a reply with picture cards from me. One will be for you and one for Chatzkaleh. Dear little brothers I have also sent a picture card to Hershaleh.

Dear and beloved little brothers, I have received a letter from the aunt Bashe in America. I have also received a letter from the aunt in Kavle. Further, my dear little brothers, I can only write you that I am not doing anything. I have learned a trade, but there is no work. Dear little brother Itzkel, write me, from you everything that you do, and how is it going with you, and how is Chatzkaleh, and why does he not write me any letters with his own little hands? Or when you write a letter why does he not send greetings. I beg you Chatzkaleh that you should send greetings with your own dear hands, in Itzkaleh's letter as I would like to see your handwriting. Dear and beloved little brothers, write me what news is in Africa. Is it winter or summer? Because, here by us it is already cold winter, everything is covered with snow and frost. Further there is no news from us. Write me if you have letters from America or not, because I am very anxious to know. I have no more news to write you. Stay well and live happily. From me your faithful sister who wishes you everything of the best.
Chaya Steiner

Please answer soon. Uncle Daniel and aunt Idel send friendly greetings. Regards from all the friends. I kiss you from far away XXXXXXXXXXX

Letter 2
This letter goes out on 21st of Cheshvan.
I wish my beloved little brothers much joy and happiness, stay safe. Beloved little brothers, I can write that we are, thank G-d, all well and hope to hear the same from you. Dear brother Hershalehk, I can write that we received your two notes. We never imagined that you would be so far away from us. Dear little brothers write us if Chatzkaleh is speaking more fluently and if he is learning. Dear little brothers, I am studying very well and soon will be able to write you a Hebrew letter. Dear little brothers Itzkaleh and Chatzkaleh, I ask you to write us with your own dear hands, because that will be a great pleasure, when we receive a letter from you and when you send regards.

Dear little brothers, I thank you many times for the postcards and I send two postcards - for Chatzkaleh a little girl and for Itzkaleh a little boy. I have no more to write you. Stay well and live happily, from me
Chaya Steiner
I send kisses to my beloved and dear little brothers, from far away.
Please reply

Letter 3
To my very loved and devoted little brothers, stay safe. Firstly I can inform you that I find myself in the best of health and hope to please G-d hear the same from you. My dear little brothers I can write to you that I received your dear letter on Friday 28th August. On the same day I had a letter from Hershaleh with a picture of all of you. My dear little brothers you cannot imagine how happy I was to see you all. I couldn't recognise you. My dear little brothers, how happy I would be if I could reach you. I can write you that I have had a few letters from Hershaleh and he writes that he always comes to you and all is thank G-d good with him He has a pleasant hand writing. Please write me about everything as I am very keen to know, dear little brothers.

What can I write you. I haven't received any letters from America for a long time and I don't know what to think. It is already about three months that I have nothing from America. My dear little brothers, I can tell you that I am thinking of travelling to Libishal to visit our father's grave [to 'Kever Avot']. Uncle Daniel told me that he has put up a headstone for our father. I don't know if this is true, that is why I want to travel to Libishal. Further, I send you two Shanah Tovah's 'New Year Greetings'. May G-d help you to have a good and healthy year and may we know no more bad times.

Also to Hershaleh, I send New Year greetings with a letter. [A few illegible words.] Stay healthy and be happy. From me your devoted sister who wishes you a good and healthy year and hopes for a good answer from you.
Chayah Steiner
I kiss you all heartily and in friendship XXXXXXX

Letters kindly translated from Yiddish to English by Bella Golubchik

Chaya (Steiner) Friedman (Fleishman)   *Chaya, her child and husband and her two children - all perished in the Holocaust*

Unknown relative   *Yentel Fleishmam*   *Feigel and Reftel Barenbo*   *Joseph Barenboim's Family in USA*

Charlie, Harry and Issy   *Charlie, Harry and Issy*   *Charlie and Issy*   *Charlie, Harry and Issy*

Chapter 47 – SAMUEL AND CECELE (OLGA) ZOLKOW – PHOTOGRAPHER AND ATTENDANT ACCOMPANYING OCHBERG ORPHANS

SAMUEL AND CECILE (OLGA) ZOLKOW
Photographer and attendant accompanying Ochberg Orphans
by Adrienne Hoberman

I have just received an email from an Aunty of mine who lives in Israel.

Her father, Samuel Zolkov and Olga Zolkov travelled with the Ochberg Orphans to South Africa.

Initially they went to South Africa and got married there. They returned to Poland at the time of the Revolution and in 1921 set out for South Africa as part of The Ochberg mission to save orphans after the slaughter of Jews during that period.

She was employed as an attendant, one of the persons looking after the children. They are both listed on the ship's manifesto (Edinburgh Castle): Olga as an attendant and Samuel as a photographer.....*see chapter three.*

Samuel Zolkov (photographer)

These are the only two photos that I have of Samuel and Olga Zolkov. Olga unfortunately passed away in 1928 from TB. My father was four years old.

Samuel remarried Naomi in 1931 and they had two children. Eli Zolkov who lives in Israel and Miriam Preiss who also lives in Israel.

Samuel died in 1948. They lived in Cape Town. Samuel worked as an accountant for the United Tobacco Co, and in 1931 he travelled to Europe to look for agencies to represent and was granted the agency for Chanel Perfumes!!!

That's all the information I have.

Olga Zolkov (attendant)

Chapter 48 – GENERAL OBSERVATIONS

OBSERVATIONS ARISING FROM COMPILING THE OCHBERG ORPHAN BOOKS
Written by David Solly Sandler

In compiling the individual life stories of the Ochberg Orphans, I encouraged descendants to write about the lives of the siblings, parents and other family left behind. Included in the index at the end of this section are the names of several siblings of Ochberg Orphans and their life stories are also told.

I encouraged descendants to include correspondence from family left behind but sadly there were many cases of correspondence ending when the Holocaust started and fruitless searches to find missing relatives after the war.

On the one end of the scale some descendants had comprehensive and well related life stories of their Ochberg Orphan forebears, while on the other end of the scale there were descendants who knew very little or did not want to share the stories they knew. While many Ochberg Orphans were successful with their lives and flourished and multiplied, others did not.

For each of the Ochberg Orphans that survived there were many children that did not. I believe the stories of those who survived must be told for the sake of, and to remember and honour the children who did not live to tell their stories.

VARIATIONS IN NAMES, DATES AND PLACES

Some children were found in terrible circumstances and there was not always an orderly handover of children in those desperate times. As a result, where the children came from and where and when they were born was not always known. Maybe a child told white lies to be accepted to go to South Africa and maybe those in charge could have told a little white lie about a child's age to help the child to be accepted.

The names of the children have been spelt in very many different ways. It is understandable, if we consider that the children were Russian, Polish or Ukraine and that their names were originally written down in Yiddish and then later different people would read the Yiddish written in the Hebrew script and then spell the name in English. Added to this are further complications and variations with of the Anglicising of their names.

Ages vary between the group passports, the registers and the many lists made out for the children. One suggestion was that on the ship the children were listed as younger to pay a lower fee.

One descendant wrote, "My mother told me that although her birth date was shown as 1911, she was born a few years earlier. Apparently when she left for South Africa, she was listed as younger than she actually was, because it was felt that younger children were more acceptable for adoption."

Names of towns vary as well as the birth places of the children. In those desperate times of wars and revolution with armies coming and going borders moved and a town in one country could easily find itself in another country. Towns in the Pale of Settlement have various spellings in Russian, Polish, Ukrainian and maybe one or two more and then there is their present day name. To add to the confusion, Jews were at times forced to move by the changing authorities and sometimes they moved from one town to another on their own accord to avoid conflict. To further complicate matters some people wanted to hide from the authorities where they did in fact come from.

SILENCE, SHAME AND SADNESS

Some descendants today would not even know that they were descendants of Ochberg's Orphans. It was not something their parents readily spoke about and indeed many of them would have tried to hide the fact from their children so as to protect them.

There was, alas, also a shame attached to being an orphan.

Arnold Rabinowitz wrote, "The general attitude of the community was that it was a mitzvah to have adopted one of those poor orphans, a good deed in a dark world, but you really wouldn't want one of them to marry into your family, would you?

"After all, you knew nothing of their parents and extended family, their health history and their genetic background. This is a generalisation that isn't true of all the adopters but it was certainly true of a fair number, nervous, insecure, only to do nothing that would jeopardise their increasing prosperity and emergent social solidity."

What is very sad to see is that some descendants are embarrassed that their parents were Ochberg Orphans and were looked after by the Jewish Community. They are reluctant to write about their parents or send photos or let it be known their parents were Ochberg Orphans or to even make themselves known.

While we should all celebrate the lives of our ancestors who overcame hardship and tell their life stories for our grandchildren and their grandchildren, I can understand that sometimes descendants find the subject too sad or distressing to deal with.

BREAKING THE RULES

The *rules* prescribed by the South African Government for the admittance of the children were broken in more cases than they were adhered to. I understand that the children had to be healthy, double orphans (both parents deceased), could not be over 14 years old and could not be separated from siblings.

The life stories reveal that many of the Ochberg Orphans had family; siblings and sometimes parents left behind and some luckier ones were brought to South Africa by their Ochberg Orphan family. Others managed to emigrate from the 'Pale' and there were reunions of family members in other countries in later years. Sadly many of the family left behind perished in the Holocaust.

While some older siblings came as *nurses and carers* other siblings did not come as they were over the age limit, not of good health or they chose not to come and ran away.

These were desperate times and at least one child denied her mother's existence to be accepted to go to South Africa. No doubt those in charge turned a blind eye to the *rules* to enable children to be accepted.

MARRIAGE

Once settled in South Africa I believe well meaning committee and care givers at Oranjia and Arcadia saw it as their responsibility to marry the girls off and that their duty ended when their charges were placed in the *bonds of holy matrimony*.

Celia Isaacman, the daughter of Regina Artman, wrote:
"At the Ladies Section at Oranjia there would be dances on Saturday nights and the girls could drop the names of young men they would like to invite into a box and those in charge of the hostel would invite the guys to come without mentioning who was actually the person asking them. In this way the hostel became a place where the young Jewish men could have a fun evening out and meet the girls. Many girls met their husbands at the Saturday Night Dances (socials) in Cape Town."

Ursula (Rosenblatt) Rembach, the daughter of Leah Altuska, wrote in Leah's Story in More Arc Memories:
"In those days the main objective was for girls to be married off at an early age and when my mother and father married at Arcadia they were given a real 'society' wedding, seemingly with no expense spared.

My mother told me that for her to get married she would have to have finished school. I have the minutes from a board of trustees meeting at Arcadia where she seeks permission to do so. Before her 18th birthday on June 8 1930, Leah married Maurice.

The Chupa took place on the lawns of Arcadia. The reception was a grand affair with 300 guests entertained at Arcadia, complete with a jazz band and children's choir from Arcadia. It was reported in *The Zionist Record* of June 13, 1930, a copy of which is one of my most treasured possessions.

The Ladies Committee set up a trousseau fund for the Ochberg orphan girls so that they would go into marriage like any other girl, with new wedding dresses and a trousseau. This fund was continued for many years and when I married in 1969, I was considered a part orphan because my father had died when I was still a young girl, I too received a trousseau. I think that my mother considered Arcadia to be her home, the place where she grew up and was cared for. I don't think she ever thought of herself as an underprivileged orphan but rather someone special who had been given the gift of opportunity."

Several weddings took place at Arcadia and were reported in the press and I suspect that many *chance meetings* were engineered by these well meaning *match makers*.

MENTAL TRAUMA AND DISEASES

There is no doubt that many of the children arrived in South Africa traumatised from the horrors they had witnessed and also sometimes endured and some of the life stories clearly reveal this.

Social workers, clinical psychologists and child care workers were only introduced four or five decades later and there was no trauma counselling.

At least two children were violent as adults, two are known to have suicided and some had recurring nightmares as adults. Others no doubt bore their memories in silence or supressed them.

Several children were described as stoic and able to endure and cope with the ups and downs that life dished out.

As the life stories reveal a few Ochberg Orphans suffered from tuberculosis (consumption) and several succumbed to TB or other diseases at a young age, and of course some suffered from malnutrition as children which restricted their growth.

THE GENEROSITY OF THE JEWISH COMMUNITY

This book is about the suffering of the Jews in the 'Pale' and the help given to these desperate people in their time of need by their brethren, the Jewish Communities around the world.

Many life stories end with concluding paragraphs similar to Celia Isaacman's. "As I look at it, it is quite a sobering thought that had it not been for Isaac Ochhberg, my mother would have perished as we believe her sister and mother did in the Holocaust, and none of us would have been here."

I believe most readers of this book owe their very existence and the existence of their families to the generosity of the Jewish Community.

The Jewish Communities around the world saw it as their duty and responsibility to help fellow Jews (our ancestors) in their time of need and they did.

We too have a duty to help our fellow Jews who are presently in need of help in the Ukraine, South Africa and in Israel.

PART 6

REMEMBERING ISAAC OCHBERG AND THE OCHBERG ORPHANS

This section tells of books and a documentary,
and the events and ceremonies
to honour Isaac Ochberg since his death in 1937

We commence with 'This Was a Man', the 'Ochberg Orphan'
Documentary and 'The Ochberg Orphans" book.

We continue with events and ceremonies in memory of Isaac Ochberg;
The Two day Ceremony in Israel and the Dedication of the
Memorial Site to Isaac Ochberg at Ramat Menashe - July 2011,
Plaque Unveiled at Arcadia Johannesburg- 1st November 2011,
Gala Dinner in Edmonton Canada - 24 June 2012,
Ochberg Orphans Exhibition in Belarus - 19 October 2012,
75th Yarzheit Commemoration of Isaac Ochberg held in Cape
Town - 20 December 2012 and A Communal Kaddish
for Isaac Ochberg held in Johannesburg - 9 December 2013

The tombstones of Ruth (daughter), Isaac and Pauline (wife) Ochberg - Maitland Cemetery Cape Town
"Isaac Ochberg's stonework has had a facelift and is looking much better than when last I visited.
His stonework is now more befitting the great mensch that he was." David Miller 2016

Chapter 49 – HONOURING AND REMEMBERING ISAAC OCHBERG

ISAAC OCHBERG REMEMBERED
Adapted from an article by Lionel Slier

Isaac Ochberg died in November 1937 on a mail ship returning to South Africa from England. The ship was two days sailing out of Cape Town and his wife, Pauline, begged the captain not to bury him at sea, as was the usual practice when a person dies on a boat.

He was later buried at Pinelands Cemetery in Cape Town age 59. His grave lies alongside that of his daughter, Ruth, who had passed away in 1933, aged 17 years.

In his will, he left money for the disadvantaged for education in Cape Town and other philanthropic causes. He also left funds for dowries to be provided for young girls living at Oranjia and Arcadia Orphanages when they married.

Also, Ochberg left a bequest to the Jewish National Fund for land to be purchased and developed for settlers to Eretz Israel. He also left money to the Hebrew University of Jerusalem.

The bequest to the JNF was about 200 000 pounds sterling and land was bought from wealthy landowners living in Lebanon and Turkey. Ochberg's bequest is the largest donation ever made by a single individual and it is estimated that in today's money, it would run into a couple of hundred million American dollars. Land was subsequently purchased on the Hills of Ephraim where three kibbutzim where established.

TWO BOOKS AND A DOCUMENTARY

Two books have been published on The Ochberg Orphans and Isaac Ochberg, *This Was A Man, The life story of Isaac Ochberg*, published in 1974, by Bertha I Epstein the daughter of Isaac Ochberg (and republished in 2014) and *The Ochberg Orphans and the horrors from whence they came* compiled by David Solly Sandler and published in 2011.

A documentary entitled 'Ochberg's Orphans' was produced with the research and information gathered by Lauren Snitcher and Lesley Friedman, grand-daughters of Ochberg orphans.

DEDICATION OF THE MEMORIAL SITE TO ISAAC OCHBERG AT RAMAT MENASHA - July 2011

In July 2011 a two day event, attended by over 200 people, mostly descendants of the Ochberg Orphans, from around the world, took place at Kibbutz Daliah and Kibbutz Gal-Ed, the kibbutzim established from Ochberg's funds. It was also an occasion for descendants of the 177 orphans that he rescued from Eastern Europe in 1921 and brought to South Africa to get together and celebrate.

At Kibbutz Daliah there was an open air welcoming ceremony on the first day. The following day ceremonies commenced at Kibbutz Gal-Ed and then later in the day the Memorial Site in memory of Isaac Ochberg was unveiled at Ramat Manashe.

There is now a mound where plaques with the names of the Ochberg orphans are placed and it will be a site in Memory of Isaac Ochberg of pilgrimage and memory for visitors to Israel.

This commemoration was initiated and driven by Bennie Penzik, whose parents were both Ochberg Orphans.

PLAQUE UNVEILED AT ARCADIA JOHANNESBURG IN MEMORY OF ISAAC OCHBERG - lst November 2011

In early November at Arcadia in Parktown Johannesburg, the early home of Jewish orphans, another event took place remembering and honouring Isaac Ochberg. This was initiated by an American journalist, Jack Goldfarb.

GALA DINNER IN EDMONTON CANADA - 24 June 2012

A Gala Dinner at the banquet hall of the local Orthodox Synagogue called the Beth Israel was held to raise funds to build two rest stops along the bike path adjacent to the Ochberg memorial site.

The event was organised by Ram Romanovsky from Edmonton, a descendant of an Ochberg Orphan.

OCHBERG ORPHANS EXHIBITION IN BELARUS - 19 October 2012

Brest Jews celebrated the 20th anniversary of the revival of Jewish life. One of the events was the opening of the exhibition, devoted to Ochberg Orphans.

This exhibition was initiated in 2011 by Lionel Slier, a descendant of an Ochberg Orphan, and brought about due to the efforts of Lionel Slier and family.

75th YAHRZEIT COMMEMORATION OF ISAAC OCHBERG - 20 December 2012

the 75th Yahrzeit Commemoration of Isaac Ochberg was held at Oranjia Children's Home in Cape Town.

This commemoration was initiated by Lauren Snitcher, a descendant of an Ochberg Orphan.

A COMMUNAL KADDISH FOR ISAAC OCHBERG - 9 December 2013

Corresponding to 7 Tevet 5774 was the 76th Yahrzeit of Isaac Ochberg and Rabbi Shaun Wingrin, himself a descendant of an Ochberg orphan, felt it appropriate to honour the memory of the man by having a communal Kaddish for him at the Great Park Shul in Houghton, Johannesburg.

Chapter 50 – BOOKS AND DOCUMENTARY: 'THIS WAS A MAN', THE 'OCHBERG ORPHAN' DOCUMENTARY AND 'THE OCHBERG ORPHANS' BOOK.

THIS WAS A MAN

This Was A Man, The life story of Isaac Ochberg, was first published in 1974, by Bertha I Epstein the daughter of Isaac Ochberg.

THIS WAS A MAN

BERTHA I EPSTEIN
St. James. Cape Province
First Published 1974
Reprinted 2014

The first publication

In 2014 with the permission of the family 'This was a Man' was reprinted by Bennie Penzik and David Solly Sandler.
Passages of the book were edited at the request of the family of Isaac Ochberg and an addendum was added.

The 2014 reprint

THE 'OCHBERG'S ORPHANS' DOCUMENTARY

Lauren Snitcher of Cape Town and her cousin Lesley Friedman of London, grand-daughters of Ochberg orphans, began intensive research in 1995. Years of intensive work culminated in the provision of vital material – including recorded interviews with a number of the original orphans - to Rainmaker Films of London.

In 2007, this production company, headed by Paul Goldin and Georgina Townsley and with Jon Blair (Academy Award Winner of the documentary 'Anne Frank Remembered') as director, produced a documentary entitled 'Ochberg's Orphans' which made it to the short list of the Oscars.

Ochberg's Orphans, the Documentary

'THE OCHBERG ORPHANS' BOOK
published May 2011
Article by Bennie Penzik

'The Ochberg Orphans and the horrors from whence they came' published in 2011 is the third in a series following **'100 Years of Arc Memories'** (2006), and **'More Arc Memories'** (2008) that had a section of 17 chapters on the Ochberg Orphans. All three volumes were compiled by David Solly Sandler, who grew up in Arcadia, the South African Jewish Orphanage, in Johannesburg.

After completing the two *Arcadia Memory* books, David decided that the Ochberg Orphans were deserving of a book dedicated exclusively to their stories. **'The Ochberg Orphans and the horrors from whence they came'** is a culmination of three years of intensive information-gathering work done mainly via the internet and also with personal phone interviews and the accumulation of knowledge gleaned from 1920's newspaper cuttings.

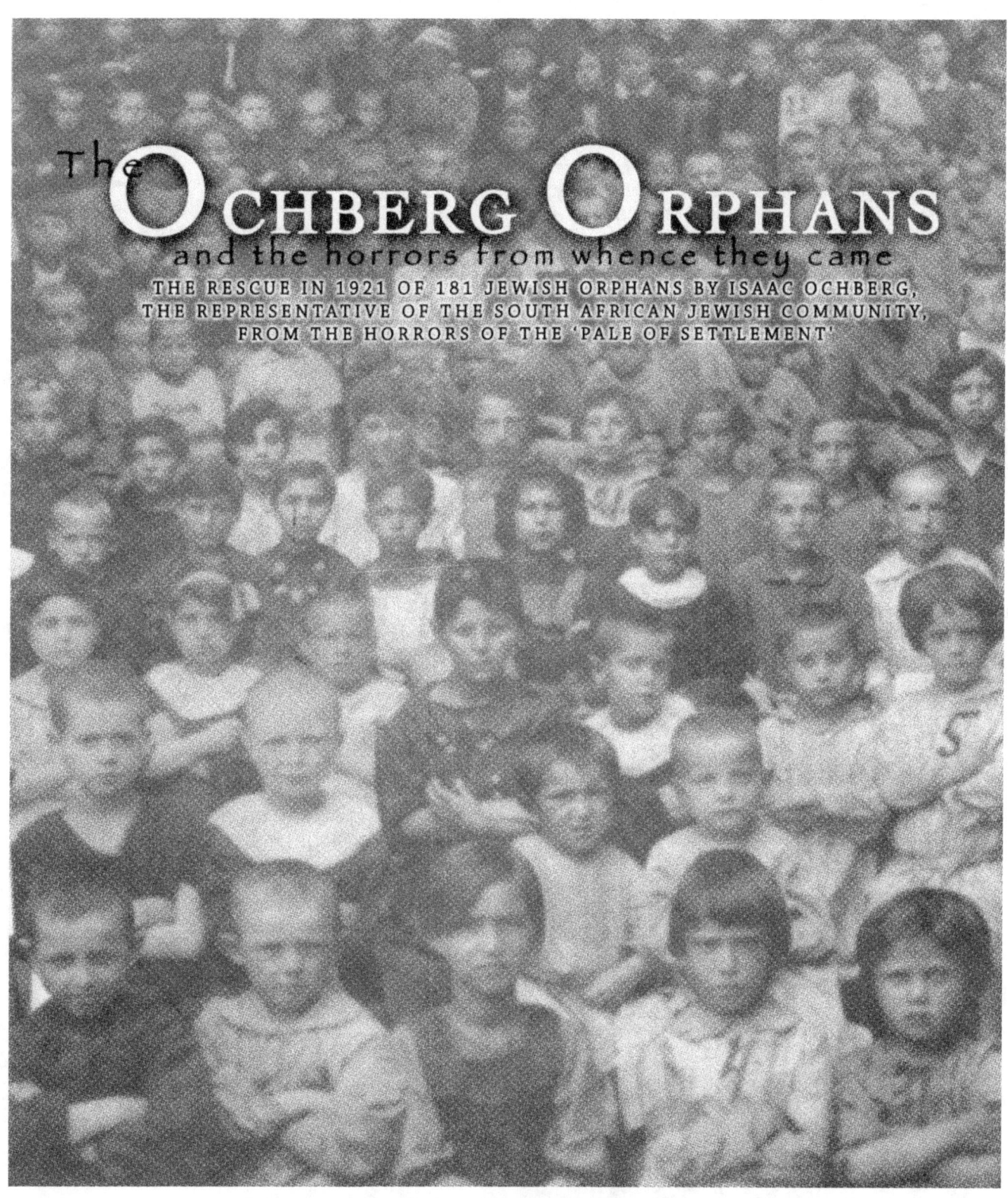

'The Ochberg Orphans and the horrors from whence they came'
The rescue in 1921 of 181 Jewish orphans by Isaac Ochberg,
The representative of the South African Jewish Community,
From the horrors of the 'Pale of Settlement'

Using contact details obtained from the Jewish *grapevine*, David spent countless hours locating and urging descendants to share their memories of stories they had heard from parents, whose past was very different from their own. Very often, recollections were either vague or sparse, but David's persistence, grit and determination produced a memorable tome.

Chapter 51 – THE WORK LEADING UP TO THE CREATION OF THE ISAAC OCHBERG MEMORIAL SITE

THE ISAAC OCHBERG MEMORIALS
Written by Bennie Penzik – February 2011

It all began in earnest in December 2008. I had read Bertha Epstein's book, *This Was a Man,* the life story of her father, Isaac Ochberg, on a number of occasions, but this time I focused on two specific issues - her descriptions of a 1950 JNF film and a 1970 JNF brochure.

I retrieved the film from the Steven Spielberg Archives - what a revelation! A well-made production - *The Immortal Road* - designed to raise funds for the Jewish National Fund (JNF) primarily in the USA with 18 minutes focusing on the close bond between Isaac Ochberg and Kibbutz Dalia. The message of the film inferred that for man to achieve immortality, he should strive to establish his bond with the Land ensuring that, accompanied by an appropriate donation, his name will last forever!

Isaac Ochberg had made the largest single donation to the JNF, a record that stands to this very day. However, I discovered that people in the area, even residents of the kibbutz, had only sparse, if any, knowledge of the existence of the man. I interpreted this as an injustice and began the quest to achieve the righting of a grievous historic wrong.

I established that the JNF had indeed erected an impressive memorial monument of stone in Ochberg's honour, of which Bertha had written when she visited in 1970, at the Elyakim junction near Yokneam but this had been removed into storage when the road required widening during the nineties.

The monument as discovered in a JNF warehouse
December 2008
Previously erected at the Elyakim junction near Yokneam

Negotiations began in earnest with the JNF and, as our small ad-hoc committee was to learn, many meetings needed to be attended, many visits were required to potential sites for the re-erection of the monument and extensive efforts on our part to convince the organisation that a debt of honour was owed and past due.

The plaque on the pergola wall in the 1960s Kibbutz Dalia
Photo from JNF brochure

In parallel, we met with the management of Kibbutz Dalia on numerous occasions to present our vision to establish the Isaac Ochberg Heritage Centre on the grounds adjacent to the pergola erected in Ochberg's memory in 1943. The story of the strong bond with the kibbutz was further covered in the 1970 JNF brochure printed in Jerusalem and thus pressure was brought to bear on the JNF management to, once again, correct a grievous historic wrong.

The plaque commemorating Isaac Ochberg
- 2010 Kibbutz Dalia
The plaque is needing attention

Fast Forward to December 2010

After constant campaigning, the JNF finally agrees to acknowledge the recognition due to Isaac Ochberg and to finance the creation of a dedicated hilltop site at Ramat Menashe, replete with the re-erection of the original stone monument, the construction of a Memorial Wall of Names in memory of Ochberg's Orphans, a watch-tower overlooking the original Isaac Ochberg Tract, explanatory ceramic plaques, benches, a mini-amphitheatre, access paths and cycle parking. Our committee agreed that this gesture indeed went a long way in complying with the terms of our quest and correcting the perceived injustice to our esteemed 'patron'.

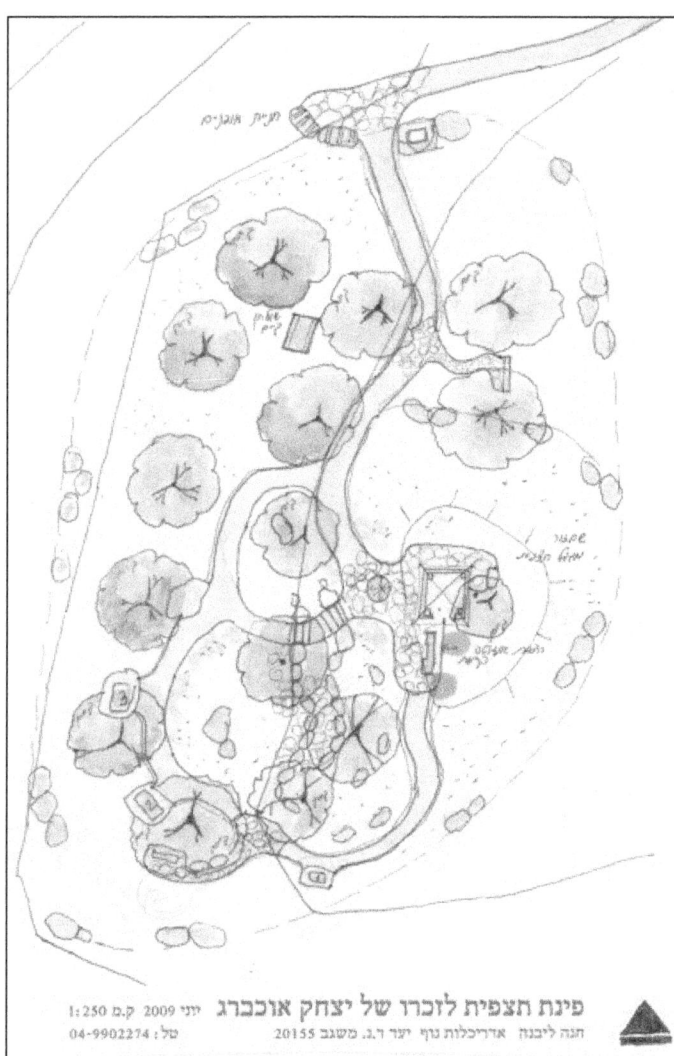

Sketch of the proposed JNF Ochberg Memorial Site at Ramat Menashe

At last!

19 July 2011 will witness the inauguration of the Isaac Ochberg Heritage Centre at Kibbutz Dalia.

The stone setting ceremony of the JNF Ochberg Memorial Site is set for 20 July 2011.

The year 2011 marks 90 years after a historic adventure which began in the orphanages of Eastern Europe via Warsaw and Danzig to Southampton and London, then southward bound on the epic voyage to Cape Town where the *Edinburgh Castle* arrived in September 1921 with its precious cargo of 177 orphans fortunate enough to have been selected to accompany Isaac Ochberg.

If I am to be permitted to end on a personal note....

My earliest recollections of my late Dad's commitment to the Arcadia orphanage in Parktown, Johannesburg, were how much he had enjoyed his sojourn, which period included both his Bar-Mitzvah and wedding. He was intimately involved in the support of Arcadia for 50 years. I recall the Sunday drives in the '34 Vauxhall with Dad and his little receipt book with its crumpled piece of carbon paper canvassing half-guinea donations from each Pretoria Jewish family.

To my everlasting chagrin, his requests of me as a teenager to accompany him on trips to the Parktown orphanage often fell on indifferent ears - after all, I had to play soccer or attend a Betar meeting so I was pressed for time.

I have ultimately joined the ranks of those who now want to ask questions and no-one is left to respond.

However, and this is the message I wish to convey to all descendants - it is never too late to pay homage. Now that I have been so intimately involved in the organisation of events in honour of his 'Daddy Ochberg', I pray that, *in absentia,* my Dad may be aware that I have endeavoured to live up to his expectations of me. It is exactly 40 years ago that he played an active role in organising the Golden Jubilee gathering of the original orphans and their families in Cape Town in 1971. I urge you all to step up to the plate and remember and honour Isaac Ochberg as befits his memory. Without him, we would not have been!

Bennie Penzik - February 2011

Bennie Penzik at the pergola 2010 – Kibbutz Dalia

Mountains of praise and thanks are due to Bennie Penzik by all Ochberg Orphan descendants for taking it upon himself to make it his business to rectify the errors of the past and to establish these Isaac Ochberg Memorials.

Bennie we all salute you!

Chapter 52 – THE DEDICATION CEREMONY OF THE OCHBERG MEMORIAL SITE - ISRAEL 19th and 20th July 2011

THE DEDICATION CEREMONY OF THE OCHBERG MEMORIAL SITE

In July 2011, a large, two-day, gathering was held in Israel of Ochberg Orphan descendants from all over the world at Kibbutz Dalia and Kibbutz Galed. The ceremonies and celebrations culminated in the dedication ceremony of the Ochberg Memorial Site, overlooking an area that had been originally named the 'Isaac Ochberg Tract.'

Bennie Penzik, son of two Ochberg Orphans, formed the Isaac Ochberg Heritage Committee that conducted extensive negotiations over a two year period with the JNF. As a result, a resolution was passed to establish a dedicated site in memory of Isaac Ochberg and commensurate with his magnanimous bequest that enabled the original JNF purchase of the land.

A major feature of the site is the re-erection of an imposing stone monument to Ochberg that had stood at the Elyakim Junction and subsequently removed into storage due to road-works many years before.

Another feature is the Hill of Names – a mound embedded with ceramic 20 cm square plaques – one for each of the original 177 orphans showing names in English and Hebrew, birth places and dates of birth. Visitors to the site will see that the traditional small stones have been placed on many of the plaques – a testament to the fact that personal pilgrimages are made, particularly on 'yahrzeit' commemorations.

Organised periodic conducted tours to the Ochberg Memorial Site are made by the JNF as well as by many tour organisers under the auspices of the Ministry of Tourism. It is hoped that South African visitors in particular will grace the site with their presence. In this respect, visits have been made by delegations from WIZO South Africa.

Bennie Penzik standing next to Monument to Isaac Ochberg

"HE WHO HAS SAVED ONE LIFE IS AS THOUGH HE HAS SAVED THE ENTIRE WORLD"

The violent attacks against the Jews of Eastern Europe in the years shortly after World War 1 caused the total destruction of entire Jewish communities. When the tragic news of the turmoil in the area was revealed, Ochberg initiated and directed the operation to rescue young, orphaned Jewish children. He managed to obtain the special permission of the South African government to bring 200 orphans from the hell of Eastern Europe. He convinced the South African Jewish community to embrace them and facilitate their absorption.

In March 1921, Ochberg set out on the long, arduous journey to the Ukraine where he travelled from village to village by truck and horse-drawn wagon. He personally organized, with the assistance of local Jewish communities, the gathering of destitute orphans, many of whom were starving and traumatized.

He arranged temporary shelter for the orphans in Warsaw, then transported them to Danzig from where they sailed by steamer to England. After a brief stay in the Jews Temporary Shelter in London, Ochberg sailed with the orphans in early September, arriving on the 19th in Cape Town. The children were placed in two orphanages - 'Oranjia' in Cape Town and 'Arcadia' in Johannesburg where Ochberg arranged and provided for their care and education. He was known to the children as "Daddy Ochberg", the name they used with warmth and respect and they honoured his memory for the rest of their lives. Years later, some of the orphans would become pillars of the South African Jewish communities. Descendants of the orphans today number some 3000 souls, many of whom retain friendly contact and maintain mutual support.

This Wall of Names has been erected by the JNF as a memorial to the exemplary accomplishments of this noble man.

1922 - Letter From a Child To Ochberg

"... Beloved father, I can write to you now that we are completely healthy and everything is absolutely fine. the only thing is that you are not here. We only hope to God that in time we will be with you..." From me Guava Gabbe

Plaque at the Ochberg Memorial Site

Bennie recently wrote -

"We think back today to the time when we discovered that very little was known, here in Israel, of the life and deeds of Isaac Ochberg.

Much to our chagrin, an alarming lack of basic knowledge was exhibited by kibbutz members living on the very land, the purchase of which was made possible through Ochberg's bequest to the Jewish National Fund. Few people on 'Kibbutz Gal-Ed - Even Yitzhak' were aware that the name Yitzhak referred to Yitzhak Ochberg and not to one of our biblical forefathers.

I believe it is fair to claim that the current situation is very different. The geographic area we targeted for our initial education projects has naturally included the schools in the area and particularly the Megiddo regional school, where we are invited to give regular lectures – all in the effort to create an awareness of the legacy of Isaac Ochberg and to perpetuate his memory."

THE PROGRAM FOR THE DEDICATION CEREMONY OF THE OCHBERG MEMORIAL SITE

The Inauguration of the Isaac Ochberg Heritage Centre at Kibbutz Dalia and The stone-setting ceremony of the JNF Ochberg Memorial Site featuring the re-dedication of the What happened nine decades ago changed many of our lives forever.

The past is alive today, embodied in the very people and their descendants who will come from all corners of the world to gather on Kibbutz Dalia and Kibbutz Gal-Ed on the 19th-20th July 2011. They will be joined by former Southern Africans living in Israel, whose descendants too, were members of a community that facilitated the miracle of 1921, one of the proudest chapters in South African Jewish communal history.

Join us in celebrating the past and embracing the future as we stand together at the inauguration of the JNF Isaac Ochberg Memorial Site. The ceremony will include the dedication of the original JNF Ochberg stone monument and the unveiling of a '**Wall of Names**', which will display individual plaques in the name of each orphan saved through the superlative efforts of Isaac Ochberg with the support of the South African Jewish community.

Here follows the program: (Subject to change)
19th July - Venue Kibbutz Dalia

4.00pm - 5.00pm - Registration and refreshments

5.00pm - 6.45pm Orientation/mingle, viewing of photos and inauguration of Ochberg Heritage Centre, photo opportunities

7.00pm - 8.15pm - Supper in the kibbutz dining hall. A kosher meal offering a selection of salads, a main course choice of fish, meat, chicken or vegetarian and dessert at NIS 45 per person (no credit cards). This is optional as people are free to bring their own snacks.

8.30pm - 10.30pm - 'A Special Evening for Special People - **Who Are the Ochberg Orphans and Why Are We Here?**' The evening's program will include speeches, movies and music.

20th July - Venues Kibbutz Gal-Ed & JNF Isaac Ochberg Memorial Site

10.00am - 10.10am - Everyone to meet at Kibbutz Gal-Ed
10.10am - 11.00am - Refreshments followed by presentation on the history of Kibbutz Gal-Ed and the inspiring association with Isaac Ochberg.
11.00am - 12.00pm - Address by **David Solly Sandler** of Perth, Western Australia, who is the author of the two monumental works on 'Arcadia' – Johannesburg's Jewish Orphanage, where half the Ochberg orphans were settled in 1921 and a 'hot-off-the-press- publication "THE OCHBERG ORPHANS - and the horrors from whence they came". This book will be available for purchase at any time over the two-day Ochberg Event.

original monument (5 kms from Kibbutz Dalia) are planned to take place in Israel on the 19th and 20th of July 2011.

THE OCHBERG EVENT 19-20th July 2011
What seemed months away, we now count in days
During years of painstaking research for this book, David uncovered little-known details of the pogroms which motivated Isaac Ochberg to seek out and rescue these young Jewish orphans and bring them to South Africa.
He interviewed many descendants of the Ochberg orphans living in South Africa, Australia, USA, Canada, UK and Israel and has gathered a wealth of information, documents, photographs and anecdotes. The presentation will be followed by a Q & A session.
12.00pm - An optional, short, guided walking tour around the kibbutz. Those not joining the tour are free to relax in the comfortable, air-conditioned kibbutz clubhouse.
1.00pm - 2.00pm - Lunch at Kibbutz Gal-Ed dining hall (NIS 40 per person, no credit cards)
2.15pm - 3.00pm - Presentation by **Solly Kaplinski**, Director of Overseas Joint Ventures, JDC, Jerusalem. A former principal of Cape Town's Herzlia School and a former Director of the English Desk of Yad Vashem, Kaplinski will speak on the association of the 'Joint' with Isaac Ochberg in 1921, when it was assisting, financially, the plight of Jewish orphans in the very region where Ochberg had arrived from SA to bring back 200 Jewish orphans.
Sadly, the saga continues today, as there remain many Jews in this same area who are living in terrible conditions and who Kaplinski will speak about. The '**Spirit of Ochberg**' is required no less today than when it was over 90 years ago.
3.00pm - 4.00pm 'Time Out' to relax
4:30pm - 6:30pm (approx.) **Official Opening of the JNF Isaac Ochberg Memorial Site**
This long-awaited ceremony will include the unveiling of the original JNF stone monument honouring Isaac Ochberg as well as the recently completed '**Wall of Names**', displaying on individual plaques, the names of all the orphans saved and brought to South Africa.

The ceremony took place over two days and in three locations and is reported in the following three chapters.
Day One 19 July 2011
    Kibbutz Dalia in the afternoon and night,
Day Two 20th July 2011
    Morning and early afternoon at Kibbutz Gal-Ed (formerly also known as Even Yiszhak)
    The late afternoon at Ramat Menashe, a hill to remember Isaac Ochberg and the Ochberg Orphans and established by the JNF. Here a monument was unveiled. These ceremonies took place due to the hard work and determination of Bennie Penzik, son of two Ochberg Orphans.

Chapter 53 – DAY ONE – KIBBUTZ DALIA – 19th July 2011

KIBBUTZ DALIA - 19th July 2011
Compiled by David Solly Sandler
Photos courtesy Anne Brest

Not only did Isaac Ochberg rescue the Ukrainian Orphans but he also made very large bequests to both the Hebrew University of Jerusalem and to the Jewish National Fund (JNF). The JNF used these funds to acquire a very large tract of land and three kibutzim were established on this land; Kibbutz Regavim which later relocated and Kibbuz Dalia and Kibbutz Gal-Ed where the ceremonies were held.

The ceremonies were in fact held in three locations; day one at Kibbutz Dalia in the afternoon and night, the morning and early afternoon of day two at Kibbutz Gal-Ed (formerly also known as Even Yiszhak - In memory of Isaac *Ochberg*) and the late afternoon of day two at Ramat Menashe, a hill to remember Isaac Ochberg and the Ochberg Orphans and established by the JNF. Here a monument was unveiled. These ceremonies took place due to the hard work and determination of Bennie Penzik, son of two Ochberg Orphans.

A group of 13 (descendants and spouses) gathered in the morning at the moadon at Kibbutz Dalia for an informal meet and greet. People introduced themselves and spoke of their Ochberg Orphan connections

19th July 2011 – Lunch in the Kibbutz Dalia dining room – above and below

The venue above and getting ready below – early afternoon Kibbutz Dalia 19th July

Shirts, flags and caps above and early arrivals (the Lipschitz family) and registration below

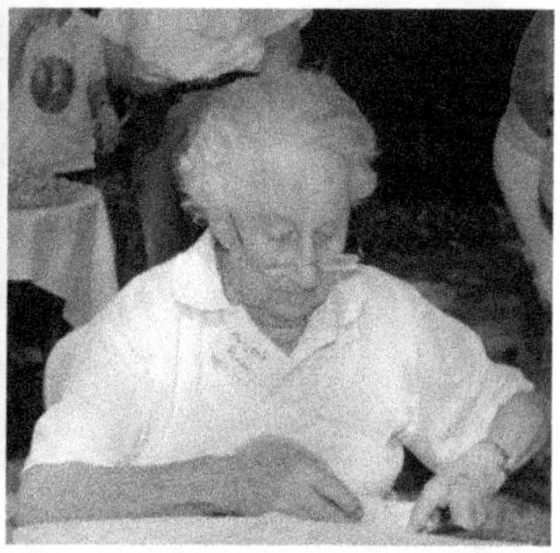

Registration and groups posing above – 19th July Kibbutz Dalia late afternoon

Cissy Harris (Zaika)   *Lizzy and Cissy*   *Isaac Ochberg's Descendants*

Isaac Ochberg's Descendants and Bennie Penzik

The Ceremony and Speeches begin – 5 pm Kibbutz Dalia 19th July 2011

Tessa Webber addressing the audience

Isaac Ochberg's Descendants, Tessa Goldin, Noreen Webber and Cynthia Zukas, address the audience

David Kaplan above and Hertzl Katz below addressing the attentive audience

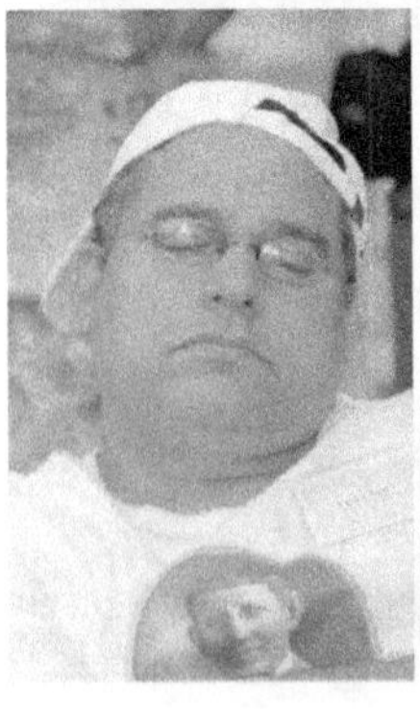

OCHBERG ORPHAN DESCENDANTS ADDRESSING THE AUDIENCE:
Ursula Rembach, Ram Romanovsky, Lauren Snitcher and daughter, the Lipschitz, the Segals, Mike Rodomsky, unidentified, Arthur Cohen, Sybel Keats, Lionel Galinsky and the Ruch Family.

Above OCHBERG ORPHAN DESCENDANTS ADDRESSING THE AUDIENCE:
unidentified, Cecil Migdal, Judy Levin and Essa Werb, Janet Shenker, Gila Weichman and Shirley Shamos, Anthony Jossel, Berisinsky (related to carers at Oranjia) and Penzik Family.

Below OCHBERG ORPHAN DESCENDANTS ADDRESSING THE AUDIENCE
Raymond and Arnold Roth, Rosie (née Schneider) Hechter and her sister
Freda (née Schneider) Sher, Gail and Arnold Nadelman and Lionel Slier and Family.

Members of the audience above and the Segal Family below

Salads above, meat and fish in the middle and vegetables below
Dinner in the dining room at Kibbutz Dalia – 19th July 2011   NIS 45 per person (no credit cards)
People helping themselves and sitting and eating

Speakers and singers – above before and below during

The last speaker, the committee and a member of the audience

Audience above listening to speakers and singers and viewing Ochberg Movie
Viewing Isaac Ochberg Photo Albums and Ochberg Orphan Book below

Chapter 54 – DAY TWO – KIBBUTZ GAL-ED – 20th July 2011

DAY TWO OF THE CEREMONIES - 20th July 2011
Compiled by David Solly Sandler
Photos courtesy Anne Brest.

After breakfast at Kibbutz Dalia, the ceremonies commenced at Kibbutz Gal-Ed and later in the afternoon moved to Ramat Menashe, a hill nearby, where the ceremony to remember Isaac Ochberg and the Ochberg Orphans was held.

Breakfast at Kibbutz Dalia Guest House and below right are the Altuska Family

Catching the bus at Kibbutz Dalia – above and below

Alighting at Kibbutz Gal-Ed – above and below

Others arriving at Kibbutz Gal-Ed above and a 'welcome to Kibbutz Gal-Ed' below

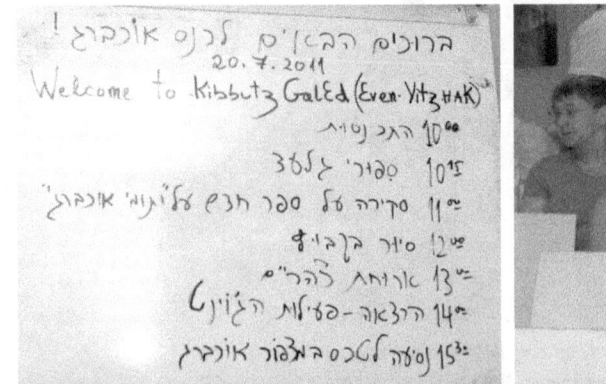

Refreshments above and the audience below

Speakers above and audience below

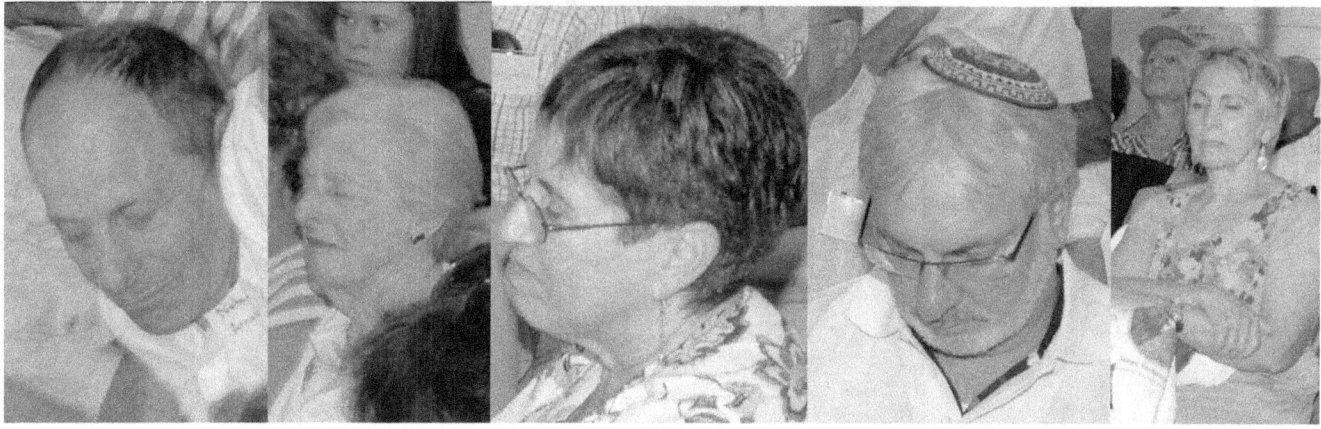

Speakers and questions above and audience below

The audience above and questions below

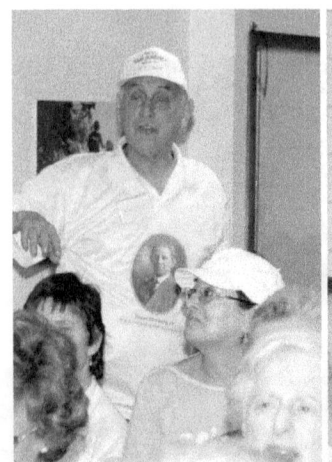

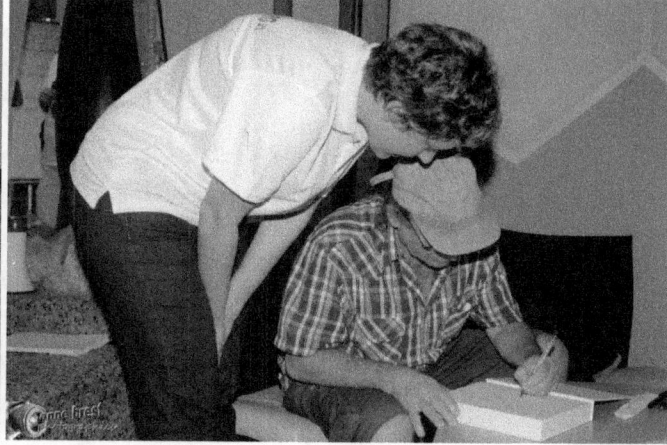

Signing and selling 'The Ochberg Orphans' books – above and below

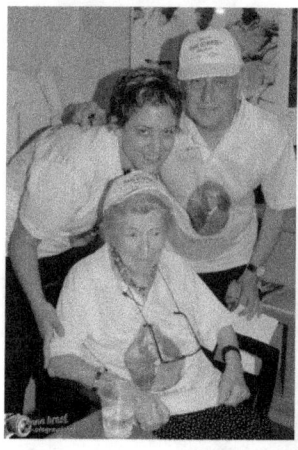

Lionel and Paula interviewing above and below plus camera man

The younger generation in the audience – above and below

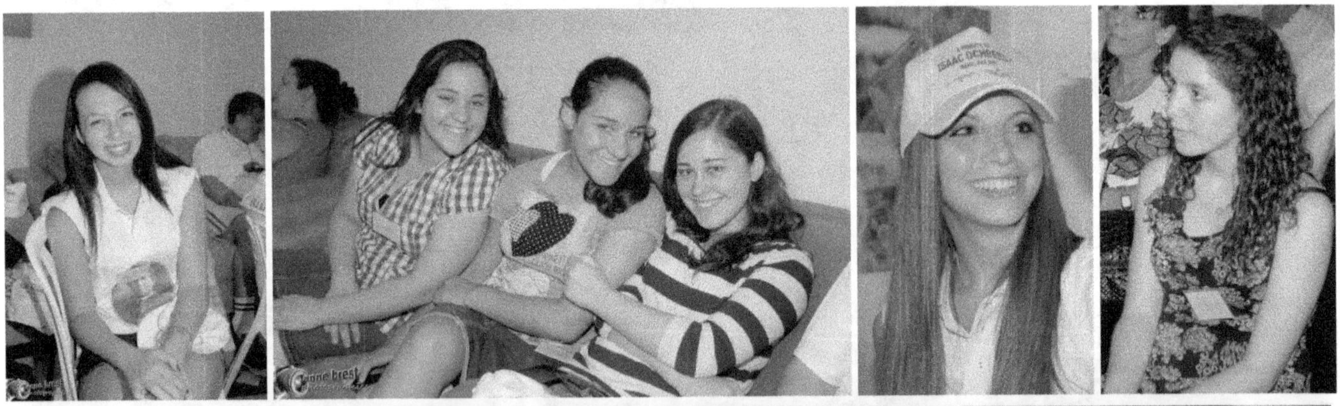

Going off to lunch

Lunch at Kibbutz Gal-Ed – above and below

Diners above and Photographers and Family and groups below and following - Kibbutz Gal-Ed 20th July 2011

Family and group photos - Kibbutz Gal-Ed 20th July 2011

Chapter 55 – DAY TWO - THE DEDICATION CEREMONY OF THE OCHBERG MEMORIAL SITE AT RAMAT MENASHE - 20th July 2011

Compiled by David Solly Sandler
Photos courtesy Anne Brest

On the tract of land acquired by the JNF using the large bequest left by Isaac Ochberg, a monument has been established by the JNF to remember Isaac Ochberg and the Ochberg Orphans on a hill, Ramat Menashe.

This event was no doubt the highlight of the celebrations and no doubt Ramat Menashe will not only become a place of interest for tourists but also a place that thousands of Ochberg Orphan Descendants will visit and remember their ancestors.

It was very appropriate that Bennie Penzik unveiled the monument as these ceremonies took place due to his hard work and determination.

Sign and the wall of names above and below

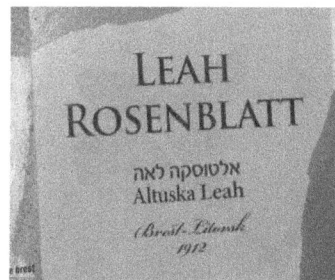   
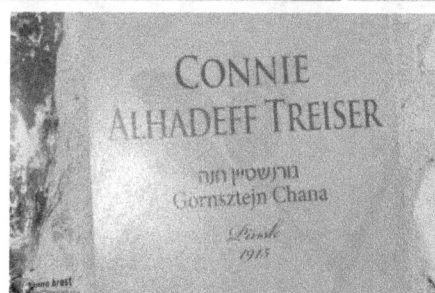  

Some of the 177 plaques above

Posing of the wall of names above and viewing the wall below

People taking their seats for the speeches

Speakers Hanan Erez (Megido area council) and JNF function organiser Andy Michalson above and audience below

Entertainers and Ms. Elizabeth Smith, the charge d'affaires of the South African Embassy above and audience below

Maish Isaacson - Telfed and Mr. Avinoam Binder - KKL-JNF talking above and the audience below

Bennie Penzik addressing the audience

BENNIE PENZIK'S ADDRESS

Betsy Smith - Effi Stenzler - Hanan Erez - Maish Isaacson, achamim, Ochberg family members, Descendants of the Ochberg Orphans, kahal nichbad

It is indeed my honour and privilege to stand before you today as Chairman of the Ochberg Israel Committee - also as the son of two Ochberg Orphans - and it is in that capacity that I offer very sincere thanks to the JNF for the construction of this magnificent Memorial site in honour of the man to whom many of us present here today owe our very existence.

This is a great day for us - a deeply memorable event - and everyone is conscious of the emotional impact of this moment, not only for those present here, among whom are direct Ochberg family - but also the many descendants of the orphans who referred to him as their 'Daddy Ochberg'. And many of you have graced us with your presence here today.

Thank you to all who made the trip from the USA, Canada, Australia, UK, South Africa, Israel and all parts of the globe. A special welcome to Cissy Harris, today a resident of Haifa and the oldest living orphan in Israel.

As the President of the JNF - USA so eloquently expressed in the 1950 JNF fund-raising movie clip (many saw this last evening) ... "that man can save his memory from oblivion by linking his name to the Land of Israel."

This stirring message continued - "The JNF...........has afforded many an opportunity to Jews all over the world to link their name with Israel and thus perpetuate their memory for all eternity."

Among the millions of donors.....stand out a few who by their generosity have made a singular contribution. One such man shall live forever in the hearts of those who shall inhabit this community for generations to come. That man is Isaac Ochberg."

It is a matter of record that Isaac Ochberg's bequest in 1937 stands as the largest personal donation ever made to the JNF. The record - half-million dollars - stands to this very day.

In recognition, the JNF has created not only a memorial to this man - returning this magnificent stone monument to its rightful place - but also to the orphans Ochberg so heroically saved. On the Hill of Names you can see a plaque for each orphan.

Although the positioning of the ceramic plaques may appear to have no specific sequence, we have ensured that, just as the children were collected from orphanages in family groups of siblings, this is the order in which they are placed here.

Obviously as time progressed, many of the original names will have been changed due to marriage or adoption, but we thought it befitting that the original family groupings be preserved. Therefore we began with "A" the Altuska family of four - who, in time, became Gordon, Rachman, Rosenblatt and Slier - these are all located one beside the other.

The seemingly erratic design of the structure itself sensitively captures the desolation and the plight of the Jewish population of Eastern Europe. It is a symbol of their struggle for life, particularly during those horrific years between 1919 and 1922 - when the pogroms so decimated entire communities. And today, in 2011, these names may now be enshrined for all eternity.

I would like to thank my committee for helping to turn our dream into a reality. My thanks to Amnon Lahav of Gal-Ed who guided me through my quest from Day One, to Shlomo Brand for his role in making this event happen to Hanna Livne for her endurance that knew no bounds and her immaculate skill in conceptualising this site and to Khalil Khoury for his dedication to its physical creation. Thank you Andy Michaelson our master of ceremonies and of course to all the dignitaries present here today.

And thank you all for attending!!

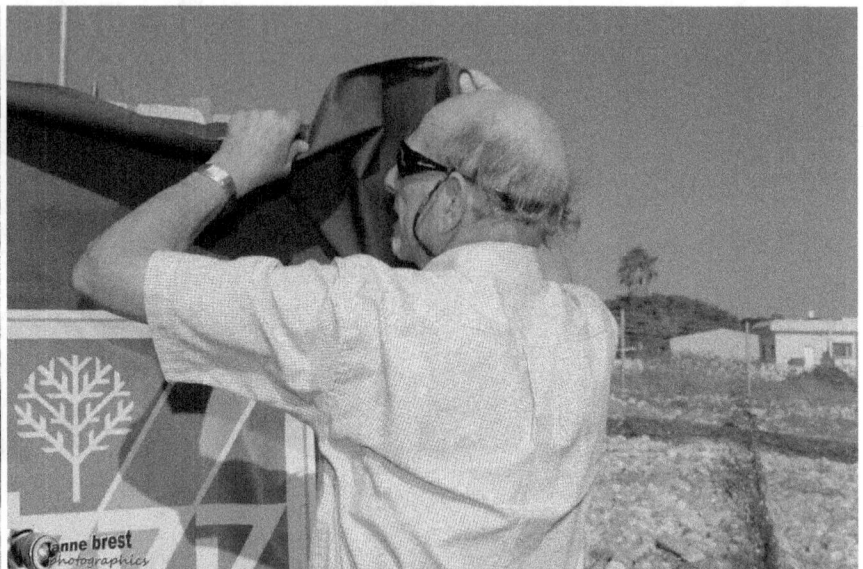

Benny Penzik unveiling the monument to Isaac Ochberg above and below.

Frank Segal and Sharon Katz above speaking and Cissie Harris, an Ochberg Orphan unveils information plaques below

ISAAC OCHBERG - 1878-1937

Isaac Ochberg, born in Uman, Ukraine, was a proud Jew and eminent Zionist. In 1895, aged 17, he travelled alone to South Africa in the footsteps of his father who had made the journey two years before. In 1906, he returned and married in the Ukraine, then journeyed alone back to South Africa. By 1903, he had succeeded in bringing his new wife, his mother and other family members to his new home in South Africa. In the following years, Ochberg became an extremely wealthy entrepreneur and highly respected businessman, making his fortune from astute investments in property, cinemas, brickfields and derelict ships for sale as scrap metal.

As one who became prominent among the foremost South African supporters of the Zionist cause, Ochberg was active in - and a generous donor to - both Jewish and non-Jewish organisations, an ardent supporter of Herzl and his policies and was a representative at the 16th Zionist Congress held in Zurich in 1929. "I deeply believe that the Jewish problem will find its ultimate solution only in Eretz Israel," he said, after his visit to Palestine in 1926. He maintained this faith all his life.

As a result of the very generous donation to the Hebrew University which he made in 1936, the Ruth Ochberg Chair of Agriculture was established at Rehovot named after his beloved daughter, who had died aged 17. His last will provided a very handsome bequest to the Hebrew University which, in recognition of his deeds, led to the establishment of the Isaac and Pauline Ochberg Wing of the Woolfssohn building on Mount Scopus in Jerusalem, which today houses the Law Faculty Library and two research institutes.

REDEMPTION OF THE LAND

The most munificent bequest in Ochberg's will was designated to acquire land for the purpose of the creation of new settlements by the JNF. This bequest remains the largest personal donation ever received by the JNF. Isaac Ochberg died at sea in 1937 and was buried in Cape Town. His bequest enabled the JNF to redeem a tract of land on which Kibbutz Dalia, established in 1937 and Kibbutz Gal-ed (Even Yitzhak) established in 1945, stand today.

This memorial site has been created by the JNF in the fields of the Megido Regional Council, in recognition of the inspirational deeds of Isaac Ochberg and in gratitude for his generosity, a contribution to the fulfilment of the Zionist vision –the creation of the State of Israel.

July 20th 2011

"HE WHO HAS SAVED ONE LIFE IS AS THOUGH HE HAS SAVED THE ENTIRE WORLD"

The violent attacks against the Jews of Eastern Europe in the years shortly after World War I caused the total destruction of entire Jewish communities. When the tragic news of the turmoil in the area was revealed, Ochberg initiated and directed the operation to rescue young, orphaned Jewish children. He managed to obtain the special permission of the South African government to bring 200 orphans from the hell of Eastern Europe. He convinced the South African Jewish community to embrace them and facilitate their absorption.

In March 1921, Ochberg set out on the long, arduous journey to the Ukraine where he travelled from village to village by truck and horse-drawn wagon. He personally organized, with the assistance of local Jewish communities, the gathering of destitute orphans, many of whom were starving and traumatized. He arranged temporary shelter for the orphans in Warsaw, then transported them to Danzig from where they sailed by steamer to England. After a brief stay in the Jews Temporary Shelter in London, Ochberg sailed with the orphans in early September, arriving on the 19th in Cape Town. The children were placed in two orphanages - 'Oranjia' in Cape Town and 'Arcadia' in Johannesburg where Ochberg arranged and provided for their care and education. He was known to the children as "Daddy Ochberg", the name they used with warmth and respect and they honoured his memory for the rest of their lives. Years later, some of the orphans would become pillars of the South African Jewish communities. Descendants of the orphans today number some 3000 souls, many of whom retain friendly contact and maintain mutual support.

This Wall of Names has been erected by the JNF as a memorial to the exemplary accomplishments of this noble man.

1922 - Letter From a Child To Ochberg

"... Beloved father, I can write to you now that we are completely healthy and everything is absolutely fine, the only thing is that you are not here. We only hope to God that in time we will be with you..." From me Chaya Gabbe

Information plaque above and Ms. Elizabeth Smith and Cissie Harris below and Tessa Goldin

Group photos above

Group photos above

Group photos above

Chapter 56 – THE UNVEILING OF A PLAQUE IN HONOUR OF ISAAC OCHBERG AT 'VILLA ARCADIA' 1st November 2011

THE UNVEILING OF A PLAQUE IN HONOUR OF ISAAC OCHBERG AT 'VILLA ARCADIA'
lst November 2011 - 22 Oxford Road, Parktown, Johannesburg
by Lionel Slier, the one time editor of the weekly Community Buzz column in the SA Jewish Report, Johannesburg

The year 2011 could be called the 'Year of Isaac Ochberg' He is the man that the *Jewish Report* famously called the 'forgotten philanthropist'. However at a dedication ceremony held in July at Ramat Menashe in Israel, a monument was unveiled in his honour for his remarkable act of humanity and bravery when he brought 177 Jewish orphans in 1921 out of the terror that swept war-torn Eastern Europe after the World War (1914-18). He had also left a bequest to the JNF which bought a large swathe of land in Central Palestine in 1943.

An American journalist, Jack Goldfarb, visiting South Africa some years ago noted that Ochberg was remembered at Orangia Orphanage in Cape Town but Johannesburg's Arcadia Jewish Orphanage, where 81 orphans were brought had no acknowledgement at all of Ochberg. Goldfarb decided that he wanted to have a plaque put up at Arcadia at his expense to rectify this. This became a dream for him and a passion.

Meanwhile Arcadia had been bought by Hollard Insurance Company and when they were approached, their Public Relations Officer, Allim Milazi was enthusiastic about the plan and an Events Team was put together to bring this about. The girls involved were excellent –Shirley Anthony, Michelle O'Neill and Caireen Gillingham who navigated the making of the plaque here.

On Tuesday 1st November the plaque was unveiled before a group of about 40 people which included eight members of Hollard Insurance and 20 descendants of the rescued orphans plus several ex-Arcadians.

Brent Wyborn of Hollard in a short speech told how the company had been dedicated to restoring the listed but disintegrating Villa Arcadia building and how sensitive they were to its history. He also spoke about Hollard's ongoing concerns about the humanitarian and social aspects of our society.

Chief Rabbi Warren Goldstein was away at a Rabbinate Conference in Poland but he sent a letter of appreciation: "On behalf of the South African Jewish Community, it is a great privilege to be able to pay tribute to the memorial being unveiled in honour of the Ochberg Orphans and in the honour of Isaac Ochberg. Allow me to wish you, from afar, Hashem's abundant blessings to all those and the descendants who participated in this remarkable chapter in our history".

Lionel Slier speaking at the Plaque Unveiling

Solly Jossel, 97 years of age and the last living Ochberg Orphan in Johannesburg unveiled the plaque. He spoke movingly about his life in Eastern Europe before being rescued by "The Man from Africa."

Solly Jossel unveiling the plaque.

Hollard Insurance has always been extremely supportive of the Jewish Community and on those occasions when they required the use of Arcadia for various functions Hollard always co-operated.

Jules Gordon wrote

There were about 50 people at the unveiling of the plaque to remember Isaac Ochberg, and many of them were Ochberg Orphan descendants as you'll see in the photos.

Lionel Slier, son of an Ochberg Orphan, opened the ceremony with a brief outline about Isaac Ochberg and thanked David Solly Sandler for all his efforts and dedication. We always mention him and praise him for his time, efforts and years of dedication.

Solly Jossel, an Ochberg Orphan, spoke of his memories as a child, how he was saved from the ravages of war and his experiences in getting to South Africa. He is truly amazing for 97 years old and it couldn't have been due to the Arc food in his case!!

Sylvia Jossel, wife of 97 year old Solly Jossel, wrote

As you know today (1st November 2011) was the big day, the plaque unveiling at Arcadia. Solly was honoured to be asked to do this wonderful task. He made a little speech and I stood 10 foot tall. Our darling children came to be with us, our daughter Bernice with her two children, Jodi and Adam and our son who went in Israel to the Isaac Ochberg ceremonies, Anthony, were at our side which was just wonderful. By the way Jodi is expecting her second baby towards the end of this month which will give us then 11 great grandchildren.

Sylvia wrote "The photo (see bottom left) shows us that in 1945 (I think) we made a donation to Arcadia of two beds. I only think it was 1945 - or maybe 1944 when we got married - as we were then living in Springs - that was before we left to go to Rhodesia (now Zimbabwe of course)."

Sylvia and Solly Jossel

First is our daughter Bernice, Jodi's Mom, next is Jodi our granddaughter, behind is Adam her brother, then its me (Sylvia) and Solly and lastly our son Anthony

Solly Jossel, 97 year old Ochberg Orphan, and family with other Ochberg Orphan Descendants
Seated is Solly with hat on and wife Sylvia next to him (white jacket). Behind Solly is Jodi his granddaughter and next to her is Solly's daughter Bernice, Jodi's Mom. Next to Bernice is Solly's son Anthony. Next to Anthony is Norma then her husand Monty Segal. Behind Jodi is Lionel Slier and on extreme left is Lionel Glinski.

Heather Rush from Johannesburg tells us who else is in the photo
The lady on the left next to Solly in white top is me Heather Rush (2nd generation descendant)
Lady on the right next to Solly's wife in blue patterned suit is Claire Rush 1st generation descendant (whose mom was Rachel Borowick an orphan) and little girl in pink (3rd generation descendant Liora Del Monte who lives in Israel) and next to her,: Robyn Del Monte (nee Rush) (2nd generation descendant who lives in Israel)

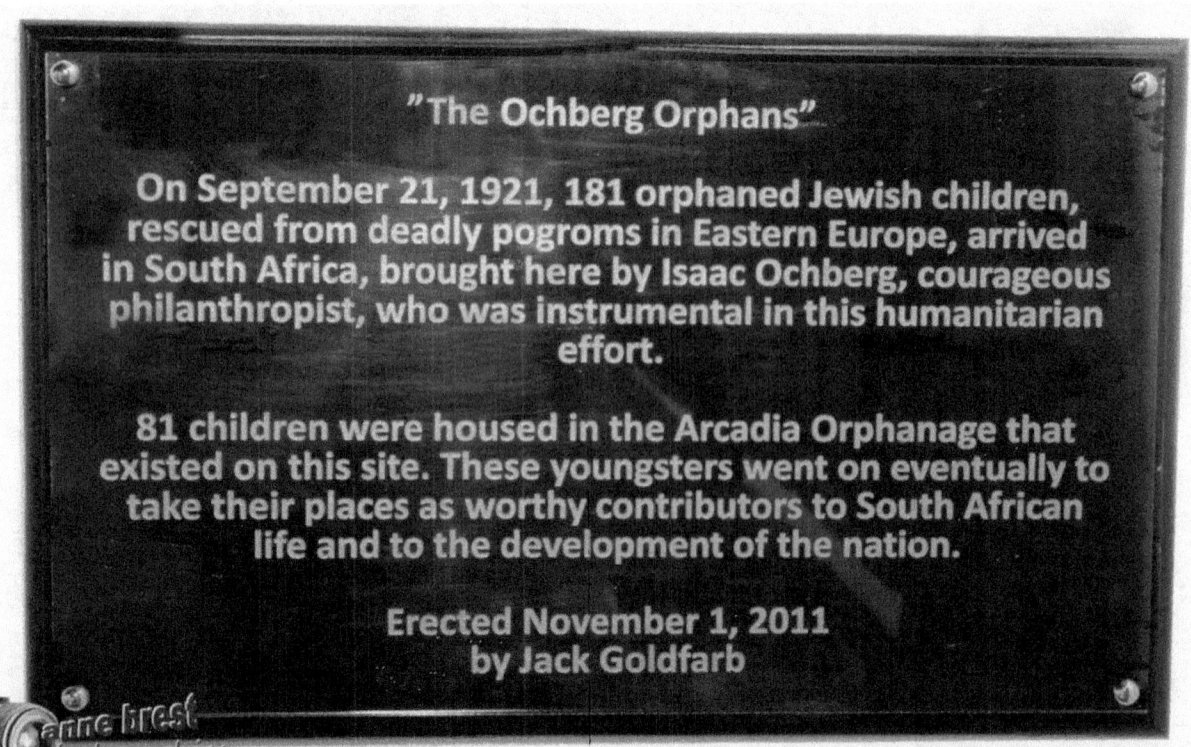

The Plaque   All photos courtesy Anne Brest

Brent Wayborne of Hollard speaking at the Plaque Unveiling

Lionel Gilinsky, Stan Smookler and Roland Kopel

Jules Gordon speaking at the Plaque Unveiling

Jules Gordon Zummy Isenberg and Max Goldman at back with Solly Jossel seated

ISAAC OCHBERG AND JANUS KORCZAK - TWO MODERN *TZADDIKIM*
by an American journalist, Jack Goldfarb from New York 2013. Jack initiated and sponsored the plaque

In the midst of the grim history of the 20th century, there are stories of singular individuals whose extraordinary courage and compassion support the belief that somehow there is always hope and promise that love and human kindness can triumph.

Two such 20th century individuals were Isaac Ochberg in South Africa and Dr Janusz Korzack in Poland. Isaac Ochberg's story lives in his adopted homeland after he came from the Ukraine as a 17 year old immigrant following his father to Cape Town.

The legendary story of how, with the story of the South African Jewish Community, Isaac Ochberg travelled to Eastern Europe in the 1920s and, against many obstacles, suceeded in rescuing nearly 200 orphaned Jewish children, shepherding them to a new homeland. Here they grew up to contribute prominently to the buidling of a new society that eventually became a South Africa that the world welcomed, while its own people raised their heads in the pride of a vibrant democracy.

In Poland, the story of the heroic Dr Janusz Korzak, his compassion concern for the education, care and future of young children is still very much alive and in practice today through his legacy of love and the principles of upbringing which he pioneered. Korczak's death in the Treblinka Concentration Camp, where he himself chose to go, so that he could accompany the doomed children, elevated him forever to the status of a tzaddik. (Henrick Goldschmidt writer also insisted on going with his children to the death camp in Treblinka).

Isaac Ochberg and Janus Korczak were two modern *tzaddikim* who have left us a brilliant legacy of the best that there is in human nature.

Article was sent in by Lionel Slier

Chapter 57 – ISAAC OCHBERG EXHIBITION IN BREST BELARUS 19 October 2012

OCHBERG ORPHANS EXHIBITION IN BELARUS

On 19 October 2012 Brest Jews celebrated the 20th anniversary of the revival of Jewish life. One of the events was the opening of the exhibition, devoted to Ochberg Orphans. This exhibition was initiated in 2011 by Lionel Slier and brought about due to the efforts of Lionel Slier and family.

Isaac Ochberg 1878-1937 - Exhibit at the Belarus Exhibition

OUR VISIT TO BELARUS IN JULY 2011
A STORY FROM THE PINSK SHUL
by Lionel Slier

In 2011 a memorable commemoration was held of Isaac Ochberg's legacy at Kibbutz Dahlia and the unveiling of the memorial to the great man on a hill overlooking land that had been purchased from his bequest in 1943. I was told that the land had been bought by the JNF from absentee Arab land-owners in Beirut and Turkey. (So much for the Jews just stealing land). It was generally agreed that it was because of David Solly Sandler's efforts and newsletters that the event was brought about.

My mother was brought out with the other orphans from Brest-Litovsk (as it was then called) and she grew up in Arcadia, in Parktown, Johannesburg. After the festival at Dahlia ended, my daughter, Paula, and I went on to Brest in Belarus to see for ourselves where she came from.

We flew to Minsk, from Tel Aviv via Vienna (!) and arrived at 1:00 a.m. We were met there by our guide and translator, Bella Velikaskaya, born in Belarus and who turned out to be a walking history book of the Jews of Belarus. We spent the night (or what was left of it) in a magnificent hotel in Minsk and next morning at ten o'clock Bella and the driver picked us up and took us to Pinsk, about an hours drive away. There was an unveiling of a monument to Jews slaughtered at a village nearby and the mayor of Pinsk, the Israeli ambassador to Belarus and other dignatories were present and also many schoolchildren and soldiers. After that we visited various areas in Pinsk which had a Jewish background. The overall feeling that one gets is one of sorrow and loss.

We then went to the shul (I believe a Chabad one) which is in two shops on Parkovaya Street where services are held daily with a lay person conducting them. Yosef Lieberman seemed to be the man in charge. He addressed us. We were told that a Rabbi comes from America from time to time, usually over chagim, to take the services. There is also a cheder class for local boys, run mostly by young twenty-somethings from England and America who teach them Hebrew and Torah. We were unable to ascertain how many Jews still lived in Pinsk. We went back to Minsk for the night.

Next morning Bella was at our hotel and said to us that she had been asked to bring "The Man From Africa" to the shul as some members wanted to meet him. When we arrived at the shul there were five elderly men sitting there waiting for us, and, of course, the usual officials going about their affairs.

It was arranged that Bella would translate the questions and answers. As we approached I heard one man say in Yiddish, "......... nicht schwartz." I know enough basic Yiddish mixed with Afrikaans to understand that and I told Bella, who is fluent in Yiddish, that there was no need to translate. They asked questions about South Africa which Bella translated and then spoke to them in both Yiddish and Belarus. I could sense, though, that they were deeply disappointed by 'The Man From Africa' not living up to their expectations.

I then told Bella to tell them that if any of them were sitting in a shul in Johannesburg no-one would be able to pick them out as not being South African Jews. At this they got slightly agitated and said repeatedly "no, no, no". They obviously thought that all the South African shul goers would be 'schwartz'. It was clear that I was an imposter and I was sorry to disappoint them.

PLANNING FOR THE EXHIBITION
AT THE JEWISH MUSEUM IN BREST

Lionel Slier writes from Johannesburg

When I was in Belarus in July 2011 with my daughter, Paula, after the Dedication in Israel, we had a guide by the name of Bella Velikovkaia. Bella was born in Minsk and she knows the story of the Jews of Belarus as completely as anyone could wish. She was a walking history book, yet strangely enough, she did not know the story of Isaac Ochberg.

However when we went to the Jewish Museum in Brest and we spoke to the curator, Regina, she and Bella expressed a wish to put on an Exbition of the Ochberg story. It is so relevant to the city of Brest, they said, and the wider province of Belarus. Just between brackets, as they say, Brest Litovsk is from the Polish connection and nobody seems to use that double name there today. Regina also, after the exhibition, wants to keep the Ochberg story as a permanent display.

Now David, this is where your help is needed. Could you make available any documents, photos, records, stories, in fact anything, which you could let them have. I will give them your wonderful book. Of course all papers will be photographed and translated into Belarussian, which I was told is not quite the same as Russian. Also perhaps you could put a request in your wonderful newsletter asking anyone who wishes to contribute a story or a photo etc.

Paula is facilitating from Israel and in fact Bella is coming to Israel in December. She has a daughter there and a grandson, who horifically, lost both his legs in the recent Gaza war. Tragic. You can email Paula at any time.

Paula Slier, the daughter of Lionel Slier, writes from Israel

Bella Velikovskaia was our amazing tour guide in Belarussia when my father and I went there to see where my grandmother came from. She and I are planning to set up an exhibition on the "Ochberg children' in Belarussia.... *this includes the children from Pinsk.*

It will be in English and Russian and Bella will be responsible for all the translation. Basically she needs info from you (although I don't know if you have extra info to what is in the books) that she can translate and she needs plenty of pictures to use in the exhibition. I know she needs everything on disc.

Bella Velikovskaia, curator at the Jewish Museum in Minsk, writes from Minsk

It is very important for us, Belorussian Jews, to learn about this event in our history. For me personally it was something I have never heard about, but I am not a historian.

So when I addressed some scholars of authority and found out that the name of Ochberg is unknown to them, I thought that it is my matter of honour to hand down this information to our people.

Next step is to get information from you. So here is the list of pages copies of which (on disks!) I would like to have:

My mail address is:
Bella Velikovskaia, 4 Glebki str. aprt.55, 220121 Minsk Belarus
Looking forward to hear from you soon.
Best wishes, Bella
"Bella Velikovskaya" <bella_v@list.ru>

David Solly Sandler wrote from Perth

I have sent Bella copies of all the pages she requested from the Ochberg Orphan Books but if there is any information you have that is not in the book please post it to her direct.

Ursula Rembach from Melbourne - mid June 2012

I can't believe that it is almost a year since we were all in Israel for the Ochberg memorial.

I was wondering if your readers were aware of the permanent exhibition being done at the Jewish Museum in Brest that will be opening on 18 October. My family (Altuska) will be included as will other orphan's families.

I am thinking of going to Belarus for the opening. Bella, the lady who has organized this amazing acknowledgment of Isaac Ochberg will organize visas, accommodation, drivers and interpreters for the event. Some of my cousins from Israel and South Africa will also be going.

Importantly, Bella is able to organize researchers from the Grodno university to assist in ancestry research. It is very cheap and you only pay if they find the information.

This exhibition is permanent and the new Jewish community in Belarus will be able to learn about the history of our families that once lived in the area before the wars and pogroms.

I would like to hear from anyone else from Australia who would be interested in making the journey.

Harold Echstein wrote from Israel

Shabbat Shalom to all,

Here is an e-mail from Bella, which is self explanatory. At the moment it looks like a trip to Brest is coming true. I am so excited, and very emotional. I will keep you all updated.

It seems that I have "struck "gold".

Bella Velikovskaya, a guide and curator at the Jewish Museum in Minsk, emailed to Harold Echstein in Israel

"On October 18, 2012 Brest Jews will celebrate the 20th anniversary of the revival of Jewish life.

One of the events will be the opening of the exhibition, devoted to Ochberg Orphans" and one of the stands will be about Echstein siblings.

My name is Bella and it was me who was with the Slier family in Brest last year.

We never met, but your family story is known to me from David Solly Sandler's book.

Meeting with Lionel and Paula opened a new and unknown (and not only to me but to many Jewish historians whom I addressed to get any information) page in the history of Brest and Pinsk Jewish communities.

I am now in Israel, but my colleagues do their best to organize everything in a proper way. Now we are trying to find something in the archives about four left behind in Poland and it is a miracle that you wrote to Paula right now!

It would be wonderful if you could come to Brest on that day. We will arrange everything - visa support, hotel, guide etc. But whatever will be your decision I would like to get information about and pictures of new generation of Echsteins.

If you have questions, please e-mail me and it would be my pleasure to answer them.

LEADING UP TO THE OCHBERG EXHIBITION IN BREST - 19TH OCTOBER 2012.

Lionel Slier emailed in early October 2012 from Johannesburg

As you know I am going to Belarus, leaving Johannesburg on the 11th October and flying via London to Amsterdam. My younger daughter is a Flight Attendant on British Airways so we always go BA if possible.

Unfortunately she will be in Singapore when we arrive in London so we are going straight on to Amsterdam.

I do not know whether I ever mentioned this to you but my father was a Hollander and he came to South Africa in 1925. He was one of nine children and they all perished in the Holocaust. In fact 34 close members of his family were killed in Sobibor and Auschwitz. There are no family members left. There is fully documented evidence. While in Amsterdam we will visit the Jewish connections including the Portuguese synagogue. I have been to Amsterdam several times and I always feel terribly sad and emotional.

There is no BA service to Minsk from Amsterdam so we are taking a Belarus airplane to Minsk on the morning of the 15th. There are nine of us coming in our own group. My wife and myself, my daughter from Israel, another from London and my son from China. Also coming is Tania Jacobson from Cape Town who is a cousin of mine. In fact her father, Isaac Bornstein and my mother were first cousins in Brest-Litovsk (as it was). Borny (as everyone called him) was an Ochberg child so was his wife Yetta. They remained in Cape Town's Oranjia. Tania has four daughters - one is coming from South Africa, another from America and a third from Holland. Her fourth lives in Australia and unfortunately cannot come. Paula has a friend in Israel, Ziona Ruth Agulnik (but always called Zinky) who is fascinated by the Ochberg saga and she is also coming. She volunteered to help at the gathering in Israel last year and handed out the special shirts. Also a cameraman is coming from Israel as a South African TV station wants the story.

We will do a tour of Minsk, of course because there is a great deal to see there. We will also go to Pinsk and I will try and get some information about the orphanages while I am there. I will contact Bella (our guide last year) who is now in Israel and ask her if she has any leads. The Ochberg Exhibition opens in Brest on Friday the 19th October and we have been invited to spend Shabbat with the community that evening. We are returning to SA via Israel.

Tania Jacobson emailed from Cape Town

I would like to let you know that with the help of Bella in Israel and my cousin Paula Slier we are embarking on a trip to Belarus. Paula's father Lionel and his wife and their children are joining us on a tour to Brest, where our parents were born and then came out to South Africa with the Ochberg Orphans. We are being accompanied by a guide arranged by Bella and the community is putting up a memorial to the Ochberg Orphans.

We have also been invited to share Shabbat with them. I think that there has been a substantial growth in the Jewish community and we will be able to see the archives which are very extensive. I can't wait to find out about my father's family as he told us very little. We leave on Sunday 14th October and will be back two weeks later. I will let you know all about it on my return. I will also be in Warsaw and Krakow.

Tanya Jacobson and Lionel Slier being interviewed by Belarus State TV

REMEMBERING ISAAC OCHBERG, FATHER OF ORPHANS
By LIONEL SLIER 11/04/2012 Jerusalem Post

"He who saves a life, saves a universe," according to the Talmud, and today there are over 4,000 descendants of the Ochberg Orphans.

2011 was the year when Ukrainian-born Isaac Ochberg, the great South African philanthropist and Zionist, was brought back from obscurity. Ochberg is best known for his journey to war-ravaged and disease-ridden Eastern Europe in 1921, from where he took 187 desperate and despairing orphans and brought them to South Africa.

"He who saves a life, saves a universe," according to the Talmud, and today there are over 4,000 descendants of the Ochberg Orphans living around the world.

Last July a memorial was established in Israel, near Kibbutz Dalya, in commemoration of Ochberg's great effort. When Ochberg passed away in 1937, his bequest to the JNF was, at the time, the largest ever made by a single person.

Hundreds of descendants and their families came to Israel to pay homage at the two-day event.

Now I must declare an interest. My mother was one of the girls rescued by Isaac Ochberg. She was 11 years old at the time. She never knew what happened to her parents.

Last year, my daughter Paula and I went to Brest in Belarus, my mother's birthplace, after the ceremony in Israel. She was taken, along with two sisters and a brother, to South Africa.

There we had as our guide, Belarusborn Bella Velikovskaya, a walking history book of the Jews of Belarus and, indeed, all Russia.

Brest Belarus - October 2012

L-R Zinky Agulnik, Kfar Saba (ex SA); Susan Jacobson, Cape Town; Jack Slier, Shanghai; Hayley Slier, London; Lionel Slier, Johannesburg; Paula Slier, Modi'in; Tanya Jacobson, Cape Town; Phillipa Jacobson, Baltimore; Leanne Jacobson, Amsterdam; Daniel Goldfine, Tel Aviv; Alicia Slier, Johannesburg

Yet strangely, Bella knew nothing about the Ochberg story; in fact, neither did Regina, the curator of the Brest Jewish Museum. There and then they determined that the story was part of Brest's Jewish past and that a permanent exhibit of it should be created.

First of all, they needed to create an exhibition in Brest and then take it to other relevant places in Belarus, such as Minsk and Pinsk.

Now David Solly Sandler comes into the story. He is a South African living in Perth, Western Australia. Sandler was at Arcadia, the Jewish orphanage in Johannesburg. He became an accountant and at some stage emigrated to Perth. There he started a weekly circular newsletter which he mailed to ex-Arcadians (Old Arcs, they call themselves) living throughout the world. Old Arcs were encouraged to contribute stories and experiences to his newsletter.

He received a wonderful response.

The name "Ochberg" cropped up from time to time and Sandler, intrigued, researched this man. He uncovered the amazing story.

After the decision was taken to have an exhibition, Sandler was approached for assistance. He is the author of three books about Arcadia and had just brought to print a massive book called *The Ochberg Orphans and the horrors from which they came*. Sandler made an enormous contribution with digital material.

So the dream that was born at the Brest Jewish Museum became a reality at the Brest Cultural Center - on Friday 19, October 2012. It was planned to coincide with a concert and celebration of the 20th anniversary of the re-emergence of the Jewish community in Brest after the "Great Patriotic War," as the Second World War is referred to in Belarus and Russia.

There were over 200 people present and short speeches were given in the foyer in front of the exhibition panels, by me and Tania Jacobson of Cape Town, whose mother and father were both Ochberg orphans. Belarus Television was present to film the opening ceremony.

The story of Isaac Ochberg, a great son of the area, will now never be forgotten there and it remains one of the great events in the annals of South African Jewish history

**Lionel Slier and Family, Tanya Jacobson and Family,
at Isaac Ochberg Exhibition - Brest Belarus - October 2012**

Photo: Daniel Goldfine

Lionel Slier in front of the

This exhibition was made possible through the generous contribution of the families of :

Tasha (Altuska) Rachman
Sarah (Altuska) Slier
Leah (Altuska) Rosenblatt
Chaim (Harry Gordon) Altuski
Isaac Bornstein and Yetta Rosier (Razu)
Chaim and Itzik Razu

And in loving memory of :
Feigel (Altuska) Milsztein who was left behind
Rochel Malka Altuska who died before the children were rescued and their parents Labe and Yetta (Pavin) Altuska

The exhibition based on materials from the David Sandler's book "Ochberg's Orphans".
The idea of exhibition belongs to Bella Velikovskaya, the design - to Regina Simonenko

Эта выставка создана благодаря поддержке семей:

Таши (Алтушка) Рахман
Сары (Алтушка) Слиер
Леи (Алтушка) Розенблатт
Хаима (Гарри Гордона) Алтушка
Исаака Борнштейна и Етты Розиер (Разу)
Хаима и Ицика Разу

И посвящается светлой памяти
Фейгел (Алтушка) Милштейн, которая осталась в Бресте
Рохел Малки Алтушка, которая умерла до спасения детей
и их родителей Лейбы и Етты (Павин) Алтушка
Экспозиция выставки основана на материалах книги
Дэвида Сандлера "Сироты Охберга".
Идея создания выставки - Бэлла Великовская.
Дизайн и оформление - Регина Симоненко.

Exhibit at the Belarus Exhibition

Chapter 58 – GALA DINNER HELD IN EDMONTON CANADA TO RAISE FUNDS FOR THE OCHBERG MEMORIAL PARK AT RAMAT MENASHE ISRAEL - 24th June 2012

GALA DINNER HELD 24th JUNE 2012 IN EDMONTON CANADA TO RAISE FUNDS FOR THE OCHBERG MEMORIAL PARK IN ISRAEL AT RAMAT MENASHE
by Ram Romanovsky from Edmonton who organised the event

On 24 June 2012 a Gala Dinner at the banquet hall of the local Orthodox Synagogue called the Beth Israel, was held to raise funds to build two rest stops along the bike path adjacent to the Ochberg memorial site.

So the time has come and gone and as promised I have emailed what transpired at the gala. The gala was a huge success and we do not want you to perceive this email as bragging, but when you have something good to say, say it loud so everyone can hear!

There were over 300 guests at the gala covering a wide section of the Edmonton community. In addition to the guests we had congratulatory letters from The Prime Minister of Canada, The Prime Minister of Israel, The Premier of the province of Alberta and the Mayor of Edmonton who graciously attended the event. It commenced with a delicious supper and then moved into the main sanctuary in the Shul for the formal presentation, followed by the entertainment, an Israeli illusionist who was very entertaining and well received by the crowd.

We prepared a very impressive and extensive brochure of over 40 pages which was handed out at the gala.

I am sure all of you are saying and asking "Enough with the preamble , so how much did you raise for the park which has been developed in honour of our hero Mr Isaac Ochberg? "

As the descendants and remaining Orphans are scattered all over the world it is best to place the results in Israeli Shekels(ILS) and South African Rands .

Gross Proceeds	891,687 ILS	R1,862,862
Net Proceeds	659,073 ILS	R1,376,898

Elaine and Ram receiving a certificate from JNF Canada acknowledging the donation made to the Isaac Ochberg memorial park in Israel

Elaine and I have had lengthy meetings and discussions with JNF Canada, where all the donations were directed, and have designated sections of the park to be developed. At an exit meeting with the representative of JNF Canada, we have been told that the funds have already been sent to KKL in Israel and hopefully construction will commence soon.

Finally if a community so far away can honour such a great man as Isaac Ochberg I would challenge you all to follow this community's example and truly ensure the name of Isaac Ochberg is never forgotten !!!

Congratulatory email from Bennie Penzik

Hi Ram and Elaine

May I add my voice to the congratulatory messages on the resounding success of your venture! Kol Hakavod.

I heartily endorse the comments you made regarding the challenge to other communities to emulate your sterling effort and we plan to publicise your event in upcoming newsletters.

You are no doubt aware of at least one delegation from Canada which visited the Ochberg Memorial Site here some months back and, as recently as last week, we hosted Josh Cooper and his wife on their brief visit. In our discussions, there was considerable interest in the group of orphans that arrived in Canada almost simultaneously with our Ochberg group to SA in 1921, an event covered by David Sandler in his outstanding volume - "The Ochberg Orphans" - refer chapter 11.

Your success will undoubtedly further strengthen the increasing level of interest and potential co-operation with the JNF in Jerusalem with whom meetings are held on a regular basis concerning issues designed to reach our common goal - to *"truly ensure the name of Isaac Ochberg is never forgotten !!!"*
Once again - well done!!

The Canadian contingent of the Romanovsky Family

The mayor of Edmonton who attended the gala with Ram

Part of the audience at the presentation portion of the gala

Chapter 59 – 75TH YAHRZEIT OF ISAAC OCHBERG
Oranjia Children's Home – 20th December 2012

THE 75TH YAHRZEIT OF ISAAC OCHBERG HELD AT ORANJIA CHILDRENS' HOME - 20 DECEMBER 2012
- report for the Jewish Chronicle sent in by Lauren Snitcher

20 December 2012 was the 75th yahrzeit of Isaac Ochberg z'l. For many decades, even according to his own great granddaughter, this great Jew, Zionist, humanitarian and benefactor had been largely consigned to the dusty pages of History. However, due to the dedicated and committed work of the Ochberg Committee in Israel and Cape Town, the memory of Isaac Ochberg z'l now seems set to live on in perpetuity.

Born in Uman, in what is now the Ukraine in 1878, Ochberg made his way to Cape Town in 1893, following his father, Aaron. Due to his unique vision and business acumen, Ochberg rose quickly to become hugely successful. He was actively involved in both Jewish and Non-Jewish communal affairs, and contributed to alleviating the harsh conditions of all disadvantaged communities in Cape Town.

His two great passions were Zionism and enhancing the lives of underprivileged children, which he was able to give great effect to in his capacity as a founding member, as well as President of the Oranjia Cape Jewish Orphanage. When he tragically passed away at sea, in 1937, he left what stands still today as the single largest individual bequest to the state of Israel. Such was the generosity of Ochberg's donation, that the JNF/KKL used his bequest as the central focus of a fundraising movie encouraging others to follow his example. It was with much gratitude for this donation that JNF/KKL Israel generously contributed towards the creation of the Ochberg Memorial Park situated close to Kibbutzim Dalia and Galed, which were established using the proceeds of Ochberg's bequest. In the same vein, JNF-SA contributed generously to the upgrading of the garden at Oranjia Childrens' Home to honour Ochberg's 75th yahrzeit.

Audience at event

> In memory of
> **"Daddy" Isaac Ochberg Z'l**
> **1878-1937**
> who, in 1921, rescued 176 Jewish orphans from eastern Europe and brought them to safety in South Africa.

Despite the soaring temperatures of a sweltering Cape Town midsummer's morning, the tent covering the garden at Oranjia was filled to capacity with over 150 people. Many had travelled from far to attend but all had come together to pay their respects to a man whose actions changed the lives and destinies of so many people, many of whom were present.

Lauren Snitcher opened the Ceremony and after a brief welcome and introduction to the Isaac Ochberg story, screened a movie made up primarily of Ochberg Orphan's never told before, firsthand accounts, of their lives in Eastern Europe before Ochberg arrived to take them to safety and the promise of a secure future in South Africa. People were visibly moved as they heard of the horrors these children had been subjected to. Also portrayed was the 90th anniversary of the Ochberg rescue mission which was marked by a two day gathering in Israel during July 2011.

A history of Oranjia was given by its chairman, Rodney Stein, who encouraged people to become engaged with and make a contribution to Oranjia.

Tessa Webber, Ochberg's great granddaughter, spoke about him as a family man as well as a passionate Zionist and tireless champion for the underprivileged.

A special message from Bennie Penzik, Chairman of the Ochberg Committee in Israel, was screened wherein the audience was able to view the Ochberg Memorial Park in Ramat Menashe. This was introduced by Michelle Scher, chairperson of JNF-Cape town. Dr Hilde Roos presented the history of the Eoan Group of which Ochberg was a major benefactor.

After an uplifting musical interlude by special Israeli Guest artist, Eitan Lewis, Chaim Cohen of JNF-SA spoke briefly of the role JNF plays in greening Israel and how Israel is the only country that has more forestation in it at the beginning of this Century than it had at the beginning of the last Century. Ben Levitas presented a brief history of the SA Zionist Federation-Cape Council, of which he is Chairperson.

The highlight of the presentations was reached when Molly Cohen, at 99 years, the oldest surviving Ochberg orphan, unveiled a beautifully worded black and silver plaque donated by the Borstrock family in honour of Isaac Ochberg. This plaque now takes pride of place on the wall of Oranjia Children's Home

The Ceremony closed with David Gordon intoning the Kel Maleh Rachamim and Rabbi Shaun Wingrin, an Ochberg Orphan Grandson, delivering a short Dvar Torah and leading the gathering in the Kaddish.

The morning ended with the singing of Nkosi Sikelele and Hatikvah after which everyone moved to the patio where they enjoyed delicious refreshments from Stan Norrie and had an opportunity to mingle and share experiences with other Ochberg orphan descendants and Ochberg family members.

Heather Blumenthal, film producer, filmed the event and conducted personal interviews which will be screened on South African TV in a program dedicated to Isaac Ochberg.

The unstinting help of, and attention to detail by Michelle Scher, Yvette Rosenberg, Phena Snitcher, Julie Berman, Bertie Phillips, Sue Lazarus and Janene Marcusen helped make the event flow seamlessly.

The Dedication Ceremony was a fitting and dignified tribute to the 75th Yahrzeit of "Daddy Ochberg", who now rightfully takes his place in the honoured annals of South African Jewish History. Of the 176 orphans Isaac Ochberg brought to safety to South Africa, there are now over 4000 descendants scattered all over the world. As our Sages say in our Talmud: "If a man saves one life, it is as if he has saved an entire universe; Isaac Ochberg was one such man!!

Lauren Snitcher talking and with, Molly and Arthur Cohen under the plaque.

Nesta Cohen (daughter-in-law of Molly and Arthur's wife), Alon Cohen (Arthur's son), Molly Cohen (Ochberg Orphan), Arthur Cohen (son of Molly), Harold Cohen and Tessa Webber grandaughter of Isaac Ochberg

Hymie Lipshitz reported

The event started with a welcome speech from Lauren Snitcher followed by her daughter who introduced the guests. There was a movie with interviews of the orphans alive at the time approx 1999-2000 with some photos of the event in Israel 2011.

Ochberg's greatgrandaughter spoke about the many charities he supported and education trusts. When she asked for a show of hands of how many present were decendants of the orphans, more than half put up their hands of the approximate 250 at the event. There was also a speech by the Zionist Federation and the non Jewish coloured song groups.

The most moving part was at the end when we all stood and said Kaddish together for Isaac Ochberg's Yartzheit. This was followed by the unveiling of the plaque by orphan Molly Cohen 99 and snacks.

David and Beth Miller selling The Ochberg Orphans books

Hymie Lipshitz and Lionel Slier

Lauren Snitcher, Molly and Arthur Cohen and Hymie Lipshitz

Photos courtesy Hymie Lipshitz

Chapter 60 – A Communal Kaddish for Isaac Ochberg
Great Park Shul – 9th December 2013

A COMMUNAL KADDISH FOR ISAAC OCHBERG held at Great Park Shul on **9 December 2013**
by Lionel Slier from Johannesburg

The 9 December 2013, corresponding to 7 Tevet 5774 was the 76th Yohrtzeit of Isaac Ochberg and Rabbi Shaun Wingrin, himself a descendant of an Ochberg orphan felt it appropriate to honour the memory of the man by having a communal Kaddish for him.

This was held at the Great Park Synagogue in Johannesburg at the Ma'ariv service on the day. The service was conducted by Rabbi Hazdan of Great Park and very impressive it was.

Rabbi Hazdan of Great Park

The 187 orphans were rescued by Ochberg in 1921 from the terror in the aftermath of the World War 1, followed by pogroms and the Spanish 'flu epidemic in the Pale of Settlement, the apartheid-like space allowed to the Jews by Tsarist Russia.

As Rabbi Wingrin wrote, "On his Yahrzeit, Descendants in Joburg will have the opportunity to bring merit to the Neshama of 'Daddy Ochberg" by saying Kaddish for him at the Ma'ariv service.

After the service, in the packed Auditorium tributes were paid to Ochberg. Rabbi Wingrin opened the proceedings with readings from the Holy Scriptures and writings from our Sages.

Before I began speaking I asked the audience how many present were connected to Isaac Ochberg and to my total surprise a forest of hands were raised, more than half of those present, it seemed.

After that I spoke about Ochberg and his courage and the 'Lessons in Jewish Leadership' which he displayed by going on his own initiative to Eastern Europe, where a civil war was still raging, where the icy weather was blowing, where danger lurked. The American Joint Distribution Board (The Joint) estimated that there could have been half a million Jewish orphans in the areas where Ochberg had gone, children who were living in the forests, or in synagogues, hungry, in rags, verminous, ill and dying. Ochberg brought 200 to London and then 187 back to South Africa.

I read up a tribute sent in by an American journalist, Jack Goldfarb. He had married Simone, a Cape Town girl. There he had visited the Oranjia Orphanage and learnt the story of Isaac Ochberg and it touched him deeply. On a subsequent visit to Arcadia Orphanage in Johannesburg where 87 Ochberg orphans were placed, he was amazed to find that there was no mention of the man at all. In 2011 Goldfarb initiated a plan to have a plaque put up in Arcadia at his expense.

Lionel Slier

In the tribute that I read out (which I have sent separately) Goldfarb wrote of two 20th Century individuals of extraordinary courage and compassion, Isaac Ochberg and Dr Janusz Korzack in Poland. Both had a connection to children in orphanages, children in need and children in peril.

David Saks

David Saks, of the S.A. Jewish Board of Deputies then spoke about the Jews still living in the lands of the Pale of Settlement, Lithuania, Latvia, Belarus, Ukraine and eastern Poland.

A video clip was shown about Solly Jossel, the oldest remaining Ochberg Orphan in South Africa who is 98 years old.

This was followed by a talk by Leonard Carr, a clinical Psychologist "Honouring the past, embracing freedom in the future."

Rabbi Wingrin wound up the event by more readings from our Holy Books. Everyone agreed that the evening had been a great success.

Anne Brest, our professional photographer, who took all the photos of the event wrote

On Monday 9th December, 7 Tevet 5744, I photographed the Ochberg Descendants Communal Kaddish held at the Great Park Shul, Johannesburg. It was the commemoration of the 76th Yahrtzeit of Isaac Ochberg. There was a nice turn out, with guests of honour Solly and Sylvia Jossel, who have to be the most beautiful couple, with Solly aged 99½ years of age! They are just the lovliest couple, and I find them an inspiration.

There was the Communal Kaddish in the Shul and then various speakers, a "Welcome by Rabbi Shaun Wingrin, Lionel Slier, himself a son of an Ochberg Orphan, a video clip by his Daughter Paula Slier, David Saks of SAJBD, and last but not least Clinical Psychologist Leonard Carr, who spoke of "Honouring the past, embracing freedom in the future.

From what I understand some Arcadia and Ochberg Orphan books were sold, one being a gift to Leonard Carr.

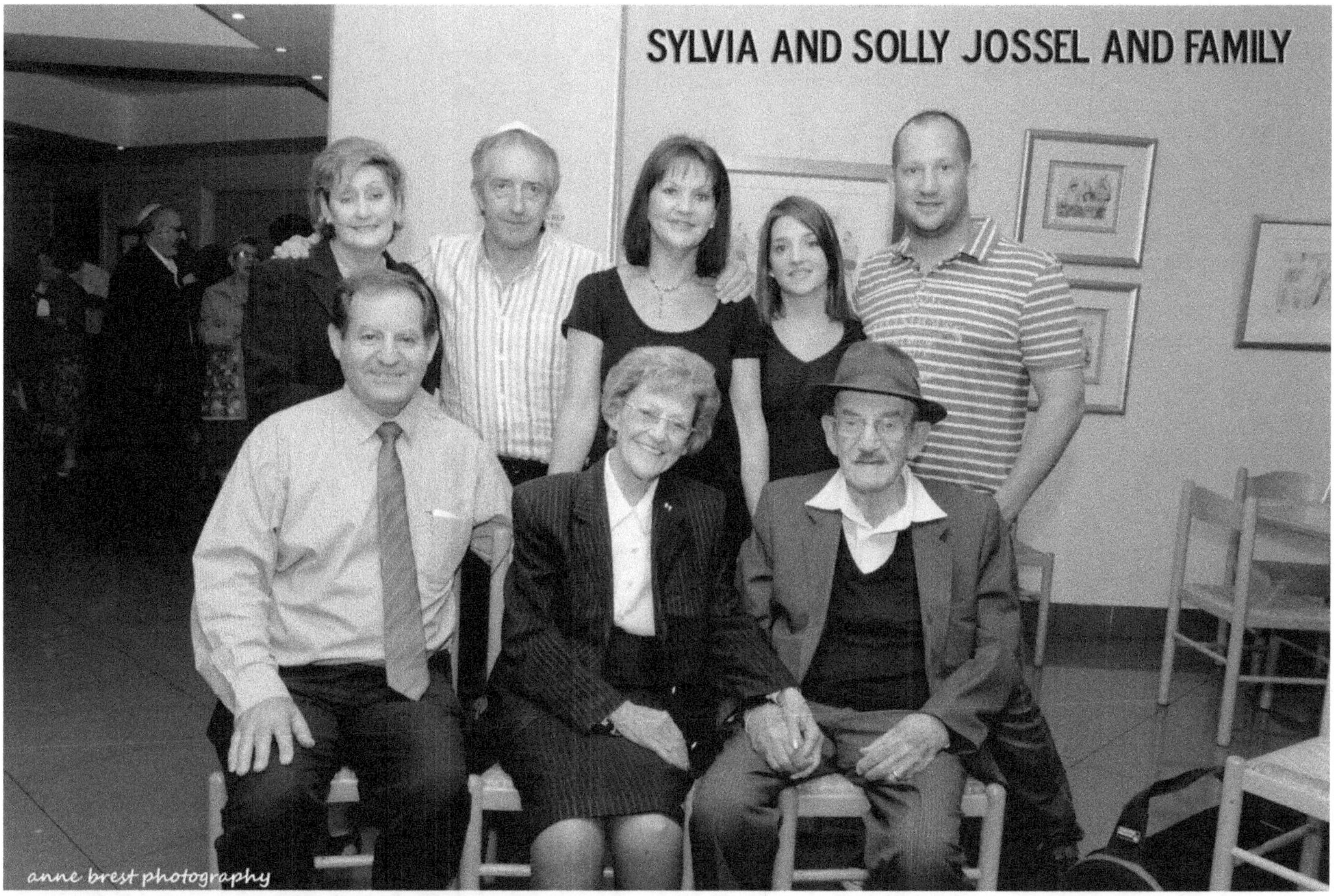
SYLVIA AND SOLLY JOSSEL AND FAMILY
anne brest photography

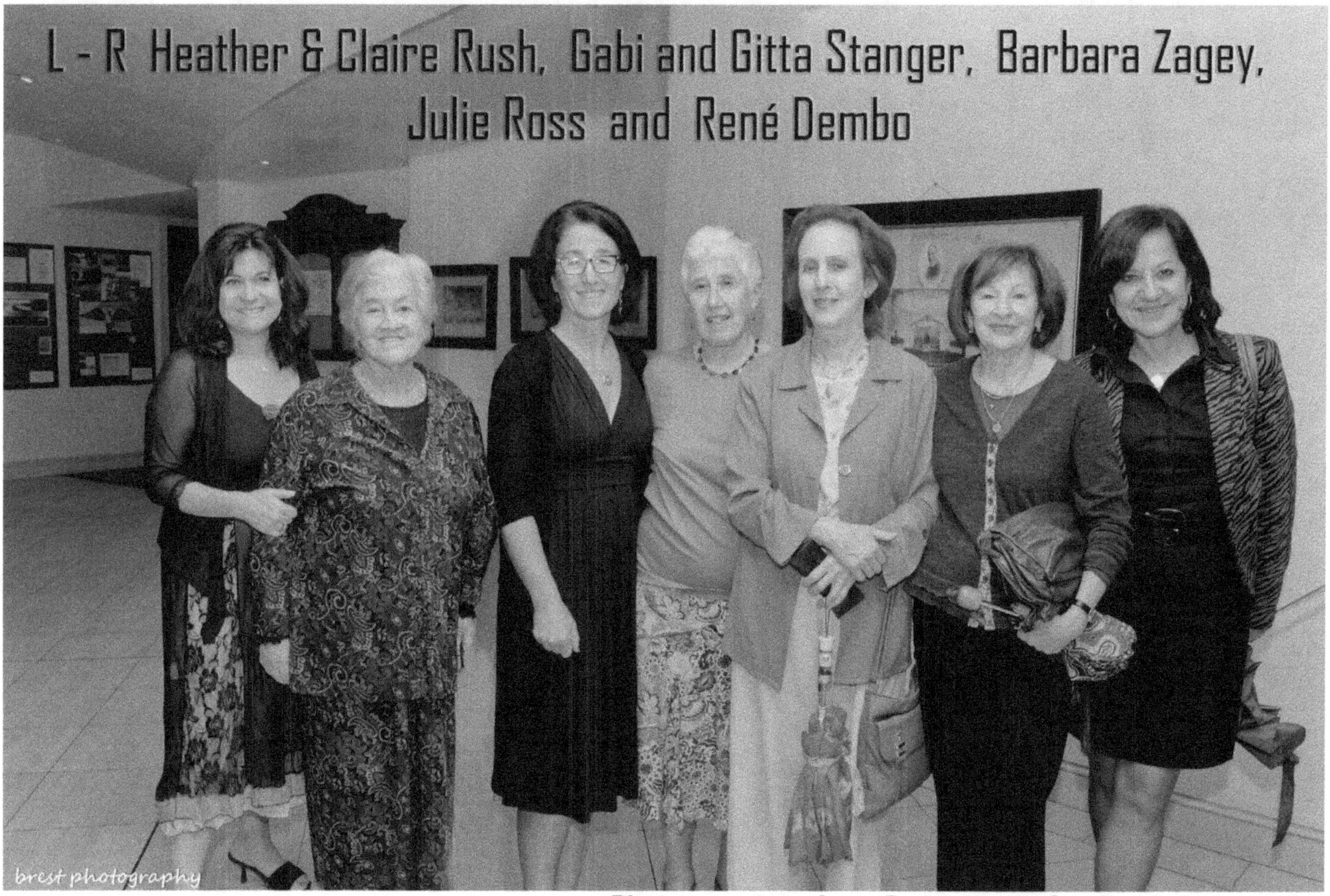
L - R Heather & Claire Rush, Gabi and Gitta Stanger, Barbara Zagey,
Julie Ross and René Dembo
brest photography

Photos courtesy Anne Brest, our professional photographer

Part 7

The Work of the Ochberg Heritage Committee

In this section we tell of the on-going work done
by the Isaac Ochberg Heritage Committee.
founded by Bennie Penzik

We share the newsletters of Bennie Penzik,
the founding chairman of The Committee, and
articles of Dave Kaplan the editor of the the Telfed Magazine

Chapter 61 – RIGHTING A WRONG

RIGHTING A WRONG
By David E. Kaplan

It was long overdue. One of South Africa's finest communal leaders – a hero and a Zionist - has finally gained the recognition he long deserved when in July 2011, Southern Africans came from all over the world to attend the opening in Israel of the KKL-JNF's Isaac Ochberg Scenic Lookout Memorial located in the Ramot Menashe Park, near Kibbutz Ein Hashofet.

Due to one man, thousands of Jews - descendants of the 1921 'Ochberg Orphans' - are alive today.

While the black and white framed portrait of Isaac Ochberg has been hanging in Telfed's offices since 1948, too few knew who he was or what he had done. And yet, this philanthropist and Zionist from Cape Town performed an act in 1921 that to this day, stands as one of the proudest chapters in South African Jewish communal history.

Born in the Ukraine and arriving as a poor immigrant to SA in 1895, he would rise to become one of South Africa's wealthiest and enterprising men. And then, when news reached the Jewish community in South Africa in the early 1920s of the plight of over four hundred thousand Jewish orphans in Eastern Europe facing starvation, disease and massacre, it was time to act.

The year was 1921.

For the Cossacks it was hunting season, and Jews were the prey!

Alone, Ochberg set out on a mission to Eastern Europe in May 1921 to rescue 200 Jewish orphans. Supported by the South African Jewish community under the auspices of the South African Zionist Federation and with permission from the SA government on the number he could bring – the figure was negotiated with Jan Smuts - Ochberg returned triumphantly to Cape Town on the Edinburgh Castle four months later with 187 orphans. Transforming fiction into fact, Ochberg - like the "Pied Piper of Hamelin' - had crisscrossed by train and horse-drawn cart, a region beset by Civil War and pogroms, plucking up orphans at cities, towns and *shtetls*. Had they not been rescued, the odds were they would have perished.

History sadly records that this was to be.

A Celebration of Life

The two-day event was organized by the Israel Ochberg Committee under the Chairmanship of Bennie Penzik – whose parents had both been Ochberg orphans and included, David Kaplan, Hertzel Katz, Leon Segal, Beryl Ratzer, Ian Rogow, Dalia Penzik and Lauren Snitcher.

Southern Africans from across Israel joined the families of the orphans and the families of the late Isaac Ochberg to participate in a jam-packed, two-day programme, which included photo exhibitions, presentations, workshops, and an evening of speeches, superb musical performances and the screening of the Oscar nominated documentary 'Ochberg's Orphans'. For many in the audience, unrelated to the Ochberg saga, it was overwhelming. They saw and heard the Ochberg orphans, most of who have now passed on, interviewed in their senior years tell their horrific stories and how they were literally clutched from the 'jaws of death' in Eastern Europe by Isaac Ochberg and brought to the safety of South Africa.

"How come we did not know about this? Why had we not been taught or told?" These were the perplexing questions plaguing many of the uninformed at the end of the event which culminated in the inauguration of the Ochberg Park.

The park *is* sponsored – it's still a work in progress - by the KKL-JNF in appreciation of the massive donation made by Ochberg in 1937, the proceeds of which, were used to buy the vast tracts of land in which the kibbutzim of Dalia and Gal'ed stand today. "Ochberg's bequest to the JNF remains the largest ever made by an individual," says Bennie. "However, it's his epic mission to the hell of Eastern Europe in 1921 resulting in the rescue of those poor children that I am most indebted. Two of those kids became my parents."

The most moving feature in the park is 'The Hill of Names', where embedded in its rock and masonry are the plaques of the names of all the orphans "Daddy Ochberg" saved and brought to South Africa. Tearfully walking along the path and stopping at her own plaque, and then the plaques of her two sisters, was Cissy Harris from Haifa. At 93, she was the only 'Ochberg orphan' to

Bennie Penzik, Chairman of the Ochberg Committee, unveiling the original KKl-JNF monument to Isaac Ochberg that he discovered in a staorage facility twenty years after it had been removed from the Elyakim Junction to facilitate roadworks.

attend the event, and was accorded the honour of unveiling the Park's information bronze plaque

Most of the orphans on arriving in South Africa in 1921 were divided between the two Jewish orphanages, Oranjia in Cape Town and Arcadia in Johannesburg. Very few were adopted by families. And yet one that had been, really had a story to tell!

The first unveiling of the Ochberg Monument at the Elyakim Junction in the 1950s

Arnold Nadelman from Melbourne emotionally approached the microphone. So overcome with emotion he had been reluctant to speak. A little over a week before, he had never heard of Isaac Ochberg. A closer look at a photo in an article advertising the Ochberg Event in an Australian newspaper followed by an observation by his wife Gail that the little boy in the photo taken in 1921 *"looks like you looked as a child, Arnold"* led him to call David Solly Sandler in Perth, who had recently published his monumental work: 'The Ochberg Orphans – *and the horrors from where they came*'. A quick investigation revealed that his father had been one of the 177 orphans and had been adopted by the Nadelman family in Johannesburg. Arnold's life was immediately put on hold as he and his wife hurriedly boarded a plane to Israel to join "my new *family*" in honoring "Daddy Ochberg".

At the ceremony, all were wearing their Isaac Ochberg T-shirts – sponsored by the Segal family in honour of their Ochberg orphan mother, Annie. On the T-shirts under the portrait of Ochberg were the words that have resonated for thousands of years and epitomize Ochberg's legacy: "He who has saved one life is as though he has saved the entire world."

If the ceremony took a while to commence, it was only because people could not tear themselves away from the 'Hill of Names' as each family crowded around "their" plaque of *their* ancestor. On this blistering mid-summer day, the tears could have irrigated the dry, thirsty land of Ramot Menashe on which the park is located.

In the years ahead, the trees planted will grow, as will the children and grandchildren of the Ochberg orphans who will come and visit the park and shelter in the shade of fully grown trees. Eighteen of those trees have been donated by Telfed, the first of which was planted at a special tree-planting ceremony, by the vice chairman of Telfed, Maish Isaacson.

"I am very happy to see that Isaac Ochberg is finally getting the recognition he deserved" says 93 year old Cissy Harris, sole surviving Ochberg orphan in Israel, in an interview with Paula Slier at Kibbutz Gal'ed. Paula the English Russian TV Middle East Bereau Chief, is the granddaughter of an Ochberg Orphan.

We are in the process of establishing an Isaac Ochberg Heritage Centre to spread the legacy of this great man,' said Hertzel Katz, who announced its launching following addresses by Ochberg's niece, Phyllis Friedlander from Cape Town and Ochberg's granddaughter, Tessa Goldin from London. The hope is that future South African visitors to Israel will include a visit to both the Centre at

Kibbutz Dalia and to the park "and should there be group missions, we in the committee, will be happy to acts as guides," says Bennie.

To understand the times and "the hell" from where these orphans came, one has only to inquire how Ochberg orphan Harry Stillerman at the Oranje Orphanage in Cape Town lost the bottom half of his arm. The Cossacks had murdered his parents in front of him, and when one of them on horseback was about to strike Harry with his sabre, he raised his arm to protect himself. Although they left him to die in the sand, he survived and was taken by Ochberg to South Africa.

Epilogue

"Isaac Ochberg was a dreamer who made dreams come true," said Avinoam Binder, representing KKL-JNF World Chairman Efi Stenzler at the ceremony. "When he purchased the land here, the scenery was nothing like what we see from the lookout today. The land was barren and desolate. Ochberg dreamt that the Jewish people would come here and establish a Jewish state. This project in his honour is to educate future generations of Israeli Jews not to take our many blessings for granted. KKL-JNF is honoured to take part in this project in memory of a man who believed in the future of Israel."

Issa and Henry Werb best summed up "The Ochberg experience in Israel" when they wrote to the Ochberg Committee on returning home to Cape Town:

"Our 18 year old grand-daughter was with us and I made her promise to come back to the forest with her own children one day to honour those who now rest in peace in such a beautiful and tranquil place. I see the memorial as the hull of a ship with the names on the plaques as portholes gazing on a wonderful vista. I know that the Ochberg children have finally all come home."

Lucky to be Alive. Descendants of Ochberg orphans walking along the path by the Hill of Names stopping to read the plaques of the 177 orphans saved by Ochberg.

Contacts for further information, particularly about visiting the Isaac Ochberg Memorial Park, viewing documentaries, organising talks: Bennie Penzik benzipen@smile.net.il or David Kaplan hildav@netvision.net.il

"Family portait. - they came from all over the world to honour "Daddy Ochberg".

Chapter 62 – IF ONLY ISAAC COULD SEE IT ALL.

OCHBERG HERITAGE COMMITTEE NEWSLETTER
by Benny Penzik <ochbergsorphans@gmail.com>
October 6th 2011

Shana Tova and Gmar Hatima Tova!

IF ONLY ISAAC COULD SEE IT ALL!

Who knows, maybe from his celestial perch, he is looking down, either crying or smiling, for he would see how loved he is; how he is so remembered; how all these who would not have been alive were it not for him, came from the four corners of the world to Kibbutzim Dalia and Gal-Ed not only to pay long awaited homage but to celebrate life itself – *"their own."*

He would see a beautiful park in his name, with trees, and paths and a hill with plaques inscribed with the name of each of the children he saved. But what would give the most joy - is all of you, all the children, grandchildren and great-grandchildren, for this remains his finest legacy – *life itself.*

The line on our T-shirt so appropriately read:
"He who has saved one life is as though he has saved the entire world."

It's been nearly three months since our memorable gathering on the 19-20th July. From the emails we have received and the enthusiasm shown of people wanting to contribute, to plant trees, to gather again, to re-visit etc, we can see how you all have connected with each other and your past and collectively imbedded this experience in the Land of Israel. This is right and fitting and we are committed to taking this project forward into the future.

Our committee has followed up with promising meetings with the JNF to explore ways of working together to enhance the park and initiate educational programs. It's all in its embryonic state and we will keep you informed as matters develop.

We are pleased to announce that upon the open area above the amphitheatre, where you all sat during the ceremony, will soon host an impressive observation tower, so symbolic of Israel's modern history. The tower will enable visitors to observe the stunning, panoramic view of the original Isaac Ochberg Tract. This will provide an even more enhanced vista of the area.

When complete, we will send you photos of the tower in a future newsletter.

In the meantime, the DVD that you have all been so patiently waiting for will still take another few weeks to complete as Paula Slier, an Ochberg descendent herself and editor of the movie, has been on constant assignments such as a TV network correspondent. We do live in an exciting and busy neighbourhood!

It should take another few weeks but we are getting there and plan to start posting them to you the moment the job is completed.

Here is a development, bristling with emotion.
Many of us live in areas remote from where our parents are buried, so come *Yahrzeit*, we are naturally far from their resting place. What we have discovered in the short time since the opening of the Isaac Ochberg Memorial Park in July, is that descendents living in Israel or visiting from abroad, will on *Yahrzeit*, visit the Park and say Kaddish standing around their family plaque. Their loved ones may not be buried here but so much of who they were and their history, is imbedded in this special place that Ochberg made possible with his generous bequest way back in 1937. These are early days, but it is becoming increasingly evident how people are, for many reasons, drawn to "Our Ochberg Park".

Kol Hakavod to Ronny Schreeuwer, an ex-Arcadian living in Sdot Yam and a close associate of - and behind-the-scenes willing assistant to - David Sandler. Ronny responded promptly to David's recent request to photograph each of the plaques individually and this is the result.

On the next page are two views of the Hill of Names on the Ochberg Memorial Site at Park Ramat Menashe overlooking Kibbutz Dalia.

Finally, these are recent messages from members of the biological Ochberg family:

Dear Bennie, Lauren, Leon, David and others whose email addresses we don't have but who helped create the Ochberg Tribute,

We are with you all in spirit at this special time of the year, but would love to be with you in presence to repeat the most wonderful experience our whole family had in July. It was truly overwhelming and unforgettable.

We cannot thank you enough for your hard work that make this outstanding occasion happen.

We wish you all a wonderful New Year and well over the fast - you really deserve it. We think of you all and of the whole event with wonder at the magic you produced with such dedication. We know that Isaac Ochberg's spirit is in you all and will continue to be spread throughout all the families.

Shana Tovah from Noreen, Ian and Tessa Goldin, Ian Webber and Olivia and Alexander Goldin
May the year ahead be one of happiness, fulfillment, good health and peace.

The Hill of Names

Dear Bennie, David and Lauren,

I want to thank you for all your incredible hard work in organising the wonderful Ochberg event. It was really worthwhile. As you know, I have always known what an incredible person my uncle Isaac Ochberg was, but to have seen and heard all the Ochberg orphans families relate their parents' or grandparents' stories was a revelation.

Those of my family, who were present, felt an immense pride in their Ochberg genes. I know also Isaacs's granddaughters and their families were also so proud.

I want to particularly thank Lauren, who initiated the interviews with the surviving orphans and made the original Ochberg DVD that inspired movie director Jon Blair to make his moving documentary, which will help further preserve the legacy.

I too would like to thank the volunteers, some of whom I knew; the JNF for the well designed Isaac Ochberg Park, including the memorable wall housing the Ochberg Orphan plaques.

I would like to make a donation of trees to the Park, but after the event there was no one to consult as to donations. Please advise?

Also if there are any future events, would you let me know, so that even if I cannot travel, my family may be able to attend.

Once again, many thanks for all your efforts. If any of you are in Cape Town I would like to see you please.
Best Wishes Lshana Tova
Phyllis Friedlander and family

And from the Werb family…..
You and your team were absolutely amazing. Thank you for your input, the wonderful organisation, and memories to last the rest of our lives.

Our 18 year old grand-daughter was with us and I made her promise to come back to the forest with her own children one day to honour those that now rest in peace in such a beautiful and tranquil place.

I know that the Ochberg children have all come home.
With warmest love and good wishes
Issa, Henry and Gabriella Werb

Chapter 63 – WIZO South Africa Visits the Ochberg Memorial

WIZO SA VISITS OCHBERG MEMORIAL
By David E. Kaplan

A WIZO SA delegation on January 21 paid an uplifting visit to Kibbutz Dahlia and the Isaac Ochberg Park, arranged by David Kaplan.

"Despite the rain, cold and even hail, we did not let it 'dampen' our spirits," WIZO SA said in a media release, "particularly remembering the hardships, so much part of the narrative that we were experiencing, being immortalised for all eternity."

The media release pointed out that it was fitting that the first two delegations hosted to date, had been the Canadians and the South Africans – the two countries that took in the orphans in 1921.

"It was truly special to have had 93-year-old Sissy Harris from Haifa join us... the only surviving Ochberg orphan living in Israel."

After listening to Harris' anecdotes, the delegation ventured outdoors to see the innovative memorial which had been constructed - a magnificent curved wall, resembling the bow of a boat, is embedded with plaques in alphabetical order of the 177 orphans saved and brought to South Africa.

"The South African Jewish community can take great pride in what has been done so far to preserve the legacy of one of its favourite sons.

Isaac Ochberg not only saved children from disease and death in the Ukraine, but also left the largest tract of land ever given by a single donor to the JNF in Israel.

"We foresee this park becoming a major tourist attraction in the future and look forward to further visits with WIZO SA."

Pictured are South African WIZO delegation to the Kibbutz Dahlia and Isaac Ochberg Lookout Memorial, with an Ochberg survivor, Sissy Harris.

Chapter 64 – Ochberg Memorial Committee Newsletters

NEWSLETTER Monday May 14, 2012
by Benny Penzik <ochbergsorphans@gmail.com>

The Isaac Ochberg Heritage Committee - Bennie Penzik - Chairman, Adv Hertzel Katz - Vice-Chairman, David E Kaplan, Leon Segal and Ian Rogow

Friends!

The past three months have seen a number of new and refreshing developments in our continuing efforts designed to perpetuate the memory of Isaac Ochberg.

The Diaspora Museum in Tel Aviv - Bet Hatfutsot - now has the story of Isaac Ochberg recorded under "Personalities" on the museum's database facility. Additionally, permission has also been granted to allow visitors to view the documentary "Ochberg's Orphans" on the museum's computers.

Visitors to the Ochberg Memorial Site in, and since, July 2011 - will have seen the square base designed to support the proposed observation tower, details of which were revealed at that time. The structure was to be a modest wooden platform some two to three meters high. We are pleased to advise that the updated plan provides for an elegant steel structure which will provide visitors with an unparalleled view of the surrounding area - including the original Isaac Ochberg Tract - from a height of almost six metres! Visitors will have access to a viewing platform five metres square - with wheelchair access - via a spiral construction supported by a central nine metre steel pillar!!

We have had a number of fruitful meetings with the education division of KKL/JNF and considerable progress has been made in our efforts to ensure that the Ochberg heritage be taught at schools and youth movements. Appropriately, the pilot project will centre on the Megiddo area schools where the Memorial Site and kibbutzim Dalia and Gal-Ed are located.

Once again, we are acutely aware of the situation regarding the proposed DVD which covered the main event of July 2011 - the memorable two days of our gathering. There have, regrettably, been a number of glitches causing incessant delays and the colour of this paragraph correctly reflects the colour of our faces. No effort is being spared to correct the situation!

An example of enterprise and positive thinking! 'Kol Hakavod' to the Romanovsky family of Edmonton, Canada for organising the upcoming Gala Dinner scheduled for June 24th. The commemorative brochure will include an article on Isaac Ochberg by Sir Martin Gilbert, the eminent historian! Attendance is hoped to reach between 300-400 guests who are prospective donors to the fund-raising effort destined for Ochberg commemoration projects in Israel.

We wish them much success in this endeavour!

We are in regular contact with various tour guide organisations here who have responded positively to our recommendations and requests to have the Ochberg Memorial Site included on the agenda for the estimated 7000 accredited tour guides operating in Israel!

Please hold the date 20-12-2012 - for Ochberg's 75th Yahrzeit!!!

There will be a commemorative ceremony on that date at Maitland Cemetery where Kaddish will be held for Ochberg as well as an appropriate tribute to his memory.

The Hill of Names

NEWSLETTER SEPTEMBER 2012
Tuesday September 4, 2012
by Benny Penzik <ochbergsorphans@gmail.com>

Shalom from Israel!

It's been a few months since we last reported to you – the wonderful global family of all those who have been touched in some way by the Ochberg orphan saga... a saga that has had a stirring beginning but happily, no end ......

And we are happy to report there has been 'no end' to our activities here as we meet frequently with the JNF/KKL, Ministry of Tourism, tour guide organisations and school boards involved in plans for the inclusion of the Ochberg saga in the curriculum for 14-year-olds. Various individuals and organizations abroad have committed themselves to be part of the future of what will finally emerge an enormous and most impressive development at Park Ramat Menashe, where the 'jewel in the crown' will undoubtedly be The Isaac Ochberg Memorial Site. We would like to think that Isaac Ochberg z"l can only nod approvingly from his celestial perch.....

Hardly a week goes by without people calling our committee members asking for directions to the park – be they locals or visitors from abroad.

When possible and when they represent leaders in communities from abroad, every effort is made to host these guests so that we may address them.

Visitors to the Ochberg Memorial Site over the past few months have included -

Dennis Rudnick (a sprightly 85!) and son and daughter from Australia. Dennis's wife, Edna, was regrettably unable to make the trip. Edna's mother was Salka Blind, Ochberg orphan, who arrived in Johannesburg in 1921 and went to live at the Arcadia Jewish Orphanage. Her name was changed to Sadie. She married and became Sadie Saus.

Dennis Rudnick

Dennis read a moving tribute from Edna while standing at the monument to Isaac Ochberg at the Site.

Dennis was a young soldier, who arrived as a Machal volunteer, during the War of Independence of 1948. He fought with Chativa 8 in Operation Yoav in the Negev. After the war, in 1950, Dennis was recruited to join a group of technicians sent to the USA in order to bring to Israel the first Super Constellations which, upon arrival to Israel, marked the foundation of El-Al.

Josh Cooper, Executive Director of JNF Canada was accompanied by Jessica Lawson-Stein, Director of the Canada Desk at Head Office - Jerusalem on his July visit.

Bennie Penzik - Dennis Rudnick - Charlene Green - Aubrey Rudnick

Bennie Penzik - Jessica Lawson-Stein (JNF) - David Kaplan - Josh Cooperof JNF Canada

Marna Meyer, daughter of Jenny Segal of Houston TX whose late mother was Rosie Hans, Ochberg orphan, who then became Rosie Flink of Bertrams, Jhbg. Marna was accompanied by her son and daughter Ayli and Darren (not pictured) and Zvi and Dot Pantanowitz who graciously assisted with facilitating the visit. Dot herself has a direct Ochberg connection via the Gonifas family.

Bennie Penzik - Zvi Pantanowitz - Marna Meyer - Dorothy Pantanowitz

The DVD of the July 2011 two-day Ochberg Memorial Event!!

Now that the DVD of the July 2011 2-day Ochberg Memorial Event finally reached those who prepaid at the time and endured the long wait, recollections have been spiked as evidenced by extracts from recent messages received.

This from Jerome Ruch of Cape Town

"I have just had my first opportunity of watching the Ochberg DVD – it really brought the memories flooding back – I only wish it had been a bit longer and more in-depth.
Thanks to all concerned for putting this piece of memorabilia together and a special thank you to you for your continuous follow-up – all in all, it was a truly fantastic effort to condense so much into around a 30 minute DVD.
A perfect ending would however have been, showing everyone singing "Hatikvah" together at the "Hill of Names" – that would really have sent shivers and goose pimples down everyone's spines."

And from Lynne Michel of Sydney -

"It was truly a mammoth task - brilliantly organised and well executed. We were all shellshocked for days after. I was so thrilled that the content of the event was so well thought out and delivered so well. We all gained much from our time spent there - it was well worth the long hike from Australia. Reconnecting with people from our past and making new friends (like the Nadelmans) who we now feel strongly connected to. It was especially meaningful for us to have three generations share that time and thankfully two of my four children were able to be there. They have learned a fortune about their (and all of the larger Ochberg descendant's collective history) and will now hopefully transmit this information to the generations below.

Thanks so much to all of you for an incredible job well done!

This presents a great opportunity to show the Hill of Names which is a major attraction of the Memorial Site:

The Hill of Names - above and below

Contacts for further information, particularly about visiting the Isaac Ochberg Memorial Park, viewing documentaries, organising talks: Bennie Penzik benzipen@smile.net.il or David Kaplan hildav@netvision.net.il

Extracts from the prominent South African Jewish newspaper,
The Zionist Record, December 1937

"AN OUTSTANDING JEW OF HIS GENERATION" -- "Zionist Record",
December 17, 1937

At the age of 16, Isaac Ochberg came to South Africa without means or influence but endowed with courage and energy.

He died at the age of 58 honoured and wealthy, a pillar of the community, benefactor of many causes, mourned by a host of friends and co-workers. His was the story of dogged perseverance and concentration. But it was not merely the pursuit of riches which animated him. He never forgot his origin; he never ignored his obligations. Nor were his substantial gifts in his lifetime merely reaction to pressure. He initiated his own benefactions. They were not confined to philanthropy. He valued above all education -- knowing from his own struggle how much the ignorant missed.

He became a leading Zionist figure in South Africa and was President of the Capetown Zionist Organisation as well as on the Cape Executive of the Board of Deputies. Zionism and local Jewish life he served equally.

That Isaac Ochberg was no ordinary personality was evinced by the public activity he undertook at no little cost of effort as well as of money when he rescued 200 pogrom-orphans from the Ukraine after the first World War. He personally selected and conducted the victims from Europe to England and thence to South Africa where he established for them a home and school. Their upbuilding was a service of love on his part.

Even as he lived, so when he made his last Will and Testament, he thought of his people and carefully planned that they should benefit constructively and handsomely from his substance.

He bequeathed many gifts to South African institutions but he realised that the core of Jewish life with which he was bound up was in Zion, and that its sustenance was the soil. He created by Will the "Isaac Ochberg Palestine Fund" with the object "to assist the settlement of poor Jewish men and women on the land in Palestine", the moneys of the fund to be paid to the Jewish National Fund (Keren Kayemeth Leisrael). The Jewish National Fund was directed

> To purchase and take transfer in its own name for the whole of the said bequest (together with any accumulated interest thereon) a tract of land suitable for agricultural settlement by Jews. It shall name the said tract of land Isaac Ochberg Settlement or an equivalent Hebrew description......It shall, whilst retaining the full and unencumbered ownership in the said tract of land nevertheless make the same available upon such terms and conditions as to the tenure and use thereof as it may deem fit for agricultural settlement by Jews.

ISAAC OCHBERG

IN Isaac Ochberg our community has lost one of its most vital figures. His untimely death closed a long period of ill-health which deprived us of much that his vivid personality, his keen brain, and his great heart could have contributed to Jewry and to humanity. In spite of this, he goes down in our annals as an outstanding Jew of his generation. The succour of the poor and distressed, the pursuit of good citizenship, and the fostering of Jewish national ideals—these were the abiding passions of his life, and to all of them he made outstanding contributions in leadership, in service, and in the substantial practical assistance which his ample means enabled him to give.

His achievement in bringing a large group of Jewish orphans from the hell of post-war Ukraine to new life and hope in South Africa, marked him as a man of rare vision, determination and large-heartedness; whilst not less felicitous was his leadership over a long period of years of the Zionist movement in the Cape Peninsula and the Western Province generally. It is almost impossible to enumerate the activities of Isaac Ochberg in every field of communal and civic life; and this in spite of that intense application to personal affairs which transformed the poor immigrant from Eastern Europe into one of the most substantial merchants of Capetown.

He has crowned a lifetime of generous giving by testamentary dispositions of princely munificence, which bear eloquent testimony to the moral stature and the feeling for true and lasting values which distinguished this devoted son of his people. *Zichrono Lebracha!*

Even Itzhak, the impressive stone monument marking the original spot where Kibbutz Gal-Ed first began

SHANA TOVA - GMAR HATIMA TOVA AND A FEW NEWS ITEMS!
Wednesday September 19, 2012
by Benny Penzik <ochbergsorphans@gmail.com>

The Isaac Ochberg Heritage Committee (Israel) wishes all descendants of the world-wide "Ochberg Family" a Happy New Year and Well over the Fast.

Our Sincere thanks for the many messages of goodwill received over the past days.

Bennie Penzik - Chairman, Adv Hertzel Katz - Vice-Chairman, David E Kaplan, Leon Segal and Ian Rogow

Along with festive season greetings from a member of Kibbutz Gal-Ed came a message that speaks of visits to Givat Even Itzhak, the impressive stone monument marking the original spot where the kibbutz first began. It is approximately two km from the present day, bustling, kibbutz and serves as a reminder of the legacy of Isaac Ochberg, albeit only in the memory of those familiar with the history of the area. It is indeed a very impressive sight, somewhat off the beaten track, and will be the subject of fresh investigation on our part soon.

Givat Even Itzhak

A message from the Gen Manager of Kibbutz Dalia, Shacham Mittler, in response to my greetings.

Hi Bennie
Good to hear from you!
Thank you for your good wishes and, on behalf of Kibbutz Dalia, I wish you, your family and all the descendants of Isaac Ochberg, a year of peace, happiness and good health.

We will remember the heritage that Isaac Ochberg granted to you, to us and to the State of Israel.
In friendship and respect,
Shacham

An important milestone was reached last Thursday with a presentation I made, together with Hanna Livne, the lady who designed the Ochberg Memorial Site and the surrounding project (more on this subject in future bulletins) to the senior 32 functionaries of the Tour Guides Division of the Ministry of Tourism. This is part of our ongoing efforts to bring the Ochberg saga to the attention of all registered tour guides and to include the Memorial Site on their planning agendas.

Tomorrow, Thursday 20th, we are scheduled to meet with the senior staff of the Megido School (250 meters from the Memorial Site) to conclude plans for the inclusion of the Ochberg story in the school syllabus.

Lynne Ruch Michel posted in Ochberg Orphans and Descendants and Friends

This group was established to share information about the Ochberg Orphans and their descendents. It is open to anyone, in particular, descendents and friends of the Ochberg Orphans. All input is welcome and can be posted directly on the wall.

Should anyone wish to join the group, they may simply request to join with a brief introduction of themselves, and they will be made more than welcome.

We look forward to flourishing as a group, held together by a common bond - a deep gratitude to the legacy left by Isaac Ochberg - a legacy that has affected the entire shape of many of our lives.
Again, 'Hag Samea'h to you all!

HAPPY PASSOVER - HAG PESACH SAMEACH
Wednesday March 20, 2013
by Benny Penzik <ochbergsorphans@gmail.com>

The Isaac Ochberg Heritage Committee wishes all descendants of the world-wide "Ochberg Family" a Happy Pesach.

May you rejoice in our traditions and always be blessed with good health, happiness, prosperity and peace.

Snippets of events over the past months:

Three members of the Aviv delegation of WIZO - South Africa - on a visit to the site in November 2012.

Khalil Houry receiving a framed photo of the Hill of Names on the Ochberg Memorial Site in recognition of his superb stone construction.

Dot Pantanowitz, Hillel Shnaps and Bennie Penzik with a class of 13-year-old pupils of the Megiddo School showing a presentation on the Ochberg Orphans.

Contacts for further information, particularly about visiting the Isaac Ochberg Memorial Park, viewing documentaries, organising talks:
Bennie Penzik benzipen@smile.net.il or
David Kaplan hildav@netvision.net.il

20-12-2012 marked the commemoration of the 75th yahrzeit of Isaac Ochberg - of blessed memory - in Cape Town. Hosting the ceremony was Lauren Snitcher and daughter Michaela together with the JNF and SAZF. Molly Cohen, the oldest living Ochberg Orphan at age 99, received the honour of unveiling a plaque to mark the event.

The Edinburgh Castle - imagine the thrill and apprehension of the Ochberg Orphans sailing on this magnificent vessel from Southampton to Cape Town in September 1921.

This presents an opportune moment to express my sincere thanks to my committee members - Hertzel Katz - vice-Chairman, David E Kaplan, Leon Segal, Ian Rogow and Lauren Snitcher (RSA) for their enthusiastic dedication to preserving the legacy of our beloved patron.

Additionally, deserving of special mention is my colleague and good friend, David Solly Sandler of Perth WA, for his major efforts at collecting and collating information and keeping us all informed on a regular weekly basis with his newsletter.

Again, Happy Passover!
Bennie Penzik
Editor and Chairman

The Megiddo schoolkids have been working on the area adjacent to the Ochberg Memorial Site - here are two examples of their handiwork in the construction of a mosaic sign - "The Path of Blooms" - and a stone resting place in the shade of a tree along the circular track.

Contacts for further information, particularly about visiting the Isaac Ochberg Memorial Park, viewing documentaries, organising talks:
  Bennie Penzik benzipen@smile.net.il or
  David Kaplan hildav@netvision.net.il

Chapter 65 – SPREADING THE LEGACY OF ISAAC OCHBERG

SPREADING THE LEGACY OF ISAAC OCHBERG
by Bennie Penzik

Together with fellow volunteers, Dorothy Pantanowitz and Hillel Shnaps, we attended the high school at Megiddo last week for another in the series of lectures we have been giving for some years to the 14-year-olds at the school, which services the nearby town of Yokneam and the surrounding kibbutzim.

The students devote two separate lessons in their study of the Ochberg story - one is the classroom talk we give them and the second is a class visit to the Memorial Site where a 'Treasure Hunt' game is conducted by the teachers which calls for answers to a list of questions for which the kids need to scour the historical plaques, the monument in Ochberg's honour and the 177 ceramic name plaques. The 20cm square name plaques reveal details for each of the orphans - original birth name, date and place of birth and the name by which each was commonly known. With the help of a PowerPoint presentation well constructed by the school teaching staff, I begin the teaching session with an apology for the quality of my command of the Hebrew language, a summary of Ochberg's early years, his arrival as a 16-year-old in South Africa - his successful business ventures - his chairmanship of the Oranjia Jewish Orphanage and the epic saga of the group of orphans he rescued in 1921 from the hell of Eastern Europe and re-located to South Africa, the event which has immortalised his name. Stress is also placed on the effect of the proceeds of his last will on the very area of the school surroundings by virtue of the redemption of the land by the proceeds of his will by the Jewish National Fund. I also explain my own personal connection in that both my parents were part of the group - and the fact the kids are exposed to three people, each with a close personal family connection is a major issue which appeals to the young audience, particularly when I am able to point to the group photos taken before departure from Europe and show the young 12-year-old in the top row who became my father.

Dorothy then tells of the hazards endured by her family members who lived in the area through which Ochberg travelled and reveals marriage certificates and other memorabilia which the kids find fascinating. Hillel ends our verbal presentation with pictures of the Edinburgh Castle, the vessel which brought to group from Southampton to Cape Town and concludes with a message that resonates well with the youngsters stating that the connection between them and we three volunteers is that Ochberg was responsible for providing them with a warm and welcome place to live and, to the three of us, he provided life itself.

We had heard much about the limited attention span of Israeli youngsters, particularly in the 13-15 year old age group, but we have found on each occasion that they are models of good and respectful behavior and ask intelligent questions when given the opportunity.

I often think back to 2008 when Dorothy and I visited the archivist at Kibbutz Galed (Even Itzhak), one of the two kibbutzim on the land once known as the Isaac Ochberg Tract. While waiting for our meeting, we asked the office personnel who the Itzhak was in the name of the kibbutz which appears thus on all maps of Israel - Kibbutz Galed (Even Itzhak). The response was - 'perhaps one of our forefathers, Avraham, Itzhak and Yaacov?'

I would like to believe that the new generation of kids growing up in the area of the Isaac Ochberg Tract will not be similarly deluded.

Bennie Penzik, Dorothy Pantanowitz and Hillel Shnaps talking to the children at the high school at Megiddo.

Chapter 66 – THE ISAAC OCHBERG HERITAGE COMMITTEE NEWS

Ochberg Heritage Committee News

While the saga of Isaac Ochberg has been well documented in numerous publications, public awareness of this great man is still sadly lacking, to say the least. Efforts to combat the lack of knowledge about the Ochberg Orphans in general and Isaac Ochberg in particular were started by Bennie Penzik. Bennie is unique in that both his mother and his father were Ochberg Orphans, making him ideally qualified to continue the legacy of the Ochberg Orphans and to do so he established the Ochberg Heritage Committee. Bennie has been ably assisted by former Telfed Chairman, Hertzel Katz, who generously made space and services in his law office in Ramat Hasharon available to Bennie. After the committee had been founded with Bennie Penzik as the first chairman and Hertzel Katz as the vice chairman, they were joined by Ian Rogow, a retired J.N.F. executive, David Kaplan, a past chairman of Telfed and Leon Segal, like Bennie, the descendant of an Ochberg orphan, together with assistance from Lauren Snitcher, also a descendant of an Ochberg orphan, based in Cape Town. Led by Bennie, this committee conceived the ambitious plan of establishing an Isaac Ochberg Memorial Park in an area adjacent to Kibbutzim Daliya and Gal-Ed/Even Yitzchak, both of which are situated on land that was purchased by the J.N.F. with funds from the legacy left by Isaac Ochberg in his will.

Needless to say, with Bennie's persistence and much hard work by the entire committee, the Isaac Ochberg Memorial Park was opened in 2011. This park commemorates not only the deeds of Isaac Ochberg, but also the names of all the Ochberg Orphans that he brought to South Africa. The Park is a tangible way of ensuring that the memory of Isaac Ochberg and his deeds will not be forgotten. Follow up visits by various communal groups have been made since then and a big event was held on the 18th May, 2016, to celebrate the birthday of Cissie Harris, the only surviving Ochberg Orphan.

I became involved in the planning for this event as a result of being the voluntary tour co-ordinator for the Telfed Tiyul committee, a small committee chaired by Joel Klotnick with Eric Glick and Robert Hyde as the other committee members. Bennie Penzik called for our assistance in arranging a visit to the Memorial Park for the birthday celebration as we have established a good reputation for organising group tours for South African expatriates to localities of particular interest to South Africans. The report of that highly successful visit follows.

South African Israelis from Raanana on Telfed Ochberg Tiyul.

South African Israelis from Raanana on Telfed Ochberg Tiyul.

The Telfed Ochberg Tiyul

A busload of South African Israelis left Raanana at eight thirty in the morning on 18 May 2016 with great anticipation for the day that lay ahead of us. The very fact that all the tour participants arrived early meant that we were able to depart five minutes earlier than planned, speaks for itself.

The tour which was a combined project of Telfed and the Isaac Ochberg Heritage Committee can only be described as having been an unqualified success in all respects. The planned itinerary of a first stop at Kibbutz Gal'ed (Even Yitzhak) with a prearranged programme, from there to Kibbutz Dalya and finally to the Isaac Ochberg Memorial Park went like clockwork.

The bus journey commenced, as always with the Tefillat Haderech prayer read by Monty Nussbaum who has become our unofficial tiyul chaplain. We were pleased to have the current Chairman of Telfed, Maish Isaacson and his wife Jocelyn, as well as past Telfed chairmen Hertzel Katz together his wife Lola, Dave Bloom and Dave Kaplan with us on the bus. Hertzel Katz is the vice chairman of The Isaac Ochberg Heritage Committee while Dave Kaplan is a committee member.

Dave Kaplan is a veritable fountain of knowledge about Israel and the South African contribution to the Israeli scene over the years and together with Peter Bailey they kept the tour group informed about the route and the many moshavim and kibbutzim we passed on the way to Gal'ed. Keeping very much to the schedule we arrived at Gal'ed in time to be met with a scrumptious spread of drinks, hot and cold, and a variety of confectionery delights and fresh fruit. At Gal'ed we were joined by our guest of honour, Cissie Harris, the only surviving

Ochberg Orphan who would be celebrating her 98th birthday with us. During a short address by Hertzel Katz, he said "it is a grave injustice to the memory of Isaac Ochberg that he has largely been forgotten by the JNF and indeed the government of Israel and other institutions". The Isaac Ochberg Heritage Committee has a duty to do its utmost to ensure that the wrong done to this great man.must be corrected.

Cissie Harris cutting her birthday cake.

This visit and a subsequent Telfed group visit of 40 people in August has gone a long way to educating many South African expatriates in Israel about Isaac Ochberg and his deeds. As a result of the success of these visits and with future activities in mind, I was approached to join the Ochberg Heritage Committee together with another Telfed Tiyul committee member, Rob Hyde, with both of us having been committee members since then. In order to allow Bennie a bit of time off, Hertzel Katz is currently the Acting Chairman while at the same time, Joel klotnick has been co-opted onto the committee.

Dave Kaplan visited South Africa where as he had been invited to participate in the Limmud event in Johannesburg, delivering a series of lectures of the subject of Isaac Ochberg and his heritage. This was followed by a visit to Johannesburg where he addressed groups of school pupils at both of the King David High Schools, Yeshivah College and the Torah Academy to rabbis, teachers and youngsters who had never heard of Isaac Ochberg or the Ochberg Orphans. One exception to this was at King David High School in Linksfield when Dave posed the question "who has heard of Isaac Ochberg", one hand went up. The respondent told Dave that he was a grandson of Ochberg Orphan, Solly Jossel z"l, and was well acquainted with the history, which was a rare exception. The important result of Dave Kaplan's visit is that a new generation of South African Jews have been made aware of Isaac Ochberg and his Orphans.

Dave Kaplan, who has really been busy spreading the Ochberg word also addressed a Telfed group of South African expats in Rishon L'Tzion during July 2016 and reported great enthusiasm from the audience on learning of the wonderful work by South African Isaac Ochberg. Subsequent to this, Dave Kaplan and I visited Rehovot where Dave addressed a gathering of T.E.A.M members on the subject of Isaac Ochberg, of which most of them were blissfully unaware. T.E.A.M is a group of English speakers in Rehovot who meet regularly for lectures and discussions in English. Our visit was very well received and we left happy in the knowledge that the Ochberg message was getting to a wider audience.

From the T.E.A.M gathering Dave and I visited the De Shalit High School in Rehovot where we met with the principal, Avi Kish and the head of his history department, who unsurprisingly had never heard of Isaac Ochberg. We are planning to take a group of about 50 senior students from the school on a visit to the Ochberg Memorial Park and educate them about Isaac Ochberg, the Ochberg Orphans and the Ochberg Bequest to the J.N.F. for the purchase of land in Israel.

Bennie Penzik, Hertzel Katz and Dave Kaplan visited Kibbutz Ein HaShofet, adjacent to the Memorial Park on 16 November 2016 where they met with officials from the Megiddo School and after that with officials from the Megiddo Region.

The meeting with the school was to discuss a suggestion to initiate a school's essay competition based on the Ochberg history with monetary prizes. The intention is to encourage young Israelis to do research about Isaac Ochberg and his contribution to Israel and thus enhance their knowledge of a unique individual. The Megiddo School would be the vehicle for a pilot project which, if successful, could be extended to other schools.

The meeting with the Megiddo Region, on the other hand was to discuss plans by the Ochberg Heritage Committee to expand the Memorial Park into a fully fledged Park of the Jewish People. The objective here is to encourage the various Diaspora communities to each develop a portion of the Park dedicated to their community and it's history. The purpose here is twofold in that the history of Diaspora communities will be on show and the Ochberg history, in particular, will become known to a far greater cross section of the Jewish global population. A park of this nature has every possibility of becoming a major tourist attraction in the future. A number of Diaspora communities also accepted orphans resulting from the pogroms in Eastern Europe after the First World War and it is also the intention that those orphans will also be suitably remembered in the Isaac Ochberg Memorial Park.

My thanks to David Solly Sandler for allowing me to include this report on the Ochberg Heritage Committee in this, his latest book on the Ochberg Orphans.

Peter Bailey December 2016

Chapter 67 – THE FORGOTTEN MAN REMEMBERED

THE FORGOTTEN MAN REMEMBERED
By David E Kaplan

While the black and white framed portrait of Isaac Ochberg has been hanging in Telfed's offices since 1948, too few knew who he was. And yet this philanthropist and Zionist visionary from Cape Town, performed an act in 1921 that to this day, stands as one of the proudest chapters in South African Jewish communal history only to be followed in 1936 by leaving the largest bequest to Israel through the JNF. It remains an all-time record.

While a part of the bequest went towards education - the fledging Hebrew University of Jerusalem - an equal bequest went to reclaim land to establish kibbutzim for new immigrants. Actuaries have calculated the current value of the bequest in excess of $60 million dollars. As was revealed at the launch of the KKL-JNF Isaac Ochberg Memorial Park in 2011, "no single individual from the USA, UK, Europe, South America or South Africa has to this day donated more!"

In the 1930s, before there was any certainty of there ever being a State of Israel, Ochberg had such a vision "and put his money where his mouth is," said Benny Penzik, whose parents were both saved by Ochberg in 1921. "Mom and Dad, like the other nearly 177 rescued orphans, used to refer to him as "Daddy Ochberg" for that was the only Daddy they knew. Many years later, he attended their wedding."

Like the many other thousands of Ochberg's "grandchildren" all across the globe, "We are only alive because of this one man," said Benny, the founder of the Isaac Ochberg Memorial Committee (IOMC) in Israel.

And yet the man and his achievements were largely forgotten, epitomized when the stone memorial to him at the Elyakim Junction was removed some years ago - to make way for the new highway - and later discovered lying abandoned in a local kibbutz shed!

Today that memorial stands at the Isaac Memorial Heritage Park, next to Kibbutz Ein HaShofet.

Proud to promote the community's illustrious history, the Telfed Events Committee together with Telfed's Head of Volunteers and Events, Dana Ben Chail, organized a tour to the park and to the kibbutzim in the Megiddo district of Dalya and Gal'ed, which owe their thriving existence to the vision and generosity of one man – Isaac Ochberg.

Piece of Cake!
Joining the over 60 participants was guest-of-honour, Cissy Harris of Haifa - the sole survivor of the 177 Ochberg orphans who arrived in Cape Town with "Daddy Ochberg" in 1921 and was that day, celebrating her 98th birthday. Marking the milestone, Rob Hyde of the Telfed Events Committee organized a large birthday cake for Cissy, who blew out the candles and later planted a tree at the KKL-JNF Isaac Ochberg Memorial Park. Defying her age, she kept amusingly admonishing a rightly-concerned Telfed Chairman Maish Isaacson to please "not grab me so tightly; I can't use the shovel to plant the tree!" Spunky Cissy was three-years-old when she was plucked by Isaac Ochberg, one of the youngest of all the rescued orphans.

Cissy Harris planting a tree at the KKL-JNF Isaac Ochberg Memorial Park on her 98th birthday - July 2016

Sissy Harris with Habonim friends on the Edinburgh Castle in the 1930s, the ship she arrived on in 1921 as an orphan.

"Daddy Ochberg"
In the early 1920's, reports filtered through to South Africa of dreadful pogroms taking place in the Pale of

Settlement – that area from the Baltic to the Black Sea where Jews were permitted to live. Following the collapse of the old Czarist Empire in 1917, cataclysmic forces were in play and Jews were caught in the middle between the rival armies of the Reds and the Whites fighting for control. Poor at the best of times owing to centuries of oppression, the condition of Jews deteriorated. Famine was followed by typhoid epidemics and into this lethal cocktail, the most toxic of ancient hatreds was added - *anti-Semitism.*

Polish and other peasants joined forces with reactionary officers and troops to massacre Jews wherever they found them. Pogroms were being reported daily - the full details and exact numbers of Jews killed are to this day still unknown.

It was hunting season and the number one prey were Jews!

Caught in the middle, were over 300,000 vulnerable Jewish orphans.

In despairing letters smuggled through enemy lines, Jews pleaded to the outside world - please save the children. One such letter found its way to Cape Town and with abounding energy and enthusiasm, one intrepid community leader formulated a plan – Isaac Ochberg - and volunteered himself to go alone and rescue the children.

Responding to the questions - *"How could the orphans be rescued from a war-torn region?"* and *"Would the South African government deny them entry?"* - Ochberg met with Prime Minister Jan Smuts, who granted permission, with three provisos – Children have to have no living parent, be under 16 years of age, and be 100% physically healthy.

Ochberg said yes to all the conditions – and ignored them all!

An example is the case of five-year-old Harry Stillerman whose arm was cut off below the elbow. Former Telfed director Sam Levin (z'l) used play as a little boy with Harry when his parents volunteered at the Cape Town orphanage. "I leant that when the Cossacks attacked his shtetl," Sam told *Telfed Magazine* in 2005, "they murdered his parents in front of him and when one on horseback was about to finish him off, Harry raised his arm to protect himself from the thrust of a sabre. He sliced off part of Harry's arm and left him to die."

Little Harry did not die. Ochberg, like the "Pied Piper of Hamelin' - who was crisscrossing this vast region by train, car and horse-drawn cart clutching orphans - picked up Harry, and despite Smut's stipulation, brought him to Cape Town.

For the remaining orphans, their futures looked bleak. Those that survived the pogroms, starvation and rampant decease as children, would later have perished as adults in the *Shoah*.

Apart from the fortunate orphans saved - such as Cissy and her two sisters, and the parents of Benie Penzik - there are thousands of descendants dispersed across the globe, many of whom attended the official opening of the Ochberg Memorial Park in 2011 when Maish Isaacson - on behalf of Telfed - planted the park's first tree. "I feel privileged to again be planting a tree," expressed the Chairman who was joined in planting trees by Cissy, the representative of KKL-JNF, Yacov Arak, the mayor of Megiddo, Yichak Holanski, and Foundation members, Bennie Penzik, Hertzel Katz, Leon Segal, whose mother was an Ochberg orphan, and the writer.

Illuminating Isaac

At Gal'ed, following addresses by Bennie, Amnon Lehav who presented the history of the kibbutz, and a presentation to Cissy by Leon Segal, the riveting documentary 'Ochberg's Orphans' by celebrated Oscar award winner Jon Blair was shown.

The audience saw and heard the orphans relate in horrific detail how they were literally clutched from the 'jaws of death' and brought to the safety of South Africa. With tears running down their aging cheeks, some related watching their parents being murdered and the horrendous conditions they lived in trying to survive alone. It was heart-wrenching listening to Charles Migdal's chilling recollections of trying to survive in freezing conditions with little clothing, and no food. "I lived like an animal; not a human being."
That was until Ochberg arrived!

Looking to Tomorrow

The Telfed tiyul was not only about learning about the past but embracing the future, and IOHC cofounder Hertzel Katz spoke about the Ochberg Heritage Programme of ensuring "immortality" for Ochberg by preserving his legacy through projects and activities. In this regard, before the park's 'Hill of Names'– where each orphan's name and place of origin appears on a plaque embedded into the hill – Chairman Isaacson announced that "Telfed was proud to be launching the Telfed Isaac Ochberg Scholarship to be awarded each year to a deserving student who embodies the values of this great South African."

Following on, there have been further presentations of Ochberg, notably at Beth Protea, in Rishon Lezion and Rehovot as well as meeting principals of schools to introduce the legacy of Ochberg into the educational system. "We had a fruitful meeting with Avi Kish, the principal at De Shalit School in Rehovot," says Peter, "where we met students and agreed to launch our programme with a *tiyul* of the older students to the Ochberg sites in November."

Back to Africa

Organised by Lyanne Kopenhager and Cheryl Benjamin, the writer during September-October addressed the Limmud Conference in Johannesburg on Ochberg, the general public at Sandringham Gardens, and spoke at the Jewish Day Schools – King David Schools (Linksfield and Victory Park}, Torah Academy (boys and girls),

Hirsch Lyons School (boys and girls) and a packed synagogue at Yeshiva College. All the school presentations were attended by the principals, teachers and rabbis.

The Ochberg motto taken from the Talmud that "*He who has saved one life is as though he has saved the entire world*" resonated with the school's rabbis.

When I asked at King David School Linksfield, whether anyone had heard of Isaac Ochberg, a youngster stood up and said, "Yes, I am alive because of him. He saved my great-grand father, **Solly Jossel**." His fellow students sat stunned – they realized instantly what they were about to learn was personal and existential. At the end of my address, the questions never stopped.

DaveKaplan at Torah Academy for Boys with Rabbi D. Hazdan, Dean of the School to the left.

When Rabbi Tzvi Chaimovitz at Yeshiva College asked the students at the end of the presentation "*What is the take-home message of what you have just seen and heard?*", one 16-year-old female student bellowed from the back row upstairs:

"I am impressed and distressed. While impressed, I am equally distressed that I did not know about an important chapter in our South African Jewish history? I ask, "why?"

How come our rabbis, teachers, principals, parents and community leaders do not know?"

Not waiting for a reply, she answered her own question with:
"I believe that it is our task as the young generation to teach our rabbis, our teachers, our parents, our friends and our leaders."

Rabbi **Yossi Chaikin** at Hirsh Lyons School for Boys concluded with: "Tomorrow, next week, next month, next year – go out and do a good deed. You never know - like Isaac Ochberg - when or where into the future what impact your deed will have on people's lives."

The rabbi had it right.

Due to one man, thousands of Jews - descendants of the 1921 'Ochberg Orphans' - are alive today.

One of this writer's most memorable moments was at my last presentation at the Torah Academy for Boys before leaving for the airport to return home to Israel.

Before parting, one young boy came forward and asked:

"*Would you like to hear me blow the Shofar?*"

Shofar for a Saviour. Following an Ochberg address in September 2016 by David Kaplan at the Torah Academy for Boys in Johannesburg, one young student spontaneously blew the Shofar honouring Ochberg and the children he saved. The Shofar blower was not much older than many of the children Ochberg saved in 1921.

"Off course," I said.

Listening to those ancient sounds that date back to the receiving of the Torah at Mt. Sinai, I reflected that the shofar blower was probably of the same age as many of the orphans that Ochberg had saved, nearly a century before.

I thought of Isaac Ochberg hearing those sounds from his celestial perch and smiling!

Isaac was no more forgotten.

SECTION 8
ADDENDUM

This section starts with photos of the plaques on the
Wall of Names and an Index of the Ochberg Orphans

It includes reviews of publications and documentaries
concerning Isaac Ochberg and The Ochberg Orphans

It tells about Arcadia and Oranjia where the
orphans were placed on arrival in South Africa
and the recipients of the proceeds of book sale.

This section ends with detail of the compilations
of David Solly Sandler

Chapter 68 – THE PLAQUES ON THE WALL OF NAMES AT THE ISAAC OCHBERG MEMORIAL AT RAMAT MENASHE

Below are 175 of the 177 plaques on the Wall of Names at the Ochberg site at Ramat Menashe in Israel unveiled on 20th July 2011.

Each plaque shows the original name of the of the orphan in English and Hebrew, and where and when they were born. The plaque also shows the current name.

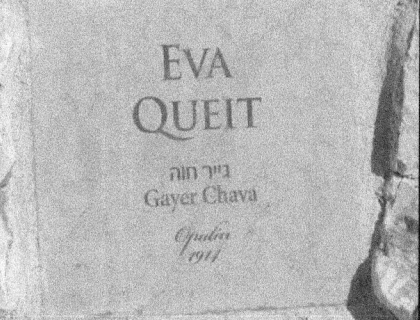

Leiba Kolodner /Singer plaque missing

Reisel Kreindel

  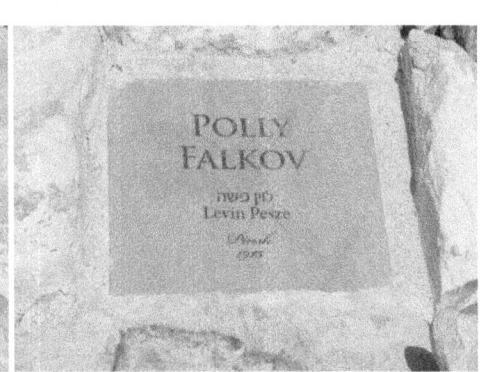

 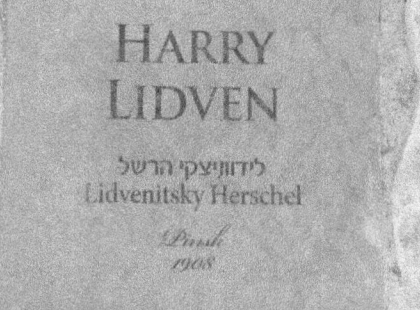 

 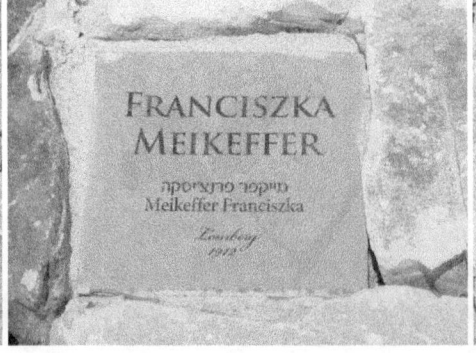 

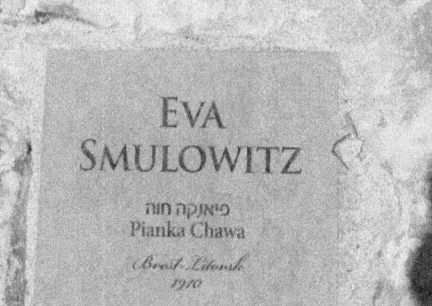

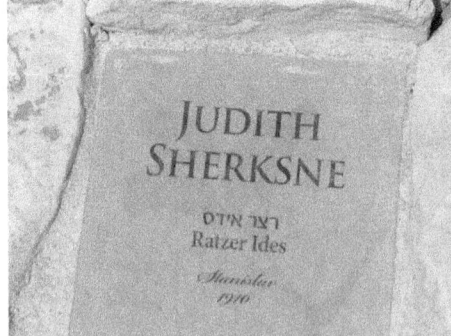
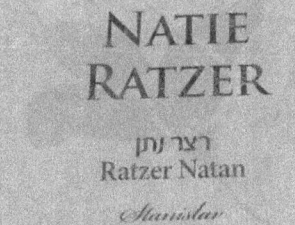

Dorah Pinsky/ Jarzin plaque missing

ABIE RICHMAN KRUGER רייכמן אברם Reichman Abram *Turow* *1910*	 **HYMIE RICHMAN ISRAELSON** רייכמן חיים Reichman Chaim *Turow* *1912*	 **RUBIN REISENDER** רייסנדר רובין Reisender Rubin *Lemberg* *1911*
 **LEYA REKLER** רקלר לאה Rekler Leya *Lemberg* *1913*	 **CHAYKEL RINZLER** רינזלר חייקל Rinzler Chaykel *Lemberg* *1913*	 **HARRY HERMAN ROTH** רוט הרמן Roth Herman *Lemberg* *1910*
 **LEON ROSENBAUM** רוזנבאום לאון Rosenbaum Leon *Lemberg* *1911*	 **GDALIA ROSENBLIT** רוזנבליט גדליה Rosenblit Gdalia *Rovno* *1912*	 **SHAMAY ROSENBLIT** רוזנבליט שמאי Rosenblit Shamay *Rovno* *1913*
 **ANN STOCK** רובין חנה Rubin Chana *Stanislav* *1913*	 **DAVID RUBIN** רובין דוד Rubin Dawid *Stanislav* *1914*	 **ARCHIE RUCH** רוכוצקי ארון Ruchocki Aron *Pinsk* *1909*
 **PHILIP RUCH** רוכוצקי פייבל Ruchocki Faiwel *Pinsk* *1911*	 **SOLLY RUCH** רוכוצקי שלום Ruchocki Sholem *Pinsk* *1913*	 **THELMA FRIEDMAN** סמורינה סימה Samurina Sima *Pinsk* *1912*

CHARLOTTE BERMAN סמורינה זלטה Samurina Zlata *Pinsk* *1909*	 **SIMON SANDAK-LEWIN** סנדק שמחה Sandak Simcha *Włodawa* *1910*	 **MOLLY COHEN** שפירא מלכה Schapira Malka *Sarny* *1913*
 **JACK SCHRIER** שרייר יעקב Schrier Jacob *Brest-Litovsk* *1908*	 **FANNY LOCKITCH** שרייר פייגה Schrier Feyga *Brest-Litovsk* *1911*	 **JOSEF SCHWARZ** שווארץ יוסף Schwarz Josef *Lvov* *1911*
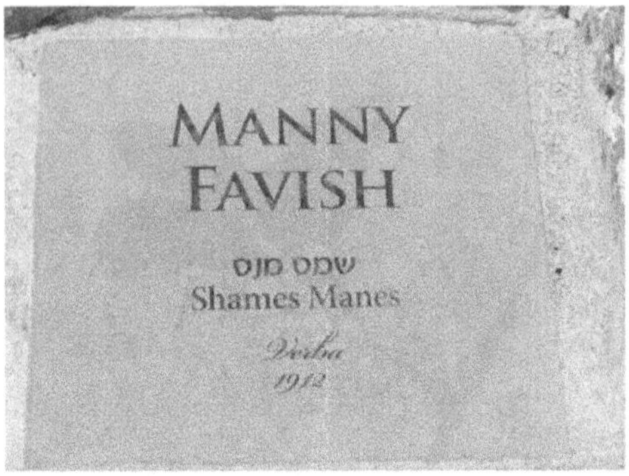 **MANNY FAVISH** שמס מנס Shames Manes *Verba* *1912*	 **ROSE MILLER** שמס רייזל Shames Reisel *Verba* *1910*	 **CHARLES STEINER** שטיינר חסקאל Shteiner Chaskel *Libshei* *1914*
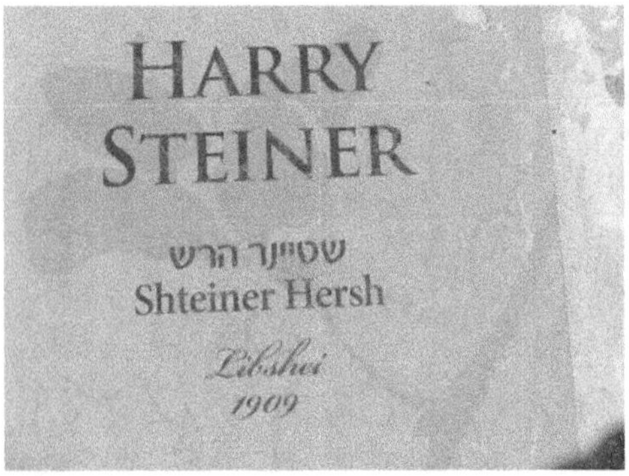 **HARRY STEINER** שטיינר הרש Shteiner Hersh *Libshei* *1909*	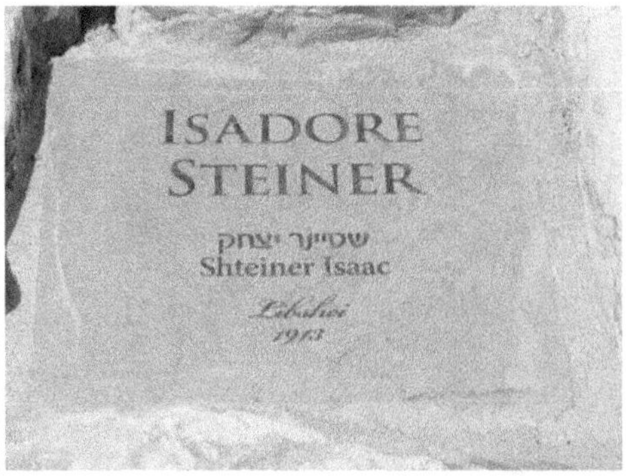 **ISADORE STEINER** שטיינר יצחק Shteiner Isaac *Libshei* *1913*	 **SOLOMON SHTERN** שטרן שלמה Shtern Solomon *Włodawa* *1912*
 **FEYGA SHTRASNER** שטרסנר פיינה Shtrasner Feyga *Stanislav* *1915*	 **POLLY JOFFE** שטנגר פפי Stanger Pepy *Otynia* *1919*	 **HARRY STILLERMAN** שטילרמן הרש Stillerman Hersh *Lemberg* *1909*

314

Above are 175 of the 177 plaques on the Wall of Names at the Ochberg site at Ramat Menashe in Israel unveiled on 20th July 2011.

Above part of the Wall of Names and below a sign at the Ochberg site at Ramat Menashe in Israel

Above part of the cycle path and below the monument to Isaac Ochberg at the Ochberg site at Ramat Menashe in Israel

חבל ארץ זה
נגאל ע"י
הקרן הקימת לישראל
לזכרו של
יצחק אוכברג
דרום אפריקה

THIS TRACT OF LAND
HAS BEEN REDEEMED BY
THE JEWISH NATIONAL FUND
IN MEMORY OF
YITZHAK OCHBERG
SOUTH AFRICA

Chapter 69 – THE INDEX OF OCHBERG ORPHANS

Birth Name			Later Name	Place Born		Born	Died	Chapters V1	V1	V2	
Altsefrum	Malka		Molly Suntup	Libov	~	1895		50			O
Altsefrum	Frieda		Freda Segal	Libov	~	1899		50			O
Altuska	Chaim		Harry Gordon	Brest-Litovsk		1914	1989	97			A
Altuska	Tasha		Tasha Rachman	Brest-Litovsk		1902	1971	96			A
Altuska	Leah		Leah Rosenblatt	Brest-Litovsk		1912	1993			32	A
Altuska	Sara		Sarah Slier	Brest-Litovsk		1910	2001			31	A
Altuska	Feiga	S		Brest-Litovsk				96		32	
Artman	Regina		Regina Weintroub	Stanislav		1914	2001	51			O
Barmatch	Sara			Brest-Litovsk	~	1909					O
Berkowitch	Chava		Eva Berkowitz	Brest-Litovsk		1912	1964	52			O
Bernfeld	Chaya		Claire Klein	Warsaw		1911	2005	30	53		O
Bernfeld	Hersh		Harry Bernfeld	Warsaw	~	1909		53			O
Bettman	Chana		Chana Schneider	Stanislav	~	1908		54			O
Bettman	Leya		Leah Marks	Stanislav	~	1902		54			O
Bettman	Sheindel		Salka Sheiham	Stanislav	~	1912		54			O
Bettman	Solomon		Solly Bettman	Stanislav	~	1913		31	54		O
Bettman	Yenta		Pearly Trapida	Stanislav	~	1915		54			O
Blind	Salka		Sadie Saus	Rawa		1910	1991	98			A
Bornshtein	Isaac		Isaac Bornstein	Brest-Litovsk	~	1909		76			O
Borowik	Chana		Annie Centner	Brest-Litovsk	~	1907	1977	99			A
Borowik	Rochela		Rachel Klein	Brest-Litovsk		1905		99			A
Borowik	Shaya		Shia Borwick Cooper	Brest-Litovsk	~	1910		99			A
Borowik	Yankel	S	Yankel Borowik	Brest-Litovsk				99			
Borowik	Alta	S	Mary Berelowitz	Brest-Litovsk				99			
Broder	Bina		Bina Stange	Stanislav		1913	1997	100			A
Broder	Sara		Sarah Levy	Stanislav	~	1915		100			A
Cwengel	Saul			Wlodawa	~	1913					O
Derlowitz	Chana		Andja Avin	Lemberg	~	1911	1984	55			O
Dreiling	Juda		Jules Fisher	Lemberg		1916	1982	101			A
Echstein	Josef		Jack Cohen	Brest-Litovsk		1915		102			A
Echstein	Toiba		Tilly Rabinowitz	Brest-Litovsk		1910		32	102		A
Echstein	Asher		Oscar Echstein	Brest-Litovsk		1913	2006	102	103		A
Echstein	Mordechai	S		Brest-Litovsk				103			
Ellman	Yankel		Joe Ellman	Brest-Litovsk		1909	1968	56			O
Ellman	Bluma		Blume Kangisher	Domatchewo	~	1916	1973	56			O
Ellman	Feyga		Fanny	Domatchewo	~	1913	1940	56			O
Ellman	Jentel		Issy Elman	Domatchewo	~	1916		56			O
Elshtein	Abo		Alf Rubel	Pinsk	~	1909		57			O
Elshtein	Shlema		Solly Rubel	Pinsk		1914		57			O
Elshtein	Leibel		Louis Rubel	Pinsk	~	1916	1988	57			O
Engelman	Jakob			Wlodawa	~	1912					A
Faifer	Liba		Lily Behrman	Slavuta	~	1910	1984	104			A
Faifer	Blume		Blume Abrahams	Slavuta	~	1911	1982	104			A
Feinschmidt	Zeidel		Sydney Jack Fine Manuel	Shershov		1909		105			A
Feldman	Mendel		Romanovsky	Shask	~	1912		58			O
Fremd	Max		Max Fremd	Lemberg	~	1911					A
Gabbe (Gaby)	Chaya		Clara Penzik	Trysk		1907	1987	61			O
Gabbe (Gaby)	Gittel		Gertie Shnaps	Trysk	~	1912		60			O
Gabbe (Gaby)	Peshe		Peggy Greenberg	Trysk		1910		59			O

Codes: S - Sibling of Ochberg Orphan, ~ approximate, V1 and V2 - Volume 1 and 2, A - Arcadia, O - Oranjia.

Birth Name		Later Name	Place Born	Born	Died	Chapters			
						V1	V1	V2	
Gayer	Moishe	Harry Friedman	Opalin		1913	1942		33	A
Gayer	Chana	Eva Queit	Opalin		1914	1981		33	A
Gayer	Sara	Sarah Gilinsky	Opalin		1909	1991		33	A
Garbus	Shmuel	Sydney Garbus	Pinsk	~	1909		106		A
Gebengolz	Rochel		Shack	~	1911				O
Gelernter	Shewa	Hilda Modlin	Brest-Litovsk		1916	2003	33	49	O
Gershenabel	Moisha	Moshe Gershbone	Brest-Litovsk	~	1909				O
Gesunterman	Braindel	Bessie Morris	Pinsk	~	1911	1982	62		O
Gesunterman	Jochevet Sheina	Jessie Sher	Pinsk	~	1913		62		O
Gesunterman	Rochel	Janie Oddes	Pinsk	~	1909		62		O
Ginsburg	Mintcha		Wlodawa	~	1913				O
Gonifas	Betzalel	Charles Gonifas	Rotne		1912	1999	107		A
Gonifas	Malka	Molly Blumberg	Rotne		1909	1939	107		A
Gonifas	Gittel	Gittel Gonifas	Rotne	~	1909		107		A
Gonifas	Leya	Leah Berkman	Rotne		1906		107		A
Gonifas	Enya	S		Rotne	~	1905			
Gornshteyn	Abram	Abram Levitt	Pinsk		1910	1999	63		O
Gornshteyn	Chana	Connie Alhadeff	Pinsk	~	1913	2002	63		O
Greenshtein	Nachman	Nathan Greenstein	Berdichev	~	1913	1989	64		O
Guber	Chaya	Annie Segal	Pnywno		1912		108		A
Guber	Tcharna	Charlotte Odes	Pnywno	~	1914		108		A
Hans	Neta	Nellie Frankal	Rawaruska	~	1912		65		O
Hans	Ruza	Rosie Flink	Rawaruska		1912	1976	65		O
Heft	Rosha	Rosie Hoffman	Domatchewo	~	1912		66		O
Helman	Aisik	Isaac Helman	Pinsk		1910	1993	109		A
Helman	Benjamin	Benjamin Helman	Pinsk		1912		110		A
Helman	Chashe	Chassia Zagey	Pinsk		1907	1983	109		A
Hurwitz	Rosa		Berdytchew	~	1911				A
Joffe	Freidl	Freda Larsen	Pinsk		1910	1995	34	111	A
Joffe	Cywje	Sylvia Chasteau	Pinsk	~	1913	1998	112		A
Kahan	Golda		Pinsk	~	1904				O
Kahan	Mordehe		Pinsk	~	1909				A
Kahan	Shachna		Pinsk	~	1911				A
Kailer/Kohler	Rywka	Becky Greenberg	Kowel		1910		67		O
Kailer/Kohler	Zippe	S	Celia Jacobson	Kowel		1915		67	
Kailer/Kohler	Moshe	S	Morris Keller Benjamin	Kowel		1913		67	
Karman	Benjamin	Radomsky	Brest-Litovsk	~	1914	1974	68		O
Kaufman	Cypora		Wlodawa	~	1912				O
Kaufman	Solomon		Wlodawa	~	1914				O
Kawerberg	Mayer		Kowel	~	1908				O
Kawerberg	Moshe		Wlodawa	~	1908				
Kigielman	Jakob		Wlodawa	~	1912				
Knuboviz	Zlata		Pinsk	~	1909				O
Kolodner	Isaac	Isaac Aronowitz	Kowel		1918		69		O
Kolodner	Lieba	Lieba Singer	Kowel		1909	1974	69		O
Kolodner	Yenta	Hetty Nick	Kowel	~	1913	1990	69		O
Kreindel	Reisel		Kowel		1912				A

Codes: S - Sibling of Ochberg Orphan, ~ approximate, V1 and V2 - Volume 1 and 2, A - Arcadia, O - Oranjia.

Birth Name		Later Name	Place Born		Born	Died	Chapters			
							V1	V1	V2	
Lerman	Dwora	Deborah Wulf	Domatchewo	~	1913	1973	70			O
Lerman	Nechama	Naomi Miller	Domatchewo		1917	1970			24	O
Levin	Chaim	Hymie Levin	Pinsk		1909	1999	113			A
Levin	Pasha	Polly Falkov	Pinsk	~	1915		113			A
Levin	Sara	Cynthia Chait	Pinsk		1913	1999	113			A
Lidvenitsky	Herschel	Harry Lidven	Pinsk		1908	1957			34	A
Lila	Rosa	Rosa Braude	Lemberg		1913	1956			35	A
Lipshitz	Moishe		Wlodawa	~	1912		114			A
Lipshitz	Perel		Wlodawa	~	1910		114			A
Mandelblatt	Pesha	Polly Kapelus	Domatchewo	~	1911	1990	71			O
Margolin	Sara		Pinsk	~	1911					
Meikeffer	Franciszka		Lemberg	~	1912					
Menkes	Debora	Dorothy Weiner	Lemberg		1914	1999				A
Migdalowicz	Chonon	Charles Migdal	Pinsk		1908	2001	35	72		O
Migdalowicz	Nachman	Norman Migdale	Pinsk	~	1986	1986	72			O
Migdalowicz	Simon	Simon Migdale	Pinsk	~	1913	1977	72			O
Miler	Braindel		Kowel	~	1913					O
Mordochowitch	Gutro		Stanislav	~	1913					
Mordochowitch	Estel		Stanislav	~	1915					
Mussman	Isaac	Jack Musman	Kostopol	~	1912		115			A
Mussman	Reisel	Ray Levin	Kostopol		1916	1995	115			A
Neishtein	Sala	Celia Rakoff	Levov	~	1914		73			O
Nemet	Beila	Judith Smith	Kyntchyn		1915				36	A
Neustein	Solomon	Solly Jossel	Drohobycz		1914	V1 16	36	116		A
Ochshtein	Salomon		Pinsk	~	1912					
Orliansky	Abram		Brest-Litovsk	~	1909					O
Penzik	Mindel	Minnie Davidow	Kupichow		1905	1956	117		38	A
Penzik	David	David Penzik	Kupichow		1908	1992	118		37	A
Penzik	Chana	Hannah Sandler	Kupichow		1911		119			A
Penzik	Chaya	Helen Green	Kupichow		1916	1990	120		39	A
Perechodnik	Szepsel	Samson Perch	Pinsk		1910	1974	74			O
Perechodnik	Yser	Oscar Perch	Pinsk	~	1907	~1970	74			O
Pianka	Chawa	Eva Smulowitz	Brest-Litovsk		1910	1983	75			O
Pinsky	Faywel	Philip Pinsky	Pinsk	~	1913		121			A
Pinsky	Feyga	Birdie Glaser	Pinsk		1916		121			A
Pinsky	Maisha	Morris Pinsky	Pinsk		1909	1979	121			A
Pinsky	Zlata	Zlata Dembo	Pinsk	~	1912		121			A
Pinsky	Dvora	S	Dora Jarzin	Pinsk						
Ratzer	Ides	Judith Sherksne	Stanislav		1910	1965			40	A
Ratzer	Natan	Natie Ratzer	Stanislav		1914				40	A
Ratzer	Perel	Phyllis Ratzer	Stanislav		1908	2002			40	A
Razu	Chaim	Chaim Rosier	Wlodawa	~	1912		78		25	O
Razu	Isaac	Itzik Rosier	Wlodawa	~	1913	1941	77			O
Razu	Yetta	Yetta Bornstein	Wlodawa	~	1911		76			O
Reichman	Abram	Abie Richman Kruger	Turow	~	1910				41	A

Codes: S - Sibling of Ochberg Orphan, ~ approximate, V1 and V2 - Volume 1 and 2, A - Arcadia, O - Oranjia.

Birth Name		Later Name	Place Born	Born	Died	Chapters V1	V1	V2	
Reichman	Chaim	Hymie Richman Israelson	Turow	~1912				41	A
Reisender	Rubin		Lemberg	~1911				42	A
Rekler,	Leya		Lemberg	~1915					A
Rinzler	Chaykel		Lemberg	~1913					A
Roht	Herman	Harry Herman Roth	Lemberg	1910	1952			45	A
Rosenbaum	Leon	Leon Rosenbaum	Lemberg	~1914					A
Rosenblit	Gdalia		Rovno	~1912				43	A
Rosenblit	Shamay		Rovno	~1913				44	A
Rubin	Chana	Ann Stock	Lemberg	1915	~1994	122			A
Rubin	Dawid	David Rubin	Lemberg	~1914	~1953	122			A
Ruchocki	Aron	Archie Ruch	Pinsk	1909	1976	79			O
Ruchocki	Faiwel	Philip Ruch	Pinsk	1911	2003	79			O
Ruchocki	Sholem	Solly Ruch	Pinsk	1913	1929	79			O
Samurina	Sima	Thelma Friedman	Pinsk	1912	1998	81			O
Samurina	Zlata	Charlotte Berman	Pinsk	~1909		80			O
Sandak-Lewin	Simcha	Simon Sandak-Lewin	Wlodawa	1910		82			O
Schapira	Malka	Molly Cohen	Sarny	1913		37	48	26	O
Schrier	Jacob	Jack Schrier	Brest-Litovsk	1908	1984				O
Schrier	Feyga	Fanny Lockitch	Brest-Litovsk	1911	2005	38	83		O
Schwarz	Josef		Lvov	~1911					A
Shamis	Manes	Manny Favish	Verba	1912	1994	123			A
Shamis	Reisel	Rose Miller	Verba	1910	1992	124			A
Shteiner	Chaskel	Charles Steiner	Libshei	1914	1959	125		46	A
Shteiner	Hersh	Harry Steiner	Libshei	1909	1999	125		46	A
Shteiner	Isaac	Isadore Steiner	Libshei	1913	~1994	125		46	A
Shtern	Solomon	Solomon Shtern	Wlodawa	~1912				27	O
Shtrasner	Feyga		Stanislav	~1915				28	O
Stanger	Pese	Polly Joffee	Lemberg	~1912	1981	126			A
Stillerman	Hersh	Harry Stillerman	Lemberg	~1909					O
Tannenbaum	Chaya	Clara Steiman	Wlodawa	1905	1988	127			A
Tannenbaum	Sara	Sally Egnal	Wlodawa	1910	1996	127			A
Treppel	Jacob	Jacob Trappel	Lemberg	~1913					A
Wachtel	Sara	Sara Glaser	Stanislav	~1912		84			O
Weidman	Sheindel		Stanislav	~1914					O
Wolchuk	Chayim	Hymie Wolchuk	Pnywno	1916	1996	128			A
Wolchuk	Feiga	Phyllis Braude	Pnywno	1915		128			A
Wolchuk	Leibel	Les Wolchuk	Pnywno	1912	2006	128			A
Wolchuk	Toyba	Tilly Karlin	Pnywno	1912	~2000	128			A
Yagolkowsky	Yakov	Jack Yagalkovsky	Brest-Litovsk	1909	1956	84		29	O
Zaika	Manya	Manya Adler	Kostopol	1911	V1-39	40	129		A
Zaika	Lysel	Cissy Harris	Kostopol	~1915		39			A
Zaika	Leya	Lisa Abend	Kostopol	~1903	~1905	39			A
Zwirin	Berner	Barry Beira	Stanislav	~1915		130			A
Zwirin	Osiach	Issy Beira	Stanislav	~1916	1991	130			A

Codes: S - Sibling of Ochberg Orphan, ~ approximate, V1 and V2 - Volume 1 and 2, A - Arcadia, O - Oranjia.

REVIEWS OF BOOKS AND DOCUMENTARIES
Chapter 70 – "THE MAN FROM AFRICA"

"THE MAN FROM AFRICA"
By David E. Kaplan

Our knowledge of history is often lazily shaped by Oscar winning movies. How many people gained their understanding of Jewish life under the Romans, fashioned by the 1960s blockbuster 'Ben Hur', or the rebirth of modern Israel by Otto Preminger's 'Exodus'? Both won *big time* at the academy awards.

And, as for the movies that don't quite cut it at the academy awards - Have as a result significant chunks of the past been relegated to the abyss of the unknown?

Such may be the case of a recent documentary by film director John Blair who had previously won the coveted statuesque for his 1995 Best Documentary Feature, 'Anna Frank Remembered'.

Ochberg's Orphans, the Documentary

His recent entry, 'The Ochberg Orphans' dealing with the rescue of Jewish children in 1921 from the war-torn Pale of Settlement and their resettlement in South Africa, failed to make the final five nominees at this year's academy award ceremony. Far more despairing than the disappointment for the film's director is that an inspiring chapter of Jewish history may now never reach a wider audience.

An aside to this little-known story is that the documentary also brought a ninety-year old former South African in Haifa out of obscurity.

Prior to making the documentary, The Jerusalem Post in 2005, carried an appeal from the film director in London for information about the South African philanthropist, Isaac Ochberg, who helped finance and personally participated in the rescue. Metro contacted Sam Levin, a former Director of the South African Zionist Federation in Israel (Telfed) who in the 1920's, had been a youngster in Cape Town. Sam recalled meeting some of the rescued children at the Cape Town Jewish Orphanage, where his parents had been active volunteers. "One particular boy I will never forget," said Sam. "His arm was cut off below the elbow. The Cossacks had murdered his parents in front of him and when they were about to finish him off, he raised his arm to protect himself from the thrust of the sword. They sliced off his arm and left him to die."

In an article that appeared at the time, Sam surmised that it was unlikely that there were any Ochberg orphans alive today, particularly in Israel. So you can imagine the surprise when this writer received a phone call from a Cecilia Harris from Haifa who in a wavering voice revealed:
"I was an Oghberg orphan."

A few months later, Cecilia was on a flight to London, where she joined the film crew en route to Eastern Europe where she stared in the documentary. Today, on a wall in her small Haifa apartment hangs a giant size poster of the movie.

THE GENESIS

In the early 1920s reports filtered through to South Africa of dreadful pogroms taking place in the Ukraine. Cataclysmic forces were in play and unsurprisingly, Jews were caught in the middle. Following the collapse of the old Czarist Empire in 1917, rival armies – the Reds and the Whites were fighting for control. Poor at the best of times owing to centuries of oppression, the condition of Jews deteriorated. Famine was followed by epidemics of typhoid and other deceases and into this amalgam of chaotic forces, the most toxic of ancient antagonism exploded to the surface - *anti-Semitism*. Polish and other peasants joined forces with reactionary officers and troops to massacre Jews wherever they found them. Pogroms were being reported daily - the full details and exact numbers of Jews killed are to this day still unknown. The Pale of Settlement became an open hunting season for Jews.

In despairing letters smuggled through enemy lines, Jews pleaded to their kinsman in South Africa and elsewhere in the world for immediate help. These pleas galvanized the Jewish communities in South Africa like nothing before. "*Why not try and mount a rescue operation and bring at least some of the children out,*" people asked at meetings across the country. Overnight an idea took shape, spreading like wildfire. Before any organization could step in, generous offers were made of financial and other help. With abounding energy and enthusiasm, Cape Town businessman Isaac Ochberg embraced the plan.

Two further questions arose: How could the orphans be rescued from a war-torn region, and would the South

African government create any difficulties in admitting them? Ochberg quickly met with Prime Minister Jan Smuts, who granted permission.

As continuous reports of the plight of Jews leaked out, the dimension of the tragedy became clearer. No fewer than 400,000 Jewish orphans were known to be destitute, so that whatever was done would only amount to a drop in the ocean. That did not deter the community who were determined to save whomever they could.

The next step was for someone to travel to Eastern Europe and make arrangements on the spot. Without hesitation Ochberg offered to undertake this hazardous mission. Fanny Frier, who would later become Chairlady of the Cape Jewish Orphanage, recalled as an orphan in Brest-Litovsk, waiting for the "*Man from Africa*" to come. In anticipation of his arrival, that is how the awaiting children referred to Ochberg. "He was going to take some of us away with him and give us a new home on the other side of the world." Understandably the youngsters had mixed feelings. While they were excited of "going to a beautiful new country, we also heard stories of robbers and wild animals and we feared we might be eaten by lions or cannibals or sold to the natives as slaves. However, when he appeared with his reddish hair and cheery smile, we all took a great liking to him and called him "Daddy". He would spend hours talking to us, making jokes and cheering us up."

The most traumatic problem facing Ochberg was how to select who to take and who to leave. In the end he decided to choose eight children from each institution making a total of 200, although only 177 made the final journey to South Africa. Since the South African government had stipulated that the children had to be of good physical and mental health, this required very careful selection. Only full orphans, i.e. those that had lost both parents were accepted. Cecilia Harris from Haifa, who was three years old at the time, was selected together with her two older sisters. As no photographs survived, she has no knowledge of what her parents ever looked like. She does remember being sick on the ship to South Africa – the Edinburgh Castle - and her sister Lisa having to look after her.

Another contributor to the documentary was Liebe Klug from Cambridge, who spends part of the year in Beersheba, where her husband Aaron - a 1982 Nobel Laureate for chemistry - is on the Board of Governors at Ben Gurion University of the Negev. Her father, Alexander Bobrow, was a key player in the drama that unfolded. "He had been an analytical chemist in a sugar factory," Liebe told Metro. Changing professions to social work during the Great War "he joined the Curatorium, which had been formed to help Jewish refugees in Pinsk. At 26 years of age he accompanied the 177 rescued orphans on the ship to Cape Town, where he settled and met my mother."

In recorded testimony before he died, Bobrow relates that "so many children were found that we set up three orphanages. At first Pinsk was so isolated by the fighting that we were dependent solely on our own resources. We had neither beds, bedding nor clothes and I recall using flower bags to make clothes for the children." Typhus broke out in one of the orphanages and in the course of his duties Bobrow relates how he had to walk through the streets as shells were exploding. Balachou, the notorious Ukrainian had descended on the city with his gangs and the pogroms raged for nearly a week. Bobrow recalled how an old lady tried to pacify the terror-stricken children by calling out: "The Almighty will keep us and save us – Now repeat after me." As order was restored, supplies began to arrive, mainly from the Joint Distribution Committee. One of the American relief workers Bobrow recalled meeting was "Henry Morgenthau, who would later become Secretary of the Treasury under President Franklin Roosevelt."

Like the Pied Piper of Hamlin, Ochberg moved from town to town, including Minsk, Pinsk, Stanislav, Lodz, Lemberg and Wlodowa collecting orphans. Three months later, with the 177 children in London, he wrote to the leadership in South Africa who were eagerly waiting for news.

"I have been through almost every village in the Polish Ukraine and Galacia and am now well acquainted with the places where there is at present extreme suffering. I have succeeded in collecting the necessary number of children, and I can safely say that the generosity displayed by South African Jewry in making this mission possible means nothing less than saving their lives. They would surely have died of starvation, disease, or been lost to our nation for other reasons. I am now in London with the object of arranging transport and I hope to be able to advise telegraphically soon of my departure for South Africa with the children."

"Never to my dying day, shall I ever forget our first sight of the lights of Cape Town and then the tremendous reception when we came ashore with half the city apparently waiting on the quay for us," Fanny Frier recorded. So large was the group of children that the Cape Jewish Orphanage was unable to house them all and a considerable number went to Johannesburg, including Cecilia and her two sisters, as well as many others whose children today live in Israel. One was Phyllis Ratzer whose daughter, Rene Simpson lives in Tel Aviv. "She often spoke of "Papa Ochberg" and died in Johannesburg at the age of 94." Another descendent of an Ochberg orphan is Yvette Shiloh of Haifa, whose mother, Andja Avin was rescued in Warsaw and came on aliya in 1960 settling initially on kibbutz Kfar Blum before moving to Kiryat Gat.

When Ochberg died in Cape Town, "he left what was then the largest single bequest to the Keren Kayemet LeYisrael," Sam Levin told Metro. "They used it to redeem a piece of land in Israel called Nachalat Yitzchak Ochberg – which included the kibbutzim Dalia and Ein Hashofet. In the course of years, the name Ochberg dropped off the signs and is now known as Nachalat Yitzchak. I am certain there is hardly anyone in Israel today who would know which Yitchak it was."

Chapter 71 – "THE OCHBERG ORPHANS AND THE HORRORS FROM WHENCE THEY CAME" REVIEWED BY LIONEL SLIER.

Book review of "The Ochberg Orphans and the horrors from whence they came" compiled by David Solly Sandler.   *Review by Lionel Slier*

2011 could be called "The Year of Isaac Ochberg." Isaac who? was what many people would have asked previously. The South African Jewish Report called him: "South Africa's long lost philanthropist."

Isaac Ochberg was born in the Ukraine in 1878 and followed his father to Cape Town as a 16 year old youth (1894). He became a successful entrepreneur and business man, involved in ship buying, ships' salvage, property, fashion shops and, in fact, built the first cinema in Cape Town. He became very wealthy and was also a philanthropist of note. He was the President of Cape Town's Jewish orphanage. (1).

The First World War (1914-18) was fought on many fronts but it was on the Eastern Front where the German and the Russian armies confronted each other, on territory that was part of the Pale of Settlement (2) Eastern Poland, Belarus, and Ukraine mainly; that caused devastation, destruction and death to the Jewish communities living there. How many died is not recorded. The fortress border city of Brest Litovsk (3) changed hands four times as the armies advanced and retreated.

When the war ended in 1918 the suffering of civilians did not. A 'flu epidemic is believed to have killed as many people again as had died in the fighting. Inevitably among the worst affected were the children. The American Jewish Joint Distribution Committee estimated that almost half a million Jewish children were left as orphans – wretched, homeless, verminous, hungry, helpless and dying, Something had to be done to help these children!

In Cape Town Isaac Ochberg was approached and he readily agreed to help. He approached the South African Prime Minister, J.C. Smuts with a proposal to bring children to this country, hoping that the local Jewish communities would adopt them. Smuts agreed but imposed conditions. The Jews here were to bear the entire cost of the operation, only orphans were to be brought, no families were to be broken up, no physically or mentally disabled children were to be taken and no child over sixteen years of age could be brought out. Ochberg accepted and the number of children as fixed at 200.

In March 1921 Ochberg set out for Eastern Europe. In London, a visa was arranged for him by Fridjon Nansen, the Polar explorer who had been involved in food relief for Russia. Russia, itself, was in chaos – the Communist revolution had taken place, followed by a civil war; hunger and disease were rife. Undeterred, Ochberg, accompanied by a British Jew, David Dainow, went to Warsaw, then on to Belarus and the Ukraine, travelling by any means he could find including a donkey cart. He visited orphanages and shuls collecting children. He ignored Smut's conditions in many cases but collected 235 children (4) and brought them to England on the S.S. Baltara. After a three week stay at the 'Shelter for Jewish Poor' in London's East End, because Ochberg took ill, he left with 187 children on the Edinburgh Castle. (5). They arrived in Cape Town on the 21st September 1921. 100 children went to the Cape Town orphanage and 87 were sent to Johannesburg, where, after some problems about accommodating them, the Jewish Board of Deputies bought 'Arcadia' in Parktown from Lionel Phillips, a wealthy Randlord.(6). The Jewish Orphanage, at that time, was in Benbow Street, Kensington, and the children there were brought to Arcadia where they lived with 'The Russians'.

Now to David Solly Sandler who by collating stories and memories from Ochberg descendants compiled this book. He had already produced two earlier books about Arcadia. Sandler was born in Johannesburg in 1952 and spent 1954 to 1969 at Arcadia. After matric, he did his National Service and then qualified as a Chartered Accountant in 1976. In 1981 he immigrated to Perth, Western Australia where he retired in 2007. As Sandler writes in the foreword of this book, "The approach of the centenary of Arcadia (2006), (7) (100 Years of Arc Memories) prompted the first book., which was published in May 2006, to celebrate the centenary, and a completed a journey of over six years and a labour of love though some call it a *meshugas*. In those years I was privileged to meet with, and get to know many Arc brothers and sisters spanning many generations across the world. Over the next two years I continued to collect more Arc Memories and at the end of 2008 'More Arc Memories' was published.

 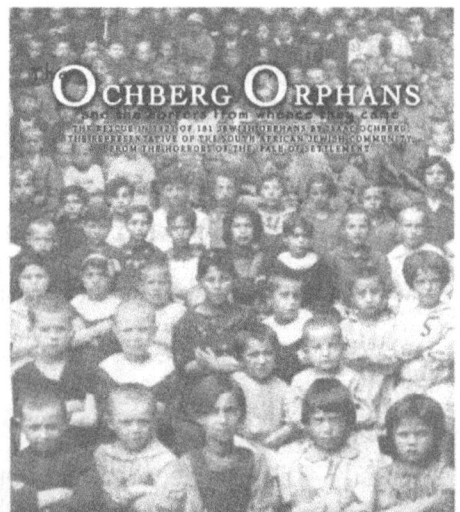

"It was only towards the completion of 'More Arc Memories' that I started to receive, via the Jewish grapevine, the life stories of Ochberg Orphans and I realized that we needed a third volume to properly record their story." (17 chapters of the second book contain stories of the Ochberg children). "And so now, after a further two years of collecting memories, I am happy to present this third volume, 'The Ochberg 'Orphans'. Subtitled 'and the horrors from whence they came.' The book is divided into three parts and eleven sections. The first part is about the Pale of Settlement and the horrors that took place there – the war, the pogroms in the Ukraine, the starvation and the death of children's parents. There is horror piled upon horror, with what "The Hebrew Standard, July 28 1922" newspaper called 'The Ukraine Gehenna.' There is some relief in the next section, which tells about the help given by Jewish communities, including 'The South African War Victims Fund.'

Section 3 is devoted to the Pinsk Orphanages and the outrages that occurred there. A sainted man is written about; he is Alter Bobrow who involved himself in looking after the children as best he could. Bobrow came to South Africa and spent time assisting at the Cape Jewish Orphanage. There is an excellent chapter about him written by Liebe Klug. David Solly Sandler has a work in progress about the three Pinsk Orphanages and inevitably Alter Bobrow will feature in the story.

Sections 4 and 5 relate some stories of Ochberg in Eastern Europe, including photos and documents, together with an extremely moving story of Feiga Mirel Shamis and her struggle written in Yiddish and later sent to her son Mannie Favish and her daughter, Rose Miller (who were both brought out by Ochberg). Mannie had the book translated into English and it fills 15 pages of this book. It is the story of the struggle to survive typical of the Jews of that place and that era.

Part 2 is about Orangia- the Cape Jewish Orphanage with 37 stories about Ochberg orphans who went there – all riveting, all similar but all with differences.

Part 3 moves to Johannesburg with a history of the Jewish Orphanage there, and the relocation to Arcadia, the stories of 35 Ochberg children, all different, all sad yet many inspiring and all gripping.

Sandler has written, "This book is about the suffering of the Jews in the Pale and the help given to these desperate people in their time of need by their brethren, the Jewish Communities around the world"

South Africa was not found wanting and in Isaac Ochberg they had a man who did not hesitate to go and give assistance. In the annals of the narrative of the Jews of South Africa this is a story that the local Community can justly be proud of. This book is a social history about some of the Jews who escaped from the horrors of their existence in Eastern Europe and who were given a new life in South Africa. All their stories are important and David Solly Sandler has collected and saved them for us. Lauren Snitcher of Cape Town, herself a grand-daughter of an Ochberg Orphan, has a database of descendants and it has currently over 3000 names who owe their lives to one man who was brave enough to go to war-ravaged Eastern Europe and bring 187 children to a new life. And of those left behind? Twelve years later, in 1933, Adolf Hitler was Chancellor of Germany!

Isaac Ochberg will now never be forgotten, and David has, with this book, presented us with a memorial to him. Besides the narratives, there are many documents reproduced as well as a great number of photographs. (8) Remember this, "No one stands so erect than when they stoop to help a child."

Footnotes.
1. The Cape Jewish Orphanage became known as "Orangia."
2. The Pale of Settlement stretched from the Baltic Sea in the north to the Black Sea in the south, through Latvia, Lithuania, Belarus, parts of eastern Poland, and western Russia, Ukraine and Bessarabia. It was established in 1772 by the Czarina, Catherine, and it was in effect a gigantic ghetto to which the Jews were restricted. A Russian census in 1897 reported 5 million Jews living in The Pale. 'Pale' is an English translation of the old Russian word 'Cheta' meaning 'an enclosed area'
3. Brest-Litovsk is in Belarus and now known simply as Brest. The Litovsk indicated that many people came originally from Litau (Lithuania). It is famous for the enormous fortress on the River Bug by the border with Poland. At the Treaty of Brest-Litovsk in February 1918, Russia (now after the Communist revolution) withdrew from the war against Germany. Leon Trotsky led the Russian delegation. By the Treaty Russia gave up a huge swath of land including eastern Poland, Baltic territories, Ukraine and Finland. At the Versailles Treaty after the war, the Ukraine and Finland sections were annulled.
4. There is some confusion about the actual number of children rescued. Ochberg wrote that he took 235 children to Warsaw originally but 37 refused to leave with him.
5. Then in London 13 children refused to go to Africa 'to be eaten by lions'. The number of children reaching South Africa is given as 187 or 181.
The confusion is caused by children's names being written in Yiddish or Russian or Polish as well as the uncertainty of their ages.
6. The original Villa Arcadia was bought by Lionel and Flo Phillips in 1909 and rebuilt by the famed British architect, Herbert Baker. When the Phillips moved into Arcadia the suburb of Parktown became fashionable for the wealthy of Johannesburg to come to live. There is some confusion about the amount paid for the building; some figures are 25,000 pounds sterling, others are 30,000.
7. Book 1.-the 2006 Centenary Book celebrating the Johannesburg Jewish Orphanage is not the centenary of Arcadia but of the first Orphanage started by the Johannesburg Jewish Ladies' Communal League in which was started in 1906 in Pretoria Street, Hillbrow. Arcadia, of course, became a Jewish children's home in 1923.
8. Such was Ochberg's foresight and confidence that he left money for a 50th anniversary reunion to be held in Cape Town. Any ex-Orphan who could be contacted was sent money from Ochberg's estate to come to Cape Town. The event duly took place in 1971.

Chapter 72 – THIS WAS A MAN - THE LIFE STORY OF ISAAC OCHBERG

THIS WAS A MAN
A message from Benny Penzik.

This message will hopefully reach all of us who owe their very existence to Isaac Ochberg z"l.
"Daddy Ochberg" was the 'father' of OUR forebears. He was, therefore, OUR grandfather!

Had YOU been granted the unique opportunity to read YOUR grandfather's biography... would YOU??

THE LIFE STORY OF ISAAC OCHBERG 1878-1937
A 2014 reprint of the original book by Bertha Epstein, (published 1974) by kind permission of the biological Ochberg family.

There are two major events indelibly engraved in our collective memories - the rescue of the Ochberg Orphans from the perils of Eastern Europe in 1921, affording them new lives in South Africa, and the mammoth bequest to the JNF which established a record that stands to this very day.

But the story of Isaac Ochberg reveals very much more than this.

Editing the script according to the wishes of the Ochberg Family and composing the addendum together with my good friend, acclaimed compiler and champion of the Ochberg legacy and 'partner' in this venture, David Solly Sandler, presented me with the opportunity to reread every word and to be inspired once again by the virtues of the man known to us as 'Daddy Ochberg'.

The author, Bertha Epstein, was Isaac's daughter so she would have been forgiven should she have embellished some aspects of her father's life. However, this is not the case. When she writes of his generosity, his character is reflected in the chapter listing his bequests. Proof indeed. Just some of the recipients of his generosity - local Jewish charities, the Hebrew University in Jerusalem, the Jewish poor of Cape Town, recreation facilities for Cape Coloured children, dowries and wedding gifts for poor Jewish girls, the Salvation Army, Old Aged Homes, Hospitals, Hebrew schools and Zionist causes.

When she describes his business acumen, the chapters dealing with his derelict ship exploits, ventures into scrap metal, cinemas, elegant stores, brickfields, astute investments - among which was the manufacture of British army uniforms in WW1 - bear eloquent testimony to his foresight.

A lesser known story is that of HMS *Penelope*, a British battleship which lay stranded for many years close to the beach near Simonstown. Isaac bought the ship, a move which brought some amusement to the locals, intending to sell it as scrap but, after a lengthy series of exploits well documented in the book, sold it in Genoa and realised a handsome profit. "He spoke of this incident as one of his best achievements".

The tragic events of his personal life - his father was killed in a railway accident, his mother stricken by a most virulent cancer, two children died young, two afflicted by an incurable disability, and his darling youngest daughter Ruth died suddenly, shortly after her 17th birthday.

The heartwarming account of the 1971 Golden Jubilee describing the overwhelming emotional event which enabled almost all the original orphans to renew acquaintance ends with this comment by the author - *"For me too, it had been a most momentous occasion. Honour had been paid where honour was due, with love and affection, in the living presence of my Father's greatest humanitarian achievement. This had indeed been a Golden Jubilee to remember; the reunion of Isaac Ochberg and his beloved pogrom orphan children. God bless them all."*

In addressing you, my fellow descendants, I am acutely aware that I am preaching to the converted when I state that most of us have a sparse record of our family history pre-1921. After all, our forebears were orphans. I know how much I would value a manuscript detailing the life and times of my biological antecedents - perhaps a forlorn wish. Possession of this book changes all that. I suggest that it warrants pride of place to grace the bookshelf of every family with an Ochberg connection.

If not for the fortitude of this one great man, we descendants would not exist. In the spirit of his legacy, proceeds of sales will be directed to Arcadia and Oranjia Jewish Children's Homes in Johannesburg and Cape Town and the American Joint Distribution Committee (The Joint).

THIS WAS A MAN
BERTHA I EPSTEIN

THIS WAS A MAN - the front cover
Contact David Solly Sandler - sedsand@iinet.net.au

Chapter 73 – THE NIGHT OF THE BURNING

"THE NIGHT OF THE BURNING"
A book written by Linda Press Wulf.
The book is historical fiction (not biography) about the childhood of Debby (Lerman) Wulf, an Ochberg Orphan.

Published by Bloomsbury in the UK in 2007 and 2008, and by Farrar Straus Giroux in the United States in 2006 (can be ordered through any bookstore in South Africa, Australia and the UK. In the USA, used copies are available on Amazon. Also narrated by author on Audible Books.)

The book is historical fiction, based on the meagre bones of fact that my husband was told about his late mother's childhood. That is, early in the twentieth century, young Dwora Lerman (later Dora or Debbie Wulf) and her even younger sister, Nechama (later Naomi Miller) were left alone after a pogrom in their village of Domachevo in Poland. Their aunt died shielding them from a Cossack. Some time later, in 1921, they were selected for rescue by an unusual visitor - a South African philanthropist called Isaac Ochberg.

When the sisters reached the safety of South Africa, they were placed in the Cape Town Jewish orphanage. In a new and perhaps avoidable tragedy, within a year they were adopted into two separate – and rather different — families, and their subsequent emotional relationship became very complicated.

Summary of Awards and Reviews

Awards

Selected for the New York Public Library's "100 Titles for Reading and Sharing, 2006"
Selected by the Forward's reviewer (USA) for "Best Children's Books of 2006"
Listed by the Financial Times (UK) as one of the (seven) teen books of 2008
A Sydney Taylor Book Award Honour Book
A Sydney Taylor Manuscript Award

Reviews

"Devorah's narration alternates between flashbacks to life in the sisters' Polish village of Domachevo and their later experiences as orphans, and both tales are equally touching and engrossing; her observations of the way black South Africans are accorded underclass status within their own country leads to provocative comparisons with her own sudden class reversal as a member of a relatively privileged white community." - *Bulletin of the Center for Children's Books*

"With bittersweet overtones, it reminds the reader of human savagery yet also shows the caring strength of one man and the power of sisterly ties." - selected and reviewed by Lesley Agnew, leading independent bookseller, for "Teenage Previews for March-June," *The Bookseller*, U.K.

"Linda Press Wulf displays great skill in her poignant handling of one of the darkest periods of 20th century history. The two sisters at the heart of her story are drawn with remarkable sympathy and understanding . A very impressive achievement, one which succeeds in conveying to young readers some notion of the depths of evil to which humanity can sink, but at the same time demonstrating to them the strengths of resilience, tolerance and love."

Chapter 74 – MY DEAR CHILDREN
THE UNTOLD STORY OF THE POGROMS

MY DEAR CHILDREN:
The Untold Story of the Pogroms
Article written by LeeAnn Dance, LeeAnn Dance the Co-Producer/Director and writer of the documentary that is in progress. She expects it to be completed by the summer of 2017.

In March 1917, revolutionaries and mutinous Russian Army forces overthrew the government of Tsar Nicholas II. The Russian Empire was over, and Jews rejoiced. Many thought it would be the beginning of a new era of freedom for minorities who had lived under decades of repression and officially sanctioned discrimination. Instead, Civil War erupted, and Jews became victims of a four-year wave of violence unlike the Jewish world had ever seen before. According to Natan Meir, co-editor of *Anti-Jewish Violence: Rethinking the Pogrom in East European History*, "It was the Holocaust of its day."

In 2012, Steve Nathan, an Ochberg Orphan descendant (Rose Miller) and friend, brought me a slim little book entitled *Shalom, Shalom My Dear Children*. It was a letter written by his great grandmother Feiga Shamis to the two children she gave up for adoption – two of the 177 Ochberg orphans. Feiga's letter was an attempt to explain why she had given them up. It was also a window into the little known humanitarian tragedy known as the Russian Civil War pogroms.

As a journalist and documentary filmmaker, I felt in my gut that Feiga's story deserved a wider audience. It was fascinating, but it was also confusing. What was all this violence she was writing about, and why had I never heard about it before? So I set it aside until I had time to dig. A year later, Steve called to say his cousin, Judy Favish (daughter of Ochberg orphan Mannie Favish) was about to embark on a trip to Ukraine to trace Feiga's story. Did I want to go along? It was the beginning of what has become a four-year passion project to ensure the world hears – and doesn't forget – what happened to hundreds of thousands of Jewish families 100 years ago – a tragedy that was the beginning of the end of a once vibrant Jewish life in Eastern Europe. It is a history shared by all the Ochberg orphans and their descendants. And it is only because of Isaac Ochberg that we are able to share this history throughout film *My Dear Children*.

Before leaving for Ukraine, I needed to better understand the history – the background to Feiga's narrative. Phone call after phone call led me to Holocaust scholars, all of whom said they knew little about this post-WWI period. Finally one directed me to Irina Astashkevich, a Brandeis scholar who had been studying this period for the past decade and who had written her dissertation on the Civil War pogroms. Jackpot.

Over the past several years, I have turned to Astashkevich repeatedly. The group of pogrom scholars

Judy Favish and her daughter Tess Peacock stand outside the building in Warsaw, Poland that once was the home to the Ochberg orphans before leaving Eastern Europe for London.

on whom we have relied has gradually grown, but it remains relatively small. For years, this history had been understudied. Many of the records had been hidden away in Soviet archives. Then the Holocaust overshadowed the tragedy that preceded it. Only when the Iron Curtain fell, and Russia opened its archives, did groundbreaking scholars begin to fill in this historical gap. Yet, many of the documents remain inaccessible but to a relative few who are able to speak Russian, Hebrew, and Yiddish, and often Polish and French, too. This band of scholars has been vital to tell the pogrom story and provide the needed context to Feiga Shamis's letter.

My Dear Children follows Judy Favish's decades-long quest to understand why her father would never talk about his past. She and her family knew that Mannie had been adopted by the Favish family from an orphanage in Johannesburg, had come with his sister Rose from an orphanage in Warsaw, but that the two were not actually orphans. Only when Mannie's wife Nora had Feiga's letter translated after Mannie's death did the family come to understand the trauma of Mannie's childhood. It would take several years of digging for Judy to reach an understanding about what had happened to her father and why he wouldn't speak of it. It is our understanding that many of the Ochberg orphans, indeed many who survived the pogroms, shared Mannie's reluctance to do so.

Since launching production in 2012, we have read everything we can get our hands on, sifted through crumbling documents in dusty archives, talked to scholars around the world, and filmed on three continents. We found the building in Warsaw that was once the orphanage where Ochberg gathered the orphans before departing for South Africa. In a little touched file at the University of Cape Town, we found one of the armbands once worn by one of the orphans during the journey -- #135. We have experienced some of the highs and lows of our professional careers, and we have laughed and cried.

One of the most memorable moments – and perhaps the most profoundly moving interview I have ever done – was with Solly Jossel. We hadn't planned on interviewing Solly when shooting in South Africa because we didn't even know he was alive. But when Lauren Snitcher, an Ochberg orphan descendant, told us during our interview with her that just two orphans remained alive, one of them in Johannesburg, we knew we needed to try. When our crew showed up at their apartment, we weren't even sure we'd be allowed in because we weren't able to adequately explain over the phone what we were doing. But Solly's wife Sylvia warmly welcomed us, and both agreed to an on-camera interview. Solly said little as we set up, and we all worried the effort would be for naught, but when the camera went on, so did Solly. He shared his memories of Cossacks killing a Jewish baby and of leaving his mother – forever. Solly died a little more than a year after we interviewed him.

My Dear Children tells a story that has been forgotten for too long. Entire families, entire villages were completely wiped out in the Civil War pogroms. Polly Zavadivker from the University of Delaware, told us before the Civil War, Jews had lived in more than 100 cities, towns, and villages throughout the Pale of Settlement. After the war, that number was 35-40. "That tells you," said Zavadivker, "that certain towns that had Jewish populations before the war were completely emptied of their populations of Jews, turned into cemeteries."

While flipping through lists of the dead in the Tcherikower Archive in New York City, I was repeatedly struck by the thought that many just simply ceased to exist, no one to even remember them.

"It's almost now when we tell Mannie's story," Lauren Snitcher said in our interview with her, "it's almost as if we are making rectification and together we're able as a community to say kaddish for all those souls who didn't have children to say kaddish for them. And I think that that's what Ochberg has allowed us to do. That's the opportunity that he's opened up for all of us."

It is our hope that *My Dear Children* will stand as a memorial to the hundreds of thousands who died or whose lives were inexorably changed forever.

The anticipated release date of *My Dear Children* is the summer of 2017. We are currently raising the funds to license the extensive archival film, photos, and artwork in the film, a necessary step to finish. Look for updates on our website at www.mydearchildrendoc.com or on Facebook at www.facebook.com/feigaschoice.

My Dear Children - the cover

"The armbands worn by one of the Ochberg orphans on the journey to South Africa found at the University of Cape Town."

Chapter 75 - THE OCHBERG ORPHANS WERE PLACED IN THE CARE OF THE SOUTH AFRICAN JEWISH ORPHANAGE (ARCADIA) AND THE CAPE JEWISH ORPHANAGE. (ORANJIA)

On arrival in Cape Town on the 24th September 1921, half the children were placed in the care of The Cape Jewish Orphanage, later known as The Oranjia Jewish Child and Youth Centre and half in the care of The South African Jewish Orphanage, later called Arcadia and now known as Arcadia Jewish Children's Home.

THE SOUTH AFRICAN JEWISH ORPHANAGE

The South African Jewish Orphanage owes its establishment to the Jewish Ladies' Communal League, which in 1899, began its activities among the small Jewish community which had ventured to Johannesburg.

It later became apparent that further expansion was essential. With the growth of the South African Jewish community applications for admission had increased considerably, but owing to limited accommodation numerous deserving cases had to be refused. This fact, coupled with the advent of the Russian pogrom orphans (The Ochberg Orphans) brought out by the SA Jewish Relief, Reconstruction and Orphans Fund, made it imperative to acquire much larger premises.

The Jewish community responded whole-heartedly in support of the movement and in 1923 "Arcadia", 22 Oxford Road, Parktown, was purchased at a cost of £30,000. The SA Jewish Relief, Reconstruction and Orphans Fund agreed to contribute £12,500 towards the purchase price, in consideration of the Orphanage taking charge of the pogrom children.

The first South African Jewish Orphanage in Kensington

A home had been acquired due to Jewish liberality, and on the 18th July, 1923, "*Arcadia*" was opened by the then Prime Minister, General the Rt Hon. JC Smuts. It was at this time that the name Arcadia was adopted.

In 1923 the Orphanage accommodated 142 children, including the 61 pogrom orphans (Ochberg Orphans). Since then admissions have continued unabated, until today there are 290 children in our care.

The Official Opening of Arcadia by Jan Smuts – 18 July 1923
Mr Schlesinger is presenting the key to General Smuts.
On the right are Rabbi Dr. J L Landau and Mr. I Heymann. On the left is Mr. M I Isaacson.

Villa Arcadia from the North - acquired by the Jewish Community in 1923

The number of children in care increased over the years and peaked at 400 in 1939 with the greatest number of children in care during the war years 1939-1945.

With the introduction of the Cottage System in 1969 the number of children in care at Arcadia dropped dramatically while the number of families supported to keep their children at home similarly increased.

In the interests of the Jewish community, and at its request, the Johannesburg Jewish Helping Hand – The Chevrah Kadisha, assumed financial, legal and management responsibility for Arcadia Jewish Children's Home in March 2002.

By 2002 only a small section of Arcadia's sprawling 17-acre property in Parktown was occupied by the children who lived there and Villa Arcadia was sold to Hollard Insurance.

As a result the children were relocated to two renovated residential houses in Sandringham so that the children enjoy a domestic, suburban environment that bears no semblance of institutionalisation. An intimate and homely atmosphere has been carefully created and nurtured.

The large, rustic log cabin on the Arcadia grounds houses a fully- equipped Day Care Centre which provides supervised care not only for children resident at Arcadia, but also for children of working parents in the community.

In residence and at the Day Care Centre, full time and well-trained child-care workers supervise and tend the children by day and night. Healthcare, education, therapy, play and homework supervision are all part of the deal.

In 2016 a new Arcadia Home and Day Care Centre were built thanks to the generosity Of Monty Koppel (an Ex-Arcadian) and family and the official opening is set for the 15th of March 2017. *(see chapter 78)*

THE CAPE JEWISH ORPHANAGE

Extracts from
AN HISTORICAL PEN PICTURE OF ORANJIA
From the 1958 Cape Jewish Orphanage Report

At the turn of the century, the seed of the idea of establishing a Home for destitute Jewish children in Cape Town had been implanted in the minds of those who, by virtue of their vision and far-sightedness, guided the destinies of the community. Their fertile brains began to explore the avenue whereby such a scheme could be implemented.

So we find a tentative start being made in 1910 by a small committee consisting of Messrs. I Ochberg, P Policansky, A Borson and a few others. Mr R Herman was Chairman and Mr Roytowsky, Hon Secretary. The committee met on several occasions, but no definite plans were formulated. It was left to a few individuals on the committees of the Jewish Philantrophic Society and the Cape Town Jewish Ladies' Society, who later merged to form what is now known as the Cape Jewish Board of Guardians, to shape and clarify the issue.

The first meeting was called on 15th July, 1911 and it finally agreed that the present name of "The Cape Jewish Orphanage" be adopted.

The first ladies meeting was held in a house in Upper Mill Street, which had been hired at a very nominal rental as the first Home for The Cape Jewish Orphanage. The first applications for admission were dealt with on the 20th December, and a second batch of five at the end of January in the following year.

By the end of 1913 the house in Upper Mill Street was found to be entirely inadequate for the needs of the Orphanage, even though an extra room in the next house had been hired. The Mill Street Home had however, served its purpose in that it had impressed on the minds of all local Jews the fact that the work of the early pioneers had not been merely a light- hearted venture providing an easy and temporary outlet for their communal energies and aspirations.

The community had realised that the demands on the Home were increasing and that it behoved them to provide more commodious and suitable premises situated in more pleasant and health giving surroundings.

After considerable negotiation, and after being compelled to decline a site generously offered by the Town Council in 1913, a large piece of ground in Montrose Avenue was purchased in March, 1914, from the Oranjezicht Estate Company, at a very reasonable figure. The plans for the building were passed the next month, but the actual construction was not completed until January 1916.

Like with Arcadia's Cottage Sytem, a Group Home was established in 1983, and the premises were sold in early 1990.

The intention was to buy a number of small homes with small groups of children being cared for by house parents.

(see chapter 77 for details of The Oranjia Jewish Child and Youth Centre today!)

Oranjia, built by the Cape Jewish Community and completed in 1916 to house the children of the Cape Jewish Orphange.
(This cover of Memories of Oranjia - The Cape Jewish Orphanage was designed by Benni Hotz).

Chapter 76 - PROCEEDS ON SALE OF BOOKS GO TO ARCADIA, ORANJIA AND THE JDC

ARCADIA CHILDREN'S HOME IN JOHANNESBURG TODAY

- Today 42 children and their families receive services from Arcadia

- There are 15 children in *residence* – all of whom are statutory placements

- An additional 22 children attend the *After School Care* program and spend their afternoons at Arcadia in a supervised, constructive and stimulating environment. These are children who have been identified as being "at risk" and in need of added supervision

- The *After-Care Program* is designed to care for the financial, educational and emotional needs of post-school adolescents who no longer live on campus. Arcadia provides them with tertiary education, accommodation and the kind of support and guidance normally provided by parents.

HOW YOU CAN HELP

Arcadia is not able to generate income in the form of fees and therefore the children are totally dependent on the facility for <u>all</u> their requirements - physical, emotional, academic and spiritual.

Private Jewish and remedial education is costly, as is counselling, therapy, dentistry and medical care.

The support of the community is essential to the ongoing care of Arcadia's children. Your donation would be deeply appreciated.

To make an online donation to Arcadia using your credit card please visit
https://www.jhbchev.co.za/pages/OnceOffDonation.aspx

For direct deposits, our banking details:
Arcadia Children's Home
Bank: Standard Bank
Branch: Johannesburg
Branch Code: 000205
Account No: 000139270
Swift Code : SBZAZAJJ
Donations are tax deductible

Please help us to identify your contribution
Email: donations@jhbchev.co.za
Or mail to: Private Bag X7, Sandringham 2131

THE JOHANNESBURG CHEVRAH KADISHA

Today Arcadia Children's Home is run by the Chevrah Kadisha in Johannesburg.

The Chevrah Kadisha is truly the Johannesburg community's Jewish helping hand. Not only does it provide all Jewish burial services, it also runs two Homes for aged people, Sandringham Gardens and Our Parents Home and cares for physically and intellectually disabled people in Selwyn Segal.

In addition to the four Organisations under the Chevrah Kadisha's management, it also provides the following nine Services to the Jewish community: Financial Assistance, Residential, Education Support, Protected Employment, Social, Emergency, Bridal, Healthcare and Burial.

With the brain drain and many of the wealthy leaving South Africa over the past 40 years those left behind are poorer and carry a heavier burden of social need.
They need our help and support.

CHAI SOUTH AFRICA SUPPORTING ORANJIA AND ARCADIA

In the USA, Canada and the UK you can make a Tax Deductible donation directly to Oranjia or Arcadia, (run by the Chevrah Kadisha) through Chai South Africa by going to www.chaisouthafrica.com and clicking on "donate now".

USA – ChaiSouthAfrica:
Mandy Katz 858-279-2740
chaisa@jcfsandiego.org

Canada - UJA Federation-Toronto/ ChaiSouthAfrica:
Athena Kay 416-631-5734 akay@ujafed.org

UK - Euro Chai: Harley Kagan 020-7190-5555
hkagan@utbank.co.uk Website: http://eurochai.com

Chapter 77 – ORANJIA JEWISH CHILD AND YOUTH CENTRE

This article has kindly been sent in by Belinda Slavin, the Programme Director of Oranjia Jewish Child and Youth Centre in 2011.

Part of the proceeds on sale of this book will go to Oranjia.

HISTORY

The Oranjia Jewish Child and Youth Centre was established in 1911 as an orphanage. With the passage of time and with advances in medical science the number of Jewish orphans decreased. However, a new need arose; children who were in need of care and who had at least one biological parent alive. And it is this type of child who Oranjia currently cares for. Indeed, not a single child at Oranjia today is an orphan and each has at least one biological parent alive. All the children at Oranjia have been removed from their families by Order of Court in terms of the Children's Act.

In the 1980s with increased research and understanding in the field of childcare, it became abundantly clear that that institutional settings epitomized by large impersonal buildings were counter-indicated for the objectives that had been set, namely to provide an alternative specialised, professional context to remediate the consequences of removal to the children placed in our care. It has always been Oranjia's objective to construct a context within which such children can continue to grow and develop physically, psychologically, spiritually and emotionally.

In 1986, Oranjia laid the foundations for a shift into a new model of childcare, away from custodial principles. A group home was opened. The success of this group house living experience lead to the old institution closing and two more group homes being opened in January 1992.

From 1996 the number of residential admissions decreased resulting in the closure of first our Gorge Road Unit and then our Gardenia Avenue Unit. Currently in 2011, we are only operating one residential unit at Frank Ave.

RESIDENTIAL CARE

Residential care is a very specialised form of intervention that happens when a family is in dire need of help, change and support and the necessary support structures in the community are not in place or not specific to their needs. To remove children from their families and place them in a residential environment, albeit a caring, therapeutic milieu, stays traumatic and requires a lot of understanding and skill from all the professionals involved; to act in the best interest of both children and their families. The ultimate aim of residential care is to help families to function optimally in their own communities therefore re-uniting children and their families after successful and intensive intervention where possible.

To change set behaviour patterns and learn new skills takes a long time and requires hard work. Children and families in our care have to face these challenges every day and often against overwhelming odds. Our job is to be there 24 hours a day, every day, every step of the way encouraging, teaching, supporting and applauding.

In the new paradigm, emphasis is placed on "prevention" and community based support structures to prevent the use of more drastic measures like residential care as far as possible. This is good and definitely the way to go in the future. Children's homes should become resource centres for the communities they serve.

But there will always be those families that will benefit most from residential care, and we owe it to them to have those facilities in place, and staff them with people who are true professionals in their field and who will provide these families with the best possible care they can offer.

Oranjia currently in 2011 has one residential home which can accommodate 10 children. In 2009 our home underwent a massive renovation in order to provide a facility that would serve the community's needs for the next 20 years.

Oranjia is managed by a group of committed volunteers who oversee the overall managing of the home and ensure by their fundraising efforts that there are sufficient finances to enable the on-going running of the home. The professional staff is accountable to the management committee.

ORANJIA'S VISION AND MISSION

Oranjia aims to provide child and youth centred services as well as residential group care to children of the Jewish Community who have been found in need of care in terms of the Children's Act.

The philosophy of care is based on the core principle that children and youth at risk need opportunities for competency, development and personal growth.

Children and youth with emotional trauma and distress present with interpersonal and social difficulties.

Our emphasis is on the development of the whole child and youth in a context that actively promotes personal growth and development by building trusting and safe relationships between professional staff and residents.

These meaningful relationships are characterized by concern for physical and emotional needs, trust, understanding and awareness of the child and youth as an individual in a social and communal context.

SERVICES OFFERED
Residential Services and Group Care

- Group home offering 24 hour residential care for children and youth of the Jewish community, operated by a team of trained and skilled youth care practioners.
- A structured but flexible therapeutic milieu and routine to meet individual and group needs.
- Management of children and youth with emotional and behavioural difficulties.
- Provision of physical, emotional, social and spiritual care.
- Clinical assessment of children, youth and families.
- Treatment programmes for children, youth and families.

The programme provides services to meet all needs in a Jewish environment for children and youth aged from two to eighteen, after which a transition can be made to an aftercare programme.

Residential Aftercare

This service is offered to residents of Oranjia who have reached the age of 18 but are unable to return to their families and are not ready for independent community living. These residents are allowed to remain at Oranjia while they are assisted to further their education, find employment and acquire the life skills necessary to make the transition into independent living.

Aftercare and Daycare

When children and youth of school going age are ready to leave the residential programme, they and their families need support in making the transition. Oranjia will continue to offer them practical and emotional support for a considerable amount of time, the period of time being determined by the needs of each individual case. This can include the child or youth coming to Oranjia on a daycare basis. This service is crucial in assisting the transition from residential care back to family living in order to prevent re-admissions.

Social Work and Counseling Services

- Individual and group work with children and youth in residence and in aftercare.
- Family work including practical, social and emotional support and crisis intervention with families.
- Parent support
- Case management and assessments and liaison with other professional.
- Recruitment of host families for residents.

DAYCARE

In 2006, Oranjia started a Daycare programme aimed at children and youth that had never been in residential care, but had been identified as children "at risk." This preventative programme was identified as a need in the community and is in line with South African Child and Youth Care Practice. Children came to Oranjia after school, returning to their parents in the evening. Currently at the moment we are not running this programme as our residential unit is full. When residential numbers decrease more children could be admitted onto the daycare programme.

We are proud of the fact that of the over 70 children who have been in Oranjia's care since the move to the Group Homes in 1992, very few have become dependent on community resources and welfare. The majority have developed into self-sufficient adults who are making valuable contributions to society. This is not only gratifying in terms of the personal achievements of our past Oranjia children but also in terms of the significant financial implications for the community, i.e. not becoming welfare dependent adults.

ORANJIA'S CENTENARY

In February 2011 Oranjia turned one hundred years old.

In order to celebrate our centenary and this auspicious occasion we are planning to hold a Gala Dinner later this year and to launch a centenary book.

We appeal to all past residents of Oranjia who would be willing to write a short paragraph or be interviewed for the book to make contact. See contact details below.

All proceeds from the Gala Dinner and the sale of the book will be used towards the running costs of Oranjia.

If you would like to make a donation, see our bank details below.

FUNDING

Oranjia relies on the generosity of members of our community for funding. A large part of our funding comes from our allocation from the United Jewish Appeal in the Western Cape, donation and bequests as well as fundraising efforts such as our Friends of Oranjia draw and our annual Golf Day.

We are indeed most grateful for all donations. Our banking details are below:

Oranjia Jewish Child and Youth Care Centre
Bank: ABSA
Branch: Heerengracht
Branch Code: 506009
Account No: 4060767290
Swift Code: absa zajj

Please help us to identify your contribution by advising us by email or fax of any direct deposits made. Fax: 021 – 461 0693, or email Admin Director Jean Mausenbaum <mausenbaum@oranjia.com>
Telephone: 021-465 5009

Or mail your contribution to:
P.O Box 1204, Cape Town 8000

Chapter 78 - THE NEW ARCADIA - OPENED 15TH MARCH 2017 AND IS RUN BY THE JOHANNESBURG CHEVRAH KADISHA

THE NEW ARCADIA HOME AND DAY CARE CENTRE

We share photos of these wonderful facilities built thanks to the generosity of Old Arcadian, Monty Koppel, and his family.

The story of Monty Koppel and his older sister Freda Koppel is told in The Arcadia Memorial books.

Old Arcadian, Jules Gordon, the head of The Old Arc Association of Johannesburg writes - February 2017.

I went past the New Arc on Friday and then went back again yesterday. They were having an open week for the public and most of Jo'burg must have pitched up yesterday with their kids, who had an absolute ball there!

I even found myself taking people on tours around the whole complex as the staff just couldn't cope with the flow.

I've been watching the place grow since they started excavations there as I live virtually around the corner. Wow what a place! It's absolutely stunning! Here are some of the photos taken

It is state of the art, very colorful, airy, ultra modern and a home that is not an institution! It's like a Hollywood house, so very comfortable!

There are kitchens where the residents can go and make themselves a toasted sandwich and a cup of coffe or a fruit juice even when they feel like it! Imagine us having that facility!

There is a lot of comfortable recreational and lounging areas in each section. Each child has their own bedroom with views of the gardens, and two roomed bedrooms share a beautiful bathroom!

There are plenty of big wall TVs so there shouldn't be any fighting about TV channels. There's an enormous patio and braai area with a mini soccer pitch which looks like a stadium with pics of crowds all around it!

There is a swimming pool and real grass, unlike the present Arc.

I was already visualizing the kids jumping from the railings on the first floor into the pool, plus I also found myself looking where they can bunk out from. I guess must have been Arc training!

THE DAY CARE CENTRE

The Day Care Centre is separate from the accommodation areas with very modern facilities.

The babies, juniors and seniors are split into their own spaces and can also be intergrated.

This is a place the the children will be so proud to say that they live. They will all hopefully flourish .

There are ultra modern jungle gyms, slides and just everything to keep the youngsters happy.

I saw Old Arcadian's Zummy and also Jerry Levy there. They both wanted to move in immediately !

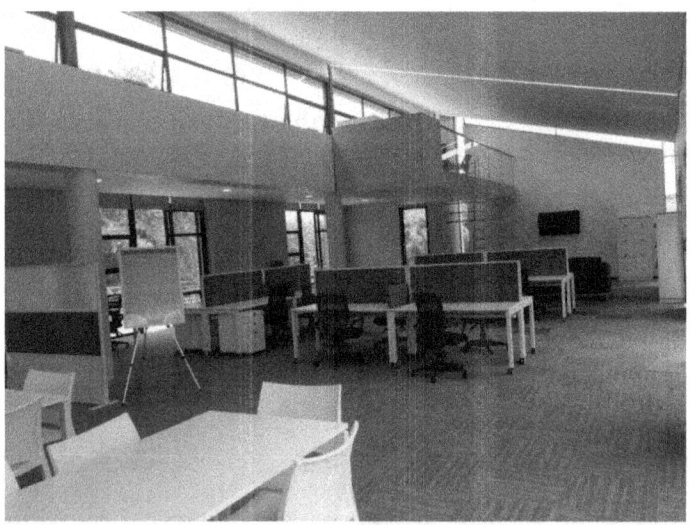

Chapter 79 - THE JOHANNESBURG CHEVRAH KADISHA

With so many of the wealthy and educated leaving South Africa over the past 40 years, those left behind are poorer and carry a heavier burden of social need.

The Chevrah Kadisha is truly the Johannesburg community's Jewish helping hand. Not only do they provide all Jewish burial services, they also run two homes - Sandringham Gardens and Our Parents Home, for the aged and care for physically and intellectually disabled people in Selwyn Segal and children in need at Arcadia.

In addition to the four Organisations under the Chevrah Kadisha's management, they also provide the following nine Services to the Jewish community: Financial Assistance, Residential, Educational Support, Protected Employment, Social, Emergency, Bridal, Healthcare and Burial.

They need our help and support.

To make an online donation to the Chevrah Kadisha using your credit card please visit
https://www.jhbchev.co.za/pages/OnceOffDonation.aspx

The Johannesburg Chevrah Kadisha Today

Nowadays the Johannesburg Chevrah Kadisha runs at an annual budget in excess of R250 million and is dependent upon the generosity of donors both locally and internationally for more than two thirds of that figure. It incorporates four major organisations and provides services under nine banners:

Four Organisations:

- Sandringham Gardens (incorporated 2000), is home to over 400 elderly people of which 250 are in the on-site Medical Centre.

- Our Parents Home (incorporated 2001), houses 200 elderly residents and has a specialised Alzheimer's ward.

- Arcadia Children's Home (incorporated 2002) is a place of safety, caring for the all-inclusive needs of children at risk and in need of protection. All the children are court placements.

- Segal Segal Centre (incorporated 2005) cares for 140 physically and intellectually disabled people in two residences, the Selwyn Segal Centre and Kibbutz Lubner. Mental illness is a growing concern and the mental health facilities, Sandringham Square and Sandringham Lodge, accommodate over 50 patients.

Nine Services:

Financial Assistance Services – R2.1 million is distributed monthly to over 2,000 needy recipients for food, rent, medication and other needs.

Residential Services – apart from the residential facilities owned by the Chev, people in need are housed in suitable accommodation at the Group's expense.

Education Support Services – approximately R6 million is paid out annually to assist students of all ages.

Protected Employment Services – over 200 people are provided with sheltered employment at our various facilities.

Social Services – counselling is provided for marriage, divorce, depression, family relationships and substance abuse. Statutory intervention is mandated when a person becomes a danger to themselves or others.

Emergency Services – available 24/7: trauma response, burial services and crisis counselling.

Bridal Services – assisting young couples with the costs of setting up home.

Healthcare Services – are available at the Sandringham Gardens Medical Centre and the Community Outpatients Department. Funding for emergency life-saving surgical procedures is regularly provided.

Burial Services – every Jew is buried in exactly the same way according to Jewish Law with the identical coffin and tahara. No-one is ever refused burial for financial reasons and the Chev absorbs all costs for indigent people without family.

The Chevrah Kadisha's Mandate

The Organisation is entrusted by the Jewish community to rehabilitate people who have fallen on hard times and into difficult circumstances and to protect and care for those unable to care for themselves. To this end it provides housing, sustenance and healthcare to people who are old, sick, disabled, mentally ill, poor and helpless.

The vast scope of its services makes it likely that every Jewish family in the city is touched, in some way, by the work of this multi-faceted Organisation. Support is provided daily through welfare and burial services and over 1,000 residents are accommodated in our various facilities – Sandringham Gardens, Our Parents Home, Arcadia, Selwyn Segal and our mental health homes. There, residents are provided with all of their needs – physical, medical, social, emotional and spiritual. Activities and outings are all in a day's work and specialised care is offered to disabled and dementia patients.

Thousands of people are assisted, supported, comforted and accommodated every day by the Chevrah Kadisha. In each situation our purpose is to improve the quality of life for those who have nowhere else to turn and no one else to turn to.

The Chevrah Kadisha's role has, since inception, been a paternal, protective and unifying one. Constantly on guard to ensure the preservation of genuine Jewish values, untainted by expedience, it has been father and teacher to the Jewish community, setting the proper example of sanctity and sincerity.

The problems of relief and rehabilitation addressed by the original Johannesburg Jewish Helping Hand were far-reaching and complex. The modern-day Chevrah Kadisha, despite having expanded its boundaries and budget extensively, has remained faithful to the high ideals and moral, ethical and spiritual tenets prescribed by its most esteemed pioneers.

Over a period of 128 years it is not possible to mention, by name, the very many humanitarian giants who have served the Organisation with so much loyalty and integrity. Suffice it to say that the culture in which they developed the Chevrah Kadisha has remained consistent and would, no doubt, be a source of great satisfaction to its founders.

When the Chevrah Kadisha assumed responsibility for Sandringham Gardens in 2000, it was completing an historical full-circle 88 years old.

That's because it was the Chevrah Kadisha that originally founded and funded the first Jewish Home for the Aged in 1912.

SANDRINGHAM GARDENS is home to over 400 residents, many of whom are, unfortunately, in need of long-term hospitalisation.

More than two-thirds of these residents are partially or fully subsidised by the Chevrah Kadisha Group as they are unable to afford the modest accommodation fees. It is for this reason that continuous fundraising is essential for the Home.

The Donald Gordon Campus, on which Sandringham Gardens is housed, also accommodates the Eric and Sheila Samson Community Medical Centre which provides professional and excellent co-ordinated healthcare for those in need of it. Its services are offered to residents at all Chevrah Group residential facilities as well as those in the community who are unable to afford visits to General Practitioners and who might sometimes neglect their health, and that of their children, rather than be faced with debts they feel unable to pay.

The Sandringham Gardens hospital, which forms part of the Chevrah's Community Medical Centre, has a full complement of nursing staff, General Practitioners and access to consulting Specialists. It also provides dentistry, optometry, audiology and speech therapy, physiotherapy, occupational therapy, podiatry and radiology services and has a fully-stocked dispensary. Hearing aids, spectacles and mobility aids are made available to patients and residents. A team of social workers offer supportive counselling to residents and family members.

For those in the residential section who are well enough to enjoy the wide range of amenities on offer, regular entertainment, outings, in-house functions, religious lectures and a beautifully maintained shul are on hand. Also available is a hairdressing salon, library and Nosh Bar which supplies tasty snacks. Meals are prepared by the professional catering team who pays faithful attention to special dietary requirements. This remarkable residential facility is a warm and caring place and sits amidst beautifully cultivated and maintained gardens which the residents, weather permitting, enjoy enormously.

OUR PARENTS HOME is located in Norwood and houses 220 residents. It was established in 1940, initially to welcome Jewish immigrants fleeing from the horrors of the holocaust, and incorporated into the Chevrah Group in 2001. At this pleasant facility, residents interact socially with each other in a safe, structured environment. Arts, crafts, concerts, quizzes, exercise classes, games and bingo are organized regularly. Guest lecturers cover a large spectrum of subjects and regular Shiurim are provided by visiting Rabbonim. The hairdresser, manicurist and podiatrist are accessible to residents and a team of social workers offers supportive counselling to them.

A Day Care program has been carefully designed for elderly people who do not need the residential services of an aged home, but who wish to benefit from the social and therapeutic advantages provided there.

Patients at Our Parents Home who are in need of hospitalization are sometimes admitted into the Sandringham Gardens hospital. Many synergies are evident as the two Homes work together to provide holistic care to the aged. An example of this is the specialised Alzheimers ward at Our Parents Home, known as the Sunshine Circle, which offers expert medical care and nursing.

THE SELWYN SEGAL HOSTEL

In 1956 the late Leon Segal and his wife, Fanny - affected by the physical disability of their only child, Selwyn - established a short-term haven for people suffering from physical or intellectual disabilities so that their care-givers could be relieved for short periods of time to take a holiday, travel or rest.

A property was acquired in Pandora Road, Kensington but before long it became apparent that the Jewish community needed a full time residential facility with therapeutic care on a scale not envisaged at the outset.

Deserving of great recognition and appreciation are three notable philanthropists who stepped forward to help carry the responsibility of guiding the new Jewish establishment through its uncharted waters: the late David Rothbart, Issie Shapiro and Simmy Silverman.

Some nine years after the organisation was established the residents were moved into new premises in Sandringham, where they remain today. It was at that time that Jack Shapiro was appointed Selwyn Segal's first Director. Under Jack's direction the organisation expanded and flourished.

To make an online donation to the Chevrah Kadisha using your credit card please visit
https://www.jhbchev.co.za/pages/OnceOffDonation.aspx

JEWISH OLD AGED HOMES IN SOUTH AFRICA

Besides Sandringham Gardens and Our Parents Home in Johannesburg both run by the Johannesburg Chevra Kadisha there are the following old aged homes:
   Cape Town: Highlands House
   Durban: Beth Shalom
   Pretoria: Jaffa House
      Zimbabwe: Savyon Lodge

Chapter 80 - BOOKS ON SOUTH AFRICAN JEWRY COMPILED/REPRINTED BY DAVID SOLLY SANDLER

ARCADIA MEMORY BOOKS *The cover of 100 Years of Arc Memories and More Arc Memories*

100 Years of Arc Memories (Published 2006)

The purpose of this book is to record the memories of the children of Arcadia (The South African Jewish Orphanage) and the history of Arcadia (the Arc). The Arc children of many different ages now live in many countries around the world and have followed many different walks of life. The common thread that binds the Arc children is that they spent some, or even all of their childhood in Arcadia.

The book also marks and celebrates the Arc's centenary. Finally, 100 years after its official beginning, old Arcs of at least five of the ten generations who passed through its gates have expressed a little of what the Arc meant to them. I feel privileged to be the recorder of their memories.

Arcadia, known as *the Arc* to all its children, started off as the South African Jewish Orphanage (SAJO). 'Arcadia' was the name of the 26-acre estate bought from Sir Lionel Phillips in 1923 by the South African Jewish community. The name remained when the palatial villa and extensive grounds were transformed into a home to house Jewish children in need of care. Thus Arcadia, 22 Oxford Road, Parktown, Johannesburg was to become the address and home of generations of children. Arcadia SAJO has cared for over three thousand Jewish children over the past 100 years. In 1975 its name was changed to Arcadia Jewish Children's Home. In 2002 the children then in residence, were relocated to Sandringham and the property was sold in 2004.

More Arc Memories (Published 2008)

The publication, distribution and sales of the Arc Centenary Book *100 Years of Arc Memories* has been a catalyst, enabling many Old Arcadians and their families to 'come out' as it were, and to be proud they were from Arcadia, and to make contact with their fellow Arcadians. I sense that for many "Coming from Arcadia" is now a badge to be shown off with pride and that the sense of shame in being an orphanage child has somewhat dissipated. This is very much like Australians, who in previous generations hid the fact that their forebears came out from England as convicts and who are now proud to show this in their family trees.

This book contains *Arc Memories* that have poured in from Old Arcs and their descendants following the publication of the Arcadia Centenary Book *100 Years of Arc Memories* in 2006. Like the first book, this sequel records the memories of the children of Arcadia (The South African Jewish Orphanage) and the history of Arcadia (the Arc).

This book differs from the first in that it more fully covers the ten decades of the previous title. Since 2006, later generation Old Arcs - by this I mean those of us who were Arc children in the 70s and later - have been sending in their memories. At the other extreme, many of the memories in this edition have come from the children of the very early generations of Arcs, including the children of the "Ochberg Orphans" who landed up in Arcadia, simply because they have wanted the stories of their late parents to be on record.

The "Ochberg Orphans" are a group of 177 orphans who were fortunate enough to be rescued in 1921 from the pogroms and poverty of Eastern Europe by the late Isaac Ochberg. Immediately after docking in South Africa, half the children were sent to Johannesburg by train and placed into the care of the South African Jewish Orphanage (SAJO). In 1923, when 'Villa Arcadia' was bought from mining magnate Sir Lionel Phillips, and the SAJO adopted the name Arcadia, 67 of the children went to live in Arcadia. Funds collected by the *SA Jewish Relief, Reconstruction and Orphans Fund* were used as part of the purchase consideration. The rescue of these orphans through the generosity of the Jewish Community of South Africa is an important part of South African Jewish history and an important part of the history of Arcadia.

This book devotes 17 chapters to the Ochberg children – six of a general nature, and eleven based on personal and family contributions. The first book did not give them the place they deserved and hopefully this book goes some way to correcting this omission. Arcadia reports of the period, referred to these children variously as the Russian pogrom orphans, the Russian orphans, or the Ukraine orphans but not as "Ochberg Orphans" as was done in the Cape.

What both books have in common is that Old Arcs are willing to express a little of what the Arc meant to them. It is nothing short of miraculous that people of so many different generations, who have followed totally different paths in life in many countries around the world, are willing to share their special status with one another and with you. I feel privileged once again to be the recorder of their memories.

The Ochberg Orphans and the Horrors from whence they came (Published 2011)

The rescue in 1921 of 181 Jewish Orphans by Isaac Ochberg, the representative of the South African Jewish Community, from the horrors of the 'Pale of Settlement'

This book tells the story of a forgotten part of Jewish History; a period completely overshadowed by the Holocaust; the horrors of war and pogroms and starvation and disease suffered by Jews in the *Pale of Settlement* from 1914 to 1922. It details the horrors and the help given to these desperate people by Jewish communities established in the USA, Canada, Palestine and South Africa.

The book then focuses on, and follows up on the lives of the 181 Jewish Orphans rescued from the 'Pale of Settlement' in 1921 by Isaac Ochberg, the representative of the South African Jewish community. Half of these Ochberg Orphans, on arrival in South Africa, were placed in the care of the Cape Jewish Orphanage (later known as Oranjia) while the rest were sent to Johannesburg and placed in the care of the South African Jewish Orphanage (later known as Arcadia).

While the firsthand accounts of the Ochberg Orphans are included in part one of the book, the secondhand accounts, as recorded by their descendants, are in part two and part three of the book. Part two, *Cape Town, South Africa,* contains the history of Oranjia and the life stories of the Ochberg Orphans in its care and similarly part three, *Johannesburg, South Africa* contains the history of Arcadia and the life stories of the Ochberg Orphans in its care

The book contains the life stories of 120 of the 181 Ochberg Orphans.

The Pinsker Orphans: The life and times of the children from the three Pinsk Jewish Orphanages in the 1920s (Published 2013)

The story of the Pinsker Jewish Orphans of the 1920s is but a small part of a much larger and forgotten part of Jewish History, the horrors suffered by the Jews in *The Pale of Settlement* between the two world wars. These horrors have been overshadowed by the Holocaust and suppressed by the Soviets who controlled the area.

These horrors commenced in 1914 with WWI and the forced relocation of Jews by the Russians. This was followed by the Spanish Influenza epidemic and pogroms committed by advancing and retreating troops. Finally complete chaos, devastation, crop failure, starvation and the diseases that accompany hunger and cold, added to the extremely harsh living conditions that continued well into the 1920s.

Jewish communities around the world were shocked by the news of the horrors of war and the pogroms, starvation and disease suffered by Jews in the *Pale of Settlement*. Especially horrific, were accounts of wholesale rape, extortion and slaughter of their brethren by Polish, Ukrainian and Belarus nationalistic armies and the Red and White (Cossack) Russian troops.

No one knows how many Jews perished in *The Pale of Settlement* between the two world wars.

The Jewish communities around the world heard the cries of their brethren whom they helped in many ways. The American Jewish Joint Distribution Committee (JDC) saved hundreds of thousands from certain starvation with their mass feeding programs and Jewish communities from Canada, The UK, Palestine and South Africa all helped.

Canada and South Africa rescued groups of approximately 200 Jewish Orphans each, by transporting them to their respective countries and caring for them.

The primary purpose of this book is to remember those Pinsker Orphans left behind and includes 135 letters in Hebrew and Yiddish written by them in 1921 to their hero, Alter Bobrow. It is most important to remember these children by publishing their letters, as no one knows how many of them perished in the Holocaust 20 years later.

The book contains details of the 44 Pinsker Orphans who went to South Africa with the Ochberg Orphans. It also includes the great work done by the Pinsker Orphans Relief Fund of London that supported the Pinsker Orphanages and that brought out to London for adoption a group of 19 children in 1924 and a further group of 34 in 1926. It also tells the life stories of some of these rescued children and of some of the committee members who supported this fund.

Lastly the book tells of the great work of the JDC, who not only supported the Pinsk Jewish Community, including the three Pinsker Orphanages, but who supported many hundreds of Jewish Communities, throughout the *Pale of Settlement,* with their orphanages, hospitals, schools, old age homes, soup kitchens, feeding programs and agricultural development and other programs.

This Was a Man (Reprinted 2014)

ISAAC OCHBERG

Isaac was born in Uman, Russia on 31 May 1878 and died on the Pretoria Castle on 11 December 1937. He was buried in Cape Town on 13 December 1937.

"He never refused to support a worthy cause; on the contrary, his creed was that since he had been enabled to achieve success in his own enterprises, he had a moral duty to help those less fortunate."

'This Was A Man' is the life story of Isaac Ochberg (1878-1937) and was first published in 1974 by his daughter Bertha I Epstein.

This is a 2014 reprint of the book slightly edited with an addendum added and reprinted with the permission of the family of Isaac Ochberg z"l.

The rescue of 200 children, orphans of the Ukrainian pogroms (later know as Ochberg Orphans), is, without a doubt, one of the most glorious chapters in the life of Isaac Ochberg.

In 1921 Isaac (know as Daddy Ochberg to the children) brought these children out to South Africa, saving them from the horrors of *The Pale of Settlement*, and half were settled in Oranjia, The Cape Jewish Orphanage and half in Arcadia, The South African Jewish Orphanage in Johannesburg

The book not only tells us of the rescue of these children, but also about Isaac's extraordinary business ventures and the many great works done by him, a once in a lifetime successful businessman and philanthropist.

"He never refused to support a worthy cause; on the contrary, his creed was that since he had been enabled to achieve success in his own enterprises, he had a moral duty to help those less fortunate."

Amongst his many bequests are two that stand out: The largest donation to the Jewish National Fund used to acquire a massive tract of land on which now stand two kibbutzim, Dalia and Galed, and a donation to the Hebrew University of Jerusalem.

The book also follows up on the Ochberg Orphans: In 1971 a Golden Jubilee Reunion of these children took place in Cape Town and in 2011 some 250 of the estimated 4,000 descendants of the children gathered in Israel at a two day ceremony at Kibbutz Dalia and Galed. This culminated in the dedication of the Ochberg Memorial Site overlooking an area that had been originally named the 'Isaac Ochberg Tract'.

This memorial site has now become a regular tourist attraction in Israel and a documentary, *Ochberg's Orphans,* and book, *The Ochberg Orphans and the horrors from whence they came*, now tell us more about Isaac Ochberg and The Ochberg Orphans.

Bennie Penzik, son of two Ochberg Orphans, formed the Isaac Ochberg Heritage Committee in Israel that raises awareness of Isaac Ochberg and his great deeds.

Bennie Penzik and David Solly Sandler (the compiler of the Ochberg Orphan book) jointly wrote the addendum of this book which tells us about resent happenings to keep alive the name of Isaac Ochberg.

Memories of Oranjia - The Cape Jewish Orphanage - (1911-2011) (Published 2014)

On 15 July 1911, a coterie of communal enthusiasts connected with the Cape Jewish Philanthropic Society [now known as the Cape Jewish Board of Guardians] assembled in the Gardens Old Synagogue to consider ways and means of establishing a Home in Cape Town for destitute Jewish orphan children.

Joseph Kadish presided at this first meeting, which a month later developed into a fully established Orphanage Committee, with himself as President, the late Adv Morris Alexander as Vice-President and Nathan Wittenberg as Hon Secretary.

By the end of that year the first orphan children were housed in a double-storey house in Upper Mill Street, and Joseph Kadish presided over the destinies of the Cape Jewish Orphanage from 1911 until 1916, when the late Isaac Ochberg became President and Joe Kadish – as he loved to be designated – acted as his efficient lieutenant for a further six years.

Mr Kadish always loved to refer to himself as 'the founder of the Cape Jewish Orphanage' as indeed he was, for it was entirely due to his unbounded energy and enthusiasm that within six months of the preliminary meeting in July, 1911, Orphanage work was started and within three years thereafter the present ground in Oranjezicht was purchased and the necessary buildings were started.

The main purpose of this book is to provide a forum for the children of Oranjia (previously The Cape Jewish Orphanage) to share their memories. My hope is that by sharing their memories, the children of Oranjia will feel better about themselves as was the case when the children of Arcadia (previously The South African Jewish Orphanage) shared their memories in the Arcadia Centenary Book - *100 Years of Arc Memories* - published in 2006.

This book is a collection of the memories of the many generations of children who were in the care of The Cape Jewish Orphanage.

The book includes good and bad memories and some very critical of those taking care of the children. Sadly, some children did not want to share their memories and some told me that it was too painful to do so. Some children bravely shared their memories in spite of the pain.

The children generally, and I too, fully realise that the intentions of current and past committee members are good and they have always sought the best for the children, however, as we are all human and even with the best intentions it is not always possible to choose the best people to look after the children.

I wish the committee success with their official *Oranjia Centenary Book* and I believe their book, which focuses on the history, and my compilation that focuses on the memories of the children, will complement each other perfectly.

The institution later adopted the name Oranjia and today is know as Oranjia Jewish Child and Youth Centre and still takes care of Jewish children in need in Cape Town.

The Memorial Section of the Yizkor-Book of Rakishok and Environs. (Published in late 2014)

This book is the English translation of the Memorial (in Rememberance) Section (Pages 539 to 620) of the Yizkor-Book of Rakishok and Environs. that was originally published in Yiddish in 1952 by the Rakishker Landmanschaft of Johannesburg, South Africa.

Translated by Bella Golubchik

As stated on its back cover this book is the English translation of the Memorial (in Rememberance) Section (Pages 539 to 620) of the Yizkor-Book of Rakishok and Environs translated into English by Bella Golubchik.

The book was originally published in Yiddish in 1952 by the Rakishker Landmanschaft of Johannesburg, South Africa and in the preface of the book is written:

"Eleven years have slipped away since the holocaust, but the wounds have not been healed, and while the enormity of the tragedy is difficult to comprehend, there are those in our midst, and many of them, for whom the annihilation was a very personal tragedy in addition to being a Jewish tragedy.

"It was, in all probability, this personal factor that partly stimulated the members of the Rakishker Landsleit Society to bring out the Yizkor Book. After all, a book is still the most enduring memorial to a past that has perished. The sponsors of this book set themselves three main tasks when they undertook to issue this tribute to the memory of their brethren in the far-off villages from which they themselves, or their forebears once came. They wanted to reflect the pattern of Jewish life in those villages up to World War II; they wanted to save from oblivion the memory of the ghastly era of Destruction; and finally they wished to place on record the activities of the Rakishker Landsleit in South Africa, during the 40 years of the existence of their Society."

Bella Golubchick, introduced me to the book and told me about her close family connection to it:

"Ethel (Schwartzberg) Aarons and Yerachmiel (Ralph) Aarons are my parents.

"I watched the book being brought to life by the members of the Rakishker Landsmanscaft in the dining room of my parents *palace* in Mayfair Johannesburg. I think every family contributed an article and (or) photographs. The book was edited by a man whose surname was Bakalczuk-Felin (Wonder of wonders- the first Jew I had ever heard of with a double-barrelled name) and his wife. They were indeed interesting times."

At the time I was collecting Jewish family histories and memories for the compilation *Our Litvak and South African Jewish Inheritance* and wanted to publish the complete book in English. Jewish Gen, who had translated about 80% of the book into English already, told me that they intended to do this themselves and so Bella and I have helped them; Bella by doing translations and I with copying photos and formatting them with the text.

This translation of the Memorial Section of the book with photos was sent to Jewish Gen in late 2014 to incorporate into the book they are publishing.

PG Jewish Gen will publish the complete *Yizkor-Book of Rakishok and Environs* book in English soon.

SOUTH AFRICA'S 800
The Story of South African Volunteers in Israel's War of Birth in 1948-1949. (Reprinted 2016)

South Africa's 800 is about Machal, the collective Hebrew acronym for volunteers from abroad and about individual volunteers, colloquially known as Machalniks.

The book reveals details never previously documented and provides a valuable new perspective on Israel's birth and struggle for survival.

It includes eye witness reports by active participants in the events. While written mainly through South African eyes, the book also contains gripping anecdotes about volunteers from the USA, Britain and other countries. It throws new light on important events and personalities of the time.

In his engaging eloquent style, Henry Katzew takes the reader on a fascinating expedition through recent historical events including:
- Adventures of eight young South Africans in their ill-fated attempt to bypass British restrictions on immigration to Palestine, by travelling overland from Pretoria.
- The purchase of ramshackle small ships and their troubled voyages to Israel.
- Six Arab armies attacking the newborn state.
- Maps of the 1948 invasion and the 1949 armistice lines.
- The appalling lack of defensive arms.
- Purchase of light aircraft and flying them over Africa to Israel.
- The airlift of volunteers from South Africa and the staging process in Rome.
- Experiences of volunteers travelling to Israel in overcrowded refugee ships.
- Light civilian aircraft with "bombchuckers" to throw home made bombs over the side.
- The dramatic airlift to Israel of Me109 aircraft inside the fuselages of C- 46's.
- The irony of Israelis flying German Me109's against Egyptians in British Spitfires.
- The incredible operation Velvetta, flying Spitfires non-stop from Yugoslavia to Israel.
- Experiences in a Greek Jail.
- The Altalena and bewildered volunteers.
- The assassination of Count Bernadotte.
- Non-Jewish Volunteers.
- Jerusalem under siege.
  Machal and Israel's first Air Force, Medical Corps, Ground Forces and Radar.
- The exploits of Ezer Weizman, now State President, Syd Cohen and other legendary fliers including non-Jewish Claude Duval and Gordon Levett.
- Personal battle experiences on the ground and in the air.
- The participation of Machal in many important battles.
- Epic adventures of ordinary men and women stirred to superhuman actions.
- West Air and Universal Airways and their role in maintaining links with the outside world before the founding of El Al.

To quote Ben Gurion, it tells how "The war was not won by heroes. It was won by ordinary men and women rising above themselves -"

OUR LITVAK INHERITANCE - Volume One of Our Litvak and South African Jewish Inheritance
(Published February 2016)

The book is of the history, life and times of the Jews in Lithuania.

Section one commences with a timeline of Jewish History, leading on to a detailed history of the Jewish settlement of Keidan and of Lithuania. It reports on the migration of the Jews from the east to the west and discusses origins, philosophies and values of South African Litvak Jews.

Section two tells of the horrors of WWI and its aftermath through reports in the foreign press and from the American Joint Distribution Committee. It also tells of the displacement of Jews from Lithuania and Latvia in 1915.

The third section tells of life in the shtetl through family histories and photographs and also articles and photographs from the *Yizkor book of Rakishok and Environs* and *The Keidan Yizkor book.*

The forth section tells of the massacre of the Jews in the second half of 1941. It includes the Jäger Report detailing Jews murdered and documents the murder of the Jews in 21 Lithuanian towns.

The fifth section consists of reports of visits back to Lithuania after Lithuanian independence in 1990. Also included is a history of Latvia, Riga and Libau and visits after independence.

The sixth section discusses the reasons for immigration, problems encountered along the way and why Lithuanian Jews chose South Africa.

Also included are memories of early immigration to South Africa.

OUR SOUTH AFRICAN JEWISH INHERITANCE published in August 2016
The matching volume to OUR LITVAK INHERITANCE

These two volumes tell of the history, life and times of South African Jews originating in Eastern Europe.

Like most South African Jews, my ancestors emigrated from Lithuania to South Africa between 1880 and 1920. We were the lucky ones escaping the horrors of the Holocaust and most of us have relatives left behind in Lithuania who perished in the Holocaust.

For about 100 years we generally prospered and multiplied in South Africa and then in the early 1970s, seeking more secure futures for our families, we commenced immigrating to Israel, the UK, the USA, Canada and Australia and by the year 2000 about 50,000 of the 120,000 South African Jews had emigrated.

Like my other books this is a compilation and not a single narrative. It is a gathering of articles, stories and histories that tell us of life and history and Jewish life and history in South Africa from 1880 to 1990. As it is a gathering of articles, stories and histories in some cases we will have two or more different views of the same event.

The purpose of this book is to tell the history of South Africa and our Jewish contribution, with its rich Litvak culture, and to share it with our children and grandchildren.

Another purpose of the book is to raise funds for Arcadia and Oranjia, formerly the two Jewish Orphanages in South Africa which still exist, and also for the JDC. All the proceeds from the sale of this book/compilation and my previous compilations will be donated to these three institutions which take care of Jewish children in need. As at the end of December 2016 over R1,300,000 had been raised for Arcadia and R60,000 for Oranjia from book sales.

This 511 paged softcovered book has the following sections
1 The early history of South Africa in the Western and Eastern Cape Province.
2 Kimberley and the discovery of Diamonds (Northern Cape).
3 The Establishment of Natal, The OrangeFree State and The Transvaal Boer Republics.
4 The discovery of Gold in the Witwatersrand and the founding of Johannesburg.
5 The Anglo Boer War 1899-1902.
6 Immigration, Yiddish, Zionism and Jewish Culture.
7 World War One.
8 The Generosity of the S A Jewish Community.
9 Landsmanschaften Mutual Aid Societies.
10 World War Two.
11 Jewish Life in Country Communities (1947 & 1948).
12 Jewish Communities and Personalities.
13 Support for Israel during the Israeli War of Independence (1948 & 1949).
14 The Struggle from Apartheid to Multi-racial elections.

Books sourced include Birth of a Community *by Chief Rabbi professor Israel Abrahams,* South Africa's 800 The Story of South African Volunteers in Israel's War of Birth *by Henry Katzew,* The Fordsburg-Mayfair Hebrew Congregation 1893-1964 *by Bernard Sachs,* The Jews in South Africa, Edited *by Gustav Saron and Louis Hotz,* The Nationwide Survey of the South African Jewish Community *by Arthur Markowitz,* The Pretoria Jewish Community up to 1930 *by Mrs Myrtle Todes, Mr Selwyn Zwick, Mrs Naomi Nowosenetz, Dr Rayme Rabinowitz, Mrs Avril Cohen, Mrs Jill Katz (editor), Mrs Mary Kropman and and Mr Ralph Lanesman,* The Vision Amazing *by Marcia Gitlin,* The War Report *by J E H Groble and* Worlds Apart *by Colin Tatz, Peter Arnold and Gillian Heller.*

Between 1981 to 2005 some 40% of Jews, about 47,000 left South Africa. About 13,000 went to Israel, 12,000 to the US, 11,000 to Australia and New Zealand, 6,000 to the UK and 5,000 to Canada.

Most South African Jews today live in Johannesburg (50,000) and Cape Town (16,000), while the other main centres are Durban (2,700) and Pretoria (1,500). Originally, the community was evenly spread throughout the country, but the rural communities began declining shortly after World War II and are today, largely defunct.

The proceeds of the sale of all these compilations go to Arcadia (formerly the South African Jewish Orphanage) and Oranjia, children's homes, (formerly the Cape Jewish Orphanage) in Johannesburg and Cape Town, South Africa, that are still looking after Jewish Children in need.

The Ochberg Orphans were placed in the care of these two orphanages when they arrived in South Africa in 1921.

On-line sales go to the JDC (The American Jewish Joint Distribution Company).

To order your books locally or have them delivered to friends and family around the world please contact David Solly Sandler on sedsand@iinet.net.au

Chapter 81 - ART BOOKS COMPILED BY DAVID SOLLY SANDLER

ELI ZAGORIA, THE ARTIST (1922-2013)

Eli Zagoria (1922-2013) by his daughter Keren Frankel

The story of Eli Zagoria is told in the Arcadia Memory Books and there you will also find some of his art.

Eli was born in 1922 in Riga, Latvia and at age 14 immigrated to South Africa. He was placed in the care of Arcadia and while still at school he was encouraged with his art.

After leaving school he served in the South African Army in the Medical Corp and was captured in Tobruk, and was a prisoner of war in Italy and Germany. There, in Stalag IVB, he met another artist who was British, and a prisoner of war too. He was Eli's first art teacher and told Eli he should take art up as a profession.

After returning to South Africa in 1946 he was given a full three year scholarship in the Art College in Johannesburg and then volunteered to go to Israel and join the Israeli Army in the 1949 War of Independence. In the Israeli Army he once again was in the medical corp helping the wounded and sick.

Eli married Estelle Kaplan in 1949 and they spent seven years in Israel and over 23 years in Zimbabwe before returning to Johannesburg for 13 years. During this time in Johannesburg he did portrait sketches at East Gate shopping centre.

Eli came to Perth in 1992. He has two sons Michael and Ilan born in Israel and a daughter Karen born in Zimbabwe.

Eli, when he passed away early in 2013, still made his living from art, doing portraits and painting in his small studio at the back of his house. He estimated that he drew over 15,000 portraits over his lifetime.

Eli leaves behind his wife of 64 years, his three children and seven grandchildren.

THE TWO BOOKLETS ON ELI ZAGORIA'S ART

The Art of Eli Zagoria

Perth and Surrounds by Eli Zagoria

DR/PROF LOUIS TOUYZ
Born 1939 Johannesburg South Africa.

The story of Louis is told in More Arc Memories therein is also some of his art. He was in the care of Arcadia for seven years and lectured to many students of Dentistry at the University of the Witwatersrand.

Touyz is a self-trained artist and is now resident in Montreal. He has worked in ceramics, batik, paints in acrylic and focuses his work mainly around Jewish themes. He was educated in South Africa and immigrated to Canada in 1990. He qualified as a teacher, is a trained research scientist, and is a specialist in periodontics, oral medicine and dental rehabilitation.

He has evolved his own unique vibrant style of painting with acrylics on canvas, using Judaic visual mantras and themes. It has been said "Judaism oscillates between 'Oy' and 'Joy'". His works are closer to 'Joy' replete with iconic Jewish images that reflect joyous Jewish life's attitudes.

He was Director and full-time tenured Professor of Periodontics at McGill University 1991-2011. He now devotes all his time to his creative work. He is a past President of Shaar Hashomayim Synagogue Men's Association as well as Past-president of the Westmount Lawn Bowling Club (2009-2011). He has three children and two grandchildren.

Jewish Festivals, Festivities and themes by Louis Touyz.
Louis' iconic Jewish art of Jewish Festivals, Festivities and themes with his detailed commentries

A few of Touyz's iconic figures. For books and prints please contact David Solly Sandler sedsand@iinet.net.au

Chapter 82 - ABOUT THE COMPILER, DAVID SOLLY SANDLER

CHARITIES BENEFITING FROM BOOK SALES

As mentioned before, the full proceeds of the sale of all compilations go to Arcadia and Oranjia, children's homes, (formerly the Jewish Orphanages) in Johannesburg and Cape Town, South Africa, that are still looking after Jewish Children in need.

On-line sales go to the JDC (The American Jewish Joint Distribution Company).

To order your books locally or have them delivered to friends and family around the world please contact David Solly Sandler on sedsand@iinet.net.au

So far we have raised over R1,300,000 for Arcadia, approximately R60,000 for Oranjia and US$1,000 for the JDC.

PG COMPILATION STILL TO COME

SOUTH AFRICAN YIZKOR BOOKS

There are two Yizkor books connected to South Africa and PG will be published in English soon.

-**The Yizkor Book of Rakishok and environs** published in 1952 in South Africa in Yiddish.

The Memorial Section of the Yizkor Book of Rakishok (see page 347) is the English translation of the Memorial (in Rememberance) Section (Pages 539 to 620) of the Yizkor-Book of Rakishok and Environs translated into English by Bella Golubchik. This booklet was translated and given to Jewish Gen to help them complete the translation of the book and PG they will publish it soon.

The Keidan Yizkor Book published in 1977 in Hebrew by the US Israeli and South African Keidan Associations.

This book has been translated partly with the help of Bella Golubchik and with the joint effort of Aryeh Shcherbakov of the Israel Keidan Society, Andrew Cassel from the US and I and PG it will be in print shortly.

Another Yizkor book originating in South Africa is **Yizkor book on Chelm - originally published in 1954 in Yiddish in South Africa.** The book has been partly translated by Jewish Gen. I offered to help them with the articles that have not been translated but they refused my help and I'm thinking how to proceed.

I also plan to re-publish with all the Yiddish articles translated into English **Krakenowo the story of a world that has passed.** This booklet on Krakenowo, a shtetle in Lithuania, was compiled by the Krakenowo Sick Benefit and Benevolent Society in 1961.

If you know of any other book or booklets from Landmanschafts in South Africa please let me know!

Kehilas (Jewish Communities) of Johannesburg and the Witwatersrand those larger Rand towns and Jewish Communities in Johannesburg that fall outside the net of the great work being done by Beyachad in their *Jewish Life in the South African Country Communities.*
I invite all South African Jo'burgers and those of the Rand to share details of their Jewish Communities - their history and photos.

From Eastern Europe to South Africa - a collection of family histories.
I invite all South Africans to share their family histories and photos.

My Inheritance - my family history - the stories of my four grandparents.

Please contact me if you need help publishing or reprinting any book on South African Jewry.

Best wishes good health and Shalom and thank you for supporting Arcadia and Oranjia.

David
David Solly Sandler
Perth Western Australia
sedsand@iinet.net.au

ABOUT DAVID SOLLY SANDLER, THE COMPILER OF THE BOOKS

I was born in Johannesburg South Africa in 1952 and all my forebears originated in Lithuania. I spent most of my childhood, 1954-1969, in Arcadia from age three until 17, when I finished school. I served in the South African Defence Force and did Articles and qualified as a Chartered Accountant in 1976.

In 1979 I married and at age 28, in 1981, I left Johannesburg and I have lived in Perth, Western Australia, ever since. I have two daughters Sarah and Esther.

In early 2007 I retired, and commenced compiling the books almost full time.

David Solly Sandler